Frank Lloyd Wright
AND THE MEANING OF MATERIALS

Frank Lloyd Wright

AND THE MEANING OF MATERIALS

TERRY L. PATTERSON, AIA

University of Oklahoma

VAN NOSTRAND REINHOLD

I(T)P A Division of International Thomson Publishing Inc.

New York • Albany • Bonn • Boston • Detroit • London • Madrid • Melbourne
Mexico City • Paris • San Francisco • Singapore • Tokyo • Toronto

I(T)P™ A division of International Thomson Publishing Inc.
       The ITP logo is a trademark under license

Printed in the United States of America
For more information, contact:

Van Nostrand Reinhold
115 Fifth Avenue
New York, NY 10003

International Thomson Publishing GmbH
Königswinterer Strasse 418
53227 Bonn
Germany

International Thomson Publishing Europe
Berkshire House 168-173
High Holborn
London WCIV 7AA
England

International Thomson Publishing Asia
221 Henderson Road #05-10
Henderson Building
Singapore 0315

Thomas Nelson Australia
102 Dodds Street
South Melbourne, 3205
Victoria, Australia

International Thomson Publishing Japan
Hirakawacho Kyowa Building, 3F
2-2-1 Hirakawacho
Chiyoda-ku, 102 Tokyo
Japan

Nelson Canada
1120 Birchmount Road
Scarborough, Ontario
Canada M1K 5G4

International Thomson Editores
Campos Eliseos 385, Piso 7
Col. Polanco
11560 Mexico D.F. Mexico

1 2 3 4 5 6 7 8 9 10 ARCKP 01 00 99 98 97 96 95 94

Library of Congress Cataloging-in-Publication Data
Patterson, Terry L.
    Frank Lloyd Wright and the meaning of materials /
Terry L. Patterson
          p.   cm.
    Includes bibliographical references and index.
    ISBN 0-442-01298-5
    1. Wright, Frank Lloyd, 1867–1959—Criticism and interpretation.
    2. Organic architecture—United States. 3. Building materials.
    I. Title.
NA737.W7P28   1994   94–28418
720'.92—dc20   CIP

To my mother, Iva Fae Patterson

CONTENTS

PREFACE

A search for meaning in the architecture of Frank Lloyd Wright cannot be complete without a thoughtful consideration of the role of building materials in his buildings. In this study, the work of Wright is examined to determine the degree to which it is sensitive to—and dependent upon—the nature of building materials. Specifically, his use of wood, stone, brick, concrete block, metals, concrete, and glass are analyzed to discover if the form, workability, strength, and durability of each material are emphasized, subdued, or misrepresented in his architectural expression. His comments on building materials are compared to his applications in order to evaluate the translation of the ideal to the real.

The basis for a material's nature used in the exploration of Wright's form and detailing is derived from a literal interpretation of substance properties so as to maximize objectivity and minimize corruption from taste, trends, and other ephemeral and subjective influences. The guidelines for evaluation are outlined and reasoning is explained so that readers can compare their own conclusions to those in the text. Conclusions are drawn regarding the role of the various components of material nature in specific details and buildings. Wright's handling of each material is summarized with regard to the importance of its nature to his architecture. An estimate is made of Wright's overall material sensitivity, which is reconciled with his reputation in this realm.

Wright's many claims for the significance of materials and his remarkable artistic success warrant a methodical study of his material use. A void in this regard exists in the analytical literature on Wright due to its intentional focus on other issues. Miscellaneous comments and insights have thus far served to verify the importance of materials but have stopped short of a comprehensive investigation into their meaning. In the response of this book to the need for such a study, certain tendencies are avoided. The power and delight inherent in Wright's remarkably moving architecture is not accepted as evidence that it also reflects the nature of materials. Although occasional praise of Wright's sensitivity to materials found elsewhere may be entirely warranted, it is intended that this study arrive at such praise or criticism through reasoning as free as possible from prejudice in behalf of Wright's genius.

ACKNOWLEDGMENTS

I am indebted to a number of people for their contributions to this work. Thanks are due Robert Bogues, Michael Brohman, Jeffrey Burquest, Samuel Callahan, Angel Cantu, Alhad Dharmadhikari, Cherie Goff, Jason Haslam, Michael Hoover, Fokruddin Khondaker, Bruce LaFleur, Matthew Lumpkin, Michael Nobert, Geoffrey Parks, Lisa Roberts, and especially Lisa Chronister, for their research assistance.

I appreciate the assistance of Bruce Brooks Pfeiffer, Director, Margo Stipe, Registrar, and Oscar Muñoz in securing access to information, drawings, specifications, and photographs in the Frank Lloyd Wright Archives. I am particularly grateful for permission from the Frank Lloyd Wright Foundation to quote from drawings and published works.

Assistance for which I am appreciative was also provided by Dr. Donald P. Hallmark, Site Administrator, Frank Lloyd Wright's Dana-Thomas House State Historic Site; Margaret Klinkow, Research Center Director, The Frank Lloyd Wright Home and Studio Foundation; Lynda S. Waggoner, Curator and Administrator, Fallingwater; Virginia Kazor, Curator, Hollyhock House; Becki Peterson, Archivist, State Historical Society of Iowa; Bob Weil, Chairman of Tours and Archives, Beth Sholom Congregation; and Jonathan Lipman.

I am most grateful for the creative expertise and special effort of Doug Carr, photographer, The Dana-Thomas Foundation; Mike Kertok, AIA; and Edward A. Young, AIA for selecting and photographing subjects specifically for this publication and for making their photographic collections available to me.

Special thanks are due to Carolyn De Witt Koenig, Managing Editor, *Architectural Record* for permission to quote from the Frank Lloyd Wright articles on building materials.

I am indebted to my University of Oklahoma colleagues, Patricia L. Eidson, AIA for sharing her photographs and information on the Meyer May house; M. Iver Wahl, AIA, Director of Architecture, for his accommodating assignment of teaching and committee duties during this project; and to Raymond Yeh, AIA, former Dean, and Jim Kudrna, AIA, Interim Dean for making resources of the College of Architecture available to me.

Many thanks to my graduate assistant, Shanyan Li, for drawing all of the graphic illustrations in this book. Her timely, accurate, and creative work constitutes a major contribution to this publication.

I am particularly appreciative of the financial support of my mother, Iva Fae Patterson, for the acquisition and production of all photographs, without which this work would not have been possible. Much thanks is due my wife, Jennie M. Patterson, not only for her constant moral support throughout this project, but also for her research, photography, and preparation of the Endnotes, the list of Cited Buildings and Projects, and the list of References.

1 INTRODUCTION

INTRODUCTION

Architects rarely comment on the expressive role of building materials in their work. Since it is often difficult to recognize a clear and consistent relationship between a building's materials (as entities in their own right) and the architectural goals of the designer, critical discourse on the subject has been limited. Perhaps many architects have not defined discrete strategies for materials use or perhaps they doubt the significance of materials in the artistic realm. Without commitments to materials ideas in both writing and architecture, many designers have kept their expressive options open. Their vagueness obscures inconsistencies between word and deed. Written and constructed materials conclusions are more difficult to challenge if they are not clearly articulated. On the other hand, neither can praise for sensitivity and insight into the realm of materials issues be forthcoming without the definition or demonstration of a materials attitude.

In contrast, Frank Lloyd Wright committed with enthusiasm to the centrality of building materials in his work and, in his opinion, to their proper use. "Bring out the nature of the materials, let their nature intimately into your scheme,"[1] he insisted in 1908. His expositions began early and continued to appear throughout his long career, yielding a record of materials discourse unprecedented in architectural literature. This written record, combined with his equally extensive built legacy, has left Wright's materials philosophy vulnerable to dissection and the inevitable claims of discrepancies and fallacies. It is difficult to imagine a 70-year discourse without contradictions, especially when both theory and applications are involved.

To understand Wright's approach to building materials requires an attempt to reconcile his written interpretation of material nature with his use of materials in architecture. The objectivity of his definitions and the directness of their influence on his architecture, however, are brought into question by his commitment to principles and goals that are not necessarily related to the nature of materials. Wright's fondness for simplicity, plasticity, honesty, nature, horizontality, and originality, all under the umbrella of his organic ideal, had the potential to affect form and detailing in ways that accommodated the expression of the nature of materials and in ways that did not. Relationships between these ideals and Wright's materials use are summarized in the concluding chapter.

The goal that appears to have superseded all others is particularly vague in meaning. Wright's claims that "...Life without Beauty accomplished is no Life."[2] and "eventually we must live for the Beautiful whether we want to or not"[3] suggest that a quest for beauty governed all goals. Because of its highly subjective nature, however, it is the most difficult of the issues to define. Wright's focus on beauty in architecture hinders the certainty with which his materials decisions might be explained. To place his material use in context, attention to this elusive ideal is necessary.

BEAUTY

Wright's use of the term *beauty* to define his ultimate focus included a broad range of issues with various degrees of subjectivity. He did not embrace all types of beauty. In his insistence that one "work with principle, and what men call Beauty will be the evidence of your joy in your work,"[4] he distinguishes meaningful beauty from beauty as a surface quality or a characteristic of imagery with no further significance. He believed, for example, that ornament, if not integral to the nature of the architecture, debases it "no matter how clever or beautiful it may be as something in itself."[5] Wright's linking of beauty with principle moves the definition of beauty into a realm that seems to be, but is not necessarily, more objective. Ultimately, he places the achievement of beauty above the legitimacy of any schemes devised to achieve it as illustrated by his warning that "...no proper excuse for 'making' anything ugly need ever be accepted from an architect."[6]

Wright's advice to "Reveal the nature of the wood, plaster, brick or stone in your designs; they are all by nature friendly and beautiful"[7] relates harmony of materials to beauty. Instead of pulling beauty into the objective arena of material properties, however, the reverse occurs. Material essence is moved beyond the scope of

its properties into the subjective realm of Wright's intuitive sense of what is beautiful. The objectivity of other otherwise tangible references is also corrupted. Appropriateness ("The inappropriate cannot be beautiful"[8]), function ("The forms of things that are perfectly adapted to their function...have a superior beauty"[9]), and need ("Human *necessity*...carries within itself the secret of the beauty we must have"[10]) could be judged by standards of some objectivity. The criteria become, instead of definers of beauty, defined by Wright's aesthetic sense.

Intuitive design yields artistically successful architecture when the designer has a universal sense of beauty such as Wright had. The intuitive nature of his genius makes identifying patterns of motivation in his work difficult as they often appear to be more spontaneous than methodically derived. In addition, the influence of his general design principles and prejudices undermine the objectivity of Wright's materials discourse and applications. His call for design sympathetic to the nature of materials establishes a clear goal, but standards less subjective than his own are needed for evaluating meaning in his materials use. Although the physical properties of materials are subject to interpretation in scope and meaning, they offer a relatively objective starting point for such standards and shall be the basis for the analysis of Wright's materials.

THE NATURE OF MATERIALS

The properties of a material are the logical basis for defining its nature since the role of opinion is thus minimized, at least in regard to their quantitative aspects. Consideration of tradition, although often relevant, is minimized because some traditional practices are rooted in long-since defunct principles and can have only a tentative grip on the spirit of a material. The economy stemming from only the repetition of a detail is not a component of material essence. Economy is central to a material's nature only if it reflects a sense of directness between a material's properties and its detailing. Limiting the basis for material nature to technical properties does not make the standard simple or entirely objective but provides a beginning point that offers the widest possible potential for agreement.

Properties manifest themselves in products and buildings by virtue of the technology available for processing the raw materials and assembling the components. Given the inseparable relationship between the nature of the technology and the potential and limitations of the material substance, analyzing the essence of a material must also include consideration of the associated technology. Consequently, it is possible for the nature of a material to change over a period of time with changes in processing and installation technologies. A conservative approach is taken in determining the approximate boundaries of property expression so as to reduce overlaps in material identities. This approach involves, essentially, increasing the normal factors of safety and focusing on uniqueness rather than sameness among materials. The scope of factors defining literal material nature is limited to the properties of the materials and the characteristics imparted by their technologies. The visual desirability of outcomes does not influence the nature of materials in the literal approach.

It appears that Wright tended to let the desirability of results affect his view of material nature. His remarks indicate that he would not have considered an unattractive attribute to be a significant part of a material's essence, that is, one worth considering as an expressive vehicle. Literal definitions of material nature, on the other hand, might include traits considered to be undesirable as their degree of attractiveness is not a factor in their identification as a property. The violation of literal material essence might, therefore, be necessary to produce acceptable results according to some tastes. Since the nature of a material has generally been considered to be a positive aspect, architects typically do not admit that their work violates the nature of a material even if such makes their buildings better. It has usually been more palatable to define the nature of materials in terms of their aesthetic contribution to the architecture, thus assuring that the design is sympathetic to its materials as long as the building is artistically successful. This is circular reasoning (the building is beautiful because it is in the nature of its materials and it is in the nature of its materials because it is beautiful) and is not an objective method of defining material essence.

In the absence of absolute rights and wrongs from the realm of architectural imagery, a comparison of material properties can yield relative conclusions regarding that which is more or less appropriate in material expression with regard to material nature. This involves comparing the like categories of properties in each material. In contrast to this balanced approach, Wright saw the categories of material properties as changing with each material. He might view one material as a strong substance and another as having a beautiful surface, thus failing to develop a hierarchy of importance or appropriateness among materials with regard to each property. This minimizes the number of his comments on like property categories (among materials) that can be examined. Consequently, his buildings become the best reflection of his thoughts in this realm.

Material properties for purposes of this study are grouped in four general categories, *Form, Workability, Strength,* and *Durability,*[11] within which characteristics

of Wright's detailing can be compared to the natural material traits. Given the differences between species, alloys, mixes, and products in each material, it is conceivable that a slightly different nature could be identified for every component of the same material. Such a system would be far too unwieldy to be useful. Traits that are reasonably representative of most variations within a material are accepted as the definers of the material's nature. Maximum precision is not achieved for every variation in substance, but a determination as to whether or not the general spirit of a material is served can be made. To be more specific would suggest that the method is more scientific than it is.

In determining the significance of compatible or incompatible materials expression in the building image, a distinction is made between structural and nonstructural materials. Expression in architecture within the main property categories is considered here to be more significant in structural components than in cladding, which establishes a bias compatible with Wright's attitude. Cladding, is, nevertheless, treated as a legitimate vehicle for expression, as Wright also considered it. It is analyzed for material sensitivity in the same way as structural components. One difference between the two realms, besides that of loading circumstances, is that nonstructural materials must be visible to play a role in the architectural expression while the nature of structural materials—by virtue of their configuration—can affect building image without being seen.

A building's compatibility with the nature of its materials can be evaluated by observing the degree to which a building's massing and detailing accommodate or, more significantly, are generated by the characteristics of each material in the four property categories. The level of sensitivity to materials is judged to increase with the degree to which architectural meaning and aesthetic order depend on the characteristics natural to each material. Although substituting one material for another will typically have some visual effect in Wright's buildings, the characters of some buildings depend more strongly on their materials than do others.

Demonstration of sensitivity to the nature of materials is dependent on the degree of clarity in each material's message. It is recognized that subtlety is not the same as vagueness and that blatancy is not necessarily significance. An expression of material uniqueness is a clearer statement about its nature than one demonstrating its likeness to other materials. It could be argued that if two materials naturally are alike, then the expression of that circumstance truly reflects part of their nature. Since no two materials are alike in all ways, however, to suggest that they are is to misrepresent their unique combinations of traits. Wright's observation that "each material has its own message"[12] supports this concept.

For example, if it is not clear whether a column is wood, masonry, steel, or concrete, the unique combination of properties of the column material have not been expressed. The actual mistaking of one material for another is not necessary to verify an absence of clarity in the material expression. Detailing that shows one material to be partially similar to another fails to express the characteristic properties of its material. However, in doing so, such detailing is only partially insensitive to its material rather than entirely insensitive. A continuous range of material sensitivity is possible from none to the maximum feasible. Although certain details clearly harmonize with their materials while others obviously do not, the line separating the two kinds of expression cannot be determined with certainty in all cases. This is a result of some interpretative latitude inherent in determining the appropriate translation of properties into their visual manifestations in architecture.

FORM

The basic products of each material have configurations and surface qualities that characterize the substance and its associated technologies (fabrication, installation, etc.). The geometries of the products can be classified as linear, blocklike, or planar according to their proportions. They can be rustic or refined, blunt or sharp, and massive or delicate and can fall between these extremes. A basic or primary form with a unique combination of substance characteristics can be identified for each product. Wright's work is judged to be most expressive of the nature of its materials (with regard to form) where the artistic message is dependent upon clearly exhibited basic material form. It is least expressive of a material's nature (with regard to form) when the material appears to have the shapes of other materials, shapes that are incidental to the aesthetic order, shapes that are obscured, or shapes that are not basic to the product.

Form appears to be the major property by which Wright defined the nature of a material as it is the property he mentioned most frequently and respected most often in his work. The Ennis House (1924) and other masonry buildings, for example, emphasize blocky unit form at the expense of system durability. Large cantilevers at Wingspread (H. Johnson House, 1937) and other houses express wood's linear form but misrepresent the actual strength of wood with hidden steel. Form is the least abstract of the properties in that its meaning is conveyed visually and immediately upon sight. The intellect plays less of a role in grasping the shape of a component than in understanding its

strength or durability. Form is a property of building materials that has a clear and immediate visual message while durability and, to some degree, strength require visualizing future consequences for their meaning. Form has the predictable and immediate kind of impact that would have appealed to Wright more than the varied effects and academic nature of the other two properties.

Given Wright's fascination with the Machine, mechanized manufacturing and fabrication techniques could be expected to affect his opinion of material form. The trend in contemporary architecture could be salvaged, he claimed, only by utilizing "the Machine as the tool of standardization."[13] He rejected handwork as obsolete and inappropriate for modern times. This attitude would seem to establish a clear cause-and-effect relationship in the production of a material and provide an objective basis for identifying forms that are logical reflections of a material's properties and its technology. The potential of this concept is not fulfilled, however, as Wright did not pursue the reasoning to its ultimate logical conclusions. His various concrete block designs, for example, required in their production a considerable amount of handwork applied to a complex assortment of steps and movements beyond the capability of mechanization of the period.

Certain of Wright's general observations respond to the nature of mechanized production such as his view that machines encourage "clean lines [and] clean surfaces."[14] A clean condition suggests straightness and uniformity that appear to be Wright's interpretation when he calls for building design in "geometrical or straight lines [because they are] natural to machinery at work in the building trades"[15] as well as "straight lines and rectilinear forms"[16] in furniture design, as these are the "terms for machine work."[17] Clean lines, it seems, are relative in that the lines of the Ennis House (1924) and the Price Tower (1952) are clean compared to Victorian design but not by standards of the International Style.

Rectilinearity is compatible with rolling mills, saw mills, and other processes where the product moves continuously past a point of applied force. The extrusion of clay for bricks is of this ilk but cast products are not. Consequently, molded brick, concrete, and concrete block can logically be somewhat less clean than lumber and steel but are limited in their contrast with this ideal because the economics of fabricating and removing formwork encourages uniformity and simplicity. Molds do not require rectilinear shapes in section or surface. Form removal, in fact, is facilitated by the tapering of mass and detail as found in the block of the Florida Southern College campus (1938–54), the precast roof decorations of the Marin County Civic Center (1957), and elsewhere.

Wright's propensity for rectangularity prior to his late work would seem to reflect his focus on the nature of the Machine but also reflects a prejudice against certain stylistic overtones. His advice to "eliminate the Decorator" who was "all curves and all efflorescence, if not all 'period'"[18] links curvilinear detailing to certain historic-period design. Wright's admission to the triangle and the T-square as the source of his favored geometry tempers the magnitude of influence that might otherwise be assigned to the nature of machine processes.[19] Wright tended to justify design decisions using only a part of a body of reasoning, apparently not feeling bound by the entire structure of a logical argument. He appeared to embrace the presence of restrictions proclaiming that accepting the limitations of "automatic industrial fabrication" was the only way "STYLE"[20] could be achieved in industry. He rejected the uniform and literal influence of these limitations, however. "It is largely the Artist's business...," he thought, "to see that the limitations do *not* destroy each other."[21] The presence of multiple limitations inevitably leads to conflict among the parameters and design goals. The designer's disregard of the most inconvenient limitations is the likely result of such conflicts. Wright's seeking of the "proper tools, proper materials for proper work"[22] is a strategy that could, by the selective definition of what is proper and what is not, minimize the influence of material limitations.

Ultimately, both the potential and the limitations of machine processes proved to be, respectively, too flexible and too severe for Wright's taste. "The Machine Age," it seemed to him, "is either to be damned by senseless sentimentality or to be sterilized by a factory aesthetic."[23] He rejected the machine's ability to copy forms that were once hand-wrought details of historic styling, not on the basis of machine incompatibility, but because the result was stylistically inappropriate. He considered machine-produced copies of historic artifacts to be "of all abominations the most abominable. Everything must be curved and carved and carved and turned," he complained, with "the whole mass a tortured sprawl supposed artistic."[24]

The economic advantages afforded by machinery in the production of curvilinear and decorative materials was problematic in Wright's promotion of the logic in machine processes. Rather than resorting to an academic argument condemning complex machine movements as failing to reflect the true machine ideal, Wright took a more direct approach in dealing with the issue. He simply rejected the legitimacy of imitative curvilinear forms and undermined the significance of their machine origins by denying that machine potential was the sole definer of form. He blamed the designer for the mechanized production of shapes he did not like because

FIGURE 1-1. Hand casting a concrete block for the Robert Levin Residence. (Courtesy the Frank Lloyd Wright Archives)

"...the Machine is only the creature, not the Creator of this iniquity!"[25] The simplifying effect of the machine could "relieve us of sentimental...abuse," he thought, "but it cannot inspire and recreate humanity beyond that point."[26]

Once the taste of the designer is brought into the equation, the range of options for legitimate material form shifts away from that defined by the potential of industrial production. Wright concludes that "by means of Imagination"[27] machines could be engaged to produce appropriate forms. Wright offered human need as the link across the gap between strict machine-logic and the logic resulting in legitimate material form. He proposed that we endeavor to use machinery and building materials "not only for qualities they possess in themselves, but to use each so that they may be beautifully as well as scientifically related to human purpose in whatever form or function we humanly choose to put them."[28] The ultimate criterion is thus revealed. It would seem that beauty superseded inherent essence of materials and technology as the criterion for the form of a material.

WORKABILITY

To work a material is to change its basic manufactured form. The ease with which a standard component may be reshaped into a new form is a measure of a material's workability. Materials that may be reshaped with less planning, less skill, less sophisticated equipment, and in less convenient circumstances have a higher level of workability than other materials having greater demands in these realms. To maximize the expression of a material's workability is to minimize the expression of its primary form. To maximize expression of primary form by failing to work a highly workable material does not violate the nature of the material per se but fails to express its full potential, thus leaving it less distinguishable from materials that are less workable.

Given the fact that workability is a kind of affinity or tendency while a material's form manifests itself physically, basic or primary material form is the dominant property among the two. Workability and primary form can be expressed simultaneously with some compromise to each. In such cases, each property typically fails to reach its highest expressive potential but the resulting intensity of material essence can be stronger than that achievable by exploitation of either property alone. A material's low level of workability is expressed by revealing the primary form of the material in architecture without changes to its shape.

Wright's attitude towards workability was complex. His recognition that some materials were more easily worked than others did not motivate, in every case, the exploitation of this potential in architectural applications. In some materials he believed that working was a violation of the sanctity of primary form and in others he thought it was necessary to fulfill the material's potential. The challenge of identifying a pattern in his attitude is further complicated by the probability that certain prejudices unrelated to material substance affected his decisions regarding workability. He wished to avoid, for example, certain kinds of historical detailing that was typically produced by the extensive working of materials. The probability that his attitude toward the working of certain materials was not based entirely on the nature of the substances involved is thus revealed.

STRENGTH

The spirit of each material is defined by a demonstration of its ability—within logical limits—to resist tension, compression, and bending. A material expresses its nature when it is shown to resist the type of stress with which the substance is most compatible or uniquely adapted. In other words, the most limited materials logically express the stresses to which they are limited and the most versatile materials logically express the stress conditions that are not suited to the more limited materials. Clarity is served by maintaining expressions of strength within boundaries that do not overlap those of other materials. If a material is weak, for example, detailing it so as to maximize the expression of its strength lacks clarity as a demonstration of its nature.

Wright claimed to respect strength in a material and demonstrated some consistency in its expression. He recognized such differences in the visual effects of material strength in his observation that "it is obvious that sticks will not space the same as stones nor allow the same proportions as steel."[29] Except for concrete, however, few of his spans and cantilevers are material-specific. This is not to say that Wright lacked interest in structural expression. He praised the powerful image of cantilevers, for example, but did not consistently distinguish between the abilities of his materials to cantilever. He seemed to view the strength of each material as being whatever was necessary to accomplish the task he assigned to it.

DURABILITY

Durability refers to the ability of a material to resist visual and physical deterioration from the forces of nature in the exterior environment. Chemical, physical, and biological decay and corrosion from water, chemicals, and living organisms are the issues. A material's natural high durability is expressed by exposing it to the elements; low durability is demonstrated by expressing the methods of protecting it from the elements. Wear resistance is not used as a measure of durability in this study. Consequently, the durabilities of materials in interior applications are not addressed in their own right. Contrasts between expressive ramifications of interior and exterior applications are examined in certain cases to provide a context for the discussion of the exterior circumstance.

Although Wright mentions the subject and upon occasion addresses durability in his use of materials, evidence of consistent design intent in this regard is lacking. In a note to the contractor on a photograph of the Pfeiffer Chapel (1938), for example, Wright complained of the contractor's addition of visible flashing on the tops of walls that he had not specified. The added detail had a visual impact on the facade that Wright did not want in spite of the practical benefits of the positive pro-

Figure 1-2. Notes to the contractor written by Wright on a photograph of the Florida Southern College Annie Pfeiffer Chapel: "Attention Harold Turner—Is it possible that you put flashing on top of this wall—to crown your efforts at Florida Southern? Please wire yes or no. FLLW." "Instructions to move this post inward 7'-0, ignored?" (Courtesy the Frank Lloyd Wright Archives)

tection from water that the detail provided. (This photograph also included a note complaining of a post that had not been set farther back, the effect of which would have been to increase the remarkableness of the cantilever.) Visible flashing was added by owners to many of Wright's buildings after leakage and deterioration over a period of years verified the need for it.

Wright's record of producing leaky structures and his subsequent disregard for their problems suggests that he had a limited concern for the forces of nature when they would affect his design goals. When, in a television interview, Wright was asked to name the building with which he was most pleased, he responded by citing his next commission, whatever it might be.[30] This forward-looking attitude does not mean that, once finished, his buildings were no longer important to him, but their problems failed to capture his interest subse-

quent to the completion of construction. Stories of leaking roofs and the witticisms he directed to complaining clients are plentiful. The lack of focus on past work is compatible with his apparent lack of concern for the ramifications of his detailing with regard to material durability.

The expression of a material's durability is more abstract than that of form and strength, because the observer of a design sketch or a new building must be able to imagine the degree to which future deterioration is likely in order to grasp the meaning of the detailing. Consequently, violations to material durability have a limited visual impact on architectural expression at the time construction is completed. This is the time that photographs are taken for publication and is the circumstance in which many designers like to remember their buildings. All properties do not require equal attention in order to establish an image of material sensitivity, but neither do the more subtle issues such as durability lack significance in this regard.

CONCLUSION

Because the properties of a material are not directly related to each other in every case, a detail cannot express all properties with the same intensity and purity. Maximizing the expression of one property can minimize that of another, as previously illustrated by the natural conflict between primary form and workability. Expressing material form by projecting components forward of the surface plane is, for some materials, in conflict with the expression of durability that might dictate a flush surface to avoid catching water. Even strength, a property closely aligned with form, can be challenged when the projections that emphasize form also induce stresses approaching the limits of the material. Pushing a material's limits tends to express the material's nature only when they are extreme in comparison to other materials. When a material's strength is moderate, for example, pushing its expression toward its maximum potential tends to blend the material's image with that of the next stronger substance. The practice hinders the expression of material uniqueness.

The selection of the properties to be emphasized or subdued is a design issue vulnerable to a designer's intuitive sense of the artistic needs of the design. Unless the design is intended to be entirely materials-generated, nonmaterial design principles influence material expression. The nature of the integration of a material's nature with general design goals ultimately establishes the level of expressed material sensitivity. Wright's materials decisions appear to have been affected by certain general principles as well as by his desire for beauty. His approach was traditional in this regard, and, although material nature is not the dominant issue in his work, a level of material sensitivity can be identified relative to that of other designers and within a range from the maximum to the minimum possible.

Although Wright claimed that his design was driven by principle, his material's decisions were not consistent with any discernable paradigm except, ultimately, the production of beauty. His response to Louis Sullivan's claim of searching "for the rule so broad as to admit no exception" is revealing in this regard. "Ever since," hearing the remark, reported Wright, "I have been looking for the exception to prove [test] the rule."[31] Having rejected outright the rules of others, those which he was intent on testing must have been his own. This would explain, in part, some apparently irreconcilable differences between his words and his work.

ENDNOTES

1. Wright, Frank Lloyd. 1908. "In the Cause of Architecture." *Architectural Record* 23(3):155–221. Reprint. 1975. *In the Cause of Architecture*, ed. Frederick Gutheim. New York: McGraw-Hill. p. 55. *ARCHITECTURAL RECORD*, (March/1908), copyright 1975 by McGraw-Hill, Inc. All rights reserved. Reproduced with the permission of the publisher.

2. Wright, Frank Lloyd. 1931. *Modern Architecture: Being the Kahn Lectures for 1930*. Reprint. 1987. ed. Bruce Brooks Pfeiffer. Carbondale and Edwardsville, IL: Southern Illinois University Press. Copyright 1987 by The Frank Lloyd Wright Foundation. p. 61. Courtesy The Frank Lloyd Wright Foundation.

3. Ibid., 113. Courtesy The Frank Lloyd Wright Foundation.

4. Wright, Frank Lloyd. 1928. "In the Cause of Architecture: IX. The Terms." *Architectural Record* 64(6):507–514. Reprint. 1975. *In the Cause of Architecture*, ed. Frederick Gutheim. New York: McGraw-Hill. p. 230. *ARCHITECTURAL RECORD*, (December/1928), copyright 1975 by McGraw-Hill, Inc. All rights reserved. Reproduced with the permission of the publisher.

5. Wright, Frank Lloyd. 1931. *Modern Architecture: Being the Kahn Lectures for 1930*. Reprint. 1987. ed. Bruce Brooks Pfeiffer. Carbondale and Edwardsville, IL: Southern Illinois University Press. Copyright 1987 by The Frank Lloyd Wright Foundation. p. 79. Courtesy The Frank Lloyd Wright Foundation.

6. Wright, Frank Lloyd. 1928. "In the Cause of Architecture: IX. The Terms." *Architectural Record* 64(6):507–514. Reprint. 1975. *In the Cause of Architecture*, ed. Frederick Gutheim. New York: McGraw-Hill. p. 230. *ARCHITECTURAL RECORD*, (December/ 1928), copyright 1975 by McGraw-Hill, Inc. All rights reserved. Reproduced with the permission of the publisher.

7. Wright, Frank Lloyd. 1908. "In the Cause of Architecture." *Architectural Record* 23(3):155–221. Reprint. 1975. *In the Cause of Architecture*, ed. Frederick Gutheim. New York: McGraw-Hill. p. 55. *ARCHITECTURAL RECORD*, (March/1908), copyright 1975 by McGraw-Hill, Inc. All rights reserved. Reproduced with the permission of the publisher.

8. Wright, Frank Lloyd. 1931. *Modern Architecture: Being the Kahn Lectures for 1930*. Reprint. 1987. ed. Bruce Brooks Pfeiffer. Carbondale and Edwardsville, IL: Southern Illinois University Press. Copyright 1987 by The Frank Lloyd Wright Foundation. p. 17. Courtesy The Frank Lloyd Wright Foundation.

9. Ibid., 62. Courtesy The Frank Lloyd Wright Foundation.

10. Ibid., 113. Courtesy The Frank Lloyd Wright Foundation.

11. This strategy and format for the analysis of materials nature appears in Patterson, Terry L. 1990. *Construction Materials For Architects and Designers*. Englewood Cliffs: Prentice-Hall. This book also includes materials critiques of Suntop Homes, the Robie House, the Ennis House, the second Jacobs House, the Morris Gift Shop, the Kaufmann House (Fallingwater), and the Guggenheim Museum, some concepts for which appear here in subsequent chapters.

12. Wright, Frank Lloyd. 1928. "In the Cause of Architecture: III. The Meaning of Materials—Stone." *Architectural Record* 63(4):350–356. Reprint. 1975. *In the Cause of Architecture*, ed. Frederick Gutheim. New York: McGraw-Hill. p. 171. *ARCHITECTURAL RECORD*, (April/1928), copyright 1975 by McGraw-Hill, Inc. All rights reserved. Reproduced with the permission of the publisher.

13. Wright, Frank Lloyd. 1927, "In the Cause of Architecture: II. Standardization, The Soul of the Machine." *Architectural Record* 61(6):478–480. Reprint. 1975. *In the Cause of Architecture*, ed. Frederick Gutheim. New York: McGraw-Hill. p. 136. *ARCHITECTURAL RECORD*, (June/1927), copyright 1975 by McGraw-Hill, Inc. All rights reserved. Reproduced with the permission of the publisher.

14. Wright, Frank Lloyd. 1931. *Modern Architecture: Being the Kahn Lectures for 1930*. Reprint. 1987. ed. Bruce Brooks Pfeiffer. Carbondale and Edwardsville, IL: Southern Illinois University Press. Copyright 1987 by The Frank Lloyd Wright Foundation. p. 35. Courtesy The Frank Lloyd Wright Foundation.

15. Ibid., 74. Courtesy The Frank Lloyd Wright Foundation.

16. Ibid., 75. Courtesy The Frank Lloyd Wright Foundation.

17. Ibid. Courtesy The Frank Lloyd Wright Foundation.

18. Ibid. Courtesy The Frank Lloyd Wright Foundation.

19. Gill, Brendan. 1990. "Frank Lloyd Wright." Keynote address for the Association of Collegiate Schools of Architecture Western Regional Meeting, October 18–20, 1990, University of Colorado, Denver, Colorado.

20. Wright, Frank Lloyd. 1931. *Modern Architecture: Being the Kahn Lectures for 1930*. Reprint. 1987. ed. Bruce Brooks Pfeiffer. Carbondale and Edwardsville, IL: Southern Illinois University Press. Copyright 1987 by The Frank Lloyd Wright Foundation. p. 30. Courtesy The Frank Lloyd Wright Foundation.

21. Ibid. Courtesy The Frank Lloyd Wright Foundation.

22. Ibid. Courtesy The Frank Lloyd Wright Foundation.

23. Ibid., 40. Courtesy The Frank Lloyd Wright Foundation.

24. Ibid., 11. Courtesy The Frank Lloyd Wright Foundation.

25. Ibid., 16. Courtesy The Frank Lloyd Wright Foundation.

26. Ibid., 40. Courtesy The Frank Lloyd Wright Foundation.

27. Ibid., 29. Courtesy The Frank Lloyd Wright Foundation.

28. Ibid., 36. Courtesy The Frank Lloyd Wright Foundation.

29. Wright, Frank Lloyd. 1928. "In the Cause of Architecture: I. The Logic of the Plan." *Architectural Record* 63(1):49–57. Reprint. 1975. *In the Cause of Architecture*, ed. Frederick Gutheim. New York: McGraw-Hill. p. 154. *ARCHITECTURAL RECORD*, (January/ 1928), copyright 1975 by McGraw-Hill, Inc. All rights reserved. Reproduced with the permission of the publisher.

30. Meehan, Patrick J., ed. 1984. *The Master Architect: Conversations With Frank Lloyd Wright*. New York:

John Wiley & Sons, Inc. p. 56. Interview by Hugh Downs at Taliesin (Spring Green, Wisconsin) for the National Broadcasting Company, May 8, 1953. Television broadcast, May 17, 1953 as a program titled, "Wisdom: A Conversation with Frank Lloyd Wright."

31. Pfeiffer, Bruce Brooks. 1986. *Frank Lloyd Wright Monograph 1887–1901*, ed. Yukio Futagawa. Text copyrighted by the Frank Lloyd Wright Foundation 1986. Tokyo: A.D.A. Edita Tokyo, Ltd. p. 69. Courtesy The Frank Lloyd Wright Foundation.

2

INTRODUCTION

Wright referred to wood in the most sympathetic terms. To Wright wood was lovable, friendly, kind, and "the most humanly intimate of all materials."[1] The linearity of lumber contributes to wood's image in this regard, as its relatively small section is of human scale, with lengths not so great as to prevent one person from easily handling a standard-size component. It is likely, however, that Wright's exploitation of the basic proportions of wood is motivated more by his desire for horizontality in his buildings. Wright ignored, for the most part, wood's high workability, a property that contributes significantly to the sense of humanity and intimacy in wood. Instead, he preferred to express the essence of the machine in plain flat surfaces.

Wright could have limited the spans of his wood in response to its moderate strength, thus affecting the scale of a building and its interior spaces. He often chose, however, to push the expression of wood strength beyond its logical limitations and to control scale by other means. The aspect of wood that appears to be most responsible for Wright's fond attention is its grain. However, Wright's partiality for wood's delicate and varied grain patterns could only be addressed with efficiency in the interiors of buildings. The inability of wood to maintain the beauty of its natural surface in the weather was a dilemma for Wright as it is for most designers. This type of incompatibility of intuitive desire with the demands of properties is common in Wright's approach to materials. It tended to generate details that upon occasion challenged the nature of wood with regard to its durability.

Figure 2-1. Ornamental post in a bedroom of the Susan Lawrence Dana Residence. (Courtesy The Illinois Historic Preservation Agency—The Dana-Thomas House and Doug Carr, photographer, The Dana-Thomas Foundation)

FORM

Wright's derivation of the forms he identified as natural to wood appears to have been driven as much by a determination to reject certain characteristics as by a desire to adopt others. The machine, conservation, plasticity, and other factors he cited to justify straight, simple, plain, and mostly rectangular shapes in wood are almost coincidental to his rejection of "old curvatures and imaging of organic-forms; the morbid twists and curious turns,

the contortions imposed on wood."[2] His reasoning favoring the simpler sections was relatively coherent compared to his rejection of curvilinear and complex forms, which was based on less logical arguments.

Wright revealed the large but controlled role of machines in his view of wood when he declared that they have enabled the designer "to realize the true nature of wood in his designs harmoniously with man's sense of beauty."[3] The statement pays homage to the machine without forfeiting the designer's prerogative to call *natural* those product characteristics considered to be beautiful. Rather than allowing the full potential of machine processing (including its ability to produce curvilinear lines) to define the nature of wood in its entirety, Wright cited compatibilities between the nature of mechanical processing and those aspects of wood he favored. In a reference to furniture he observed that "clean straightline effects…are characteristic of the machine."[4] This approach falls short of synthesizing the characteristics of processes in sawmills and shop fabrication into a definition of wood form.

The standard sawmill produces long, narrow, straight, and flat components with 90-degree corners in all planes. Wood production is a machine-dominated process characterized by straight movements parallel and perpendicular to each other. The basic manufactured geometry defines the nature of lumber with regard to form. Its expression in architecture calls for a demonstration of wood's linearity in the large scale and rectangularity in the small scale. Since there are no other options for product geometry from the basic processes of the standard mill, the nature of wood form generated at this level is relatively clear. Utilitarian and economical demands are the primary influences. Wright's commentary and use of wood are generally compatible with this objectively based version of the nature of wood form.

Subsequent processing in specialty mills and shops is characterized by changes in the nature of machines and product movement with a corresponding increase in human handling. This increase facilitates the production of a greater variety of component shapes, often having the increased refinement that is the purpose of secondary manufacturing. Unlike those of the sawmill, many of the product forms of specialty mills are taste-driven, with utility and economy maximized only after they have been compromised to achieve the desired image. It is in this realm that Wright's embracing of machine potential was the most selective. The machine will teach us, he said, "that certain simple forms and handling serve to bring out the beauty of wood, and to retain its character, and that certain other forms and handling do not bring out its beauty, but spoil it."[5]

Wright rejected certain profiles that had become standard machine products by virtue of their popularity.

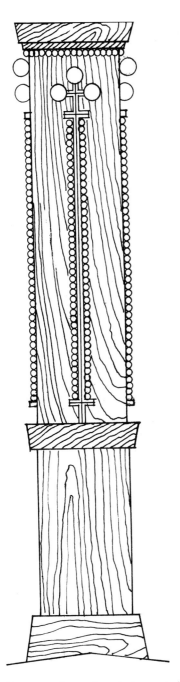

FIGURE 2-2. Ornamental newel post at an exterior stair of the Frank Thomas Residence. (From Frank Lloyd Wright Archives drawing 0106.007.)

He lamented the preference of manufacturers for molded and turned sections in response to the market demand since it drove up the cost of his simpler but unique woodwork.[6] He did not consider the machine to be the definer of natural wood form when it produced nonrectangular or complex curvilinear sections. Wright generally favored simple geometric forms, especially rectangles, but small circular and angular sections were also included in

FIGURE 2-3. Block ornaments on top of fascia and perforated plywood glazing panels at the Kundert Medical Clinic.

his detailing. He went so far as to list shapes that were acceptable in wood, which predictably included a variety of straight flat rectangular components. He also included, however, round sections and block forms and allowed for the ornamental treatment of poles and timbers.[7]

Some of his approved shapes were less common in his work than others. Ornamental poles appeared in the library of his Oak Park Home and Studio (1895), in the master bedroom of the Dana House (1902), and adjacent to exterior stairs at the Thomas House (1901) and other locations, but were not used extensively. Accent blocks contrast in their lack of linearity with the other shapes Wright used. The form of blocklike wood overlaps into the spirit of masonry although Wright's blocky wood detailing is smaller than a typical masonry unit. They appeared periodically in many of his buildings in a number of formats. Series of block shapes occur as dentils along the ceiling trim of the Winslow House (1893), D. D. Martin House (1903), and his Oak Park Home (1889). Slightly larger, and more widely spaced versions can be found at such locations as the exterior at Taliesin

FIGURE 2-4. Extensive expression of wood grain in walls, ceilings, screens, and furniture at the Carlton Wall Residence. Linear expression in ceiling and walls. (Courtesy The Frank Lloyd Wright Archives)

West (1937), the M. M. Smith House (1948), and outside and inside the Hagan House (1954) where they run along the lower edges of the fascia as well as around hexagonal openings in the roof overhang. Occasionally they appear on top the fascia such as at the Kundert Medical Clinic (1956).

Wright's many favorable references to the appearance of wood grain revealed that this characteristic was, like the nature of the machine, central to his reasoning for justifying flat and other simple geometries as being the most appropriate for wood. Flatness, he thought, was in the nature of wood because it exhibited grain characteristics better than surfaces that were not flat. This was not an argument based on any natural affinity in wood for flatness but on the ability of flatness to enhance beauty. His claim that "the beauty of wood lies in its qualities as wood"[8] is a reminder that to express

a material property was, by his definition, to express beauty. Limitations or weaknesses in materials were recognized occasionally but were not considered in the same way as were properties contributing to beauty. Wright's definition of the nature of wood did not include its shortcomings.

A uniform derivation of the nature of a material would logically compare like properties among all materials. It would be expected, therefore, that if the internal structure of wood embodied the essence of wood, expressing this aspect of other materials would reveal their nature also. To Wright, however, it was not the internal structure but the beauty of it that was the common property. This attitude is illustrated by his failure to promote the expression of the internal patterns in clay, concrete, and steel which, according to Wright, lacked the beauty required to qualify as a property. Beauty as

FIGURE 2-5. Plywood panels expressed in linear format with horizontal projected battens in the second prefabricated house design for the Marshall Erdman Company. Metal poles at stairs, with block ornaments attached. Subdued vertical joints and emphasized horizontal joints in concrete block at fireplace. No lintel expressed at concrete block fireplace. (Courtesy The Frank Lloyd Wright Archives)

the basis for reasoning typified his materials discourse as well as his commentary on other issues in architecture.

If a flat board surface reveals the beauty of wood grain, simplistic reasoning suggests that a larger flat surface would do so even more. Although Wright typically did not follow literal reasoning such as this to its extreme conclusion, he did so with regard to wood grain. He considered machine-cut veneers to be a kind of paper that revealed in their surfaces the beauty of wood grain and that could be adhered to large surfaces. He accepted sliced and sawn veneers as well as the rotary-cut version, in which he observed a new configuration for grain[9] that he considered to be in the nature of wood in spite of its flamboyant character.[10] The continuity of these broad surfaces was important to the clarity of the grain as well as to the plasticity that he favored. Consequently, he thought, that once this property had been liberated so clearly in the form of a broad flat

plane, it would be "folly to mold it, and join it, and panel it painfully any more."[11] Apparently, bending the veneered plane such as that found on the balcony fascia in the living room of the H. Johnson House (1937) was not problematic in this regard as the large curve of the surface does not obscure the grain.

The lack of homogeniality of veneered components appeared to pose no dilemma for Wright with regard to honesty in materials representation. He accepted veneers in strips (which might resemble boards) as well as sheets laminated to other veneers or other substances.[12] In his commentary there was no confusion about the nature of the veneer. It was something to be appreciated in its own right, a product which he praised for its own characteristics without regard to what other products it might resemble. The fact that the surface material could differ in quality, size, or substance from the substrate was addressed only in terms of its favorable economy and efficiency.

FIGURE 2-6. Lack of continuity and structural logic in ceiling bands at the Avery Coonley Residence. Expressed lintel at brick fireplace. (Courtesy The Frank Lloyd Wright Archives)

Wright noted that the use of veneers could save trees.[13] The implication is that surface grain is wood's most important characteristic, as he seemed willing to eliminate its other aspects in the interest of conservation. His several references to the minimal waste associated with veneers are a kind of justification for their use but do not appear to be excuses for imitating thicker wood (which they tend to do). Perhaps he considered imitation (which he held in contempt) to be defined in the mind of the perpetrator rather than the beholder. He did not entertain the possibility that veneers might be dishonest in their misrepresentation of reality.

In the same spirit he also claimed the minimization of waste to be a benefit of using long bands of ceiling trim, which he thought yielded "the charm of timbering without the waste."[14] By some definitions, this constitutes an imitation of timbers that seems incongruous with Wright's promotion of architectural honesty. Rather than a lapse in expressive integrity, however, the statement suggests an ambivalence towards the strength of wood as a significant property. Most of his ceiling trims lack credibility as imitations of timber due to the absence of structural logic in their configuration. The wood on the Coonley living room (1906) and Unity Church (1905) ceilings, for example, lack the continuity necessary in real timbering. It is too plastic in such installations as the bedroom of the Wright's Oak Park Home (1889), in the second Little House (1913), and in the studio of Taliesin II (1914) as it follows the breaking planes of the ceilings, turns down onto the walls, and/or forms decorative patterns. The wood strips of the gabled ceilings in the Heurtley dining room (1902) and Cheney living room (1903) lack a ridge beam as do those at Taliesin II (1914), the dining room of the Thomas House (1901), and in the Dana House (1902) and numerous other locations that are also too plastic as they follow breaks in the surfaces.

The vaulted ceiling trim of the Dana House (1902)

FIGURE 2-7. Wood banding follows planes of ceiling and walls in a bedroom of the Susan Lawrence Dana Residence. No ridge beam expressed. Ornamental wood poles. No lintel expressed at brick fireplace. (Courtesy The Illinois Historic Preservation Agency—The Dana-Thomas House and Doug Carr, photographer, The Dana-Thomas Foundation)

and Wright's Oak Park Home Playroom Addition (1895) suggest massive wood arches which are not generally thought of as timbers. A convincing timber image occurs at the Davenport living room ceiling (1901), which appears to have a reasonable span, adequate width, and the straightness typical of large beams. Present also is the structural logic necessary to be convincing as the wood aligns with thick mullions between the windows, suggesting the transfer of beam loads downward. Of course, as with all such trim, it lacks the expressed depth typical of real timbering. The beamlike ceiling trim of the Robie House (1906, due to some plasticity) and Bradley House (1900, with an excessive apparent span) are slightly less timberlike. If they exist at all, images of timbering in the structural sense are in the minority among the banded ceilings of Wright's buildings.

Given the lack of structural integrity displayed by the trim patterns, it is the form of wood rather than the strength of wood in Wright's view that emerges as the property providing the timbers with their charm. The relative lack of depth in the ceiling strips nearly limits the expressed form to the bottom surface of the would-be timbers. The focus thus directed to the grain of the wood is shared only by the linearity of the strips, two characteristics that Wright exploited in much of his wood detailing. In any case, a commitment to saving trees by forfeiting the use of real timbers is neither convincing nor needed as a justification for his use of ceiling bands. Wright also alluded to the trim as a modulator of scale and texture which, alone, is adequate justification for it.

Wright also complained of the waste inherent in the production of the complex shapes of certain historically

FIGURE. 2-8. Arched ceiling bands in the gallery of the Susan Lawrence Dana Residence. (Courtesy The Illinois Historic Preservation Agency—The Dana-Thomas House and Doug Carr, photographer, The Dana-Thomas Foundation)

FIGURE 2-9. Wood ceiling bands turn down face of dropped ceiling at perimeter of Frederick C. Robie Residence living room. Lintel expressed at brick fireplace.

inspired woodwork that he claimed was absent in the production of straight simple wood elements. His urging the use of simple round spindles (alternating with flat or square strips)[15] would not eliminate the waste generated by cutting round sections from square stock. Wright's square or rectangular balusters are in the majority, appearing in such houses as the Charnley (1891), Winslow (1893), Willits (1902), D. D. Martin (1903), Davidson (1908), Gilmore (1908), and other buildings, thus establishing that profile geometry as the preferred one. Examples of round and/or tapered and decorative balusters that are as wasteful as Victorian versions occur in the Blossom House (1892), W. M. Gale House (1893), his Oak Park Home Playroom Addition (1895), Heller House (1896), and the C. E. Roberts House (1896). These early round sections are thus chronologically bracketed in his work by the use of square stock.

The focus on waste among the various products seems unnecessary and appears to signify, especially for veneers, a lack of faith in their general acceptance in their own right. The fact that waste in other materials is not addressed (the shortage of steel after World War II was not an issue of discussion for Wright), may not be significant given Wright's general lack of consistency in attention to issues among different materials. Wright tended to confront only those issues in a material that he thought to be important in that material. The waste of trees may have been of greater concern to him than the waste of clay or iron. If waste was inconsequential in

concrete, for example, its lack of preciousness produced no tendency toward overt extravagance in its use or comments on the concept. The purposeful expression of a material's abundance or a commentary on its appropriate affect on design has an academic abstractness about it that was not Wright's style. He approached the theory and practice of material use more directly.

A true commitment to the conservation of wood could dictate the substitution of concrete or steel for wood entirely or, at least, in hidden locations. The enormous amount of wood in the sanctuary roof of the Unitarian Church (1947) is lost for any visual purpose as it is entirely hidden above the ceiling. As a principle, the conservation of wood was unable to supersede, in this case, the influence of economics and general design goals that dictated the use of wood and the hiding of it from sight. (Once wood is selected, expressing it is an act of conservation as more use is gained from the material.) The failure to let conservation govern when it did not serve Wright's design goals reflects a commitment to architecture in the broadest sense instead of to issues narrow in scope.

Wright's claim that the use of veneers was real conservation because only the beautiful aspects of wood were used[16] reveals less about his commitment to conservation than about his view of wood. As a veneer, wood has lost nearly all of its properties save the appearance of its surface. Consequently, this aspect is revealed to represent, to Wright, the essence of wood. Thus an ambivalence is indicated towards the visual impact available from wood's other properties such as strength, durability, and workability. (A veneer might be considered by some to be a product of working wood but the working is not readily apparent in the final component.)

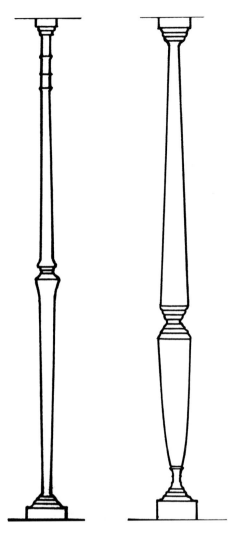

FIGURE 2-10. Balusters at the Walter M. Gale Residence (left) and the George Blossom Residence. (From photographs, *Frank Lloyd Wright Monograph 1887–1901*, pp. 18, 36.)

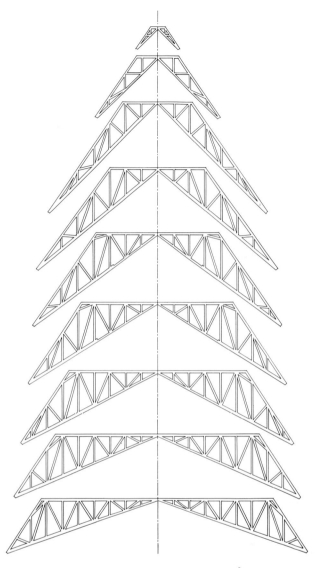

FIGURE 2-11. Roof trusses of the Unitarian Church. (From Frank Lloyd Wright Archives drawing 5031.048.)

Although Wright's desire for plasticity in wood did not originate in the nature of the substance, he appreciated a particular uniqueness in wood's relationship to plasticity. He recognized that the flow of grain across the surface was a plastic effect not found in other materials.[17] Enhancing the expression of the grain would increase the plasticity of the image and elevating the plasticity of the detailing would strengthen the appearance of the grain. Wood's potential for plasticity of form is a relatively new phenomenon Wright observed, as without the machine, the production of broad flat and flowing surfaces of wood would not be characteristic of the material and would be too expensive to be accessible.[18] The emphasis of plasticity tends to subdue the identities of individual components, in effect, denying some or all of their dimensions. Making wood plastic

meant making it "light and continuously flowing instead of the heavy 'cut and butt' of the usual carpenter work," he thought.[19] The length of lumber and millwork stock loses its identity as the joints of butted pieces are concealed.

The specific length of lumber has some established identity due to its well-known two-foot increments, its even-numbered nominal dimensions, and its influence on design that is sometimes planned around standard lengths to minimize cutting. Millwork traditionally has no identity with regard to specific length as it does not influence room dimensioning and is treated as being virtually continuous once installed. In both lumber and millwork, however, length plays a role in component image in that its many variations are typically long

FIGURE 2-12. Roof construction of the Unitarian Church. (Courtesy The Frank Lloyd Wright Archives)

enough to establish a proportion that is relatively slender (linear). The very large increase in apparent length is typical in Wright's plastic detailing does not change the essence of the basic geometry. The wood is still linear and still contrasts with the form of nonlinear materials such as masonry. A veneer's length and width do not establish a preinstallation identity except possibly in the case of standard plywood. After installation, veneers usually remain rectangular—which is as much of an identity as it ever had to most observers.

Although Wright's use of wood in a great variety of thicknesses and surface widths ignores the exact manufactured dimensional identity of wood, it tends to maintain the general image. Linear stock typically retains a linear image after installation, albeit a more intense linearity. Typically it gains a significant increase in apparent length due to the virtual invisibility of butted end-joints while its original width remains apparent. The condition is common in the detailing of most designers. In contrast to the tendency to obscure board length there appears to be a desire to celebrate board width in Wright's detailing. This is evident in his praise of the joints between the edges of board-paneled walls that, because of their ornamental nature, define each board as an individual unit.[20]

The thickness of Wright's flat-roof overhangs express the depth of their structural lumber. The expressive intensity of the lumber dimension is given a boost where the overhang changes thickness in steps equal to the depth of the wood. Although the fascias on the stepped soffit of the Sondern and Goetsch-Winckler houses (1939) are slightly deeper than the cantilevering lumber, the detail ties the character of the architecture to a property (depth) of the wood used. The rectangularity of the wood is also expressed in the right-angled steps of the soffits, which seems no more than logical but is significant when compared to the more plastic changes in the thickness of cantilevered concrete as in such locations as the Johnson Wax complex (1936, 1944) and the Price Tower (1952).

Board widths are slightly less apparent when the edges of millwork are assembled in contact with each other compared to single strips isolated in a field of plaster such as in Unity Church (1905) and in most of Wright's banded ceilings. The apparent length of the trim is typically far greater than the width of a single unit or the entire assembly of parallel pieces, thus assuring the expression of linearity of the whole. As in the interior plastered surfaces, the natural linearity of exterior wood in a field of stucco is unmistakable. The strongest

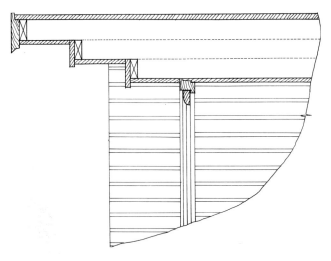

FIGURE 2-13. Section at roof overhang showing stepped soffit of the Clarence Sondern Residence. (From Frank Lloyd Wright Archives drawing 4014.010.)

FIGURE 2-14. Wood bands isolated in plaster field in the sanctuary, Unity Church. (Courtesy Mike Kertok)

FIGURE 2-15. Parallel series of vertical wood trim isolated in field of stucco at the Thomas P. Hardy Residence. (Courtesy The Frank Lloyd Wright Archives)

linear statements occur when several parallel trim pieces are separated by stucco as in the horizontal strips in the Henderson (1901) and Fricke (1902) houses and the vertical strips on the Hardy House (1905) and in the gables of the Moore House (1923). Compared to trim on stucco, the individual boards of wood siding have a lower intensity of linear expression due to the absence of contrasting background for them. An entire wall of wood siding may be more intensely linear than a few boards on a stuccoed wall, however, depending on the detailing.

Although clapboard siding as in the Blossom House (1892) and the W. M. Gale House (1893) maintains a degree of linear expression by virtue of its shadow lines, the fact that the product is so common prevents it from being the vehicle for a profound statement about the form of wood. The product was not favored by Wright after his earliest houses; thus there are no signs that beveled clapboard siding had any particular significance to him. The intentionality of Wright's emphasis of wood's natural form is more certain in three other devices he used to express board width.

His use of projected battens clarifies board width in a field of wood cladding the most intensely among his joint treatments. The detail can be found at the Pitkin (1900), Davenport (1901), Gale (summer house,

FIGURE 2-16. Parallel wood bands isolated in field of stucco at the William G. Fricke Residence. Wood trim rests on water table. (Courtesy Mike Kertok)

1905), Glasner (1905), and Stewart (1909) houses as well as the "Ocatillo" Desert Compound (1929), and a number of other examples. Unusually large and widely spaced battens cover the horizontal joints of the plywood wall panels in the second Erdman prefab design (1957). Projected battens were eventually supplanted as

FIGURE 2-17. Horizontal projected battens at the George Stewart Residence. (Courtesy The Frank Lloyd Wright Archives)

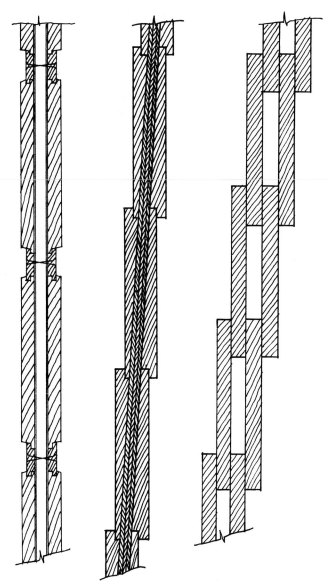

FIGURE 2-18. Wall sections at the Paul and Jean Hanna Residence (left), John C. Pew Residence (center), and Rose Pauson Residence. Exterior surface on right side of each. (From Frank Lloyd Wright Archives drawings 3701.023, 4012.19, 4011.050.)

FIGURE 2-19. Plastic configuration of projected ceiling battens and wood grain at the Carlton Wall Residence. (Courtesy The Frank Lloyd Wright Archives)

the favored detail by inset battens. Having less of a shadow line, the narrow strips inset between wider boards are physically less emphatic than are projected battens but regain some emphasis through their appearance of deliberateness. The absence of a utilitarian function in the inset battens such as is inherent in projected battens elevates the intensity of their artistic message as they appear to exist only for expressive purposes. Shiplap boards such as inside and outside the A. P. Johnson House (1905) have much the same image as the inset battens except in the closest view. Once they are under-

stood to be the more common shiplap product, their sense of deliberateness is significantly diminished.

The Hanna (1935), Pope (1940), and Baird (1940) houses are among many having exterior board and inset-batten-sided elements. The initial linearity, plasticity, and horizontality of the first Jacobs House (1936) was boosted considerably by the contrasting colors of its pine boards and inset redwood battens over houses incorporating a single species of wood. The contrast of this strong board-definition with the lesser clarity of boards and strips of the same color is illustrated by comparing the image of the raw wood in the Jacobs House to the same surface after weathering and a coating of creosote had rendered the walls a uniformly dark tone.

Inset-batten walls in the interior such as the inside surfaces of the exterior walls as well as the interior partitions of the Sturges House (1939) and the ceilings at the Anthony (1949), Zimmerman (1952), and Hagan (1954) houses have no shadow lines to emphasize their linear expression. Their proximity to the viewer and their striking natural wood finishes are enough to draw attention to the slight change in surface plane between the boards at the inset-battens. The importance of proximity to the reading of linearity defined by conditions of low contrast is further illustrated by the absence of battens or laps in the flush board ceilings at the Rebhuhn (1938), Sturges (1939), Wall (1941), Lovness (1955) and other houses. Only a small groove at the joints defines board width in these houses but it is enough for the linearity of the wood to dominate the ceilings. On another ceiling of the Wall House projected battens clearly define boards but plasticity rather than linearity is emphasized because of the complexity of the pattern.

FIGURE 2-20. Broad fascias step out the thickness of a board with each horizontal strip at Suntop Homes. Wood mass is linear and is held high above grade. (Courtesy The Frank Lloyd Wright Archives)

Wright's lapped and partially lapped horizontal-siding boards installed with vertical (plumb) faces define their edges in a way similar to that of the slightly sloped faces of clapboards but have a greater sense of artistic purpose. The unusual relationship between boards—wherein the plumb face of each board is set forward of the one below—defines their edges both by the change of plane and the shadow line created. Unlike tilted clapboards, Wright's lapped plumb-faced boards cause exterior walls to step outward as each board face is positioned forward of the one below. The highly expressive condition brings attention to the boards as individual units and, therefore, emphasizes their natural linear form. The Sturges (1939), Pew (1938), and Affleck (1941) houses, among others, enjoy a remarkably strong linear quality in their wood cladding due to this type of detailing.

Board siding such as that of Suntop Homes (1939) and the Pauson House (1939) was detailed so that each entire board was set forward of the one below. The fully lapped units boost the form expression to a nearly literal level by showing the entire board thickness in con-

trast to the partial thicknesses revealed by partially lapped boards. Consequently, the projection of the top of the wall beyond the bottom becomes an exact multiple of the thickness of a single board (thickness times number of boards above the bottom board). This produces the clearest definition of board form (deepest shadow line) among the lapped variations and yields the strongest tie between the nature of a board and the design of a building element. The small dimensions that are involved and the fact that the observer's recognition of this detail's achievement is not assured, however, temper the intellectual impact of this remarkably direct link between a material's nature and architecture.

Extensive use of lapped boards at the Sturges House (1939) yields an intense expression of the nature of wood through the clear boardlike linearity covering the house inside and out. Several variations of the detail help reduce the monotony that might otherwise desensitize one to the expressiveness of the wood. Lapping units of exterior walls emphasizes their long lines on both their interior and exterior surfaces. Horizontal battens project through the joints of the battered (inward leaning) walls at the

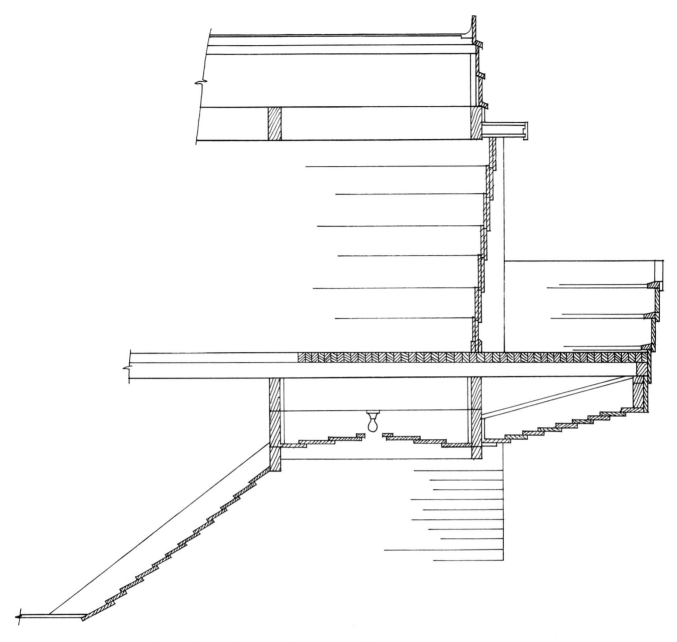

Figure 2-21. Section of George Sturges Residence showing four different details emphasizing board proportions in the facade. (From Frank Lloyd Wright Archives drawing 3905.017.)

top of the house. Inset battens occur in interior partitions. Fully lapped boards, cover the large sloped and highly visible soffits around the lower part of the house.

The Sturges soffits include units with parallel faces as well as boards in an inverted clapboardlike configuration. If the clapboard laps were right side up (units overlapping the exterior faces of those below) in these sheltered surfaces, their apparent linearity would be much subdued in the absence of shadow lines. In the inverted position on the sloped soffits, the edge of each board is more or less perpendicular to the observer, thus yielding the most clear view of them possible. The maximization of linearity and expressed thickness that results from this

detail is further intensified by its sense of purposefulness. Since it is a unique variation of a standard clapboardlike detail, it appears to have been generated in order to achieve a particular expressive goal. Such apparent purpose diminishes any sense of utilitarian function in the detail that would have rendered the visual effect incidental and therefore less important to the message of the architecture and the material.

Lapped board ceilings occur in a number houses including Pew (1938) and L. Lewis (1940) where, since the laps change direction at the center of the living room, one can see emphasized linearity for at least half the surface from any point in the space. The boardlike

Figure 2-22. Horizontal lapped boards applied in long and short radius curves at the Robert Llewellyn Wright Residence. Fascias step out with each higher board. (Courtesy The Frank Lloyd Wright Archives)

linearity of the ceiling at the David Wright House (1950) is interrupted slightly by the turns of the boards necessary to emulate the curve of the exterior wall but is enhanced by the contrast afforded in the juxtaposition of the lines with the blockiness of the concrete units in the walls.

The partially lapped siding of the H. Johnson House (Wingspread, 1937) emphasizes linearity at the expense of reality. A routed strip at its lower edge makes each single board appear to be two boards. A surface thus clad appears to be alternating wide and narrow boards each overhanging the one below. The expression of linearity is thus elevated above that of lapped boards and battens, having more shadow lines than either plus the sense of purposefulness that comes with a special composition.

The boards are highly worked but without expressing workability, since the complex edge configurations are not apparent as installed. This condition is the same for all the edge joints of the board siding except where the boards remain rectangular in section. The workabil-

ity of wood is shown here and elsewhere to be exploited in the service of other properties (enhancing the clarity of wood form, preventing water penetration) but is not expressed in its own right. The misrepresentation at Wingspread of board width and the number of boards present cannot be reconciled with Wright's promotion of honesty unless the issue is deemed too insignificant for concern. Long slender boards are shown in the facade to be long and slender, albeit by means of exaggeration, a common tactic in artistic expression.

The expression of wood width is not essential to plasticity where the absence of clearly defined unit edges can facilitate multidirectional flow. In Wright's wood, multidirectional plasticity was typically an interior phenomenon because veneers that best express this type of plasticity do not weather well. Given the relatively small size of interior surfaces, cabinets, and furniture, veneer plasticity is necessarily limited in scale. With lumber's linear identity, its use plastically produces directional visual flow that tends to be larger in scale than the multidirectional flow of veneered surfaces. This is because

FIGURE 2-23. Horizontal board siding on the Romeo and Juliet Windmill with projected battens after every third board. (Courtesy The Frank Lloyd Wright Archives)

lumber needs significant length only in one direction, while veneers need two large dimensions if they are to avoid a linear image. Typically, interior surfaces are longer in one direction than the other and exterior walls are typically longer than those inside to which veneers

are largely restricted. Lumber and its unidirectional flow, therefore, tends to overshadow the multidirectional plasticity of the smaller veneered surfaces in Wright's work.

Plasticity suggests the presence of turns in the flowing plane, standard practice in Wright's wood walls and fascias. Long runs of board surfaces usually continue around one or more corners, thus adding three-dimensional plasticity to the expression but is unidirectional within each plane. The R. L. Wright House (1953) provides a rare example of curved wood siding and therefore of plasticity in the more traditional (curvilinear) sense. It could be argued that since straightness is an inherent property of boards, some expression within the nature of wood form is forfeited in behalf of plasticity here. If so, any loss of form-identity is at least partially compensated by the added expression of wood's workability inherent in curved wood. Expressed workability is always in at least partial conflict with primary form but can combine with form to express the nature of the material more intensely than can either property alone.

The potential conflict between wood's basic form and its ability to be reshaped has been resolved here in an unusual way. The bend in the wood is so gentle that the new configuration is not so far removed from its original shape thus the basic sense of wood form is not significantly obscured. Normally a large radius bend would express workability only slightly as minimal effort is reflected. In this case, however, the expression of workability is elevated by the exaggerated length of the arc which represents an accumulation of many small efforts to bend individual components. The large arc also boosts the importance of the working by showing it to be the root of a physically imposing form that is a significant part of the aesthetic strategy for the building. A small sacrifice in the expression of one property has yielded a large return in the expression of another for a net increase in attention to the nature of wood. The expression of worked wood here is more likely to have been a by-product of a quest for plasticity than a desire to express workability in its own right. The expression of workability, nevertheless, remains a component of the building character.

The plasticity of the Romeo and Juliet Windmill (1896) is not curvilinear but is similar in its three-dimensionality. Wright achieved plasticity in the flow of its board siding (substituted for the original shingles in 1938)[21] around the many bends of its small polygonal plan. Some linearity is developed in the surfaces due to the many parallel lines and its unusual combination of inset battens at every joint combined with periodic projecting battens. Without a long horizontal dimension the horizontal boards have difficulty in doing more than tempering slightly the verticality of the tall slender structure. The horizontal proportions common in much of

FIGURE 2-24. Horizontal projected battens and building proportions, Bitter Root Inn. (Courtesy The Frank Lloyd Wright Archives)

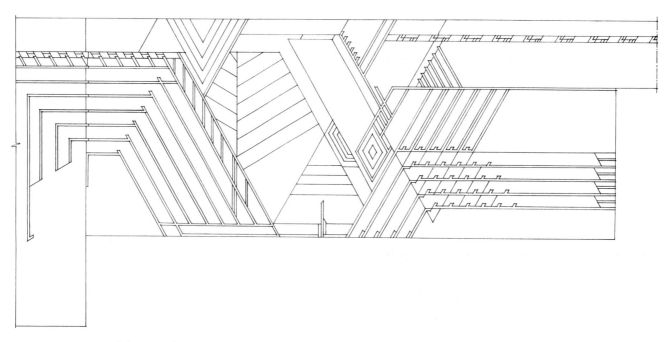

FIGURE 2-25. Parallel series of wood strips in variety of orientations at the office of Edgar J. Kaufmann, Sr. (From Frank Lloyd Wright Archives drawing 3704.002.)

Wright's work are philosophically and physically compatible with a horizontal linearity in lumber. Boards butted end to end can seem to flow endlessly on his long facades with the possibility of returning on themselves as they might pass entirely around a building, if so desired, as they actually do in the Romeo and Juliet Windmill. Vertically oriented siding would typically produce a plasticity more limited in the length of its flow (except in tall

structures such as the windmill) and would counter rather than support the horizontal image Wright sought for many of his buildings.

Wright praised board and batten detailing in all orientations[22] but failed to make extensive use of any but the horizontal version. An unusual combination of directional patterns appears in the plywood paneling of the Edgar J. Kaufmann, Sr., Pittsburgh Office (1937).

The fact that the patterns are unlike boards or panels and are reminiscent of compositions that Wright produced in fabric, metal, and stone indicate that the assembly is related to wood only in its workability and surface qualities and so is an expression of only those aspects of the nature of wood. A rare installation of slanted boards occurs on the exterior of the Stevens buildings (1939) in a reverse-batten wall that is also battered and on the Griggs House (1946), which also incorporates horizontal boards. Diagonal lapped boards can be found on the walls of the mezzanine in the second Jacobs House (1943). Surface configurations usually prevent long runs in diagonal wood and thus significant plasticity is not achieved in Wright's few applications. Given the subdued plasticity in diagonal boards and their opposition to horizontality, it not surprising that they are rare in Wright's wood.

Although individual shingles are rectangular, Wright's use of them in the standard format yielded surfaces with a linear rather than a rectangular quality. The flush vertical joints are less prominent than are the long shadow lines of the lapped horizontal joints thus producing an image similar to that of clapboards. The fact that this is the standard installation for shingles diminishes but does not completely eliminate the significance of his decision to allow the form of individual components of this particular product to remain subdued in his buildings. Charles and Henry Greene showed that the rectangularity of shingles could be emphasized in their design of the Gamble House (1908) where shingles were installed with their bottom edges slightly misaligned and with small spaces between units. As a result the expression of shingle rectangularity was elevated slightly above the norm.

The fact that standard shingle detailing gave surfaces the horizontal emphasis that Wright favored is a likely reason why he did not alter it to express more strongly the nature of individual shingle form. Installing shingles out of alignment or with spaces between units clarifies the identity of each thus increasing their contrast with clapboards. Wright's overlooking of unit form in this instance seems more purposeful than incidental in light of his occasional willingness to alter a standard detail for a greater sense of horizontality. Placing wood strips under periodic courses of the original shingles of the Romeo and Juliet Windmill (1896) and on the roof of the C. Brown House (1905) indicates that even with the horizontal shadow lines of standard shingle detailing, the horizontality of the surfaces was not intense enough. The unusual combination of horizontal battens and shingles on the Porter House (1907) is further evidence of this probability. The addition of the battens increases the horizontal linearity of the facade and further subdues the rectangularity of the shingles.

FIGURE 2-27. Horizontal bands of roof shingles and horizontal projected battens, Charles E. Brown Residence. (Courtesy The Frank Lloyd Wright Archives)

Like his variations on the standard shingle composition, Wright's variations in board siding detailing tended to emphasize horizontality rather than diminish it. Regardless of whether or not his detailing of board cladding was motivated by a desire for plasticity and horizontality, it is consistently linear and therefore reflects the spirit of basic wood form. The focus on the natural form of lumber suggested by the cladding, however, is tempered by Wright's lack of an equally strong record in the expression of linearity in structural wood.

The linearity of structural lumber is easily expressed. Unless it is hidden by cladding, its normal use brings it into minimal contact with other materials thus minimizing the visual blending of its form with its surroundings. For structural purposes, columns need contact other construction only at their ends. Although beams typically touch other materials along their top edges, they project downward from the other surfaces to maintain a linearity that is more three-dimensional than that of cladding. Cladding components usually touch components on all four edges, are flush or nearly flush with the surrounding surface, and require special detailing (such as battens) if the expression of form is to be more than minimal. The expression of structural wood's basic form, then, becomes a function of the degree to which the components are exposed and arranged to emphasize their linelike quality. Like cladding, series of uninterrupted parallel structural lines tend to boost the sensation of linearity and, consequently, the presence of basic wood form.

Wright's tendency to hide structural wood reflects an attitude about building in general as much as it does about wood. Nevertheless, it may be concluded that, to Wright, the appearance of structural wood was not often desirable to a degree sufficient to supersede his goals for a particular building image. For example structural wood's three-dimensionality and periodic placement would tend to interrupt the visual flow that was so important to plasticity. More continuity, and therefore plasticity, could be achieved by covering the structural members with a relatively smooth surface than would result from exposing beams, columns, and bracing.

Wright's covering of rafter ends with fascia boards increased the visual flow of the eave but may have also been a reaction to the craftsman-style (which he did not like) overtones of the exposed rafters. In the rare example of joists exposed under the roof overhang at the Stevens (1939) and second Jacobs (1943) houses, the ends of the members are covered with a fascia board, effectively obscuring the periodic rhythm of the joists.

His desire for original and plastic architecture was not always compatible with a routine use of wood structures as the expressive vehicle. It may also be significant that the most structurally remarkable parts of Wright's wood-framed construction were composites of wood and steel, a combination sometimes lacking the neatness and clarity usually considered necessary for exposure.

While the continuity of surface is largely a matter of choice on the face of a building, it is less so in the interior. The smaller surfaces and greater number of corners, built-ins, stairwells, and openings make the achievement of plasticity more difficult. Exposed structure would be, therefore, less disruptive to the already compromised interior than to the exterior. Although Wright was willing to expose more structure inside than outside, he did not consistently do so.

Beams running through the living room of the Sturges House (1939) are unique in their nearly total three-dimensional exposure, thus maximizing the sense of linearity in the expression of the wood. Their tops are not in direct contact with the roof construction thus their linear geometry is particularly clear. (They provide support to the structure above through a few thin decorative posts on top the beams). The wood beams of the Storer House (1923) enjoy some emphasis and, therefore, clarity of form because they contrast in color and shape with the concrete block of the walls. At the other extreme, the blocky pattern along the bottom of the wood strips on the Lovness ceilings (1955) obscures the linear statement, which is already limited by the shallowness of the components.

Unique combinations of both interior and exterior expression of wood structure occurs at the Stevens House and the second Jacobs House, where the exposed ceiling joists pass through the exterior walls and remain visible under the overhang of the roof. In addition, joists are exposed in the Teater House (1952) and trusses in the Griggs House (1946). The most unusual and powerful statements of wood form are made at the two Taliesins, one inside and the other outside. At Taliesin West (1937), the gently sloping exterior wood roof structure demands attention by its contrast in color with the roof, by its large depth, by its uniqueness, by its repetition, and by its significant role in the aesthetic order of the building. Since the intensity of a material's expression is related to the importance of the material to the architectural statement, this configuration maximizes the importance of the wood.

Linearity, the characteristic property of basic wood form, enjoys an exceptionally strong presence at Taliesin West. Unlike the few other exposed beams, however, the cross-section of the units is not the simple rectangle of primary wood form. The assembly which is thicker at its base and steps inward to a thinner top edge is wood-

FIGURE 2-28. Horizontal projected battens between groups of five shingled courses, Andrew Porter Residence. (Courtesy The Frank Lloyd Wright Archives)

like in the solidness of its parts and the 90-degree corners of its configuration. The overall proportions of the section, however, and the relative thinness of edge compared to the total structure are reminiscent of steel. During restoration, steel flitch plates were revealed to be hidden within the exposed roof beams of the administration wing and are also suspected to be in the other exposed wood roof beams of the complex.

A clearer statement of the simple rectangular section typical of lumber occurs in the wood structure of the drafting room of Taliesin at Spring Green (1933). The linearity of the wood is slightly obscured by the multiplicity of triangulated members overlaid in the field of vision. The apparent crossing of lines tends to shorten them, as well as prevent a clear rhythm of parallel lines from dominating the composition. Nevertheless, a linearity is apparent that, combined with the clarity of section and surface quality afforded by the proximity of the wood to the viewer, maintains the spirit of wood in the assembly.

A freestanding column expresses wood's natural linearity three-dimensionally but alone cannot establish a significant presence of the woodlike geometry. Such columns must appear in a closely spaced series to establish linearity as a significant part of a building's aesthetic order. Use of the much-favored cantilever typically rendered exposed columns unnecessary in Wright's buildings. A cantilever develops more of its potential for psychological impact if columns are absent from sight. It is logical, therefore, that columns and the woodlike linearity they bring to a building are not commonplace in

FIGURE 2-29. Wood beams span virtually through open space in living room of the George Sturges Residence. Beam appears to bear on brick grille. Linear surface at ceiling. Rowlock lintel at fireplace. (Courtesy The Frank Lloyd Wright Archives)

Wright's work. Rare column series appear in such early works as the Blossom House (1892), the Lake Mendota Boathouse (1893), and in the interior of the Winslow House (1893).

Of the exterior installations, the Blossom and Boathouse columns appear to be the most necessary for structural purposes. Their support of porch roofs, however, renders them slightly less significant than if they were supporting building masses. The historical implications of the colonnade format (the Blossom House and Mendota Boathouse are historically reminiscent) might have been problematic for Wright after his earliest work. He saw the ancient stone temples of Greece as being essentially wood imagery. They seemed to imitate "wooden beams, laid over vertical wooden posts,"[23] he thought.

Mullion systems are the most plentiful source of visible parallel structural lines in Wright's buildings but two circumstances hinder their expression as such. Although they are flanked by smooth broad surfaces of glass, their visibility remains below that of freestanding columns. Their significance is also compromised as it is typically not clear that they are structural instead of trim.

Even the relatively clear structural configuration of the second Jacobs House (1943), where joists are visible as they pass over the mullion system, requires a more than casual examination to understand the nature of the mullions.

Wright rejected certain assemblies of wood as "laborious joinery."[24] The joinery of historic heavy timber (and its subsequent imitations), being less dependent on metal fasteners than contemporary light framing, tended to be more bulky and less plastic than Wright's ideal. The fitting of one piece into another with mortises, tenons, holes, dowels, dovetails, etc., emphasized the individual member. Wright complained of such assemblies as having too many parts. He envisioned a better joint that was more flush in nature and that would interrupt to a lesser degree the flow of the eye over the surface. Wright complained, that constructed-looking assemblies were less plastic than those of his own joinery.[25] The implication is that, to Wright, the plasticity of joinery was a measure of its compatibility with the nature of wood. His favoring of plasticity appears to have superseded the properties of the substance as the motivation for joinery design.

Wright's fondness for turning veneers down over the edges of table tops and other horizontal surfaces[26] is a tactic that obscures substance characteristics when the substrate is lumber. The appearance of end grain in the substrate is eliminated in lieu of veneer face grain, which would cover the ends as well as the sides and face of an object. This signifies either Wright's preference for face grain over end grain or the subjugation of grain to the demands of plasticity or both. The visual effect in this case is small but large enough to draw Wright's comment and it represents a loss of apparent reality in wood. Wright recommended covering ceilings with veneer sheets arranged so as to create any desired pattern with the grain.[27] The minimal perceptibility of a veneer's relationship to its former natural state is further reduced by cutting and rearranging the grain pattern. Like the obscuring of end grain, this diminishes the integrity of the more basic forms of wood. It is an exercise in working wood which, if it is apparent that the new grain pattern is a fabricated phenomenon, is an expression of wood's workability.

Wright's many references to plasticity, including a claim that it would reenergize the spirits of both wood and people, illustrate its importance to him. He was not faced with reconciling any potential mismatches between wood properties and the characteristics of plasticity, since he defined the nature of wood by its ability to be plastic. This is apparent in his declaration—in reference to wood's unique properties—that "treatments that fail to bring out those qualities, foremost, are not *plastic*, therefore no longer appropriate."[28]

Based on common products of the sawmill, the primary form of lumber can be described as linear in elevation and rectangular in section with flat plain surfaces. Wright's interior and exterior lumber consistently exhibits these characteristics and, therefore, reflects the essence of wood in the realm of form as defined by contemporary technology. The intensity of the expressed spirit with regard to the form of wood is both magnified and tempered by detailing intended to produce plasticity. The expression of wood's linearity is enhanced in the cladding and interior trim as the end joints between units are subdued. The hiding of most structural wood, although it maximizes visual continuity by reducing the number of apparent pieces and producing a smoother surface, nearly eliminates the linear contribution of this significant part of architecture. Since this is a lost opportunity rather than a challenge to wood's nature, Wright's net overall expression of lumber, boards, and millwork with regard to form is in the spirit of wood.

Rectangular veneered components such as plywood do not naturally reflect the linearity associated with lumber and millwork. A pure treatment of their basic form would focus on their rectangularity. Often Wright's

Figure 2-30. Wood 'bents' exposed above roof at Taliesin West incorporate flitch plates. Corners mitered across width of lumber. Dentils along edge of roof at right

installation of plywood did not do so, resulting in a limited expression of the product. In the ceiling of the Bazett living room (1940), for example, plywood panels are butted with only the imperfections of the joints expressing the product's form. In the second Erdman prefab design (1957), large horizontal battens dominate the joints, giving the installation a strong linear appearance both from the battens and the appearance of long strips of plywood between them. On the other hand, the joints between plywood on the ceiling of the Pratt House (1948) are covered with battens that clearly delineate the rectangular panel form.

Since veneers were used mostly in interior applications and in nonstructural roles, their impact on the character of Wright's buildings is less than that of the linear forms that occur both inside and outside as structure, cladding, and paneling. The measure of Wright's architecture in its sensitivity to the nature of wood, therefore, is—for the most part—a judgment regarding his use of lumber. Since Wright's veneers are neither imitative nor particularly difficult to distinguish from boards, their vagueness does not detract from the overall essence of the form of wood in his architecture.

WORKABILITY

Wright described wood as a "workable, fibrous material"[29] but rejected the extensive expression of this property in certain realms. He observed that "wood is willing to do what its designer never meant it to do."[30] Arguments in favor of exploiting wood's workability as the logical expression of this aspect of its nature can be countered with complaints about the loss of wood's

FIGURE 2-31. Wood arcade on series of columns at inglenook of William H. Winslow Residence. Alternating rectangular and round balusters at left. (Courtesy The Frank Lloyd Wright Archives)

primary form. The more wood is worked increasing the expression of its potential workability, the further the shape of wood is removed from the plain, linear, and rectangular characteristics that define its basic image. His reference to wood's "beauty of marking, exquisite texture, and delicate nuances of color that carving is likely to destroy"[31] cites a loss in the clarity of surface characteristics as a justification for not working the material. He thought that working wood expressed the tool rather than the substance.[32]

"Carving usually did violence to the nature of wood," he claimed.[33] To Wright, the extensive working of wood is "butchery and botchwork,"[34] and he pitied the material for being "gored and ground and torn and hacked."[35] The sense of injustice was further magnified, he thought, because the outrageous treatment of wood

was encouraged by its nature.[36] Wood, he believed, was by virtue of its workability, helpless in the hands of its violators, or in other words, those who would express this characteristic property.

His rejection of "all wood-carving," which "is apt to be a forcing of this material likely to destroy the finer possibilities of wood,"[37] is most credibly justified by what he considered to be the improprieties of handwork. Handwork, he thought, was not only tedious[38] and costly,[39] but also lacked sophistication. It was no longer necessary or appropriate to depend on handwork, he believed, as machinery could yield detailing that reflected the nature of the material due to its plasticity.[40] He advised us to "forget ancient models that are especially made to suit freedom of the hand"[41] because in most cases the wood is overworked and, consequently, fails to reflect the nature of the substance. The comment reveals that, to Wright, even in ancient models truly dependent on hand processes, the working of wood had its limits, which were usually superseded. The appropriate degree of shaping wood, therefore, is shown to be not so much a function of the nature of the substance or the technology available but of artistic judgment.

The necessity for aesthetic judgment is revealed by several of Wright's comments which tolerate the hand-working of wood. He thought that the expression of wood's properties was enriched by an old Japanese practice of rubbing the palm of a hand on the wood which wore down the softer parts and left oil from the hand in the material.[42] This rubbing and grinding would enhance the appearance of the grain (the favored property) without significantly affecting the profile of the wood, which could remain essentially rectangular. He tolerated a small amount of ornamental handcarving on wood[43] and thought that machines could not successfully imitate certain kinds of fine handwork. The implication was that, although handwork was superior to the machine for certain kinds of woodwork,[44] it was not accessible to the architect for broad application because the machine, not the hand, was the appropriate mechanism for the production of architecture in a modern age.

Wright's embracing of certain machined forms and the rejection of others seems less arbitrary in light of his recognition that "elaborate machinery has been invented for no other purpose than to imitate the wood-carving of early handicraft patterns."[45] Unless one believes that technological achievements are self-justifying, it is feasible for machines to perform processes that lack compatibility with the basic characteristics of mechanization. It could be argued that a machine designed to produce a particular product, the shape of which was determined without a primary regard for mechanical characteristics, compromises the machine's ability to define natural forms.

Wright's reference to certain characteristics that could be produced in wood by "good machine methods"[46] implies that there are also bad machine methods. Given certain principles of mechanization such as the need to minimize moving parts and to maximize simplicity in general, the production of the straight, plain, and simple forms that Wright favored could be claimed as the logical product of the ideal machine. Any distortion of the most logical machine processes (necessary to work the basic forms into more complex shapes) could therefore be called bad machine methods, those that are philosophically inappropriate. According to this theory, not all shapes, even though produced by a machine, would necessarily reflect the essence of the machine.

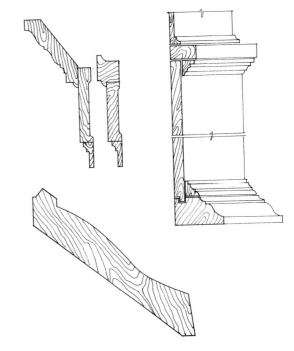

FIGURE 2-32. Curvilinear or "molded" profiles in woodwork at the Warren Hickox Residence (upper left), William H. Winslow Residence (upper right), and Taliesin I. (From Frank Lloyd Wright Archives drawings 0004.002, 9305.001, 1104.008.)

If Wright engaged in any such reasoning, he did not dwell on it publicly. Intricate syllogistic argument was not his style and could not be used to justify many of his conclusions, anyway. For example, the rejection of all but the most simplistic machine processes could rule out the use of lathes that produce both the curvilinear spindles that he disliked and the rotary-cut veneers of which he was fond. To save the latter and be rid of the former would then require a distinction between the nature of lathe blades, another step in an exercise of reasoning fraught with opportunities for losing control of the outcome. There were fewer pitfalls in the rejecting of certain products directly without bothering with a methodically reasoned basis in the philosophy of manufacturing.

In Wright's effort to establish the machine as an important influence on proper wood shapes, he also found it necessary to denounce the machine for its role in the production of improper shapes lest it wrest from him the ultimate authority to define form in every case. Certain machines, he complained, brutalized wood in their cutting and shaping of it[47] that resulted in "horrible glued-on botch-work meaning nothing" with "weird or fussy joinery."[48] His judgmental vocabulary indicates his disgust in colorful ways but without the benefit of reasoning. The lack of apparent objectivity in his narrative on the subject makes the discovery of principle in his approach difficult. He justifies his disgust by

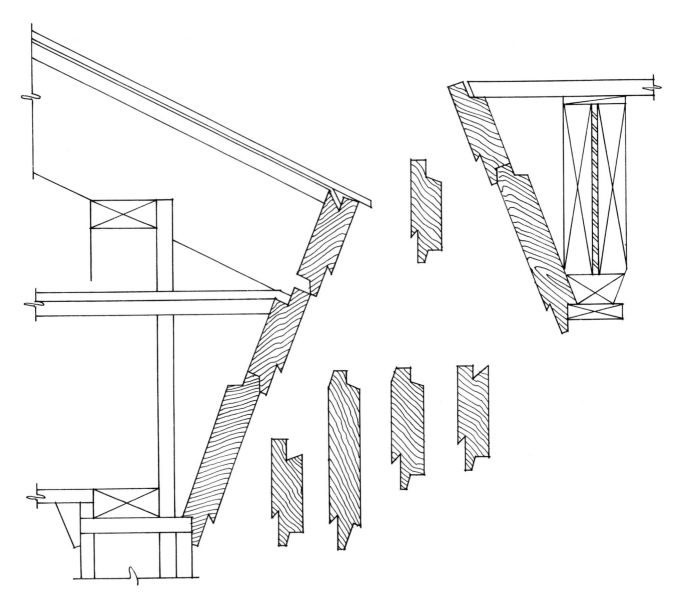

FIGURE 2-33. Sections of fascias and fascia boards of the Herbert F. Johnson Residence. (From Frank Lloyd Wright Archives drawing 3703.059.)

describing the potential damage he envisioned. "The miserable tribute to this perversion yielded by Grand Rapids alone," he warned of the highly decorative wood, "would mar the face of Art beyond repair."[49] (Grand Rapids was a furniture manufacturing center in the early 20th-century.) The prediction is of a disaster in terms not universally defined.

Although in giving credit to the machine for producing good forms, he stopped short of assigning to the machine the ultimate blame for producing bad forms. Ultimately, he blamed the designer for using machines to produce inappropriate forms in wood.[50] This is not only logical but also tends to salvage the machine as a legitimate influence on shape. If the machine's ability to

influence the nature of form was entirely undermined by faulting it for producing complex products, its simple products would also lack credibility having come from a flawed source. Its ability to produce simple shapes adds credibility to Wright's desire to use those forms so long as the machine's general credibility is not undermined. The logic lacks consistency but characterizes his comments on the subject.

His thought that the machined elaboration of wood done "to outdo in sentimentality the sentiment of some erstwhile overwrought 'antique'"[51] is, compared to his other more animated observations, a gentle reminder of his antihistoricism. He was especially critical of the curvilinear decorative wood of Queen Anne architecture as well as other Victorian, Colonial, Neoclassical, and Gothic styles.[52] Wood cut into complex curvilinear forms is reminiscent of the historic styling that Wright so much detested in contemporary architecture. Whether or not it was intended to recall any particular style, the presence of such wood was unacceptable to Wright as he considered it to be historically imitative.[53] The antihistorical and anti-imitative argument alone could have justified the rejection of complex curvilinear wood except that it did not address material properties. Historically based arguments would have been convincing to only other anti-historicists, while the enlisting of machine processes and a focus on the grain of wood, etc., would have had credibility with a broader audience.

Since the bulk of Wright's written works appeared after his earliest buildings were constructed and since the character of his architecture continued to evolve, some occasional difficulty can be anticipated in reconciling his discourse with the earlier architecture. On the other hand, his comments often addressed circumstances surrounding his earlier work that tends to link his written philosophy to them. In some instances, he explained the circumstances that led to ideas which he later rejected (i.e., historical references) but did not, as a rule, disown the early works or often confess to their failure to live up to his subsequently stated ideals.

For example, millwork, having some of the complexity and curvilinear characteristics about which he later complained, can be found in several of the early buildings such as the Hickox (1900) and Winslow (1893) houses and Taliesin I (1911). Later, wood, as at the H. Johnson House (1937), was less curvilinear and appeared to be more plain but in fact had greater complexity in the configuration of the joining edges than did the earlier trim. What may be Wright's most successful chair and one of which he was especially fond was a barrel-shaped unit designed for the D. D. Martin House (1903). The chair expresses the working of wood to a relatively high intensity in the curvilinearity of its plan and section and in the tapered thickness of certain elements.

A general desire for simplicity (plainness) in architecture could justify the use of simple (plain) forms of wood regardless of the material's natural characteristics. Wright's claim that simplicity was not merely plainness but a significant relationship between the parts, does not mean, apparently, that plainness is entirely undesirable. His periodic favorable descriptions of various wood shapes as being plain indicate that there was a place for plainness in his wood detailing. Wright's early works indicate that plainness in a single piece of wood was more desirable than plainness in the entire assembly of wood pieces, which could be called simple only if simple was defined as a purposeful relationship between the parts.

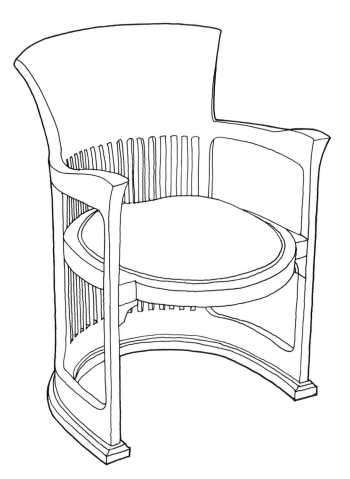

Figure 2-34. Wood chair for the Darwin D. Martin Residence. (From a photograph, *The Prairie School Tradition*, p. 59.)

In later work, as both the detailing and whole assemblies in wood became plainer, a unique method of working wood appeared that seems to reconcile the material's highly workable nature with Wright's desire for rectilinear and rectangular geometries. Instead of cutting the edges of rectangular stock—thus changing the geometry of its perimeter—the central areas of boards and plywood were perforated, leaving the edges straight and rectangular. With this technique, the perforated units in such houses (among others) as the Schwartz (1939), Stevens (1939), Pope (1940), M. M. Smith (1948), Weltzheimer (1948), Hagan (1954), and A. Friedman (1956), Bott (1956), and the Kundert Medical Clinic (1956) maintained their flat surfaces as well as their rectangular perimeters. In this system individual boards first lost their linearity as they were cut into relatively short segments but regained it upon their installation, which usually aligned the short members in long rows. By the same token, plywood tended to lose its basic two-to-one proportion once cut for a particular pattern and installed in rows.

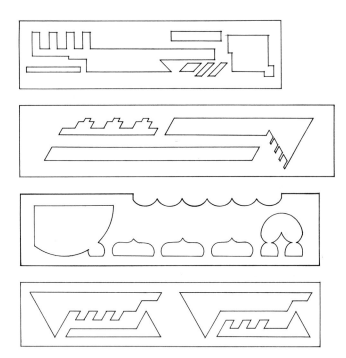

FIGURE 2-35. Perforated glazing boards (top to bottom) for the Bernard Schwartz, C. Leigh Stevens, Charles T. Weltzheimer, and Frank Bott Residences. Lengths from 42 to 50 inches. (From Frank Lloyd Wright Archives drawing 3904.024, photographs in *Frank Lloyd Wright: Preserving an Architectural Heritage*, p. 104, and *The Decorative Designs of Frank Lloyd Wright*, p. 160, and Frank Lloyd Wright Archives drawing 5627.007.)

The cut patterns of the perforated boards are not simple but are simpler than Wright's earliest fretwork and grilles. The ceiling grilles of his Oak Park Home and Studio (1899, 1895) were intricate curvilinear and complex patterns of stylized oak leaves cut in an assembly of oak veneers. The reproduction of missing grilles for restoration of the building required 155 hours of work for each grille with hand and power tools.[54] Neither the early grilles nor his perforated window boards were compatible with Wright's later rejection of handwork. Both are within the nature of wood with regard to its workability, however.

The pattern in the perforated boards of the Hagan House strayed from the norm for this type of component with their irregular but straight-sided polygons, as did the rare curvilinear shapes in the pattern at the Weltzheimer House. The highly rectangular cuts in the M. M. Smith boards define the more rigid extreme of Wright's perforated patterns and seem, ironically, to be among the more difficult to produce. The inconvenient relationship between the nature of machine processes

and the shape of the pattern suggested in the Smith units is the antithesis of that often claimed by Wright for his materials. When working within the interior of a board, cutting is facilitated by curvilinear patterns and made more difficult by rectilinear patterns. It is apparent that in this method of expressing both the workability of wood and the basic form of wood, the nature of the machine has been overcome rather than accommodated, both in the shape of the perforations and the decision to cut within the interior rather than on the edges of the wood.

The Victorian version of perforated wood accommodated the nature of the saw to a far greater degree, which, given Wright's disdain for historic precedent, would encourage him to proceed in a different direction regardless of the intellectual ramifications. Compared to the complexity of patterns in his metals, concrete block, stone, glass, and fabric, those of this perforated wood are relatively simple (in the plain sense). The potential influence of several of his design principles on the nature of the perforated patterns complicates the identification of the governing issue. Given the high workability of wood and the relatively moderate level of working apparent in the perforated wood, it appears that the nature of the substance was not the central force determining the patterns.

In addition to the perforated glazing boards in the M. M. Smith House (1948), an unusually bold demonstration of worked wood is present. A wall of floor-to-ceiling perforated wood panels are similar in character to certain worked wood patterns of the Greene brothers except Wright's cutting is within the interior of the component rather than on its edges. The forms of the panels are, for the most part, obscured by the flush fit of their edges with adjacent panels. The pattern dominates the wood in this screenlike assembly more so than in the smaller perforated units at windows because the geometry of the wood plays less of a role in the composition. Consequently, the workability of wood is emphasized to an unusually high level for Wright at the expense of basic component form. It is significant that the general form of the wood is sacrificed in the working but not the grain, which remains visible in the relatively broad flat surfaces.

The spherical dentils on the Weltzheimer House (1948) are a rare example among his later works of working wood in three dimensions. The numerous small globes lining the bottom of the fascia are unified with the curvilinear perforations of the glazing boards but, according to Wright's precepts rooted in rectangularity and conservation, constitute overworking. The spheres are simple, which tempers the sense of working in an individual unit, but numerous, which boosts the sense of worked wood in the facade.

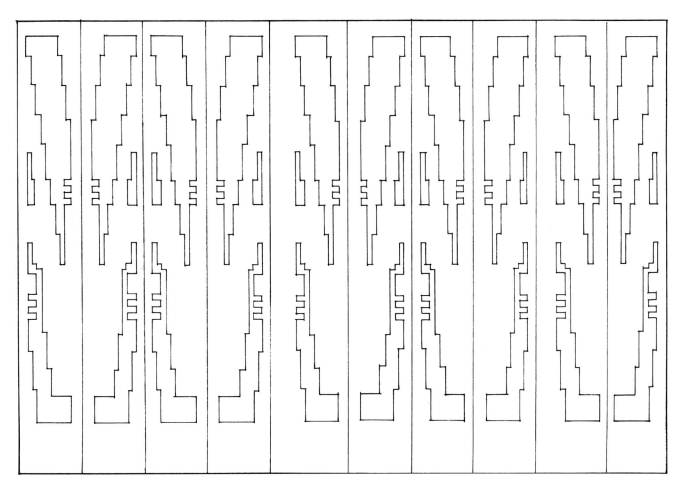

Figure 2-36. Perforated wood screen at the Melvin M. Smith Residence. (From a photograph, *Frank Lloyd Wright Selected Houses* vol. 6, p.173.)

STRENGTH

Wright commented little on wood's strength. This, in itself, reflects a particular attitude toward the material. His discussion of materials is characterized by a visual orientation. Issues that are essentially nonvisual (machine processing, waste, etc.) are discussed in terms of their visual manifestations. For example, Wright observed that "sticks of wood will have their own natural volume and spacing."[55] In the statement, appearance-oriented words are used to mean size and span, which are more strength-oriented terms. He concluded the comment by reporting that these aspects are "determined by standards of use and manufacture and the nature of both,"[56] each of which is related to strength but does not refer to strength directly. It is significant that strength is not mentioned in the statement although the comment is, to large degree, about this property.

Since wood's strength falls between the extremes among structural materials, it is neither remarkable in greatness nor limitation. It is logical, therefore, that wood's relatively moderate strength would draw from Wright few expressions in his work that are more than incidental. With the exception of some columns in early work, there are nearly no exterior expressions of wood structure. Exposed beams inside the Storer (1923) and Sturges (1939) houses are deep enough to be convincing as structure while the beamlike strips on ceilings at the A. Adelman (1948) and the Lovness (1955) houses are not. Much of Wright's wood does not reveal readily its structural role. It commonly appears to be undersized because it indeed is or because it is supplemented by hidden steel. The true role of the wood components is overshadowed by their apparent role. If they look too small to carry a real load, their visual message tends to be about form while their statement about strength remains ambiguous. The range of characteristics accepted as indicating real structure varies between professionals and laypersons, but even the untrained person has limits as to what is perceived as feasible. Depth is not the

FIGURE 2-37. Decorative spacing pattern of wood at ceiling of the former Hillside Home School II. "Structural" relationship between ceiling bands and beams.

only mechanism, however, for establishing the sense of real structure necessary for wood to express its strength.

The shallow ceiling bands at the A. Adelman House span from walls to ridge beams in several rooms thus imparting to the whole an image of structural logic. Shallow bands in the ceiling of what is now the living room at Taliesin also reflects a common structural format. When this space was the assembly room of the Hillside Home School II (1901) the roof structure was entirely exposed revealing pairs of rafters equally spaced, an artistic but also a more utilitarian composition than the pattern of the present ceiling bands. The fact that the wood members visible on the subsequently installed ceiling appear to rest on beams near the perimeter of the room gives them a sense of structure. The pattern of the bands on each plane of the hipped ceiling consists of a set of three strips on either side of the center line, with pairs of strips occurring beyond them. This variation of the normal rhythm of repetitive spacing suggests an artistic purpose rather than a structural one. The sense of structural logic is compromised somewhat as the strips rise from the four edges of the ceiling to meet

shallow bands at the hips instead of larger, more beam-like, members. The lack of structural clarity diminishes the role of the rafterlike structure and—consequently—the strength characteristics of the wood in the character of the architecture. The large beams at the perimeter remain reasonably convincing as real structure and reflect upon the nature of wood by their size and span.

The relationship between a beam in the living room of the Sturges House (1939) and the brick grille in the wall to which it spans undermines the structural credibility of the beam. The trim on the bottom of the beam obscures the top brick of the grille over which the wood passes so that it appears that the beam is resting nearly on an air space in the grille. The detail implies that the beam carries no load and therefore cannot express the strength of wood. If the brick were not obscured, little credibility would be gained by the beam because the single brick spanning the air space in the grille itself lacks the sense of a structural support. The other beams in the space that appear to have sound supports lose some sense of structure by their association with the questionable beam. The structural image of the beams is further undermined because they do not directly contact the construction above. Loads from the roof are transferred to them through slender decorative spindles that appear to lack the capacity for significant weight. This relationship between elements has prevented a clear expression of wood's strength; thus the nature of wood does not participate to its full potential in establishing the character of the architecture.

The imposing presence of the large wood structure in Taliesin's drafting room expresses wood's structural potential in several ways. The close proximity of the wood forces it into the consciousness of the observer. This, its extensiveness, and its mass make it difficult to ignore either intellectually or emotionally. The significant size and large quantity of the wood clearly expresses the moderate nature of its strength. If it were a material of greater strength such as steel, a thinner, lighter system with components spaced farther apart could be anticipated.

The message regarding the strength of wood at the second Jacobs House (1943) is less clear than the expression of its form. Lack of clarity occurs in wood wherever steel is hidden, a condition occurring in two formats here. The steel rods from which the mezzanine hangs introduce ambiguity into the wood structure but do not necessarily misrepresent the strength of the wood. Hidden rods hang from the roof structure to support one end of several mezzanine joists while the other end rests on the stone wall. The free ends of the joists meet a beamlike mezzanine rail that approximates the curve of the plan and is too long to structurally span from one end to the other. It seems unlikely that the

FIGURE 2-38. Wood trusses in the drafting room at Taliesin III.

FIGURE 2-39. Wood and steel roof cantilever of Frederick C. Robie Residence exposing no structural material.

joists might cantilever from the stone wall due to the long distance. The doubtful feasibility of either possibility, even to the untrained observer, leaves the expression of the nature of wood strength in a vague, rather than misleading, state.

The steel flitch plates in the beams and fascias at the ends of the roof make the double overhangs (over perpendicular walls) possible and push the apparent strength of the relatively thin roof system upward. The spans are not excessive for wood but the complexity of the double cantilever would tend to force the thickness of the roof overhang to a larger dimension if wood alone were the structure. Given the visibility of the wood in the soffit and the near invisibility of the thin steel sandwiched between the wood, the detail suggests that only wood is present and that it is stronger than wood actually is. The exposed beams over the roof of the administration wing at Taliesin West (1937) express the moderate strength of wood by virtue of the large depth of the members. In addition, the low end of the system brings the wood close to the viewer, thus emphasizing the significant depth and mass of the section at the roof line. On the other hand, the section is relatively thin for the long span, a characteristic made possible by the steel flitch plates in the beams. Flitch plates were also used in the cantilevered carport roof of the first Jacobs House (1936) and in other projects.

The structural wood in Wright's pitched-roof cantilevers is often neither visible nor acknowledged by the surfaces that house them. His frequent push of the cantilevers (and simple spans) to lengths superseding the strength of wood required the addition of steel. Both wood and composite roof systems typically show only shingles, soffit, and fascia, none of which are convincing as structural elements. Thus any hidden steel that is present does not directly misrepresent the strength of the hidden wood framing. Cantilevered plastered framing—regardless of span—is structurally neutral as the plaster

obviously carries no load. Instead of a strong misrepresentation of wood strength, vagueness prevails in these structural statements. Wood cladding, however, suggests the presence of wood framing although the cladding itself does not necessarily appear to be structural. When hidden steel helps wood-clad elements to cantilever farther than could wood alone, the strength of the material is misrepresented even if no structural wood is apparent.

The doubt that the builder and Wright's uncles expressed regarding the structural stability of the 60-foot Romeo and Juliet Windmill (1896)[57] was not unfounded. The issue was one of material expression since the tower seemed too tall and slender for wood, which it appears to be but which it is not entirely. Iron straps project six feet out of the foundation serving as considerably more than anchor bolts. They make the 10 percent of the structure at the point of largest overturning moment into a composite material able to provide a moment-resisting connection to the foundation. The effect of the iron on the wood structure was the same as that of steel in Wright's later buildings. The composite section allowed a taller, more slender, building form than wood alone could support while maintaining an appearance of only wood. Wood's strength was misrepresented and the uncles protested. They accepted all-steel towers that had considerably less visual mass than the wood tower because the expression of the steel was compatible with the thinness of those structures.

Wright's use of the arch in wood framing was often vague in its structural meaning and consequently expressed little about the nature of wood with regard to strength. A true arch, like the cantilever, generates a particular kind of stress associated with certain materials because of their ability to accommodate the structural

FIGURE 2-40. Wood and steel building cantilever at the Herbert Johnson Residence clad in wood siding. (Courtesy The Frank Lloyd Wright Archives.)

challenge. Consequently, based solely on strength, wood lacks a compatibility of maximum logic with the arch that, in ideal circumstances, requires only wood's compressive ability. Wood's tensile ability and bending strength go unused and unacknowledged in such a form. The true arch, therefore, only partially expresses the nature of wood with respect to strength.

To build an arch, the various methods by which the natural straightness of wood can be overcome are generally compatible with wood's high workability but not with its other properties. To overcome the strength of wood by bending it in order to produce the necessary curve is to violate that property. The vulnerability of joints to weathering limits to interior applications the viability of extensive cutting and laminating as a way to curve the wood. Since Wright did not expose the structural wood in many of his interior or exterior arched forms, the practical and philosophical problems associated with the mismatch of nature of material and nature of arches is less apparent than it otherwise would be. The positive aspect of expressed workability is also diminished where the worked wood is not visible.

The most structurally vague arches are those surrounded by plaster as at the McArthur House (1892), the upper story of the Mendota Boathouse (1893), the entry of the Williams House (1897), the entry of the Thomas House (1901), and at a high window in the Dana gallery wing (1902). Except for the presence of wood framing implied by any wood trim present, the structures could be masonry, steel, or concrete. The workability of wood is expressed in these examples to the extent that wood trim was shaped to follow the curve of the arch. In the absence of a strong structural-material statement, the arches fail to significantly misrepresent the nature of the wood, since the role of the wood is vague.

The shingled arches at the Hillside Home School (1887) and Lake Mendota Boathouse (1893), as well as those at the clapboard covered MacHarg (1890) and Blossom (1892) houses, suggest slightly more strongly that wood framing is present as it is the usual substrate for wood cladding. The implication of hidden wood, however, only promotes a sense of a structural mismatch between material and form since the spans are so small

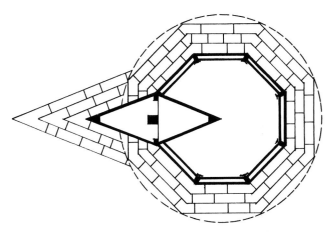

FIGURE 2-41. Floor plan of the Romeo and Juliet Windmill. Iron straps at the vertices. (From Frank Lloyd Wright Archives drawing 9607.003.)

FIGURE 2-42. Segmental arch at center of Lake Mendota Boathouse. Shingle cladding. Series of arches on second level. Top of colonnade visible at the top center of back facade. (Courtesy The Frank Lloyd Wright Archives.)

as not to take the span-advantage that true arches offer. The working of the hidden wood is implied by the arched form, and the cutting of the cladding to fit the curves adds visible working to the expression of this property.

Arches in interior partitions are generally plastered, as at the Charnley (1891), Blossom (1892), and Winslow (1893) houses, but a wood-clad arch occurs in the hall of the playroom at Wright's Oak Park Home (1895). Interior arches have implications regarding their hidden wood similar to the exterior examples, except that the interior arches are structurally more vague. Exterior walls are generally perceived as being load-bearing, even if they are not; interior partitions are generally perceived as nonload-bearing, even when they carry loads. Consequently, the structural capacity of arches seems to be more necessary in exterior walls than in interior partitions where they tend to appear to be only decorative.

Any absence of structural logic perceived in wood arches and the spirit of insensitivity to wood that it brings is stronger in exterior arches than interior arches. The degree to which interior arches express the nature of wood, therefore, can be judged, for the most part, by their expression of workability. An exception to this idea occurs in the arcade at the inglenook of the Winslow House. The fact that the arches rest on columns and that they occur in a series across a relatively large opening to the inglenook suggest that they serve a structural function. The arcade's expression of the nature of wood, therefore, is confused with regard to its strength potential and limitations.

Large segmental vaults and arches at the Mendota Boathouse (1893) and the F. B. Jones House (1901) have the characteristics of true arches. Further con-

FIGURE 2-43. Stuccoed arch with wood trim at entry, Frank Thomas Residence. Wood trim rests on water table. (Courtesy Mike Kertok)

tributing to the image, the Mendota Boathouse had three courses of shingles acting as visual voussoirs over the vault. The presence of true arch-action in the assemblies is highly doubtful, but whether or not they are true arches is not the issue. Analysis of the expression of a material necessarily focuses on the visual message rather than the reality of the hidden conditions. Because of their large sizes, the arches are more significant in the architectural expression of the buildings than the smaller doors and windows of the other examples, thus magnifying whatever message arches offer about wood. The significant spans of the arches tend to justify the use of wood instead of masonry, but they are not so large as to call for steel. There is adequate apparent mass on either side of the arches that could resist the thrust that a true arch would develop. The presence of such buttresslike framing does not assure that thrust is present, but the absence of such framing makes arches seem less real, even if tie-rods (which typically have little visual impact) are present. Without buttressing, the sense of a true arch would have been significantly undermined in each case.

Regardless of the reality of the structural conditions, apparent structural vagueness is much reduced in the arches of these examples. The focus on compression in wood afforded by the arches is only part of the story of wood strength, however, so that any structurally convincing arch can only partially express the nature of wood. The curves of the arches express some workability but not so much as to draw attention from the apparent structural assignment of the material. Consequently, the usual sense of violation that occurs when the strength of wood is overcome in the fabrication of a curved component is diminished.

The vaults in Wright's Oak Park playroom (1895) and the Dana House (1902) offer mixed messages about the strength of wood. The vaults are large enough to warrant (but not demand) steel so that the appropriateness of wood and possibly the existence of wood is brought into question. The presence of a wood structure is not denied, but any message that the hidden structure might offer about the material is weakened by the possibility that the structural achievements are not due solely to wood. Arched wood bands cross the ceilings in the gallery at the Dana House and terminate in deep elements that suggest structure. The detailing does not necessarily reflect reality, but the arches seem more real than in the dining room and in the Wright playroom, where no thickness is suggested beyond that of the surface trim. If the Dana base detail makes the structure more convincing, the result can be no more than a partial expression of wood's nature as in the case of the boathouse vault.

The questionable presence of thrust resistance undermines the structural reality of these vaults and their apparent arches. Since true arches have only partial compatibility with the nature of wood, the presence of a nonstructural arch is not a necessarily a sign of insensitivity to wood. The edges of the vaults in the Dana gallery appear to rest on very shallow segmental arches.

The nature of these very long, slightly arched, shapes is truly mysterious as they appear to be too flat to develop any real arch action and too shallow to act as beams. The structural integrity of these odd components is only slightly more feasible than the wide but very shallow beamlike components appearing to support the edges of the playroom vault over the windows at Wright's Oak Park Home.

The ethical implications of presenting a structure as something that it is not is a subject in the realm of honesty and is not a focus of the wood analysis. The element of this circumstance that pertains directly to wood is the resulting confusion that prevents a clear presentation of the nature of wood with regard to strength. The implied message is that Wright was not concerned about the strength of wood. Given modern technology's diminishing dependence on arches as utilitarian structures and their subsequent drift toward a purely decorative roles, Wright's use of the form in wood construction does not yield a sense of flagrant violation of the spirit of wood. On the other hand, neither can his arches serve as evidence of elevated sensitivity to the nature of the material.

Wright's frequent use of steel in his otherwise wood-framed structures indicates that wood's strength was often inadequate for his demands on the material. Sagging cantilevers at the Ingalls (1909), Mrs. T. Gale (1909), and other houses reflect this circumstance, as do houses in which owners subsequently added steel to bolster failing wood structures. The Goetsch-Winckler House (1939) is an example of such a case.[58] Edgar Tafel reports that he was tentatively fired (but reinstated) because he added steel to the structure of the Schwartz House (1939) during construction without Wright's knowledge.[59] The collapse of a similar roof during the construction of another house in which no steel was added verified its need at the Schwartz project.

Given the inability of wood's strength to meet Wright's needs, it is understandable that he rarely spoke of this property. The limited amount of visible structural wood in the presence of strong structural statements throughout Wright's work indicates a low interest in the strength of wood as an expressible property. The nature of wood with regard to strength failed to affect Wright's architecture, for when it proved to be inadequate, steel was often added to achieve the desired span. If steel was not added in these cases, the eventual sagging of the structure was likely. Wood does not have great strength but Wright wished to express great structural achievements with it. Consequently, if the simple spans or cantilevers of his wood framing are at all remarkable, it is likely that hidden steel is present. The nature of wood with regard to strength is misrepresented in such detailing.

DURABILITY

Although it is Wright's attitude toward the challenges of weathering that is of interest, interior wood is also addressed when its detailing reflects pertinent values. Much of Wright's commentary on finishes occurs without an indication as to whether the wood is outside or inside. His few distinctions in this regard are adequate, however, to establish his view of exterior and interior wood as deserving of some differences in handling.

The delicate subtleties of grain pattern, texture, and color that Wright saw as the nature of wood are most apparent where the surface of wood is least obscured. This commonly occurs indoors where viewers are in close proximity to floors, walls, ceilings, woodwork, and furniture and where the wood is protected from the weather by the building enclosure. Here, in the absence of weathering, minimally treated wood may be seen at a relatively close range and slow pace. Wright favored a minimal finishing of wood, a tendency which he admired in the Japanese.[60] Minimally finished wood on the exterior, however, soon loses its sensitive and intimate qualities through visual and physical deterioration from weathering. Every designer who is focused on wood's natural (raw) appearance faces this dilemma as the transparency and longevity of a protective finish are inversely related.

Wright's advice to "strip the wood of varnish and let it alone—stain it"[61] blurs the distinction between an ideal of wood and the reality of wood. His promotion at another time of a wide range of colors in which to stain interior inlaid veneers[62] suggests that the protection of exterior wood was not his motivation to stain wood. Transparent artificial coloring, misrepresents the nature of individual species if it is decorative rather than protective. It appears that, to Wright, staining was simply another option for producing beauty in wood and as such was compatible with its nature.

His desire to let exterior wood alone suggests that, if in practice the beauty of raw wood must be obscured for its own good, the philosophical correctness of doing so and possibly even the act of doing so must be denied. Based on a literal interpretation of tangible properties, this approach (letting exterior wood alone) is insensitive to the nature of wood with respect to its durability. Oddly, Wright once appeared to accept the painting of wood in his claim that wood "may be polished, or painted, or stained."[63] Paint was subsequently rejected in strong terms. It was seen as a substance that not only obliterated grain entirely but also had overtones of historicism. In the name of taste, "the precious efflorescent patterns of wood," Wright complained, were "to be painted out of sight; its silken textures vulgarized by varnish."[64] Varnish was excluded, apparently for its unacceptable sheen.

His advice to leave wood alone could also be taken literally as indicated by his thought that exterior wood could be rough sawn and "be color-stained or allowed to weather."[65] The weather should have little effect on shaping wood, he thought, as the forms outside are similar to those inside "allowing wood to be wood but coarser in scale with an eye to weathering in the joinery."[66] His willingness to let wood weather is an optimistic view of weathering or a short sighted view of architecture. Alexis J. Panshin withdrew from his proposed house project in 1939 complaining, among other things, that the two species of untreated wood that Wright intended to use would neither weather well nor maintain their contrasting colors.[67] He was right, as Kathrine Winckler verified by her complaint to Wright's office six years after completion of her house (in the same area) that the (untreated) siding was discolored and not holding up to the weather.[68]

Wright's focus on future projects could have affected his outlook regarding the natural but temporary appearance of raw wood. The creamy and delicately textured surface of newly cut wood has a universal attractiveness (supplemented by a temporary pleasant scent) that is difficult for many designers to cover with the protective coating that it needs. Wright's thought that wood requires "no painting at all," that "wood best protects itself," and that "a coating of clear resinous oil would be enough"[69] does not reflect an understanding of the technical nature of wood. The natural surface of wood begins to deteriorate immediately upon contact with the weather and eventually turns dark and loses its tautness. If the image of wood is defined at the completion of a building rather than five years later, raw wood exposed to the weather would seem simultaneously beautiful and respectful of the nature of the material.

Since practices that challenge rather than accommodate the properties of wood violate its nature, the exposure of raw wood to the weather is not in the spirit of wood. After a year the weathering challenge to raw wood becomes apparent. A year of expressed uniqueness and beauty is not long enough to define the image of the wood in architecture. Although Wright did not call for the natural weathering of wood in all cases, he offered it as an option without further qualification. This further indicates that his focus on wood's grain was highly influential in his definition of the nature of the material.

It would seem that Wright's desire for a year of visible raw wood supersedes any desire to provide for its survival. This illustrates his tendency to treat negative aspects of materials as obstacles to be ignored or overcome with the least disruption to the quest for the ideal. The attitude contrasts with one that is accepting of negative characteristics as part of the nature of wood and

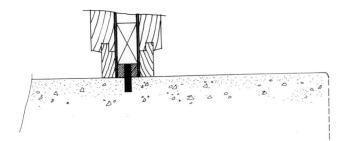

FIGURE 2-44. Section at base of exterior wall, Paul and Jean Hanna Residence. (From Frank Lloyd Wright Archives drawing 3701.023.)

views their recognition in architectural expression as being appropriate and desirable. In the latter case the application of an effective protective coating such as paint would be clearly in the nature of wood, as it speaks to a significant property, albeit a weakness or limitation.

Wright's focus on horizontality and its relationship to the earth negatively affected the expression of wood with regard to its limited durability in much of his work. His horizontal inset battens produce more joints in the cladding than is otherwise necessary and, like projected battens, slow the drainage of water from the surface. Both conditions challenge the durability of wood. The expressive and physical ramifications of this reality are limited but real, as indicated by the joints of several installations that have loosened due to weathering.

At the long window-walls of houses such as the Hanna (1935), first Jacobs (1936), second Jacobs (1943), M. M. Smith (1948), Mossberg (1948), and many others, wood is set on or near paving, which expresses a lower priority for the durability of wood than the desire for a particular architectural character. In the literal approach to material nature, the long rows of doors and windows that place wood close to or on the pavement (and the moisture collected there) would constitute a violation of the spirit of wood with regard to its durability. In Wright's approach, this detailing would be considered to be within the nature of wood because it benefits the artistry of the architecture. He seemed to define the nature of wood by how it was able to serve his architectural goals rather than by the potential and limitations of its tangible properties.

Horizontal bands of wood either as cladding or as trim on stuccoed walls were often placed close to the destructive agents of the earth. The wood siding of the River Forest Tennis Club (1905) and the G. Millard House (1906) was placed about an inch above grade, while the bottom trim of the stuccoed Boynton (1907), Evans (1908), Davidson (1908), Stockman (1908), and Greene (1912) houses was detailed to be a fraction of an inch above the earth. For all practical purposes, the

wood appears to be set on soil, a condition foreign to the nature of wood. The issue is not only the actual threat to the wood but also the apparent threat (certain pressure treated woods today are not threatened by earth contact). The question is whether or not the wood is expressed to be more resistant or less resistant to the agents of deterioration than it appears to warrant. Although the expressive message of the trim at the bottom of stuccoed walls is one of insensitivity, the small amount of wood thus expressed indicates only a minor lapse of attention to the nature of wood.

The bottom board of horizontal wood siding is a very small percentage of the whole, but for expressive purposes, it is the entire wall that appears to be threatened at its base when the bottom strip approaches grade. The fact that a horizontal orientation threatens only one or two boards, while in a vertically oriented siding the ends of all the siding would be jeopardized is more pertinent as a practical matter than for expressive purposes.

The earth's physical challenge to wood was often abated in Wright's early houses by setting the wood on a concrete or stone base called a water table. Since the bases projected beyond the framing, their tops could collect water unless they were significantly sloped. The bottom wood trim at the stuccoed Thomas (1901), Willits, (1902), and Fricke (1902) houses, among others, is set on bases that collect water which contacts the wood. The wood siding of the Glasner House (1905) has a similar detail. Sloped tops on some bases discharge water at a speed proportional to the angle of the slope but cannot prevent snow from contacting the wood if it is higher than the base. Unless the slope is steep enough to perceive in casual observation, it will not contribute to an image of sensitivity to the nature of wood.

Variations on the base detail include the lifting of the low horizontal wood band a couple of inches above the spread base, which would seem to reduce the peril of the wood. At the M. Adams (1905) and Coonley (1906) houses, such an improved condition was compromised by placing a thinner strip of wood below the raised band, thus reducing the challenge to the higher but not the lower wood. A stronger visual and practical adjustment occurs at the Tomek House (1907), where the bottom trim is raised above the base and overhangs a concrete lip projecting upward from the concrete base. Consequently, no wood touches an exposed horizontal surface at the water table. The concrete lip is just visible below the trim and thus it verifies a desire to protect the wood. Revealing the intent boosts the apparent respect of the nature of wood embodied in the expression. The apparent protection to the exterior wood afforded by the concrete bases is not, as it appears to be, also afforded to the framing behind the cladding. Typically in these houses, the wall studs pass down behind the concrete

FIGURE 2-45. Wood wall bases in contact and near contact with grade, Robert Evans Residence. (Courtesy The Frank Lloyd Wright Archives)

base to a wood plate resting on the top of the foundation at grade level as does the concrete base itself. Because it is not visible, the questionable detail does not affect the expressed sensitivity to wood's durability in spite of its susceptibility to water penetration.

A more visually prominent juxtaposition of wood and a masonry base occurs in several of Wright's later houses. In the Suntop (1939), Pew (1938), Pauson (1939), Sturges (1939), and Affleck (1941) homes, narrow building elements sided in wood are mounted high above the ground in masonry walls. Extending the wood siding to grade in these houses would adversely affect the horizontality of the buildings, as the loss of the directional force of the horizontal masses would not be compensated by the increased number of siding boards. The distance between the wood and the earth that simultaneously protects the wood and expresses its durability limitations would also be lost. In spite of the fact that no intent to express the limited durability of wood is apparent in this detailing, the property is, nevertheless, expressed.

Miscellaneous details in Wright's work have various relationships to the durability of wood but cannot be profound in the absence of their significant repetition. Horizontal trim on the Baldwin (1905), Gilmore (1908), and other houses, for example, is separated from the surface of the wall by a space. Both the three-dimensionality of the horizontal line and the size of its shadow are thus increased. Theoretically, water could drain behind the strip rather than collect on it. Regardless of

the actual intent, the detail increases the apparent sensitivity of the building to the nature of wood in the realm of its limited durability. The visual result rather than the practical benefit of the spaced trim is the significant aspect of the detail, since it is the degree to which material concerns affect architectural expression that is the measure of a building's expressed sensitivity to materials. In actuality, the space behind the trim can provide some protection to the wood only if it remains free of obstructions and if the back side of the wood can be painted periodically.

In alterations to the south facade of the Coonley House, the tops and ends of lumber exposed to the weather were clad with copper. The copper is highly visible because of its contrasting color and relatively large size. Its importance is elevated by the decorative patterns in the end caps that secure the role of the devices in the aesthetic system. The combination of the copper characteristics express, with a sense of artistic purpose, the protection copper gives to the wood. This uniquely strong expression of wood's vulnerability does not illustrate a continuing sensitivity to the nature of wood, however, because it is a unique example. If most of Wright's lumber was so protected, the importance to him of wood's nature in the realm of durability would be clearly established.

Roof overhangs protect the walls below them, a circumstance to which Wright referred on more than one occasion. The degree of protection varies with the size and height of the overhang. Since overhangs also pro-

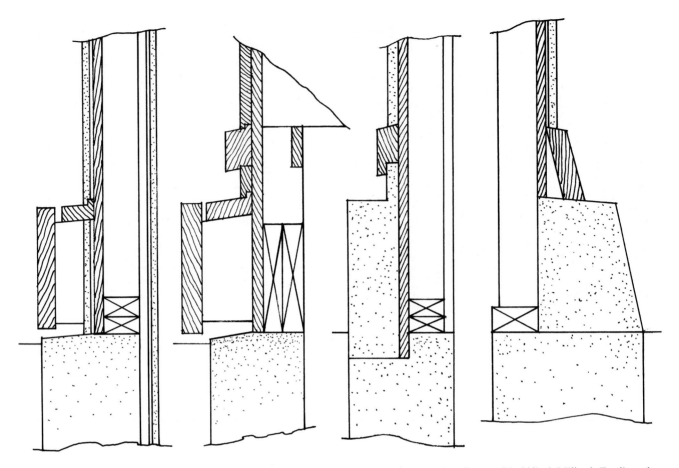

FIGURE 2-46. Sections at bases of walls at (left to right) the Eugene A. Gilmore, Mrs. George M. (Alice) Millard, Ferdinand F. Tomek, and Frank Thomas Residences. (From Frank Lloyd Wright Archives drawings 0806.017, 0606.010, 0711.22, 0106.07.)

vide shade, employ the favored cantilever, and express horizontality, their ability to express a concern for the limited durability of wood in the wall below is impaired somewhat. In other words, they do not appear to be generated only by a need to protect wood. The absence of roof overhangs above all the perforated plywood glazing boards of the Kundert Clinic (1956) undermines the possibility that overhangs are in any way inspired by the durability limitations of the material. The especially vulnerable edges of the perforated plywood patterns are partially protected by small overhangs in some places but not protected at all in others where no overhangs exist.

Upon occasion, Wright mitered the corners of exterior wood such as across the width of the lumber in the exposed roof beams at Taliesin West (1937) and across the thickness of boards in the trellis system of the Rebhuhn House (1938). The precision of such details is difficult for wood to maintain, due to the dimensional instability of the material and the thinness of the wood that occurs at the most critical point, the apex of the corner. While three miters on the horizontal end-unit

of the trellis are on obtuse corners and therefore are thicker at the apex, one is an acute angle and thus more vulnerable to warpage and deterioration than are right-angled corners. The use of exterior mitered corners indicate Wright's expectation for the wood to act in an ideal way, as it could perform indoors. The nature of the wood with regard to durability has not governed such details.

An occasional comment indicated that Wright recognized a difference between exterior and interior environments as they related to wood's durability. Characteristically, however, he resisted any consistent influence from this aspect of wood in its use and detailing. Wood's tendency to discolor, warp, and decay detract from its natural beauty, as do the protective measures available. Apparently, in having to choose between two conditions, both flawed by some definitions, Wright opted for temporary maximized beauty rather than a more permanent compromised beauty. The tendency illustrates the relatively low priority he assigned to the nature of wood with regard to its durability.

FIGURE 2-47. Wood base trim raised above top of water table, Ferdinand F. Tomek Residence. (Courtesy The Frank Lloyd Wright Archives)

CONCLUSION

Wright's use of wood was always compatible with its nature—according to his own definitions. In a more literal interpretation of wood's properties, however, distinctions can be made between issues of greater and lesser concern to him. It is apparent that he was more sensitive to the grain of wood than to any other property. His opinion that wood was really treated as wood when it was applied as a veneer[70] reveals that the

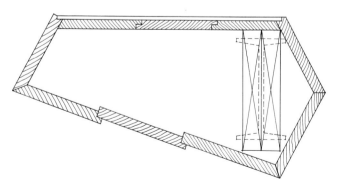

FIGURE 2-49. Section showing mitered joints of cladding on outer trellis beam, Ben Rebhuhn Residence. (From Frank Lloyd Wright Archives drawing 3801.016.)

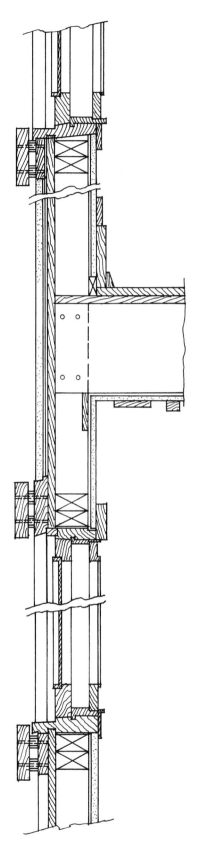

FIGURE 2-48. Wall section showing space behind wood trim on facade of Eugene A. Gilmore Residence. (From Frank Lloyd Wright Archives drawing 0806.017.)

strength, durability, and basic form of the material are secondary in his definition of the material.

His desire for plasticity and horizontality had both positive and negative effects on the expression of wood's nature. Wood's form, strength, workability, and durability were periodically revealed and obscured by these and other design themes. Consequently Wright's expressions in the nature of wood seem to be largely the by-product of his general architectural goals rather than a purposeful intent to honor wood. Although putting architectural achievement first is not unreasonable, the practice brings into perspective the more idealistic claims of Wright's dedication to the nature of wood made by himself and others.

ENDNOTES

1. Wright, Frank Lloyd. 1928. "In the Cause of Architecture: IV. The Meaning of Materials—Wood." *Architectural Record* 63(5):481–488. Reprint. 1975. *In the Cause of Architecture*, ed. Frederick Gutheim. New York: McGraw-Hill. p. 179. *ARCHITECTURAL RECORD,* (May/1928), copyright 1975 by McGraw-Hill, Inc. All rights reserved. Reproduced with the permission of the publisher.

2. Ibid., 185. *ARCHITECTURAL RECORD,* (May/1928), copyright 1975 by McGraw-Hill, Inc. All rights reserved. Reproduced with the permission of the publisher.

3. Wright, Frank Lloyd. 1931. *Modern Architecture: Being the Kahn Lectures for 1930.* Reprint. 1987. ed. Bruce Brooks Pfeiffer. Carbondale and Edwardsville, IL: Southern Illinois University Press. Copyright 1987 by The Frank Lloyd Wright Foundation. p. 17. Courtesy The Frank Lloyd Wright Foundation.

4. Wright, Frank Lloyd. 1927. "In the Cause of Architecture: II. Standardization, The Soul of the Machine." *Architectural Record* 61(6):478–480. Reprint. 1975. *In the Cause of Architecture,* ed. Frederick Gutheim. New York: McGraw-Hill. p. 137. *ARCHITECTURAL RECORD,* (June/1927), copyright 1975 by McGraw-Hill, Inc. All rights reserved. Reproduced with the permission of the publisher.

5. Wright, Frank Lloyd. 1931. *Modern Architecture: Being the Kahn Lectures for 1930.* Reprint. 1987. ed. Bruce Brooks Pfeiffer. Carbondale and Edwardsville, IL: Southern Illinois University Press. Copyright 1987 by The Frank Lloyd Wright Foundation. p. 17. Courtesy The Frank Lloyd Wright Foundation.

6. Wright, Frank Lloyd. 1908. "In the Cause of Architecture." *Architectural Record* 23(3):155–221. Reprint. 1975. *In the Cause of Architecture,* ed. Frederick Gutheim. New York: McGraw-Hill. p. 56.

7. Wright, Frank Lloyd. 1928. "In the Cause of Architecture: IV. The Meaning of Materials—Wood." *Architectural Record* 63(5):481–488. Reprint. 1975. *In the Cause of Architecture*, ed. Frederick Gutheim. New York: McGraw-Hill. p. 185.

8. Wright, Frank Lloyd. 1931. *Modern Architecture: Being the Kahn Lectures for 1930.* Reprint. 1987. ed. Bruce Brooks Pfeiffer. Carbondale and Edwardsville, IL: Southern Illinois University Press. Copyright 1987 by The Frank Lloyd Wright Foundation. p. 16–17. Courtesy The Frank Lloyd Wright Foundation.

9. Wright, Frank Lloyd. 1927. "In the Cause of Architecture: II. Standardization, The Soul of the Machine." *Architectural Record* 61(6):478–480. Reprint. 1975. *In the Cause of Architecture,* ed. Frederick Gutheim. New York: McGraw-Hill. p. 137.

10. Wright, Frank Lloyd. 1928. "In the Cause of Architecture: IV. The Meaning of Materials—Wood." *Architectural Record* 63(5):481–488. Reprint. 1975. *In the Cause of Architecture*, ed. Frederick Gutheim. New York: McGraw-Hill. p. 184.

11. Wright, Frank Lloyd. 1927. "In the Cause of Architecture: II. Standardization, The Soul of the Machine." *Architectural Record* 61(6):478–480. Reprint. 1975. *In the Cause of Architecture,* ed. Frederick Gutheim. New York: McGraw-Hill. p. 137. *ARCHITECTURAL RECORD,* (June/1927), copyright 1975 by McGraw-Hill, Inc. All rights reserved. Reproduced with the permission of the publisher.

12. Wright, Frank Lloyd. 1928. "In the Cause of Architecture: IV. The Meaning of Materials—Wood." *Architectural Record* 63(5):481–488. Reprint. 1975. *In the Cause of Architecture*, ed. Frederick Gutheim. New York: McGraw-Hill. p. 184.

13. Ibid., 185.

14. Ibid., 183. *ARCHITECTURAL RECORD,* (May/1928), copyright 1975 by McGraw-Hill, Inc. All rights reserved. Reproduced with the permission of the publisher.

15. Ibid.

16. Ibid., 185.

17. Ibid., 184.

18. Ibid., 185.

19. Wright, Frank Lloyd. 1931. *Modern Architecture: Being the Kahn Lectures for 1930*. Reprint. 1987. ed. Bruce Brooks Pfeiffer. Carbondale and Edwardsville, IL: Southern Illinois University Press. Copyright 1987 by The Frank Lloyd Wright Foundation. p. 72. Courtesy The Frank Lloyd Wright Foundation.

20. Wright, Frank Lloyd. 1928. "In the Cause of Architecture: IV. The Meaning of Materials—Wood." *Architectural Record* 63(5):481–488. Reprint. 1975. *In the Cause of Architecture*, ed. Frederick Gutheim. New York: McGraw-Hill. p. 182–183.

21. Storrer, William Allin. 1993. *The Frank Lloyd Wright Companion*. Chicago: The University of Chicago Press. p. 35.

22. Wright, Frank Lloyd. 1928. "In the Cause of Architecture: IV. The Meaning of Materials—Wood." *Architectural Record* 63(5):481–488. Reprint. 1975. *In the Cause of Architecture*, ed. Frederick Gutheim. New York: McGraw-Hill. p. 185.

23. Wright, Frank Lloyd. 1931. *Modern Architecture: Being the Kahn Lectures for 1930*. Reprint. 1987. ed. Bruce Brooks Pfeiffer. Carbondale and Edwardsville, IL: Southern Illinois University Press. Copyright 1987 by The Frank Lloyd Wright Foundation. p. 57. Courtesy The Frank Lloyd Wright Foundation.

24. Wright, Frank Lloyd. 1927. "In the Cause of Architecture: II. Standardization, The Soul of the Machine." *Architectural Record* 61(6):478–480. Reprint. 1975. *In the Cause of Architecture*, ed. Frederick Gutheim. New York: McGraw-Hill. p. 137. *ARCHITECTURAL RECORD*, (June/1927), copyright 1975 by McGraw-Hill, Inc. All rights reserved. Reproduced with the permission of the publisher.

25. Ibid.

26. Wright, Frank Lloyd. 1928. "In the Cause of Architecture: IV. The Meaning of Materials—Wood." *Architectural Record* 63(5):481–488. Reprint. 1975. *In the Cause of Architecture*, ed. Frederick Gutheim. New York: McGraw-Hill. p. 183.

27. Ibid., 184.

28. Wright, Frank Lloyd. 1931. *Modern Architecture: Being the Kahn Lectures for 1930*. Reprint. 1987. ed. Bruce Brooks Pfeiffer. Carbondale and Edwardsville, IL: Southern Illinois University Press. Copyright 1987 by The Frank Lloyd Wright Foundation. p. 17. Courtesy The Frank Lloyd Wright Foundation.

29. Wright, Frank Lloyd. 1927. "In the Cause of Architecture: II. Standardization, The Soul of the Machine." *Architectural Record* 61(6):478–480. Reprint. 1975. *In the Cause of Architecture*, ed. Frederick Gutheim. New York: McGraw-Hill. p. 137. *ARCHITECTURAL RECORD*, (June/1927), copyright 1975 by McGraw-Hill, Inc. All rights reserved. Reproduced with the permission of the publisher.

30. Wright, Frank Lloyd. 1928. "In the Cause of Architecture: IV. The Meaning of Materials—Wood." *Architectural Record* 63(5):481–488. Reprint. 1975. *In the Cause of Architecture*, ed. Frederick Gutheim. New York: McGraw-Hill. p. 180. *ARCHITECTURAL RECORD*, (May/1928), copyright 1975 by McGraw-Hill, Inc. All rights reserved. Reproduced with the permission of the publisher.

31. Wright, Frank Lloyd. 1931. *Modern Architecture: Being the Kahn Lectures for 1930*. Reprint. 1987. ed. Bruce Brooks Pfeiffer. Carbondale and Edwardsville, IL: Southern Illinois University Press. Copyright 1987 by The Frank Lloyd Wright Foundation. p. 17. Courtesy The Frank Lloyd Wright Foundation.

32. Wright, Frank Lloyd. 1928. "In the Cause of Architecture: IV. The Meaning of Materials—Wood." *Architectural Record* 63(5):481–488. Reprint. 1975. *In the Cause of Architecture*, ed. Frederick Gutheim. New York: McGraw-Hill. p. 180.

33. Wright, Frank Lloyd. 1927. "In the Cause of Architecture: II. Standardization, The Soul of the Machine." *Architectural Record* 61(6):478–480. Reprint. 1975. *In the Cause of Architecture*, ed. Frederick Gutheim. New York: McGraw-Hill. p. 137. *ARCHITECTURAL RECORD*, (June/1927), copyright 1975 by McGraw-Hill, Inc. All rights reserved. Reproduced with the permission of the publisher.

34. Wright, Frank Lloyd. 1928. "In the Cause of Architecture: IV. The Meaning of Materials—Wood." *Architectural Record* 63(5):481–488. Reprint. 1975. *In the Cause of Architecture*, ed. Frederick Gutheim. New York: McGraw-Hill. p. 180. *ARCHITECTURAL RECORD*, (May/1928), copyright 1975 by McGraw-Hill, Inc. All rights reserved. Reproduced with the permission of the publisher.

35. Ibid. *ARCHITECTURAL RECORD*, (May/ 1928), copyright 1975 by McGraw-Hill, Inc. All rights reserved. Reproduced with the permission of the publisher.

36. Ibid.

37. Wright, Frank Lloyd. 1931. *Modern Architecture: Being the Kahn Lectures for 1930*. Reprint. 1987. ed. Bruce Brooks Pfeiffer. Carbondale and Edwardsville, IL: Southern Illinois University Press. Copyright 1987 by The Frank Lloyd Wright Foundation. p. 17. Courtesy The Frank Lloyd Wright Foundation.

38. Wright, Frank Lloyd. 1927. "In the Cause of Architecture: II. Standardization, The Soul of the Machine." *Architectural Record* 61(6):478–480. Reprint. 1975. *In the Cause of Architecture*, ed. Frederick Gutheim. New York: McGraw-Hill. p. 137.

39. Wright, Frank Lloyd. 1928. "In the Cause of Architecture: IV. The Meaning of Materials—Wood." *Architectural Record* 63(5):481–488. Reprint. 1975. *In the Cause of Architecture*, ed. Frederick Gutheim. New York: McGraw-Hill. p. 184.

40. Wright, Frank Lloyd. 1927. "In the Cause of Architecture: II. Standardization, The Soul of the Machine." *Architectural Record* 61(6):478–480. Reprint. 1975. *In the Cause of Architecture*, ed. Frederick Gutheim. New York: McGraw-Hill. p. 137.

41. Ibid. *ARCHITECTURAL RECORD*, (June/ 1927), copyright 1975 by McGraw-Hill, Inc. All rights reserved. Reproduced with the permission of the publisher.

42. Wright, Frank Lloyd. 1928. "In the Cause of Architecture: IV. The Meaning of Materials—Wood." *Architectural Record* 63(5):481–488. Reprint. 1975. *In the Cause of Architecture*, ed. Frederick Gutheim. New York: McGraw-Hill. p. 179.

43. Ibid., 182, 184.

44. Ibid., 186.

45. Wright, Frank Lloyd. 1931. *Modern Architecture: Being the Kahn Lectures for 1930*. Reprint. 1987. ed. Bruce Brooks Pfeiffer. Carbondale and Edwardsville, IL: Southern Illinois University Press. Copyright 1987 by The Frank Lloyd Wright Foundation. p. 16. Courtesy The Frank Lloyd Wright Foundation.

46. Wright, Frank Lloyd. 1928. "In the Cause of Architecture: IV. The Meaning of Materials—Wood." *Architectural Record* 63(5):481–488. Reprint. 1975. *In the Cause of Architecture*, ed. Frederick Gutheim. New York: McGraw-Hill. p. 186. *ARCHITECTURAL RECORD*, (May/1928), copyright 1975 by McGraw-Hill, Inc. All rights reserved. Reproduced with the permission of the publisher.

47 Ibid., 180.

48. Wright, Frank Lloyd. 1931. *Modern Architecture: Being the Kahn Lectures for 1930*. Reprint. 1987. ed. Bruce Brooks Pfeiffer. Carbondale and Edwardsville, IL: Southern Illinois University Press. Copyright 1987 by The Frank Lloyd Wright Foundation. p. 16. Courtesy The Frank Lloyd Wright Foundation.

49. Ibid. Courtesy The Frank Lloyd Wright Foundation.

50. Wright, Frank Lloyd. 1928. "In the Cause of Architecture: IV. The Meaning of Materials—Wood." *Architectural Record* 63(5):481–488. Reprint. 1975. *In the Cause of Architecture*, ed. Frederick Gutheim. New York: McGraw-Hill. p. 182.

51. Wright, Frank Lloyd. 1931. *Modern Architecture: Being the Kahn Lectures for 1930*. Reprint. 1987. ed. Bruce Brooks Pfeiffer. Carbondale and Edwardsville, IL: Southern Illinois University Press. Copyright 1987 by The Frank Lloyd Wright Foundation. p. 16. Courtesy The Frank Lloyd Wright Foundation.

52. Wright, Frank Lloyd. 1928. "In the Cause of Architecture: IV. The Meaning of Materials—Wood." *Architectural Record* 63(5):481–488. Reprint. 1975. *In the Cause of Architecture*, ed. Frederick Gutheim. New York: McGraw-Hill. p. 180.

53. Ibid.

54. Kalec, Donald G. 1982. *The Home and Studio of Frank Lloyd Wright in Oak Park, Illinois 1889–1911*, ed. Jean P. Murphy. Oak Park, IL: Frank Lloyd Wright Home and Studio Foundation. p. 11.

55. Wright, Frank Lloyd. "1928. In the Cause of Architecture: I. The Logic of the Plan." *Architectural Record* 63(1):49–57. Reprint. 1975. *In the Cause of Architecture*, ed. Frederick Gutheim. New York: McGraw-Hill. p. 154. *ARCHITECTURAL RECORD*, (January/ 1928), copyright 1975 by McGraw-Hill, Inc.

56. Ibid. *ARCHITECTURAL RECORD*, (January/1928), copyright 1975 by McGraw-Hill, Inc. All rights reserved. Reproduced with the permission of the publisher.

57. Wright, Frank Lloyd. 1932. *An Autobiography*. Revised. 1943. New York: Duell, Sloan and Pearce. Copyright by The Frank Lloyd Wright Foundation. p. 134. Courtesy The Frank Lloyd Wright Foundation

58. Brandes, Susan J. 1991. "Introduction." *Affordable Dreams: The Goetsch-Winckler House and Frank Lloyd Wright*, ed. Susan J. Brandes. *Kresge Art Museum Bulletin* 6:xvi.

59. Tafel, Edgar. 1979. *Apprentice to Genius: Years with Frank Lloyd Wright*. Reprint. 1985. *Years with Frank Lloyd Wright: Apprentice to Genius*. New York: Dover Publications. p. 191.

60. Wright, Frank Lloyd. 1928. "In the Cause of Architecture: IV. The Meaning of Materials—Wood." *Architectural Record* 63(5):481–488. Reprint. 1975. *In the Cause of Architecture*, ed. Frederick Gutheim. New York: McGraw-Hill. p. 179.

61. Wright, Frank Lloyd. 1908. "In the Cause of Architecture." *Architectural Record* 23(3):155–221. Reprint. 1975. *In the Cause of Architecture*, ed. Frederick Gutheim. New York: McGraw-Hill. p. 55. *ARCHITECTURAL RECORD*, (March/1908), copyright 1975 by McGraw-Hill, Inc. All rights reserved. Reproduced with the permission of the publisher.

62. Wright, Frank Lloyd. 1928. "In the Cause of Architecture: IV. The Meaning of Materials—Wood." *Architectural Record* 63(5):481–488. Reprint. 1975. *In the Cause of Architecture*, ed. Frederick Gutheim. New York: McGraw-Hill. p. 185.

63. Wright, Frank Lloyd. 1927. "In the Cause of Architecture: II. Standardization, The Soul of the Machine." *Architectural Record* 61(6):478–480. Reprint. 1975. *In the Cause of Architecture*, ed.

Frederick Gutheim. New York: McGraw-Hill. p. 137. *ARCHITECTURAL RECORD*, (June/1927), copyright 1975 by McGraw-Hill, Inc. All rights reserved. Reproduced with the permission of the publisher.

64. Wright, Frank Lloyd. 1928. "In the Cause of Architecture: IV. The Meaning of Materials—Wood." *Architectural Record* 63(5):481–488. Reprint. 1975. *In the Cause of Architecture*, ed. Frederick Gutheim. New York: McGraw-Hill. p. 180. *ARCHITECTURAL RECORD*, (May/1928), copyright 1975 by McGraw-Hill, Inc. All rights reserved. Reproduced with the permission of the publisher.

65. Ibid., 185. *ARCHITECTURAL RECORD*, (May/1928), copyright 1975 by McGraw-Hill, Inc. All rights reserved. Reproduced with the permission of the publisher.

66. Ibid. *ARCHITECTURAL RECORD*, (May/1928), copyright 1975 by McGraw-Hill, Inc. All rights reserved. Reproduced with the permission of the publisher.

67. Senkevitch, Jr., Anatole. 1991. "Usonia II and the Goetsch-Winckler House: Manifestations of Wright's Early Vision of Broadacre City." *Affordable Dreams: The Goetsch-Winckler House and Frank Lloyd Wright*, ed. Susan J. Brandes. *Kresge Art Museum Bulletin* 6:12,25.

68. Brandes, Susan J. 1991. "Introduction." *Affordable Dreams: The Goetsch-Winckler House and Frank Lloyd Wright*, ed. Susan J. Brandes. *Kresge Art Museum Bulletin* 6:xvi.

69. Wright, Frank Lloyd. 1932. *An Autobiography*. Revised. 1943. New York: Duell, Sloan and Pearce. Copyright by The Frank Lloyd Wright Foundation. p. 491. Courtesy The Frank Lloyd Wright Foundation

70. Wright, Frank Lloyd. 1928. "In the Cause of Architecture: IV. The Meaning of Materials—Wood." *Architectural Record* 63(5):481–488. Reprint. 1975. *In the Cause of Architecture*, ed. Frederick Gutheim. New York: McGraw-Hill. p. 179.

CHAPTER ▣ STONE

INTRODUCTION

Stone, clay brick, and concrete block, all being types of masonry, are similar in their blockiness of form, their limited strength beyond compression, their high resistance to deterioration somewhat compromised by joints, and their limited receptiveness to alteration of basic form beyond simple breaks and cuts. Given their differing substances, expression of their nature in architecture could be expected to be similar but not identical. Although some of Wright's detailing appears to have been influenced by forces outside the realm of materials, certain treatments common to the masonries can be associated with like properties, while certain variations in detailing relate to differences in properties.

Both stone and brick have long histories, but only the history of stone interested Wright. Stone has contributed unique characteristics to several historical styles, whereas brick, having had essentially the same appearance throughout history, is not associated with any particular epoch. Historical treatments provided examples that were, according to Wright, in the nature of stone and others that were less so. The Egyptians and Chinese used stone sympathetically, he thought, while the Greeks and Romans did not.[1] The fact that stone is the only masonry made of a natural substance also influenced his commentary and use of the material.

FORM

A material's form is largely a function of its substance strength. Wood's bending strength, for example, allows trees and the lumber they yield to maintain linear shapes. While stone, clay, and (unreinforced) concrete can be shaped into long slender forms, to do so would yield units too fragile for routine use and economic handling. Wright observed that in history stone had often been forced into the shape of wood. In China, for example, stone can be seen to "imitate literally great wood towering of poles and posts, [and] beams."[2] The Romans cut stone "into wooden cornices," he observed.[3] The stone forms in the Greek temples, he thought, were "only derived from wood."[4] He sensed logic in the fact that the woodlike shapes were "now crumbling to original shapes of stone," whereas originally "there were no stone forms whatever."[5] Justice had prevailed, it seemed, in the stone's inability to maintain the linear woodlike form into which it was originally forced by man. The more compact masses into which much of it had broken were, he thought, more natural to the material.

Wright saw stone as "a solid material, heavy, durable and most grateful for masses" and was therefore compatible with its nature when used in massive assemblies.[6] From his rejection of slenderness (a woodlike form) and his promotion of mass, Wright's ideal of the natural form of stone as a block emerges. Stone blocks, he believed, should be "true to square and level"[7] so that they can be securely stacked to high levels and carry heavy loads. Thus the logical format for stone as being blocklike and weight-bearing is established. His stone usually carried building live loads but when it did not, it at least carried its own weight.

Wright thought that the nature of stone (meaning, in this context, the type of stone) would influence the character of the wall surface. He accepted a variety of textures including "a natural face" (rough), "a face characteristic of the tool" that shaped the stone, a "flatly smoothed" face, and "sometimes a honed or polished" face.[8] Logically, polishing was to be limited to stone that could take a polish. Given the inability of certain stone to accept a polish and the ability of others to yield attractive patterns when polished, his textural preferences conformed to the limitations and potential of the material. Although most of his stone was sedimentary and therefore limited in its textural options, his preference for rough-faced blocky masses is, nevertheless, significant. The shape and texture of his stone conform to that promoted in his commentary and to that logically generated by a combination of physical properties in combination with the most basic manufacturing processes.

Although it is formed by nature, fieldstone, or rubble, does not embody in its entirety the nature of building stone, just as a tree with limbs and leaves does not entirely reflect the nature of the wood for construction framing. The use of rubble in itself, therefore, does not constitute sensitivity to the nature of building stone.

Since the stacked format typical for building walls is not a natural condition for rubble, the expression of its nature is especially sensitive to its detailing as a wall. Wright used an unusually large amount of rubble for an architect of his stature, a circumstance related, in part, to the nature of his projects. The variety in his rubble detailing produced a range of expressions that reflect the nature of stone to varying degrees.

A unique and relatively pure use of small boulders in the spirit of Charles and Henry Greene occurs at the Williams House (1897). Large rough stones are set at the base of the exterior brick wall of the house. They are stacked part-way up the sides of the entry door in a random pattern having a natural and stable appearance except for one or two stones supported by the adjacent brick into which they extend. The close proximity of the units to the earth and their limitation to essentially a wall-base are conditions compatible with their nature for reasons of form, structure, and durability. The large odd-shaped masses would not stack efficiently (in theory) to form an entire wall and having originally developed as part of the earth's crust, their merging with the grade reflects a physical and philosophical compatibility with it. Although the detailing is highly compatible with the nature of boulders, the installation is little more than a curiosity. Unlike the Greene brothers, who demonstrated serious consideration of these issues in several constructions, Wright did not pursue the idea much further.

The issues regarding rubble in its traditional detailing are nearly moot, given Wright's limited exploration of its standard format in building. His use of rubble in the F. B. Jones boathouse (1900), main house (1901), and gate house (1901), yields mostly structural issues (subsequently discussed in the section on strength). Issues relating to the expression of rubble form are similar to those of any product. The question is whether or not unit form is revealed and to what degree the detailing accommodates or exploits its unique characteristics. Wright's use of traditional detailing at the F. B. Jones buildings expresses the form of rubble to the degree typical of the standard approach. The shape and dimensions of the stone faces can be seen clearly in the surface. The thickness of the units is revealed at corners. The sense of thickness is reinforced slightly in the walls where the stones project slightly forward of the mortar. The irregular and rounded form of the stone is not reflected in the relatively flush surfaces, however. The form of the rubble would seem to call for less precise surface planes than exist in traditional walls. Random bulges, bumps, and other irregularities would be a more natural response to the rubble, although they would not reflect the standard concept of what a constructed wall should be.

Figure 3-1. Boulders surround the base of the Chauncey Williams Residence. Bricks lap at obtuse corners to yield texture. (Courtesy the Frank Lloyd Wright Archives)

Boulders or irregular masses of stone reappear occasionally in Wright's work, as at the fireplace lintels at Taliesin (1925) and the Pew House (1938) and as an outcropping in the Kaufmann House (1935). After the brief use of rubble as an expressive material at the F. B. Jones complex and a lengthy abstinence from its use in quantity, he returned to the substance with a unique detailing strategy. In 1937 Wright developed a variation of rubble construction that he called "desert rubble masonry,"[9] which he used periodically through 1958. In its first use at Taliesin West, rubble was placed into concretelike formwork with the flat faces against the wood. The cavity between the outer rubble of the thick wall masses was then filled with rubble and concrete.

The uniqueness of the hybrid assembly is reflected in the variety of names given to the material. A caption in a 1948 article signed by Wright in *The Architectural Forum* refers to the material as "Desert Rubble Cast in Wooden Boxing."[10] Bruce Brooks Pfeiffer called it "cast-in-forms masonry"[11] and "poured rubblestone masonry"[12] in the *Frank Lloyd Wright Monograph* series. Four variations of the term can be found in notes on working drawings. It is called "concrete rubble"[13] on the floor plan sheet and "poured masonry"[14] on elevations of the

Austin House (1951). It is referred to as "poured rubble masonry"[15] on the elevations and "poured conc. & stone masonry"[16] on a section of the Bott House (1956). More recent references to the material have been "desert rubblestone"[17] by William Storrer and "desert concrete"[18] by Meryle Secrest.

The handling of stones as individual units during construction and their exposure in the surface imparts to the assembly certain masonry characteristics in process and image. Also, the wall masses have characteristics that are like concrete. The concretelike aspects of the image cannot be said to reflect an insensitivity to the nature of masonry as they are due to the use of concrete as an equal partner with the stone rather than as mortar (a masonry component). The fact that the concrete was, for the most part, poured into formwork rather than being applied by troweling and that the ratio of binder to stone is far greater than typical of masonry construction makes the assembly truly a composite of two materials. The material was addressed in the general masonry notes rather than in the general concrete notes on the floor-plan working drawing sheet of the Austin House,[19] thus verifying that it was viewed in Wright's office more as a masonry than a concrete substance at that time.

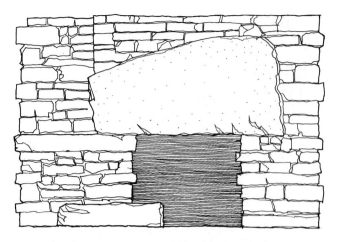

Figure 3-2. Single irregular stone as fireplace lintel, John C. Pew Residence. (From a photograph, *Frank Lloyd Wright Selected Houses vol. 6*, p. 52.)

Figure 3-3. Varied sizes and relatively large proportion of concrete to stone in surface of the Taliesin West Music Pavilion.

Nevertheless, the detailing of the desert rubble masonry cannot be evaluated by standards that are entirely masonry- or entirely concrete-based. An irregular mass constructed from only irregular stone would reflect the nature of the individual units in both a practical and philosophical way. The irregularity of units would facilitate their fitting together in an irregular configuration and make entirely straight geometries difficult to achieve. The straight edges and flat surfaces, however, at Taliesin West were facilitated by concrete, which filled the voids between the stones. The sloped surfaces as well as acute and obtuse corners reflect a nonrectangularity that is compatible with that of stone in a general way. They also express the plasticity of concrete as it simultaneously assumes the irregularity of the stone and forms straight edges.

For the most part, the stone is expressed as a two-dimensional substance, for the units are flush or slightly recessed in the surface. The corners of the masses are typically shaped by the concrete rather than by the stone. Consequently, the sense of depth and mass usually afforded units by their routine appearance at corners in traditional masonry walls occurs infrequently at Taliesin West and most other installations of this type. The few stones that appear on corners are too small to reflect a sense of mass. Although rubble is not expected to have a cubelike geometry, the placement of tapered or thin stones on either or both sides of a corner that itself has a concrete edge, contributes further to the sense of two-dimensionality in the units. An exception to this method of detailing can be found at the Berger House (1950), where large stones are routinely exposed on corners and thus reveal their mass in three dimensions.

The stone faces revealed in the desert rubble masonry systems are clearly real stone, but their being entirely dependent on their face images to bring to mind a sense of mass weakens the expression of the nature of stone. The overall sense of mass in the walls is compatible with the massiveness of stone, but it does not seem to be generated by the masonry. The units seem too small to force the walls into their great thicknesses. Consequently, the mass of the whole has limited ability to reflect on the thickness of the stone. It allows the possibility of significant stone thickness but does not prove that it exists. An analysis of the rubble as a kind of large exposed aggregate might yield different conclusions, but its size and method of placement tend to define the stone more as masonry than aggregate. As simplistic as it seems, the occasional large boulder placed about the Taliesin West complex as part of the landscaping lends a sense of mass by association to the similarly shaped and colored unit faces in the concrete. Perception of the encased rubble would be significantly different if similarly colored and textured thin, slatelike, or flagstone-shaped rock was stacked among the landscaping in place of the boulders.

Most of the spread-based masses at Taliesin West are low to the ground, thus emphasizing the compatibility of the concrete and stone with the earth. Although the concrete and rubble of other installations are also in extensive contact with the earth, the lengthy perimeter and relatively low profile of the Taliesin West compound exaggerate the relationship beyond that present at other locations. The Pauson (1939) and Bott (1956) houses have a greater percentage of their wall masses farther from the ground, which dilutes slightly the otherwise expressive relationship of the material to the earth compared to Taliesin West.

The desert rubble masonry at Taliesin West is generally more expressive of the nature of its components than are subsequent installations. The reduced proportion of concrete to stone, the more uniform sizes of stone, and the more uniform orientation of the stone at other desert rubble buildings gives the stone a tighter, more mechanical, sense that is less natural looking than the detailing at Taliesin West. The varied sizes, shapes, and orientations of the Taliesin West stone with the hand-packed appearance of very small stones in occasional gaps against edges of the larger units has a variety and randomness reminiscent of nature. The labor-intensive look of the Taliesin West surfaces, although not reflecting nature itself, embodies an organic spirit missing from the greater uniformity found elsewhere.

Except in comparison to Taliesin West, the Pauson installation does not appear to be particularly uniform. It seems more random and natural than the highly uniform and somewhat mechanical surface of the Bott House which, except for its fireplace, looks the most artificial of all the desert rubble masonry projects. This is no doubt related to the relative thinness of the matrix, which is shown in the drawings to be essentially a veneer thinner than the eight-inch wythe of concrete block to which it is applied. The Oboler (1941), Berger (1950), Austin (1951), Boomer (1953), and Pilgrim Congregational Church (1958) projects fall between the extremes in their reflection of the naturalness of the stone and the plasticity of the concrete.

Typically, drawings for these projects show very large rubble (varying in character with each apprentice's drawing style) and very little concrete. The character of the drawn images was never achieved in construction, which must be partially due to the role of the drawn stone as a symbol rather than as a proposal for reality. The availability of material and the degree of artistic sensitivity of the builders doubtless affected the outcomes. The working drawing instructions for the builder of the Austin House to prepare a 100 square-foot sample of the wall for approval of the texture[20] indicate an intention to control the image, which could never be as closely directed as it was at Taliesin West where Wright was in attendance literally around the clock.

In several projects Wright used mixtures of rubble and roughly squared units. Although most of these are shown in the working drawings as large, rounded, and irregular rubble, none of the projects were constructed with stone in that form. The significance of this phenomenon is limited because of the relative ease of drawing the rubble symbol versus drawing actual shapes. Also, Wright's practice of using local stone makes the installed shape somewhat independent of the drawn shape. Nevertheless the failure to insist that the drawings reflect the actual image of the stone suggests a certain amount of tolerance for appearance of the walls. The circumstance is a reminder that the link between intent

FIGURE 3-4. Bottom of wall battered, top of wall reverse battered, stones approach corners but are not set on corner, horizontal V-grooves irregularly spaced in kitchen wall at Taliesin West.

and outcome is too loose in these cases to draw other than the most general conclusions about intent.

The roughly squared stones at the S. Friedman House (1949) look rather natural, and their mixing in large numbers with field rubble expresses a broader variety of natural-looking forms than would irregular rubble alone. The greater variety here is more informative about the nature of stone form than are installations with less variety, as more of stones' potential is demonstrated. The random slight projections add a sense of mass and coupled with the absence of coursing, give the walls a natural looking texture.

A series of windows in the house has sills that curve downward into the stone. The precise half-circle that the stone defines at the sills detracts from the natural appearance of the whole. The absence of inverted voussoirs give the curve an appearance of having been precisely cut out of the stone mass rather than having been assembled—an odd condition for rough stone. The horizontal joints maintained while fitting various shapes to

FIGURE 3-5. Rubble mixed with more regular stone at the Sol Friedman Residence. No lintels expressed at lower windows. Cantilevered roof slab approximates circle with multiple straight segments. (Courtesy The Frank Lloyd Wright Archives)

FIGURE 3-6. Irregular stone mixed with squared stone at the Henry J. Neils Residence. Some stone projected. (Courtesy The Frank Lloyd Wright Archives)

form the curve is more natural to the stone than the radial joints of inverted voussoirs would have been. A less natural appearance is projected, however, as voussoirs (albeit inverted) have a construction logic that would have forced the basis for judgment of the detail from one reasonable in nature to one reasonable in construction.

A similar sense of precision occurs in the recess in the stone by the fireplace of the Kaufmann House, which was constructed to store a large spherical cauldron. A constructed wall is not a natural formation and can tolerate detailing that does not duplicate stone outcroppings in nature. In this case, however, the walls are more natural in image than the precise geometry of the recess, which nearly seems to have been carved. Curves in masonry express the smallness and individuality of units, but a spherical surface of small radius suggests a mechanical precision unlike the nature of hand-cut and hand-placed stone.

The curved walls of the S. Friedman House are compatible with small units, which may be easily positioned out of alignment to produce a wall that is not straight. The irregularity of units edges facilitates a curved alignment, as right-angled corners are not present to force the stone faces apart (to create a large vertical mortar joint) when turned relative to the adjacent unit. Because of its particular combination of form and structural expression, the S. Friedman House constitutes one of Wright's uses of stone that is more expressive of the material's nature. (Lapses in the structural purity of this stone are subsequently addressed.)

The stone of the Serlin (1949) and Walker (1951) houses is uncoursed but has fewer irregular units than

have the S. Friedman walls. Irregularity is typically limited to the ends of the units, which occasionally slant. The predominate proportions are compact like those of the Friedman. The greater regularity of unit form reduces slightly the sense of naturalness in the Serlin and Walker walls compared to those of the Friedman House. The Walker House is slightly less expressive of stone's naturalness than the Serlin because of its particular combination of form characteristics and structural expression. The Walker stone approaches a coursed format in certain zones but does not appear coursed overall. A slow and tedious fitting of the fairly regular units is suggested by the large variety of sizes, which—combined with the their flush condition and the very large expanse of wall surface—imparts a sense of unnatural rigidity to the whole. The Serlin stone has a more casual (unforced) appearance, thus reflecting to a greater degree a characteristic associated with natural things.

The marble walls of the Neils House (1950) are among the least expressive of the nature of stone in Wright's work. The fact that the units were culls from the client's business explains their selection but does not alter conclusions regarding their expression. The roughness of the marble fails to distinguish the stone from types of stone that cannot be polished; thus the potential of marble is misrepresented or, at best, confused with the less versatile stones. The narrow-faced rectangular units have an appearance of precision and regularity that is unlike a natural material in its natural state. This aspect could be interpreted as an expression of stone technology or stone in the service of building except that further evidence of applied technology (such as polishing) is not present to support this strategy.

Scattered broad-faced stone in the wall is not integrated into the surface composition. Because of its contrast in proportion and value with the narrow stones, it appears to be superimposed on the established pattern and thus fails to become part of a continuum of alternatives in marble form. The broad stone is an intruder in a self-contained system. This image is exacerbated by the absence of sizes and shapes between the thin- and broad-faced units. The occasional projection of thin units serves only to create a visual tension in the apparent struggle of the broad units to fit between the projected stones. The overall appearance is the most artistically rigid of those in Wright's rough-faced stone. The stone, lacking the apparent casualness and randomness of nature and natural things in general, has a machined sense about it. It fails to exploit the potential of this expressive strategy, however, as it does not present a comprehensive demonstration of the potential of stone-processing technology, from the simplest level to the most sophisticated. Its character falls somewhere between the two ideas but is not successful in integrating or contrasting their significant aspects.

The unique mix of rubble, roughly squared thick stones, and thin rectangular stone at the Reisley House (1951) generates both advantages and disadvantages in the expression of stone. The thinner units frequently project forward of the wall surface, bringing in to the mass the sense of unit depth typical of this detail. Although the variety provides a broad range of information about stone form, the rubble prevents the projected rectangular units from emulating the spirit of sedimentary rock deposits as the natural formations do not include embedded pieces of rubble.

Consequently, the rubble becomes a kind of academic presentation of one extreme of stone form juxtaposed against another common form. This constitutes an expressive device or strategy that derives its validity from the expression of options in stone technology rather than from the expression of the naturalness of stone. As such it falls short of its potential, having failed to exhibit dressed stone as the extreme of processing. The fact that the original drawing of the stone shows it as large rounded rubble dilutes the credibility of the installation as purposefully expressing the nature of stone technology. When considering all aspects, the stone forms as constructed appear to be a compromise between ideals and material availability. This does not mean that the detailing fails to respect the nature of stone, since many properties of stone are exhibited. However, there is a lack of unity and clarity in the expression of the stone, thus diminishing the significance of miscellaneous property-sensitive details.

The majority of Wright's stone was rough-faced, rectangular, relatively slender in various sizes, and coursed. This combination of characteristics, including the coursing, is similar to the faces of certain natural outcroppings and stone deposits exposed by road construction. Thin layers of sedimentary stone deposits are visible in various landscapes that have weathered and broken into segments resembling stacks of randomly protruding and receding units. Various patterns of projected units in Wright's walls of rough-faced narrow rectangular units emulate, to various degrees, the projections and recesses of the exposed surfaces of such natural deposits. It is not necessary to imitate forms in nature to demonstrate sensitivity to the nature of a material, in which the relationship between lumber and trees is a reminder. (That is, it is not necessary to reproduce the image of trees in a building to be sensitive to wood. Emphasizing the characteristics of lumber is not only adequate to this end but preferred.) The characteristics of this particular format of building stone, however, describe a condition that accommodates the limitations and potential of sedimentary stone as a building product and, therefore, reflects the nature of the material in this role. The resulting image seems highly natural in form and structure even without direct comparison to the natural deposits in the earth. The intensity of the expression of stone's nature in this format, however, varies with the slightly different detailing of each project.

The rectangular rough-faced stone of the Hillside Home School II (1901) and the Smith Bank (1904) was unique for several reasons. These were Wright's first buildings (after the mixed masonry of the Charnley House) in which stone was the predominate expressive vehicle. The stone was set with its faces flush in the surface of the walls (to the degree that rough faces allow). The flushness of the stone imparts a rigidity to the surfaces that seems somewhat artificial in its precision. This is not to say that the stone of the Hillside Home School II looks artificial, as this is only one aspect of the image. The treatment of the stone in the Smith Bank is less accommodating to its nature than at the Hillside Home School II, due mostly to its structural expression. This flush detailing was the last before a variation emerged wherein selected stones were projected forward of the wall plane.

The projected detail first appeared at Taliesin I (1911) and was used in most of the rough-faced rectangular stone to follow. The projected stones of the Kaufmann House (1935), the second Jacobs House (1943), the Unitarian Church (1947), and a long list of lesser-known houses extending to the late 1950s express the nature of stone form more intensely than do the previous flush surfaces. The three-dimensional expression of randomly distributed units emphasizes unit thickness and face shape by virtue of the shadow created and, to a smaller degree, the observer's depth perception. The randomness of the placement of the projections further contributes to the sense of naturalness. Flush stone has

Figure 3-7. Relatively flush squared rough-faced stone at the Hillside Home School II. Prominent copings and caps. Buttressed arch at lower level. Battered walls. Tooled vertical corners. (Courtesy The Frank Lloyd Wright Archives)

an inherent sense of thickness, especially if it is revealed at corners, but the projected units eliminate with certainty any possibility that thin panels are present.

Like the desert rubble masonry of Taliesin West, the rectangular rough-faced stone of Taliesin I produced a particular combination of natural and human-generated characteristics that was not matched in other projects. The pronounced projections are distinct enough to suggest purposeful (human) manipulation and are numerous enough to develop their own identity as a special set of units. The small dimension of their projection limits the emphasis of their regularity or uniformity (which is greater than units in a natural deposit) and avoids an expression of excessive preplanning and control. They reflect a nearly accidental quality that might come from a struggle to manipulate stones of widely varied depths without intent to force a condition of flushness where it was not convenient. Accidental and casual characteristics reflect the aspect of human manipulation closest to nature or, at least, furthest from the mechanical kind of

uniformity afforded by technology. The masonry at Taliesin I expressed the nature of stone as a building material at a high level. The relatively thick and slightly varied proportions of the long rectangular stones contribute significantly to this expression, as they appear to be less fragile and less the result of human intent than the more narrow units common in other projects.

A generally rectangular stone with a very low sense of human manipulation occurs at the second Jacobs House. The randomness and shortness of projections there prevent any particular group of stones from developing an identity separate from the mass. The detailing is more of a rough texture than a set of projections due to the subtlety in the surface undulation and the lack of a distinguishable pattern. This texture has the most natural appearance among the variations of this type. (Naturalness is not a measure of interest or attractiveness and is acknowledged only to report the dominance of a naturelike randomness and casualness over the regularity typical of calculated control.) This detailing may lack

FIGURE 3-8. Rough-faced roughly squared stone at Taliesin I. Random projection of units. (Courtesy The Frank Lloyd Wright Archives)

the richness and interest of more manipulated patterns at other installations such as the Kaufmann House (1935), but such does not warrant attention here as aesthetic achievement is not the focus. Without an identifiable pattern or the large variation in position, the artificiality that is characteristic of human influence is subdued in the Jacobs stone. Stone is not forced to perform in a particular way that requires certain sizes of certain lengths. The sense of preplanning, a major human characteristic, is not nearly as strong here as in other examples. Although the curve of the wall is based on a single specific radius, which is an artificial and a rigid condition, curves generally conceal irregularities more readily than flat surfaces and are, therefore, visually less rigid than straight walls. The sense of naturalness in the stone is enhanced by the curve.

Much of Wright's rectangular projected stone masonry is similar to that of the Unitarian Church. This particular detailing provides the large-scale roughness associated with stone in nature and has a reasonably random and casual look. The stones have a significant projection and are few enough in number to appear as a pattern within a field. These characteristics add a human quality largely absent from the stonework of the second Jacobs House. (References to human qualities and artificial characteristics are not value judgments here but describe an order typical of humans and construction, as

opposed to a more random order typical of nature.) The relatively long length of the narrow units suggest an aesthetic choice, as well as imparting a fragility to the stone not long tolerated by nature when extreme.

Like that of the Unitarian Church (1947), the rectangular projected stone of a large number of houses of the late 1940s and 1950s (H. Anthony, J. Gillin, R. Smith, P. Kinney, E. Arnold, M. Hoffman, A. Jackson, F. Iber, J. Mollica, S. Peterson) appears to be a thoughtful effort to produce a balanced but natural randomness. The buildings succeed in this regard but, because of the appearance of intent in their surfaces, fall short of the naturalness at Taliesin and the second Jacobs House. The Hagan (1954) and Lovness (1955) houses are similar to this group but are distinguished by their stone having a greater variety of proportion and being generally more compact than the narrow units at the other houses. Greater compactness and variety seem more natural than would less.

Certain other house of this ilk fall at the lower extreme of the reasonable naturalness reflected by the whole category, due to detailing variations that emphasize human manipulation. The long length of each projected unit at the Shavin House (1950) seems odd, not something anticipated in nature. The large projection of the stone at the Elam House (1951), the wide spacing of the projected units, their long length, and the

FIGURE 3-9. Roughly squared stone with a variety of proportions at the IN. Hagan Residence. Wood dentils above windows. (Courtesy The Frank Lloyd Wright Archives)

relatively uniform and laborious-looking spacing produce the most mechanical appearance of the various installations. (Copies of Wright's projected stone detailing by other designers typically fail to capture the natural spirit inherent in the idea because of characteristics in their construction that are like those at the Elam House.) The Staley House (1951) projects its larger stones while holding back the more slender units. Any pattern between face-proportions and the stone's position relative to the wall surface imparts a sense of human decision to the image. The Staley arrangement is the opposite of the more natural (and structurally logical) version found at the Kaufmann House (Fallingwater, 1935).

In a letter to Mr. Kaufmann, Wright described his vision for the stones at Fallingwater being several feet long mixed with other lengths. He hoped for a variety of heights but was willing to accept what resulted from their quarrying.[21] The stone he described lacks the compactness that accommodates the materials' lack of tensile strength. The subsequent installation of stone of Fallingwater yielded a variety of proportions, which, in general, seems more natural than the repetition of a single size. An unnatural aspect of the selection is that, while large units and very thin units are present, the sizes between the extremes are limited. Another artificial circumstance is the fact that only the thin units are projected. An aesthetic decision is strongly implied. On a philosophical level, it makes more structural sense to project the thin stones while the larger ones secure the cantilevered units in the wall. This particular logic demonstrates a sensitivity to the nature of stone in the role of a construction material with regard to strength.

Most of the rectangular rough-faced stone in

FIGURE 3-10. Relatively narrow squared stone at the Edgar J. Kaufmann, Sr. Residence. Random thinner stones project. (Courtesy The Frank Lloyd Wright Archives)

Wright's work was installed much as it was shown in the working drawings. The Kinney (1950) and Reisley (1951) houses are exceptions, having been drawn as large rounded rubble. The existence of greater control of the final image is suggested for the slender rectangular rough-faced stone, than for the projects with rubble mixed with near-rubble or roughly-squared units. This suggests that the appearance of the slender rectangular stone was not only more predictable but may have also had a more definite role in the architectural expression of the buildings.

The notes to the contractor on the Blair House (1952) working drawings call for "rock or quarry faced

Figure 3-11. Smooth stones assembled as 'expressed' lintel at fireplace in contrast to rough wall stone at the Hillside Home School II. Wording cut into smooth stone. Tooled joints on vertical corners. (Courtesy The Frank Lloyd Wright Archives)

(no draft) squared stone masonry."[22] Further instructions call for varying thicknesses of stone and for occasionally projecting it two or three inches. The contractor is instructed to "see photos of Kaufman House, Architectural Forum [sic], January 1938."[23] A 100 square-foot sample of stone wall is requested so that the stone can be approved prior to installation. Enough tolerance exists in the note to render the character of the stone vulnerable to the mason's taste and judgment. The final controlling device, the sample, failed to fulfill its potential, as the pattern of the Kaufmann stone was not emulated. Fine distinctions between the images of the stonework in the various projects are analyzed as products, if not of the architect's hand, of the architectural process at his disposal. As it turned out, the Blair House is not one of the projects most expressive of the nature of stone. The spottiness of the reddish and off-white coloring combined with the sharp-edged units yield a relatively artificial and mechanical looking installation.

Although most of Wright's rectangular stone reflects, to some degree, the spirit of stone in nature and stone in the service of construction, the strongest com-

bination of these qualities is found in the original installation, Taliesin I. Like the desert rubble at Taliesin West, the expressive achievement in the nature of stone at the installation for which the detailing was invented was never duplicated in projects more remote from the architect.

WORKABILITY

Thus far, the stone examined has been rough-faced. This texture is considered here to be the most central to the nature of stone, as it is the texture found in nature and the one produced by the most basic stone shaping process of splitting. A smooth flat face is not foreign to building stone but neither does it result from the most basic processing. The degree of smoothness in the surface of modern stone is directly related to the degree of processing, measured in terms of time, effort, and/or sophistication of technology. Wright's aforementioned observation that stone can have many textures was directed to all varieties of stone rather than a single type. Since all types of stone are rough as found in nature and rough as initially quarried, Wright's comment addresses the variety of potentials available through working the stone beyond the most basic processing.

Worked stone is that in which the most basic shape or surface has been changed by processing subsequent to the initial steps that produced the first usable mass. For purposes of this study, smooth stone is considered to be worked stone. Although stone can be worked into shapes that are too fragile and delicate to be reflect the nature of the material, Wright avoided such shapes. His worked stone, like his rough stone, tended to be reasonably compact and massive. In some instances, however, detailing subdued the actual form of the units. Wright's brick was sometimes trimmed with smooth, rectangular stone copings, lintels, sills, and bases. Where single-unit forms were isolated from each other, the stone trim is reasonably blocky, although lintels and window sills are usually too slender to be called blocks. Where continuity was achieved, as in a long wall coping or base, the compact blocky sense of the stone was lost in the butting of units with joints of minimal visibility. The resulting linear strips share a geometry with wood, metal, and concrete copings.

The Waller Apartments (1895), the Larkin Building (1903), the Morris Gift Shop (1948), and several older houses have trim of long runs of butted units that make the stone look linear rather than blocky. The most pronounced of the examples is the Robie House (1906), which has, in the prominent street facade, four continuous parallel stone strips running uninterrupted for almost the full length of the house. In these cases the stone expresses the nature of linear materials with regard to form. Only its color distinguishes the trim from wood and metal, while it is virtually identical to concrete. The need for continuous coverage by a coping would seem to excuse the forfeiting of stone form in the building expression. It should be noted, however, that the decision to do so is an aesthetic one, not one forced by conditions beyond the control of the designer. Alternating two colors of stone in any strip would maintain the identities of the individual blocks and thus express more clearly the basic form of each. To reject this image as being too busy or otherwise unattractive is to subdue the nature of the material on behalf of a goal that is not derived from material nature.

Wright's acceptance of smooth (unpolished) stone does not stray far from the heart of stone's nature, as such is a standard texture produced by modern stone technology. It is, nevertheless, a small step away from the most basic roughness typical of both stone found in nature and the primitive process of splitting. This small step becomes particularly significant when precast concrete or cast stone is considered. The simplest formwork yields a smooth flat surface in precast copings, sills, lin-tels, and other trim. Given the similarity in substances, smooth flat stone and smooth flat precast are practically identical. Although a smooth surface is a small step away from roughness, its presence places stone into the expressive realm of other smooth materials, especially concrete.

When rough stone and smooth stone are used together, as at the Hillside Home School II (1901) and the Smith Bank (1904), the rough stone tends to clarify the substance of its smooth counterpart. In these cases, nearly the full potential of stone processing technology is expressed for the sedimentary stone that reflects the nature of the material as a modern building product. Although it could be argued that smooth stone by itself expresses one extreme of stone technology, it does so only if the observer mentally compares it to rough stone. Without the rough stone as a reference, the smooth stone cannot represent a point in a range of options. It can only present itself as the nature of stone. No doubt every observer, when viewing smooth stone, can visualize rough stone for a comparison if the identity of the smooth stone is certain. The physical presence of rough stone with the smooth version provides a more positive reference that can be controlled in intensity, quantity, and composition, thus securing the expression of smooth stone within the nature of stone and its technology. The presence of rough units is particularly helpful in clarifying the expression of the stone at the Smith Bank. The ambiguity in the identity of the smooth, long, slender units appearing as lintels and horizontal divisions in the openings of the facade is diminished by the presence of rough-faced units.

Corner details express the reality that the stone, as installed at the Hillside Home School II, is a construction material rather than a deposit occurring in nature. Tooling of the building corners yielded narrow smooth corners on the otherwise rough stone. The detail runs vertically across many units, thus establishing a specific relationship between them and distinguishing them from other stones in the wall surface. As such ordering characteristics are typical of humans, a sense of labor and purpose is imparted to the construction. Since the working is minimal but occurs in significant locations, the potential of stone technology is revealed without subduing the natural sense of the material. A broad expanse of smooth stone occurs over a fireplace in a rough-faced stone wall of the Hillside Home School II. The cutting of words into the smooth stone takes the expression of stone processing a step further than the usual juxtaposition of smooth and rough components. The sense that this installation represents a special condition is further secured by the fact that the smooth stone seems to form an exaggerated lintel over the firebox, its intermediate joints notwithstanding. The extremes of processing pos-

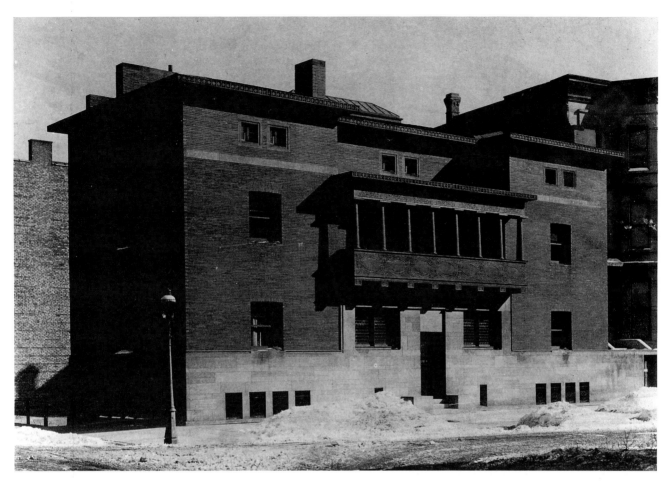

FIGURE 3-12. Smooth stone as base of brick facade at the James Charnley Residence. Trim frames windows at upper level. (Courtesy The Frank Lloyd Wright Archives)

sible in sedimentary stone are revealed without seeming to establish the more highly processed form as the most natural state of the material. The smooth surface with its cut letters shares an image with concrete into which words have been cast. The joints in the stone help separate the two images but do not eliminate the possibility that individual blocks were cast.

Wright rarely used smooth stone as a wall surface. In the Charnley House (1891), which incorporated the largest expanse of smooth stone of any building designed by him, the stone covered only about one-fourth of the main facade in the visual role of a tall foundation or building base. Although an analysis of the house can reveal the relationship of the detailing to the nature of stone, Sullivan's influence and Wright's limited experience at the time dilute the significance of specific details. It is more notable that for the most part, Wright discontinued this use of smooth stone as Sullivan's influence diminished and Wright himself gained more experience. The closest Wright came to building in smooth stone again was in two Japanese projects, the Hayashi House (1917) and Jiyu Gakuen Girls'

School (1921). The pitted surfaces of the lava stone blocks are not smooth to the degree of the Charnley stone, but they are smoother than the split and chipped faces on the majority of Wright's stone. Corners of the Hayashi House were tooled in the manner of the Hillside Home School II so as to yield narrow vertical strips of smoother stone on both faces of the corner. The smooth corner detail emphasizes the relative roughness of the fairly smooth blocks, which also show diagonal marks of the dressing tool.

A small amount of smooth stone occurs as a wall surface around the south entry of the Heller House (1896), which also includes two columns. The columns are relatively short—only a little taller than door height—but are, nevertheless, linear in image rather than blocklike. Since they are about the mass that would be expected of wood, they are distinguished from wood only by their color. Neither color nor mass distinguishes them from concrete. The absence of characteristics that identify them beyond a doubt as stone push the columns at least to the periphery of the nature of stone, if not beyond it. In light of Wright's rejection of ancient

FIGURE 3-13. Smooth stone flanks entry in brick facade at the Isidore Heller Residence. Carved stone over entry and at column capitals. (Courtesy The Frank Lloyd Wright Archives)

FIGURE 3-14. Profusely carved stone trim at the Imperial Hotel in variety of shapes. (Courtesy The Frank Lloyd Wright Archives)

Greek columns as forms appropriate for stone, it is not surprising that this form was the exception in his stone work rather than the rule. Smooth white marble columns occur on either side of the highly figured flat marble panels of the fireplace at the F. Bagley House (1894), but the fact that the owner was a marble merchant diminishes the significance of the material selection.

Marble and granite are rough as they occur in nature and when split. Roughness is in the nature of these stones but, alone, does not reveal their uniqueness among the various types of stone. Marble and granite, Wright observed, can produce "a brilliant surface, finally polished until its inner nature may be seen."[24] (His conclusion that "polished sophistication is not at home with stone"[25] was a reaction to the fluted, molded, painted, and gilded stone of the Greeks rather than to the polishing of marble and granite.) Uniqueness is the basis for material identity and is logically exploited in the expression of material nature. The simultaneous expression of rough and polished versions of this type of stone would maximize the information presented about

the nature of the material, but Wright rarely used this tactic. His extensive use of the rough-faced marble at the Neils House (1950) verifies nothing more significant than a tolerance for marble in this format because of the circumstances of its availability, as previously discussed.

The traditional broad, highly figured panels around the fireplaces of the Charnley (1891) and McArthur (1892) houses conform to his promotion of polishing marble. Given its appearance, it was logical he thought, to saw marble so as to produce sheets to cover walls, thus "revealing and accenting its own pattern and color."[26] Although the two examples indicate his capacity for a wide range of detailing, Wright's use of marble was too limited to establish any particular trend or pattern of use. The figuration in marble and granite (like the figuration in wood) led Wright to a conclusion similar to his attitude toward wood. "To carve or break its surface…," he thought, "is a pity."[27] Further applications of marble could have been expected to be flat and polished. Cutting into highly figured surfaces was not in the

FIGURE 3-15. Extensively cut stone in interior of the Imperial Hotel. (Courtesy The Frank Lloyd Wright Archives)

indicates his recognition of fewer restrictions imposed by the properties of terra-cotta than by the properties of stone.

Softness allowed but did not demand of Wright the working of stone. The lava stone at the Hayashi House (1917) and the Jiyu Gakuen School (1921) is in the form of plain blocks, as is nearly all of his sedimentary stone. Given Wright's statements supporting the decorative cutting of limestone, his limited exploration of this realm would be more surprising if it were not for the emergence of his decorative concrete block. Prior to his decorative concrete block, terra-cotta as at the Roloson (1894), Francisco Terrace (1985), and Francis (1895) apartments, and plaster as at the Winslow (1893) and Dana (1902) houses, provided opportunities for decorative surface relief. Both curvilinear and geometric patterns were included. Several materials competed with stone as the choice for exterior surface decoration. Wright's willingness more often to produce relief by molding rather than by cutting indicates his sense of greater propriety of the former over the latter technique.

STRENGTH

Masonry strength is most intensely expressed when it appears to be securely compressive. Units stacked one upon another are in compression, the expression of which can be diminished or enhanced by detailing. Characteristics that enhance the sense of stability such as battering, large mass, and low profile reflect masonry's aversion to the tensile stresses that would occur should the stack of units lean or tip. Although single stones can perform in bending for short spans, significant tensile stresses cannot cross a joint of (unreinforced) unit masonry under bending loads. Arched spans of unit masonry maintain a compressive appearance so long as adequate buttressing and other assurances of stability are present. Hiding steel behind masonry so that the units appear to perform structurally in a way that they otherwise could not does not express the nature of masonry even though the practice is common. Expression, being a visual phenomenon, is defined by what is apparent.

Although having a highly natural-looking shape and texture, rubble lacks the flatness and regularity of form that facilitates a structurally stable assembly. Given the dependable quality and reasonable strength of modern mortars, this is mostly a visual issue, but, as such, is appropriate for the distinction between the philosophical meaning of various masonries and their detailing. Since rounded irregular stone is relatively unstable, expression of its nature in the realm of strength logically addresses methods of accommodating this structural shortcoming.

nature of the material, according to Wright, as it interfered with rather than enhanced natural beauty.

Wright complained that carved stone in ancient China was essentially a copy of the carved wood that preceded it. The carving seemed to have been transferred from wood to stone without consideration of the nature of stone, he thought.[28] He accepted, however, certain carving in his observation that stone such as limestone is a material without a strong personality of its own, "on which it is appropriate to cut images."[29] Wright's highly worked lava stone at the Imperial Hotel (1914) and the Yamamura House (1918) conforms to his implication that soft stone is more appropriately carved than hard stone. Apparently, the spotty surface pattern of the lava stone was not beautiful enough in its own right to discourage cutting into the face of the relatively soft material. The geometric shapes cut in the lava stone reflect his disapproval of realistic life-forms as a motif for stone.[30] His praise of Sullivan's terra-cotta design, which included plantlike forms, suggests his acceptance of the shapes without his actually committing to the idea for himself.[31] His thought that "terracotta chiefly lives by virtue of the human imagination,"[32]

Figure 3-16. Circular and free-form pattern in repetitive terra-cotta cladding on lower level of the Francis Apartments. (From a photograph, *Frank Lloyd Monograph, 1887–1901*, p. 79.)

The failure to install the forms of field rubble that were drawn for the design of the F. B. Jones complex (1900, 1901) produced shortcomings in the structural expression of the material that are not present in the drawings. The drawings for the complex show slightly flattened massive stones with small mortar joints. The image is massive, compressive, and stable due to selected battering, the extensive stone-to-stone contact depicted, and the use of the stone generally in positions low in the building. The drawings, consequently, show natural-looking stone in a relatively natural-looking format. The nature of the stone as built, however, varies in significant ways from the drawings, yielding walls less in the compressive spirit of masonry.

The actual stone is smaller, rounder, and is set in larger mortar joints. The rounded stone and the thick mortar that appears to hold the stones apart lack the massive and compressive sense that the drawings project. The substantial-looking battered mass drawn for the rubble wall of the small water tower by the gate house is reduced to a low and unconvincing wing wall in the actual construction. The absence of the batter, which is physically logical and psychologically needed for the tall stack of imprecise units, further draws the image away from the stable structural circumstance compatible with the spirit of stone. Wood siding, which partially clads the upper part of the tower, meets and partially covers the stone at the corners leaving only a few inches of rubble thickness exposed. The resulting appearance gives the impression of a thin stone veneer, which is a format particularly unsuited for rounded stones stacked this high.

The convincing form and structural image of the original design was reduced to tokenism in the building, the condition that must ultimately be judged. The general sense of compression in the drawings was translated to a sense of near-tension, as visually the small spheres appear to be on the verge of being squeezed out of the wall. Only the mortar seems to hold them in. The absence of a hierarchy of unit size in the walls contributes a sense of structural artificiality. This condition is particularly apparent in comparison to the more structurally natural detailing of the Greene brothers, in which the size of boulders and stones diminish with height.

The detailing of the larger flatter stone was not changed when the smaller rounder stone was substituted. Consequently, the structural expression of the stone as constructed fails to reflect with the greatest possible efficiency the nature of the material. For example, more significant (lower sloped) battering would have addressed the inherently less stable nature of the rounder rubble. Large concrete sills and other elements could have helped visually stabilize the walls. Although Wright's use of rubble here failed to reflect adequately the nature of the material with regard to its strength, his quick abandonment of the format prevents it detracting significantly from his record in this realm. The F. B. Jones buildings emphasize, by their contrast, the greater sensitivity to the structural nature of rubble inherent in his subsequent detailing.

His rubble innovation at Taliesin West (1937) expressed the structural shortcomings of the stone by visibly eliminating dependence on the forms of individual units for stability. Surrounding the relatively widely spaced irregular rock with masses of concrete only demands of the stone that it transfer compression between the nearly perfectly fitting bearing faces of the concrete above and below. The stone is no longer responsible for the stability of itself or the construction. The sense of stacking typical of traditional rubble walls is absent. The stone is visually suspended in the walls as a component of a concrete system. This significant expressive advantage of desert rubble masonry over traditional rubble wanes with a reduction in the visible proportion of concrete to stone. This proportion varies throughout the masses at Taliesin West. Unlike other projects that tend to be more uniform, at Taliesin West those elements where there is less concrete—sometimes showing physical contact between stones—fail to dilute the stability of the image, because of the extensive presence of concrete nearby.

The reduced proportion of concrete visible at the Pauson House (1939) and the Oboler complex (1941) pushes their images away from concrete and toward stacked stone, as the units come closer together and the binder approaches the role of mortar. The flat faces of the rubble suggest less of a tendency to roll forward than do the rounded faces of the F. B. Jones units but these have a thinner sense (although they may not actually be thinner), which adds a precarious quality to that already suggested by the irregular perimeters of the faces. The

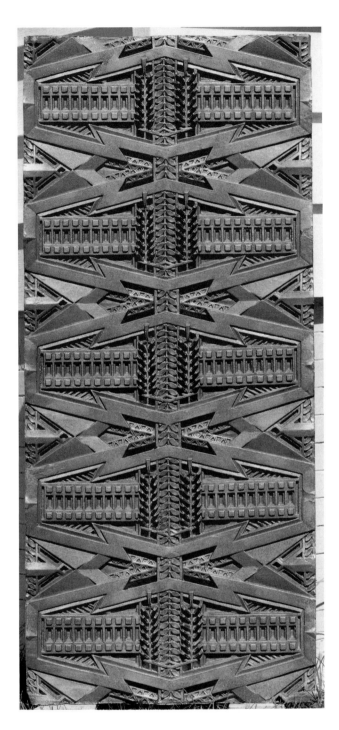

FIGURE 3-17. Portion of plaster frieze at the Susan Lawrence Dana Residence. (Courtesy The Illinois Historic Preservation Agency—The Dana-Thomas House and Doug Carr, photographer, The Dana-Thomas Foundation)

FIGURE 3-18. Section through roof of breezeway and elevation of water tower at the Fred B. Jones gate house. Large, flattened boulders in battered wall. (From Frank Lloyd Wright Archives drawing 0103.007.)

thus stabilizing slightly the wall image. The surface proportion of concrete to stone in the Boomer House (1953) comes closest to that of Taliesin West but falls short of the original version in certain aspects that express structural sensitivity to rubble.

The Boomer House, like the other desert rubble masonry examples, fails to achieve the ground-hugging spirit of Taliesin West. The low, battered masses of Taliesin West express, through their highly stable image, the structural nature of unreinforced masonry and concrete. The spread bases and limited heights in the complex eliminate any sense that tipping or leaning is possible. The elimination of tensile or bending stresses that such movement would induce makes the masses entirely compressive in spirit, a condition strongly associated with the nature of unreinforced masonry and concrete.

The other desert rubble projects do not appear to be unstable, although the reverse battered terrace wall at the Pauson House did not help stabilize the image. The angle of the leaning or projecting wall surface is steep and well within the angle of structurally sound corbeled masonry, but the projection of the top beyond the base cannot have the same compressive sense as that of a spread base. Reverse battering also occurs at Taliesin West, but in the case of a wall at the kitchen, the

sense of stability is slightly enhanced at the Oboler installation, which has a greater variety of stone sizes than does the Pauson construction. Small units filling the gaps between large units yield greater visual density,

Figure 3-19. High desert rubble mass at the Jorgine Boomer Residence. Large dynamic roof. (Courtesy The Frank Lloyd Wright Archives)

battered bottom-half of the wall prevents the reverse-battered top half from projecting beyond the base of the construction. In comparison to Taliesin West, the other desert rubble applications generally have a greater proportion of tall masses to low masses and have less significant battering, although battering is a common characteristic among the subsequent installations and always contributes a sense of stability and compressiveness.

An exception to the predominant compressive image at Taliesin West is its sign structure at the entrance gate (1953). The leaning form of the tall, relatively slender, mass lacks the stability that is compatible with its materials. It appears to almost purposely defy the compressive nature of its matrix. The precarious condition is abated somewhat by a lower buttressing mass that opposes the lean of the structure. Thus recognition, if not elimination, of the visually challenging circumstance of the structure is accomplished. A hammer cast in the surface of the concrete along with the stone serves as a reminder that, after all, this is not stacked masonry but a material cast in wood formwork. Being a small percentage of the desert rubble expression and, therefore, an exception to the rule, the structure fails to undermine the overall compressive sense of the complex.

Another curious structural circumstance occurs on the roof of the Cabaret Theater (1949). Exposed beams were cast as desert rubble on the roof to bolster a sagging slab that had been placed the year before. The result is an unusual exposed concrete beam structure, the continuity of which is interrupted by the periodic faces of the rubble in the surfaces. The beams are broad enough to fit tension steel between the stones, but the appearance of spanning-rubble (albeit a composite kind of rubble) seems less in the nature of the material than that which rests in compression on the ground. The detail is less troublesome than unit stone, which is not expressed as a composite but which appears to span over glass or through space without assistance. Such stone was detailed at the Imperial Hotel (1914), Robie House (1906), and virtually all other houses incorporating stone trim on brick.

Taliesin West's glazing and roof structures are generally low shapes of minimal silhouette, which lets the desert rubble walls dominate the image. The character of the architecture is, therefore, largely the character of the concrete and stone matrix. The nature of the material, consequently, dominates the composition. The relatively large glazing areas and flamboyant roof structure of the Boomer House yield an overall character that is generally less massive and more dynamic than Taliesin West. Although it is not violated by the flighty image of the house, the nature of the desert rubble is somewhat subdued and, therefore, is not as significant in the architectural expression as it is at Taliesin West.

FIGURE 3-20. Low battered masses at Taliesin West.

FIGURE 3-22. Desert rubble beams exposed on roof of Taliesin West Cabaret Theater. Steel bents of Music Pavilion visible at left background.

FIGURE 3-21. Tall, leaning mass at the Taliesin West Sign. Hammer embedded in concrete.

Consequently, the architecture seems less sensitive to the nature of the desert rubble.

Other installations fall between these extremes of participation by the desert rubble in the building image.

The desert concrete at the Oboler Retreat (1941), Berger House (1950), and Austin House (1951) fails to dominate the elevations due to the presence of glazed walls and large roofs. The matrix as a substantial base in contact with the earth and positioned below the lighter superstructures makes intellectual sense but does not achieve the same feeling of material "rightness" on an emotional level as it does at Taliesin West. The projection of matrix masses above the roofs as chimneys places a significant percentage of the desert rubble high in the air, thus further diluting the opportunity for an exaggerated stability and compressive sense. The significant widths of the tall masses helps visually stabilize them but, unlike the tall Taliesin West sign structure, the chimney masses do not appear to be aberrations. Appearing to be a legitimate component of the architectural message, they dilute slightly the sense of mass and compression in their respective houses.

The concrete and rubble of the Bott House (1956), being located on a steep incline, takes the logical form in such cases and reaches down the hill as the grade drops away from floor level. Although the house is not tall in the entry elevation, the desert rubble wall on the low side of the site is tall. The sensation of significant height in the side and back elevations is not as intense as that of a typical two- or three-story house but the spirit of mass and compression of Taliesin West is remote from the image. In addition to the tall chimney mass, the height of the matrix is also increased by its extension to the underside of the roof except where interrupted by glazing.

The one other nonresidential application of desert rubble masonry, the Pilgrim Congregational Church (1958), falls short of the Taliesin West standard as constructed but would have been closer to the standard if built as originally designed. The design shows a tall

FIGURE 3-23. Stone trim appears to span over glass and space at the Imperial Hotel. (Courtesy The Frank Lloyd Wright Archives)

central mass that increases the average elevation of the material. This has the usual effect of diluting the relationship of the desert concrete to the ground and reducing slightly its compressive sense. As constructed, the highest mass reaches no higher than the roof, thus avoiding the height issue. The failure to build the main part of the complex, however, left the project without the large sanctuary volume that would have been particularly expressive of the material.

The long prow of the main sanctuary as drawn shows a low mass with battered sides gently rising from the grade toward the building in a slope of about 30 degrees. The image of exaggerated stability is not matched by the reality of the design, however, as a large part of the prow was to be hollow. The mass, therefore, becomes a relatively thin roof slab over the space below. This would not be an expressive problem for observers who did not understand the nature of the building section, that is to say, the general public who would see—but not use—the church.

The significant reinforcing required in the roof of the prow, although entirely compatible with concrete, would have been less compatible with the masonry characteristics of the concrete and rubble matrix. The spanning role would have signified an abrupt change of direction for this material that had previously been presented as essentially a compressive substance (the roof beams of the Cabaret Theater at Taliesin West notwithstanding). The large stones in the matrix would make physically difficult the insertion of steel in a slab-like form.

A difference in the superstructure of the relatively small segment that was built and the larger sanctuary volume as designed has a significant effect on the structural expression of the matrix base. The wood A-frames exposed above the roof in the design drawings rested directly on the base and thus demonstrated a transfer of compressive loading to it. This verification of compressive service in the desert rubble was compatible with the battered surfaces and the low profile of the base as an

FIGURE 3-24. Perspective of original design for the Pilgrim Congregational Church. Low, battered, desert rubble masses at walls. Tall central mass. Exposed wood A-frame structure. (From Frank Lloyd Wright Archives drawing 5818.02.)

expression of an unreinforced masonrylike material. Some of the concrete bents that were built in the partial completion of the project bypass the desert rubble base and rest directly on the ground. The compressive role of the matrix is, therefore, diminished, diluting the expression of the material with regard to its strength potential.

Due to an assortment of compromises, the installations subsequent to Taliesin West seem like textural imitations of the original. As the system became more sophisticated, the results seemed to become more artificial. (The dessert rubble at the Austin House, 1951, includes half-inch vertical and horizontal temperature steel absent from the original version.)[33] The use of the rubble from a farmer's field wall[34] in the matrix of the Bott House (1956) placed small stones of relatively uniform size into a system originated for much larger stones of more varied shapes, sizes, and colors. It is doubtful that the thin veneer of the matrix on a concrete block backing is the logical variation of the Taliesin West detailing given the differences between Kansas and Arizona rubble. Although the thinness of the system is reflected only at the narrow windows that pierce the matrix, the installation is one of the examples most remote in appearance and physical reality from the orig-

inal concept of the material. This illustrates a circumstance where a material concept preceded the selection of the actual material, which was subsequently challenged to conform to the original idea as best it could.

No doubt programmatic requirements, site considerations, material availability, the nature of the labor force, and the nature of the construction supervision made a number of the achievements at Taliesin West inconvenient or impossible in other buildings. The fact that desert rubble masonry was invented specifically for the conditions at Taliesin West is reflected in its expression there, which is, among all the installations, most sympathetic to the nature of the material. The lack of visual stability inherent in the irregularity of rubble is solved by the addition of concrete in desert rubble masonry.

In several stone buildings of the 1940s and 1950s, visual stability of the traditional rubble used was enhanced by mixing it with units that are more rectangular. Although the percentage of rubble in the S. Friedman House is relatively high, there are enough roughly squared units intermingled to eliminate any sense of precariousness in the stack. This accomplishment is unique among related examples, as it is brought

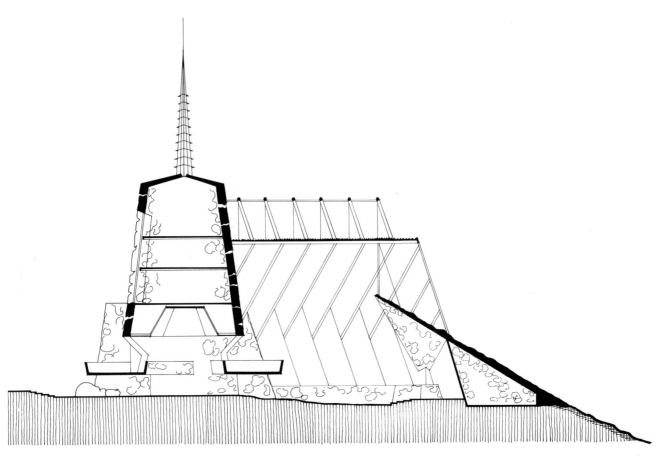

FIGURE 3-25. Section of original design for the Pilgrim Congregational Church. Low battered desert rubble mass at end of sanctuary on right shown to be relatively long thin slab. (From Frank Lloyd Wright Archives drawing 5818.09.)

about without generating the spirit of artificiality that typically comes with increased stone processing. The battering of the walls in a curved footprint and the low position of the stone in the elevations also contribute to a sense of naturalness, in that the significant tensile stresses beyond the capability of stone are missing and clearly will not be a threat in the future. Reverse battered or slightly outward-leaning walls, which Wright used occasionally, are also present. Although the lean is slight and well within the range acceptable for corbeling, the effect is somewhat visually destabilizing. Outward-leaning stone masses are present in nature but enjoy some dynamacy because of their precarious appearance. If such formations seem natural when they occur in nature, it is largely due to their great mass, not present in architecture. The curved form of the reverse-battered wall at the S. Friedman site bolsters slightly the fragile stability of the reverse-battered mass as it imparts some sense of balance missing in straight walls that lean outward.

At the low extreme of rubble content are the Neils (1950) and Reisley (1951) houses. In the latter, the relatively small number of irregular units cause the stones to be no more than intruders in an otherwise stable stack

of roughly squared units that continue to maintain their secure compressive condition. In the former, there are so few irregular units among the field of precise rectangular stone that they develop no relationship with the ashlar. The rectangular stone maintains, through its tightly fitting bearing faces and battered configuration, a clear stability from which the sparsely scattered rubble is unable to detract.

The reverse batter of the terrace wall at the Walker House (1951) has a greater destabilizing effect on the image than usual because of its large size and its domination of some elevations. The sense of stability is enhanced by the limitation of irregularities in the stone to the ends of the roughly squared units. The snug fit of the straight bearing surfaces add to an image of stability, although the absence of coursing detracts from it. The few trapezoids and parallelograms mixed among the essentially rectangular-faced units do not affect the structural expression. Although much of Wright's other stone is more regular, these slight irregularities do not establish a sense of rubble in the wall thus avoiding the structural image that comes with that shape of unit.

The large variety of rough rectangular stone in the

Miller House (1950) looks more casually stacked and therefore more natural than the Walker stone. The greater proportion of narrow units in the Miller House give the stone a less forced look, as it is set in the neat stack forming the house wall. This is essentially a structural issue, as a sense of stability without effort is projected. The achievement of the Miller House stone is emphasized by its contrast with the garden walls adjacent to the building. The low freestanding walls consist of, for the most part, irregular rubble, with broad flat faces in the wall surfaces. Although the stone shapes look natural, they appear to be stacked on edge, thus seeming somewhat precarious. The juxtaposition of the two sets of walls in some views emphasizes by contrast the basic character of each. That is, the house walls appear as being more compressive and the garden walls appear to be less so in comparison to each other. The smaller expanses of stone surfaces at the Miller House also contribute to its appearing to be more stable and, therefore, more compressive than the terrace walls of the Walker House.

The rough-faced rectangular stone appearing in a large number of Wright's buildings, such as the Hillside Home School II (1901), Taliesin I (1911), Kaufmann House (1935), the second Jacobs House (1943), the Unitarian Church (1947), and over a dozen lesser-known houses to 1958 maintains a slightly higher sense of stability than do the less regular shapes previously discussed. Although dimensions vary, the generally horizontal proportions stabilize individual stones while the broad contact of their parallel bearing surfaces does the same for their assemblies. Battered walls at the Hillside Home School II (1901) and Anthony House (1949) and the curved plans of the second Jacobs House (1943) and the Dairy Shed (1943) at Taliesin add a sense of stability to the stone masses.

If the notion that greater regularity of unit form generates greater stability was followed to its logical extreme, the precisely dressed ashlar stone of the Charnley House (1891) would express a maximum sense of compressiveness in stone. Although the stone is held low in the building, which contributes to a sense of stability and compression, expression of the structural nature of stone is not maximized. The flush, tight joints subdue unit identity and contribute to the extreme smoothness of the entire assembly that projects an image of tautness. The suggestion of a kind of tension in the surface dilutes slightly the sense of units pressed together by gravity.

Two examples of stone slightly less perfect than the Charnley units combine the most expressive aspects of uniformity and irregularity. The Hayashi House (1917) stacks highly rectangular and flush blocks that are each about three times wider than high. The horizontal, thick

FIGURE 3-26. Butted stone lintels over windows at the Isidore Heller Residence. (Courtesy Mike Kertok)

proportions and the secure contact of flat, parallel, bearing surfaces lend a sense of mass and stability to the assembly. This is tempered slightly by the expression of unit thickness at building corners, which is about one-half the block height. (A slightly stronger sense of stability would have been established if a square or horizontal proportion in section would have been revealed in the blocks at the corners.) Although dominated by the vertical dimension, significant thickness is, nevertheless, revealed for the stone. The pitted surfaces and the rough bevels at the edges eliminate any sense of tautness or tension in the surface and reflect the reality that these units have significant thickness and are more than a surface application.

The stone at the Jiyu Gakuen School (1921) is essentially the same. The restriction of its use to a low band across the base of the building reflects the stability inherent in that format but does not develop a sense of great compression because of the limited stone weight on the lower units. The band is so narrow that it fails to demand attention, which limits its influence in the larger architectural expression. The linear overtone of the narrow strip is not helpful to the expression of block form. Corbeling at the apparent lintel of the fireplace, although projecting a strong sense of material form, is structurally questionable, thus subtracting rather than adding to the general sense of stone used within its natural limits of strength.

Wright's glazing often extends to the roofs of his buildings, which eliminates the need for stone to pass over the glass. Where this detail prevails, stone is almost restricted to the simple stacking format necessary to form blank walls. Stacking, being compressive in nature, expresses stone's essence with regard to strength in degrees of intensity varying with the detailing of the stack, as previously described. The majority of the stone in Wright's buildings expresses its compressiveness in this straightforward way. There are many examples of this circumstance, the most notable of which is the Kaufmann House (Fallingwater, 1935).

In addition to being almost entirely expressed in the most basic form of compression (units in simple stacks), stone's limited structural potential is further emphasized at Fallingwater by its contrast with reinforced concrete, which performs nearly all of the more sophisticated structural challenges. Concrete's dynamic cantilevers juxtaposed against stone's simple compressive stacks simultaneously emphasizes the structural limitations of masonry and the greater potential of reinforced concrete. The contrasting form and texture of the two materials secures the distinction between them. A minor exception occurs at openings on a minor elevation, where stone lintels appear. Although within the realm of stone bending-strength, the rough-faced lintels blends with the surrounding field. This fact, combined with their obscure location, fails to draw attention away from the ubiquitous and more basic demonstration of the essence of stone with regard to its compressive nature.

When there was need for openings through Wright's stone, treatment of the lintel provided an opportunity to express or violate the nature of the material with regard to its strength potential. When stone or any unit-material is supported over an opening by a hidden steel component, the masonry appears to span the distance in a level line and with the ends of units adhering to each other in a way that masonry cannot structurally perform. The thin steel flange on which such masonry sits is visible only upon close inspection and consequently makes a negligible contribution to the image. The nature of stone is violated by the appearance of this detail. The intensity of the violation varies directly with the span and inversely with the visibility of the steel.

The suggestion that there are bending stresses in the small stones that appear to span over some glazing at the S. Friedman House dilutes slightly the generally compressive sense of the stacked stone. Since this glazing is not an important or prominent feature of the house, the loss to the nature of stone caused by the hidden steel is minimized. When Wright supported unit stone over an opening with hidden steel, it was usually limited to a few locations of low importance and visibility. This does not

diminish the violations to the nature of stone but it prevents them from significantly affecting the overall image of the masonry. This circumstance is illustrated by the commonly published photographs of his buildings, which are selected to show views embodying the essence of each building. Stone "floating" over openings is rare in such photographs. The Staley House (1951) is an exception to this pattern, with its rough-faced rectangular stone units appearing to span over a sequence of three prominent windows.

The difference in Wright's attitude toward unit stone versus brick and concrete block in this regard is notable. He did not hesitate to prominently express concrete block and, in his later buildings, brick "floating" over openings. If one of the three masonries deserved to be treated in a visually more pure way, stone would be the logical choice, being the one least dependent on technology in its production and the one most often solid in section. (The solid section prevents hiding steel inside the unit.)

As important elements in Wright's architecture, his fireplaces warrant comment. They have a variety of lintel expressions ranging from single massive stones to hidden lintels supporting small units. The rough-faced units seeming to hang over the firebox at the Hagan House (1954) are particularly unlike the structural nature of masonry, as the weight suggested by their thick proportions emphasizes the compressive nature of the assembly. Since the fireplace is open on two sides, the large stones over the firebox turn the corner in midair. The image is unsettling, given the large mass of stone above the pseudo-lintel that seems to hang from the ceiling.

The Hillside Home School II fireplace, previously mentioned, has a unit-masonry lintel that is far less combative with the spirit of the material. The smooth-faced stones define a large rectangular mass set in a field of rough-faced units as it passes over the firebox. The juxtaposition of the smooth mass against the rougher field obscures the joints and lets the pseudo-lintel read nearly as a large single unit. The quotation carved into the smooth stones crosses their joints further diminishing the individuality of the stones. Structurally, this apparent lintel differs little from the Hagan House fireplace. (All single-stone lintels, whether real or false, are referred to here as apparent lintels or, simply, lintels.) Visually, however, the Hillside Home School II detailing is far more compatible with the structural spirit of stone, as the beamlike mass emulates a spanning element and thus refers to the need for a lintel in that location. There is no sense of intent to let the smooth band of stone appear to be the actual lintel. The detailing does not maximize the expression of stone strength, however, because it seems that units pass over the firebox without assistance.

The limited bending strength of stone is legitimately expressed by short lintels that are deep compared to their span. This expression of stone as lintels was more common in Wright's early brick houses than in his stone buildings, whose arrangement of masses minimized the need for visible lintels. The expression of stone strength, regardless of its degree of purity, is intensified by Wright's common use of light-colored stone lintels against darker brick walls. The expression of strength was more compatible with the nature of stone in the lintels of his earliest masonry work compared to later projects. The smooth stone lintels of the Charnley House (1891) are realistically proportioned, although this positive expression of the nature of stone is much subdued in the smaller windows at street level because they occur in a field of stone that has the same texture and color. The larger spans by the entrance are framed, more or less, in a contrasting field. The stones of these longer lintels have greater depths than those over shorter spans, as logic would dictate.

The stone lintels at the Roloson Apartments (1894) are similar in circumstance except the walls are entirely brick. Small windows in the attic have small light-colored lintels surrounded by darker brick. The stone lintel-like trim over the trios of windows on the top floor in each unit has significant depth, which is nearly reasonable for spanning the entire grouping without intermediate support. In fact, intermediate support appears to exist between each window, boosting the intensity of the visual statement through exaggeration of stone's spanning limitations. The entire expression, although not representing reality, expersses the nature of stone. It fails to reach its maximum potential in this regard, however, due to the appearance of faint joints in the large lintel-like trim that fall within the span rather than over the apparent mullions.

The reasonable structural statement of the stone lintels at the Heller House (1896) is obscured slightly by their detailing. Several lintels butt end-to-end over series of lower-level windows. Although it is an issue of form rather than strength, the apparent continuity of the strips is reminiscent of concrete. Faint joints over the brick mullions weakly define the lintels as individual units rather than one long member. Both the positive and negative aspects of the expression are emphasized by the contrast between the color of the brick wall and the lighter stone lintels.

The reasonable reflection of stone's natural bending strength diminishes in subsequent buildings. The length of the smooth stone over the openings in the facade of the Smith Bank (1904) is long compared to its height, the slender proportion of which is emphasized by the butting of several units. Coupled with the relatively slender columns and thin strips passing across the openings, the assembly has the appearance of a post-and-beam system, which is not the structural format most central to stone's nature. As building shapes emphasizing horizontality stretch apparent spans far beyond the potential of stone in both strength and form, the ability of trim (supported by hidden steel) to reflect the spirit of stone strength by its service as a visual lintel is severely hindered.

Among the several examples where stone trim reaches too far over openings to be true lintels, the Robie House (1906) is the most flagrant. Although clearly not pretending to be structural in most cases, long strips of light gray stone underlie masses of darker red brick, thus visually providing a place for the brick to set. The stone pulls the apparent violation of masonry strength away from the brick and into itself. The comprehensive expression is more reflective of the nature of masonry strength than if the stone were absent, because this would cause brick to pass, apparently unsupported, over lengthy glazing or open space. Even with its unrealistic slenderness in many locations, the stone does respond to the need for lintels, albeit in a more philosophical than real way. A sense of violation is thus tempered slightly.

Occasionally, Wright spanned openings with arches, the structure traditionally associated with masonry's compressiveness. Most of his arches are in brick, but a particularly convincing stone example occurs at Hillside Home School II (1901). Arches seem most compressive when their spans are short, when they have significant ability to resist thrust, and when there is a demonstration of considerable load present. Exaggeration of these conditions intensifies the sense of compression and diminishes the threat of other types of stress that would result from movement in the stone. The small arch at a lower level of the school secures its compressive expression through these devices.

Durability

Building stone is typically resistant to normal weathering and requires no protection of its vertical surfaces. Wright's failure to paint stone, while compatible with stone's weatherability, was likely to have been motivated by aesthetic considerations. His reluctance to paint exterior wood and his insistence on using soft lava stone (of dubious weathering capability) in his Japanese projects indicates that durability was not a prime concern. Nevertheless the absence of paint from his stone reflects the nature of the material with regard to durability. More revealing than this common treatment of stone surfaces is detailing that either acknowledges or ignores the vulnerability of joints to water penetration.

Stone trim on lower edge of balcony refers to hidden lintel at the Frederick C. Robie Residence. Butted stone trim, copings, and water table yield linear forms. (Courtesy The Frank Lloyd Wright Archives)

Although, upon occasion, Wright protected joints on the tops of walls, he often left them unprotected. The varied levels of attention to joints in this particularly vulnerable location undermine the possibility that the copings specified were primarily in response to the nature of stone in the realm of durability.

A variety of coping details exist at the Hillside Home School II (1901) and is generally expressive, although to varying degrees. The large smooth copings on the tops of chimneys are reasonably apparent by their contrast with the rough stone below. Since they are flush with the chimney surface, their presence is slightly subdued. Rough stone windowsills that overhang the wall surface are emphasized by the shadows they create but fail to achieve maximum expressiveness since they do not contrast with the adjacent wall in texture or color. Projected copings, unlike flush units, also tend to drip water forward of the wall face rather than on it. Smooth stone caps on the tops of piers overhang the rough wall stone and are, consequently, the strongest expression of joint protection. The absence of an apparent coping on a garden wall denies the vulnerability of its joints. The fact that this inattention to the durability of stone masonry occurs in a structure remote from habitable space indicates an understanding of the nature of the material, if not the highest respect for it.

The copings and sills of the Smith Bank (1904) express attention to joint vulnerability in standard ways. The smooth trim contrasts with the rough stone of the wall surface for increased visibility. The overhang of the trim creates a shadow line that emphasizes its presence.

The color of the copings and sills does not contrast with the wall stone nor are these elements unusually large. Without more purposeful signs of focus on durability, the bank detailing fails to supersede that common for the times, which happens to be reasonably responsive to the need for protection of joints. Taliesin I (1911) and subsequent construction on that site incorporated rough-faced projected copings on chimneys and walls that were not covered by roofs.

The wall units that project forward of the surfaces at Taliesin and other locations express component unit form and mass but also catch water and temporarily hold it against the mortar joint at the top of each stone. The detail, therefore, challenges the integrity of the joints to a greater degree than do flush units. Because of this fact, all of Wright's stone walls with random projected units demonstrate a slight neglect of the nature of stone masonry with regard to durability. The gain afforded by the detail in the expression of unit form prevents the overall expression from violating the nature of stone. In this case, that which promotes material form to some degree also denies material durability to some degree. Although the gain in form expression seems to be more significant than the challenge to durability, flush detailing as a response to the threat of water is not without precedent and expresses an aspect of the nature of stone that is appropriate and worthy of consideration.

At the Kaufmann House (1935), the tops of stone masses (not covered by roofs) are left without expressed protection, as is a cylindrical mass at the second Jacobs House (1943). The Jacobs House also expresses another type of challenge to joint integrity. The juxtaposition of the stone against the earth on the north side of the building, without apparent protection of the joints, misrepresents the durability of the masonry system. The fact that cement plaster coated with waterproofing protects the joints from moisture does not abate the misrepresentation, because the protective layer is not visible. The disrespect to the nature of stone masonry (in the realm of durability) is magnified by the presence of windows on the north side just above grade. They verify that a habitable space occurs behind the wall, which increases the consequences of a joint failure compared to those in a retaining wall that does not enclose space. It is not suggested that visible waterproofing or an expressed concrete foundation wall would yield better architecture. Such detailing would, however, indicate a commitment to clear expression regarding the nature of stone masonry.

Subsequent stone projects randomly include—or omit—copings and sills projecting slightly over the wall surface. The Unitarian Church (1947), the most significant work of the later stone buildings, has rough stone

FIGURE 3-28. Stone merges into earth berm with no expressed water proofing at the second Herbert Jacobs Residence. Random roughly squared stones project from surface. Flitch plates support the roof's double overhangs at each end of the building. Floor to roof glazed wall. (Courtesy The Frank Lloyd Wright Archives)

copings and sills that slightly overhang the rough wall surfaces below. The Shavin (1950), Hoffman (1955), Iber (1955), and Jackson (1955) houses have similar details. Regardless of the specific motivation for the details, these projects carry a sense of respect for the nature of stone with regard to its joints, because the copings contribute to the character of the architecture. The Walker (1951), Anthony (1949), Reisley (1951), Hagan (1954), and Petersen (1958) houses do not project this sense, due to the absence of expressed protection of the joints on the tops of exposed walls.

In most of Wright's stone works, the tops of many walls are protected with roofs and other construction. Although such protection is entirely compatible with stone, it is doubtful that the nature of stone inspired the detailing. This compatibility should be acknowledged, but without detailing, which establishes a sense of intent to honor durability limitations, the intensity of respect for the nature of stone is not maximized. The wall tops that are not protected by roofs are a more revealing indicator of Wright's attitude towards the nature of stone. Since the general popularity of overhanging stone copings diminished as the century progressed, it might be expected that Wright's use of them would also diminish in later years. This does not appear to be the case, in spite of the fact that his last stone house did not have expressed copings. The continued use of overhanging copings after they were no

longer fashionable suggests some level of sensitivity to the nature of stone with regard to its durability.

CONCLUSION

The property of stone that plays the largest role in the character of Wright's buildings is its form. Its natural blocky mass often established building character and was rarely forced into shapes of unnatural delicacy or precision. Generally, the strength of stone is respected in structural and apparent structural expressions. Upon occasion, units are "floated" over openings, or apparent lintels are too long for their depth. Wright's stone is, for the most part, however, expressed in compression, the format most compatible with its nature. Although many of his buildings in various materials have leaked, deteriorated, and have been subsequently altered because of his inattention to issues of durability, his stone work is not known for failure in this realm. Even with a mixed record of joint protection, his buildings generally do not challenge the durability of stone beyond its potential to function visually in a satisfactory way.

Wright's record of stone construction is, on the whole, highly reflective of the spirit of the material. Among other architects, however, most violations of the spirit of stone occur in tall buildings, which Wright did not build in stone. His thought that marble could be cut into thin sheets for wall coverings[35] suggests that his approach might not have been entirely free of the form and structural inconsistencies inherent in stone curtain walls. If the tall buildings of other designers are omitted from the comparison, Wright's expression of stone is still slightly more compatible with its nature than stone work of the modern movement, due to the common deletion of expressed lintels and copings in that arena. His advantage over his contemporaries diminishes as the comparison moves back in time, because of the greater frequency throughout the building industry of cornices, copings, arches, and the use of thicker stone, the mass of which is revealed at corners and jambs.

ENDNOTES

1. Wright, Frank Lloyd. 1928. "In the Cause of Architecture: III. The Meaning of Materials—Stone." *Architectural Record* 63(4):350–356. Reprint. 1975. *In the Cause of Architecture*, ed. Frederick Gutheim. New York: McGraw-Hill. p. 174.

2. Ibid., 173. *ARCHITECTURAL RECORD*, (April/1928), copyright 1975 by McGraw-Hill, Inc. All rights reserved. Reproduced with the permission of the publisher.

3. Ibid., 175. *ARCHITECTURAL RECORD*, (April/1928), copyright 1975 by McGraw-Hill, Inc. All rights reserved. Reproduced with the permission of the publisher.

4. Wright, Frank Lloyd. 1931. *Modern Architecture: Being the Kahn Lectures for 1930*. Reprint. 1987. ed. Bruce Brooks Pfeiffer. Carbondale and Edwardsville, IL: Southern Illinois University Press. Copyright 1987 by The Frank Lloyd Wright Foundation. p. 57. Courtesy The Frank Lloyd Wright Foundation.

5. Ibid. Courtesy The Frank Lloyd Wright Foundation.

6. Wright, Frank Lloyd. 1928. "In the Cause of Architecture: III. The Meaning of Materials—Stone." *Architectural Record* 63(4):350–356. Reprint. 1975. *In the Cause of Architecture*, ed. Frederick Gutheim. New York: McGraw-Hill. p. 173. *ARCHITECTURAL RECORD*, (April/1928), copyright 1975 by McGraw-Hill, Inc. All rights reserved. Reproduced with the permission of the publisher.

7. Ibid. *ARCHITECTURAL RECORD*, (April/1928), copyright 1975 by McGraw-Hill, Inc. All rights reserved. Reproduced with the permission of the publisher.

8. Ibid. *ARCHITECTURAL RECORD*, (April/1928), copyright 1975 by McGraw-Hill, Inc. All rights reserved. Reproduced with the permission of the publisher.

9. Pfeiffer, Bruce Brooks. 1986. *Frank Lloyd Wright Monograph 1937–1941*, ed. Yukio Futagawa. Text copyrighted by the Frank Lloyd Wright Foundation 1986. Tokyo: A.D.A. Edita Tokyo, Ltd. p. 45. Courtesy The Frank Lloyd Wright Foundation.

10. Wright, Frank Lloyd. 1948. "Frank Lloyd Wright." *The Architectural Forum* 88(1):152.

11. Pfeiffer, Bruce Brooks. 1986. *Frank Lloyd Wright Monograph 1942–1950*, ed. Yukio Futagawa. Text copyrighted by the Frank Lloyd Wright Foundation 1986. Tokyo: A.D.A. Edita Tokyo, Ltd. p. 310. Courtesy The Frank Lloyd Wright Foundation.

12. Pfeiffer, Bruce Brooks. 1986. *Frank Lloyd Wright Monograph 1951–1959*, ed. Yukio Futagawa. Text copyrighted by the Frank Lloyd Wright Foundation 1986. Tokyo: A.D.A. Edita Tokyo, Ltd. p. 221. Courtesy The Frank Lloyd Wright Foundation.

13. Wright, Frank Lloyd. Frank Lloyd Wright Archives. Drawing #5102.03. Courtesy The Frank Lloyd Wright Archives.

14. Ibid., #5102.04. Courtesy The Frank Lloyd Wright Archives.

15. Ibid., #5627.06. Courtesy The Frank Lloyd Wright Archives.

16. Ibid., #5627.07. Courtesy The Frank Lloyd Wright Archives.

17. Storrer, William Allin. 1974. *The Architecture of Frank Lloyd Wright*. Cambridge: The MIT Press. p. 241.

18. Secrest, Meryle. 1992. *Frank Lloyd Wright: A Biography*. New York: Alfred A. Knopf. p. 453.

19. Wright, Frank Lloyd. Frank Lloyd Wright Archives. Drawing #5102.03.

20. Ibid.

21. Pfeiffer, Bruce Brooks, ed. 1986. *Letters To Clients.*

Fresno, CA: California State University Press. p 90.

22. Wright, Frank Lloyd. Frank Lloyd Wright Archives. Drawing #5203.05. Courtesy The Frank Lloyd Wright Archives.

23. Ibid. Courtesy The Frank Lloyd Wright Archives.

24. Wright, Frank Lloyd. 1928. "*In the Cause of Architecture:* III. The Meaning of Materials—Stone." *Architectural Record* 63(4):350–356. Reprint. 1975. *In the Cause of Architecture*, ed. Frederick Gutheim. New York: McGraw-Hill. p. 173. *ARCHITECTURAL RECORD*, (April/1928), copyright 1975 by McGraw-Hill, Inc. All rights reserved. Reproduced with the permission of the publisher.

25. Ibid., 174. *ARCHITECTURAL RECORD*, (April/1928), copyright 1975 by McGraw-Hill, Inc. All rights reserved. Reproduced with the permission of the publisher.

26. Ibid., 177. *ARCHITECTURAL RECORD*, (April/1928), copyright 1975 by McGraw-Hill, Inc. All rights reserved. Reproduced with the permission of the publisher.

27. Ibid., 173. *ARCHITECTURAL RECORD*, (April/1928), copyright 1975 by McGraw-Hill, Inc. All rights reserved. Reproduced with the permission of the publisher.

28. Ibid.

29. Ibid. *ARCHITECTURAL RECORD*, (April/1928), copyright 1975 by McGraw-Hill, Inc. All rights reserved. Reproduced with the permission of the publisher.

30. Ibid., 175–176.

31. Wright, Frank Lloyd. 1928. "In the Cause of Architecture: V. The Meaning of Materials—The Kiln." *Architectural Record* 63(6):555–561. Reprint. 1975. *In the Cause of Architecture*, ed. Frederick Gutheim. New York: McGraw-Hill. p. 194. *ARCHITECTURAL RECORD*, (June/1928), copyright 1975 by McGraw-Hill, Inc. All rights reserved. Reproduced with the permission of the publisher.

32. Ibid., 193. *ARCHITECTURAL RECORD*, (June/1928), copyright 1975 by McGraw-Hill, Inc. All rights reserved. Reproduced with the permission of the publisher.

33. Wright, Frank Lloyd. Frank Lloyd Wright Archives. Drawing #5102.03.

34. Storrer, William Allin. 1974. *The Architecture of Frank Lloyd Wright*. Cambridge: The MIT Press. p. 404.

35. Wright, Frank Lloyd. 1928. "In the Cause of Architecture: III. The Meaning of Materials—Stone." *Architectural Record* 63(4):350–356. Reprint. 1975. *In the Cause of Architecture*, ed. Frederick Gutheim. New York: McGraw-Hill. p. 177.

4

INTRODUCTION

Wright's discourse on clay brick was surprisingly limited in light of his belief that it is "the material we in Usonia know and love best."[1] Considering the many brick buildings he had already built by 1928, the year his observation was published, his claim to have done little work with the material was significant in its understatement. Unlike the creative detailing in certain other materials, his brick work had yielded only minor advances. In this context the previous brick work might have seemed to him to be limited in quantity because it had not yet produced major technical or stylistic innovations in detailing. His view that "we use it, on the whole very well"[2] could have been an obstacle to his technical and stylistic progress in brick detailing. There was no outrageous condition to rebel against; little needed to be corrected.

Wright thought that terra-cotta offered "the greatest opportunity for the creative artist of all materials,"[3] but he was preoccupied with Sullivan's use of the material, which seemed to discourage his own continued exploration of it. Wright's use of terra-cotta was limited, especially after his early work.

FORM

Compared to materials shaped by nature, Wright thought, clay should "be nearer man's desire—molded, as it is, by himself."[4] Most of Wright's praise for clay's flexibility was directed to terra-cotta, suggesting that he saw brick as being less versatile. Terra-cotta depended on the artist for its personality, he thought, as it "lives

FIGURE 4-1. Lapped brick at obtuse corners yield texture at the Frank Lloyd Wright Residence and Studio. Flush copings. Linear expression in shingled surface. No lintels expressed at lower windows. (Courtesy Mike Kertok)

FIGURE 4-2. Smooth obtuse corners at the Joseph Husser Residence. Prominent copings. Expressed lintel, arches, or roof above windows. (Courtesy The Frank Lloyd Wright Archives)

only as it takes the impression of human imagination."[5] His reference to brick as "inexhaustible in texture and color and shape"[6] describes a potential that was to remain largely unexplored, as most of his brick is smooth, of a few basic colors, and has the traditional form.

Wright neither described the form he thought to be appropriate for a brick nor offered reasoning as to how it should be determined. He complained of the numerous special shapes of brick needed in Burnham and Root's Monadnock Building (1891) for which the "flowing contours, or profile, unnatural to brick work was got by forcing the material."[7] His routine use of specially shaped brick with curved or angled faces suggests that his complaint about the Monadnock installation was more in regard to the building design than the brick. Otherwise, the shape of brick does not seem to have been an issue to Wright, although his frequent use of Roman brick indicates a preference for its relatively slender proportions (which, when installed, yielded

more horizontal lines than standard modular brick). The percentage of rectangular brick in his work was neither unusually high nor greater than that typical of other architects. Wright did not limit his brick construction to the rectangular geometry that is entirely compatible with the shape of a standard unit. His detailing of non-rectangular building forms included elements that were expressive of brick form and those that were not sympathetic to the nature of the material.

Obtuse angles appeared in Wright's plans intermittently throughout his career. Most obtuse building corners in his early brick work were formed by overlapping rectangular units (uncut) producing a texture of protruding brick corners alternating on either side of the junction. The detail appeared in such buildings as his Oak Park studio (1895), the Winslow House and Stable (1893), the Francis Apartments (1895), the Williams House (1897), and the G. Furbeck House (1897). Allowing the shape of the standard unit to affect the character of the building in this way demonstrates sensitivity to the nature of brick with regard to its form. In these cases the character of the brick (small, blocky, rectangular) is imposed upon the building, rather than a design idea (i.e., an obtuse angle in plan) forcing brick into a shape that is not natural (basic) to it. Notable

FIGURE 4-3. Smooth obtuse corners on projected breakfast nook of the Susan Lawrence Dana Residence. Prominent copings and water table. In background, windows with no expressed lintels. (Courtesy The Illinois Historic Preservation Agency—The Dana-Thomas House and Doug Carr, photographer, The Dana-Thomas Foundation)

exceptions to this trend were the prominent octagonal masses of the Husser House (1899), which had smooth-faced obtuse corners, and the projected breakfast alcove of the Dana House (1902) with similar detailing. Angular units were used in these cases to achieve the relatively tight, smooth corner joints.

The effect of the textured brick corners on the character of the early buildings was limited by the visual roles of the octagonal masses. These elements tend to be more or less incidental to the facades as are, consequently, their textured corners. The octagonal brick pilasters flanking the entry to the Winslow stable significantly affected the character of the entry but were a small part of the whole facade. Their relatively small diameter (compared to building masses) yielded corners very close to each other. The several vertical stacks of overlapped brick on the corners of the pilasters produced a highly noticeable texture. The quantity of over-lapped corner-brick was not greater than that of other early buildings, but the close proximity of the units and their position at a building focal point elevated the intensity of their expression within a small zone of the facade.

This application is of particular interest because Wright, in a note on an elevation, specifically called for

FIGURE 4-4. Lapped brick at obtuse corners yield texture at the Paul and Jean Hanna Residence.

a special bond[8] for the pilasters. The rare reference indicates Wright's desire to have this specific detail constructed unlike most of his other works with similar details, where the rustic corners are neither shown nor noted in the drawings. Wright's tolerance for rustic corners elsewhere is reasonably certain, given his supervisory control of the construction, but there is little evidence that he, rather than the mason, initiated the detail. In any case, he must be credited with the strong respect for the nature of brick form that the rustic corners represent.

A variation of the overlapping brick corners appears at the Hanna House (1935), which is only slightly less expressive of brick than the earlier examples. The hexagonal grid of the building (known as the Honeycomb House) generates numerous obtuse corners that offer an opportunity to subdue or express the basic form of brick. The brick generates gaps at the ends of every other course on each side of the corner. Unlike the earlier details, these units do not extend beyond the surface plane of the adjoining wall. The result is a texture that expresses the rectangularity of brick but less aggressively than the earlier overlapping/projected version. The texture of the gaps caused by rectangular brick at the numerous obtuse corners is apparent in most interior and exterior views of the building. Consequently, the textured corners affect the building character in a uniform and balanced way to a degree greater than the less frequent and more random applications of the earlier version of the detail. Because of the omnipresence of the detail, the rectangularity of brick is expressed more intensely at the Hanna House than in previous nonrectangular building elements.

Another indication of elevated respect for brick's form in this house is the use of the textured connection for inside corners (which recede from the viewer) as well

Figure 4-5. Lapped brick yield texture at obtuse corners of fireplace of Stanley Bazett Residence. Rowlock lintel at fireplace. Tight joints of plywood ceiling yield minimal expression of panel form. (Courtesy The Frank Lloyd Wright Archives)

as outside corners (which project toward the viewer). Smooth, obtuse, inside corners can be produced with rectangular units, while smooth, obtuse, outside corners cannot. The choice to use textured inside corners when not forced to, suggests a focus on the rectangularity of brick. The greater element of choice for inside corners make them slightly more revealing of designer attitude than their outside corner counterparts. Inside corners adjacent to the fireplace of the Rebhuhn House (1938) and in the Harper House (1950) are detailed with smooth surfaces rather than with the texture of the gaps typical of the Hanna House. The corners do not challenge the nature of brick but represent a missed opportunity to emphasize its blocky rectangularity.

At the Winslow House an octagonal bay is pushed out from the main wall far enough that the sloped wall, which might have met the main wall to form an obtuse inside corner, forms an outside corner before meeting the main house. Consequently, the bay wall meets the house wall at a right angle. The result is a bay with four, obtuse, outside corners and two right-angled inside corners. This arrangement is slightly more expressive of the rectangular blockiness of brick than having half the

number of outside corners, which would have resulted from abutting the house wall with the slanted bay walls.

Use of the textured corner detail dropped off sharply after the Hanna house. Its appearance in hexagonal chimney masses of the Stevens House (1939) and in walls at the Armstrong (1939) and Edwards (1949) houses mixes chronologically with a series of applications utilizing special units. The obtuse- and acute-angled corners formed with specially shaped brick have flush surfaces on either side. The fact that a unit has a special shape does not, in itself, violate the spirit of brick, although the form of such a unit is not central to the basic spirit of the material. The specific relationship of a nonstandard unit to the nature of brick is defined by the particular characteristics of the special shape. Curved units and units with obtuse angles in their faces maintain a compactness compatible with the strength characteristics of burned clay and the traditional mass of brick. Only the sense of rectangularity is lost in these kinds of special units.

Detailing at the Bazett House (1940) verifies Wright's preference for the textured corners in their own right, that is to say, as more than an inexpensive

FIGURE 4-6. Specially shaped brick visible in foreground at Stanley Bazett Residence construction. Smooth obtuse corner on end of wall in background. (Courtesy The Frank Lloyd Wright Archives)

solution. Specially shaped bricks were manufactured and used in the house but textured corners were also incorporated. Once a commitment to having special units was made, it would have been easy and reasonably economical to produce those necessary to form smooth obtuse corners in every case. The fact that some corners are textured when economy was not the central motivation for their use gives importance to the property of blockiness (illustrated at each textured corner) in the aesthetic order. Blockiness motivated by economy is a legitimate expression of the nature of brick, but the expression of blockiness where other options are as economical demonstrates a more intense appreciation of the nature of the material.

The flush-surfaced acute and obtuse corners among the Wall (1941), Palmer (1950), Mathews (1950) Glore

(1951), Kraus (1951), and A. Friedman (1956) houses—as well as in the Meyers (1956) and Fasbender (1957) clinics—are formed with specially shaped (non-rectangular) units, some of which were molded and some of which were cut. The resulting smooth-surfaced corners subdue the unique blocky nature of brick with an image reproducible in certain other materials. Special units that have acute angles fail to reflect the essence of brick not only because of their lack of rectangularity but also because of their delicacy and sharpness. The image of such brick, if cut or molded so as to form a mitered corner, is further removed from the spirit of the material by the joint on the apex of the corner. Mitered brick joints impart a sense of thinness rather than mass. Also, in these cases, the most delicate part of the units (the sharp edge) is placed in a position most vulnerable to damage (on the corner). When mitering occurs at obtuse corners, acute angles are also produced in the units. The mitered corner lacks philosophical and practical logic. The effect of the less material-sensitive detailing on the overall images of the buildings varies with the prominence and number of the corners.

Although there is some chronological mixture of corner details more and less sensitive to the form of brick, a general trend is apparent. There is a greater sensitivity to the rectangularity of brick in Wright's earlier work, as demonstrated by the limited use of brick that was not rectangular. There is a greater disregard for the basic rectangularity of brick in the later work, as demonstrated by the frequent use of special units. The trend of diminished sensitivity is exacerbated by the greater frequency of acute-angled corners in the later brick houses, such as the Kraus House (1951). Although Wright demonstrated a willingness to overlap rectangular units at obtuse corners, he did not show an equal willingness to do so at acute corners, which typically project a knife-edge image remote from the spirit of brick.

Wright's arches incorporate a considerable amount of specially shaped brick. The strong historical association of arches with brick is rooted in the strength and size of the material. The small size of the units make possible the construction of a curve that approximates the flow of compressive stresses across the span of the arch. That is to say, smallness allows the slight turning of each unit without disruptive consequence to the construction. The rectangularity of brick is not compatible with the geometry of arches, however. The detailing in two realms of incompatibility between unit shape and arch shape are potentially revealing of Wright's attitude towards brick form.

His use of nonrectangular units to solve the interface of the extrados (the convex or upper edge of the arch) with the stretchers of the wall is traditional. He cut the stretchers that meet the extrados at the angle necessary

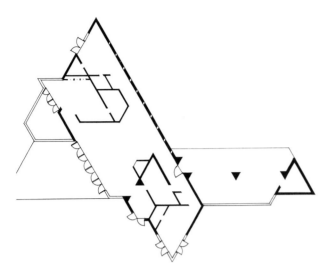

FIGURE 4-7. Floor plan of the Russell Kraus Residence showing acute angles in brick. (From Frank Lloyd Wright Archives drawing 5123.001.)

FIGURE 4-8. Strips of tapered and butted brick form a fireplace arch at the Susan Lawrence Dana Residence. (Courtesy The Illinois Historic Preservation Agency—The Dana-Thomas House and Doug Carr, photographer, The Dana-Thomas Foundation)

for a smooth tight junction. The resulting trapezoidal stretchers become more slender and delicate with positions higher on the arch. Occasionally, triangular units result. A loss in expression of brick's blockiness corresponds to the increase in sharpness and thinness of the units. This demonstration of diminished sensitivity to the form of brick is not profound, however, because of the detail's common use throughout history. It reveals only that Wright was no less or more concerned with the rectangularity of brick than other designers before and after him. It is likely that—to the casual

FIGURE 4-9. Tapered bricks (not aligned) in four off-set arches of the V. C. Morris Gift Shop. Brick lighting grille at left of entry.

observer—the strong historical association between arches and brick overshadows the material implications of the detail.

In another realm of general incompatibility between brick form and arch form, Wright reveals a preference for compositional goals over concern for the basic form of brick. The compatibility of arches and rectangular brick "voussoirs" varies with the relationship between unit size and arch radius. Compatibility increases as unit size diminishes and as arch radius increases. Although Wright's brick is not extraordinarily large, he created great depth in many of his arches by aligning several units end-to-end on radial lines. The detail has the effect of increasing unit length. The radii of his brick arches are relatively small, as they typically span entrances and fireplaces. The use of aligned rectangular bricks radiating from the center of a deep arch that has a small radius requires large wedge-shaped mortar joints between the units. The use of such joints would reflect a desire to maintain the basic brick form in lieu of other design goals. Wright sacrificed brick rectangularity, however, in order to maintain mortar joints of uniform width.

The assembly of tapered units in the reception room fireplace of the D. D. Martin House (1903) is particularly unlike brick. The deep arch is formed by a radial pattern of brick strips, each two and one-third units long. The tapering of each strip as a single entity yields a very small thickness at the intrados (the concave or lower edge of the arch). The identity of the multiple-brick radial strips as individual entities is further secured by the radial gold mortar joints between them. The bricks are not aligned so as to form concentric arcs. The mortar joint within each radiating strip is not gold in color and is much subdued when compared to the radial joints.

The Dana and Heurtley fireplace arches (1902) are similar but do not have gold colored mortar joints. The large upper arch (three and one-half bricks deep) at the Heurtley fireplace is trimmed at its intrados with a slightly recessed arch that is one brick in depth. The continuous taper of brick across the depth of the upper arch does not continue into the lower arch. The units of the lower curve are tapered from full-sized units. This avoids the extremely thin slivers of brick that would have occurred if the taper had continued across both parts of the arch. Consequently, some sense of mass is salvaged in the detail compared to the use of a continuous taper.

The deep arch at the entrance to the Dana House is segregated from surrounding brick by concrete trim, which hinders the comparison with the adjacent standard units. Consequently, the lack of blockiness in the tapered bricks of the arch is not emphasized to the degree that would have been apparent without the trim. The detailing of the brick in the arch is also subdued by the scale of the facade and competing features. The loss of brick rectangularity in the arch, therefore, is not as pronounced in the composition as in the previous examples. The Heurtly entrance arch is not as deep as the others and so its brick does not taper to as thin a dimension. The brick form there is emphasized, however, by strips of radial brick that contrast in color with adjacent units and project forward of them. The tapered bricks of the inglenook and drafting room fireplaces of Wright's Oak Park Home and Studio (1889, 1985) are also less sliverlike because the depths of the arches are less than in the other examples.

The deep tapered-brick arch at the Morris Gift Shop (1948) is reminiscent of the raised arch at the entry of the Waller Apartments (1895). The arch consists of four distinctly separate concentric arches (the Waller arch had five) each formed with a single band of brick. Unlike the units in the Martin fireplace, the identity of the brick lies with each arch rather than each radial line. The slight projection of each arch beyond the face of the one below emphasizes the definition of each course and disrupts radial continuity. This reduces the possibility of establishing a radial identity by aligning units with a continuous taper across the full depth of the arch. The bricks in each course have the same dimension across their widest end and taper as required by the radius of their individual arches. The units therefore do not align radially. The taper is not perceptible to the casual observer, leaving their blocky and apparently rectangular image reasonably intact.

A continuous taper of brick across such a deep arch would have produced visually and physically awkward slivers at the intrados. Although physical demands may have been the motivation, the Morris detailing represents a change in the trend in Wright's arches towards greater sensitivity to the rectangularity of brick. If practical considerations (often related to a material's nature) forced the change, it would still seem that Wright had to have a reasonable level of appreciation for the more blocky image in order to eliminate the continuous tapering of units across the full depth of the arch.

Curved walls have a relationship with the brick form similar to that of arches. The smallness of unit size allows the construction of a curve by slight differences in the orientations of adjacent units. Curves, therefore, express smallness of size, a unique characteristic of masonry among the structural materials. Although curves are not related to rectangularity, the combination of rectangular brick and mortar joints between units that are wedge-shaped in plan, establishes, within certain limits, a compatibility between the material system and curved geometry. The degree of compatibility increases as the radius of the curve increases and as unit size diminishes.

Wright built relatively few curved walls in brick. Early examples include a terrace wall at his Oak Park Home (1889) and a room on the back of the Winslow House (1893). There is no apparent texture of protruding unit corners that would indicate a confrontation between the units and the curved surfaces. On the other hand, unit geometry is subdued, as it is in any curved structure where the rectangularity of brick does not assert itself in the image. A radius that is too short for the length of the brick will cause the corners of units to project noticeably forward of the unit below, thus creating a texture of corners and their shadows. In such cases the rectangularity of brick is expressed, but, because it is not intended and would be eliminated if possible, it indicates a lack of sensitivity to the material.

The rectangularity of brick is forfeited in the curved ends of the central brick mass of the H. Johnson House (1937). The small-radius curves are constructed with curved brick that maintain the mass and compactness of the units but not their basic rectangular geometry. The detailing indicates an awareness and control of the nature of brick but does not maximize its expression. The curve of the individual units at the Johnson Wax Administration Building (1936) is less noticeable, as the various radii of the curved walls are larger than those of the H. Johnson fireplace. The rectangularity of the general nature of brick is challenged more by the clearly perceptible curved geometry of the walls than by the curved faces of the units themselves, which are difficult to perceive as such.

A very large-radius curve occurs at the brick-clad cylindrical volume projecting from the Gammage Auditorium Building (1959). The curve of the wall is

FIGURE 4-10. Specially shaped brick in curved surfaces at the S. C. Johnson and Son Administration Building. Flush copings. Concrete lips under brick over open space. No support for brick over glass expressed.

FIGURE 4-11. Drum-shaped brick clad mass at the Grady Gammage Memorial Auditorium. Tinted flush concrete coping and similar trim around semicircular windows.

gentle enough to obscure the actual geometry of the units and is, therefore, compatible with both flat and curved bricks. Consequently, the large radius wall expresses brick's unit nature by its ability to form the curve and its structural nature by the stabilization the curve affords the stacked units. Absent is the sense of mismatch between wall and unit geometries that more abrupt curves exhibit.

Wright's belief of the "brick pier and mass…to be natural in brick construction"[9] is illustrated most vividly in his early buildings. His thought that brick was particularly suited to the formation of building corners,[10] doubtless influenced the design of many corners in the early work which, in turn, express the right-angled nature and blocky character of the brick. The Dana House (1902), Heurtley House (1902), D. D. Martin House (1903), Larkin Building (1903), Robie House (1906), and May House (1908) are among his many brick buildings with blocky masses and piers. The Allen House (1917) was the last of the brick buildings characterized by the piers and moderately scaled blocky masses that so clearly reflect the rectangularity and blockiness of individual units. For sixteen years following the Allen House, no brick projects were designed and built. It was during this period that Wright's statement praising piers and mass was published. It is now apparent that the comments described previous brickwork rather than that which was to follow.

When brick reappeared in 1934 at the Willey House it showed signs of a new sleekness which was to typify subsequent detailing. Generally, smooth brick surfaces, extending without interruption to borders of glass or other materials, have a tautness that emphasizes neither the compressive nature of brick construction nor the smallness and individuality of units. Rectangular brick

masses do appear in the later buildings, but their scale and detailing express the nature of brick form to a lesser intensity than the earlier work. Although the later detailing does not violate the nature of brick form, its contrast with the more sympathetic early work emphasizes its average sensitivity to the material.

Nearly all of Wright's brick was set in running bond or one-third running bond (vertical joints at third-points of adjacent stretchers instead of midpoints). Upon occasion, Wright set his brick in a Flemish bond. The expression of brick form in bond patterns of a single color is subtle, but any bond pattern which includes both stretchers and headers reveals more of the nature of brick than does running bond. In the G. Furbeck House (1897), the glazed headers of the Flemish bond have a slightly darker appearance than the stretchers, thus the face and sectional characteristics of the brick are slightly emphasized, as are the faces of the stretchers between them. The orderly distribution of units in the pattern yield an orderly and blocky sense, a spirit closely aligned with the nature of brick. The use of running bond in parts of the building reveals, by comparison, the slightly greater sense of blockiness in adjacent areas of the Flemish pattern. A variation of Flemish bond was used on the German Warehouse (1915), an unusual choice for an industrial building. Flemish bond appears in the

FIGURE 4-12. Blocky brick piers and masses at the Darwin D. Martin Residence. Prominent copings and water tables. Trim refers to hidden lintel over wide opening at lower center. (Courtesy The Frank Lloyd Wright Archives)

semicircular volume on the back of the Winslow House (1893), while the remainder of the building is in one-third running bond.

Wright's use of texture and color in brick shows restraint, given his expressed admiration for the broad range of options. Individual units were typically smooth, as was most surface detailing. (Brick at the Bogk House, 1916, and the Imperial Hotel, 1914, was slightly textured with vertical striations.) The effort and intent embodied in flush surfaces reflect the precision of human-generated forms rather than those of nature. This seems appropriate for brick, which is entirely shaped by manufacturing processes compared to some stone largely shaped by nature. On the other hand, projected units reflect a built condition rather than a natural condition, if they are in a clear pattern instead of randomly placed. Projected bricks emphasize the form of the unit and express, to degrees varying with the pattern, the nature of brick construction.

Wright created only a few patterns in his brick surfaces with color or texture. Early patterns of projected brick are found inside the Thomas House (1901) and on the exterior of the Heurtley (1902) and the May (1908) houses. Courses of units project to create hori-

FIGURE 4-13. Blocky brick piers and masses at the Frederick C. Robie Residence. Prominent copings and water tables.

zontal stripes on the Heurtley facades. The contrasting colors of the projected and flush courses enhance the visibility of the striped pattern. Although the projections create a sense of material thickness, a wood- or steel-like linear shape is expressed in the continuity of the horizontal lines. The expression of brick form in such strips

FIGURE 4-14. Flemish bond with dark headers in lower walls at the George Furbeck Residence. Lapped brick at obtuse corners yield texture. Running bond at upper level of wall. (Courtesy Mike Kertok)

FIGURE 4-15. Pairs of projected courses (contrasting in color) create horizontal lines on the facade of the Arthur Heurtley Residence. Prominent (tinted) concrete copings and water table. Deep arch with projected brick on radial lines. Battered walls. (Courtesy Mike Kertok)

FIGURE 4-16. Alternating projected and recessed brick courses at upper level of Meyer May Residence. Prominent copings and water table. Blocky piers and masses. (Courtesy Patricia L. Eidson)

varies with the visibility of the vertical joints. When viewed from any distance, the image of the head joints tends to be weaker than the long, thin, horizontal, shadow lines below the projections. As the distance between the observer and the house increases, the expression of the nature of brick as defined by its face shape diminishes. The loss of definition is more complete than in plain brick walls, because the domination of the stripes over the rectangularity of the texture increases with distance.

An opportunity to compare the visual effect of alternating projected and recessed brick courses with that of flush brick surfaces occurs at the May House. The projected courses on the upper level look more linear than the traditional surfaces below, which have a subtle blockiness in spite of the raked horizontal joints. Consequently, the lower surfaces seem slightly more bricklike than the upper detailing. All the brick is the same color. In the Thomas House, the projecting of every other course on the fireplace creates a series of horizontal lines in the brick. A sense of unit thickness is established, but, as in all courses where every unit is projected, rectangularity is subdued by the stronger pattern of linearity. The vertical joints in the bands maintain at least a minimal level of visibility, as the size of the room limits the distance at which one can observe the pattern. A similar phenomenon can be seen in the G. Furbeck fireplace (1897) where every seventh course is recessed instead of projected.

A few buildings have isolated bands (not part of a striped field) created by units oriented in the soldier or rowlock position and/or projected slightly forward of the wall surface. The Francisco Apartments (1895), Waller Apartments (1895), and Lamp House (1904) have such bands, which extend across the facades and pass over openings as pseudolintels. The three bands of projected stretchers at the R. Furbeck House (1898) align with windows but do not form lintels. Their widely spaced positions cause them to read as individual lines rather than as a texture, thus emphasizing their linearity at the expense of the rectangularity of individual units. As in the striped surfaces, the linear patterns emphasize only certain aspects of brick and emulate forms typical of linear materials.

Occasionally, in Wright's work, a three-dimensional manipulation of a brick surface occurs that emphasizes the rectangularity of individual unit form. Utilitarian patterns such as the omission of every other unit to form

FIGURE 4-18. Brick grilles on fireplace at the Isabel Roberts Residence. Expressed lintel at fireplace. (Courtesy The Frank Lloyd Wright Archives)

FIGURE 4-17. Brick grille on the main (south) facade of the Susan Lawrence Dana Residence. (Courtesy The Illinois Historic Preservation Agency—The Dana-Thomas House and Doug Carr, photographer, The Dana-Thomas Foundation)

small grilles on the facades of the Dana House gallery wing (1902), Robie chimney (1906), May chimney (1908), Sturges House (1939), and Walter House (1945) and at the fireplaces of the I. Roberts (1908), Hanna (1935), and Sturges (1939) houses (among others) are significant materials statements, although minor in scope. The omission of bricks in a pattern of holes defines the face form of the both the missing units and those that remain, as well as their depth (as seen in the depth of the holes). Selecting such a detail for a grille in the presence of other options reflects sensitivity to brick properties as expressive vehicles. An early drawing of the Dana House gallery wing, for example, shows a large blank rectangle in the location where a brick grille appears in the actual construction, as if the selection of the detail was still pending at the time of the drawing. The brick grille that was built (which emits light into a small room) expresses more of the nature of brick than other options for the opening, such as a window or louvers.

The pattern forming the grille at the top of the May chimney continues in the solid brick on either side of the open holes on the long face of the chimney and also appears on the end where there is no grille, thus establishing that this expression based on the form of brick is generated partially for its own sake. Courses of stretch-ers alternate with courses of headers, every other header being recessed, or—in the area of the grille—omitted. The height and thickness of the units is clearly expressed as is the width of the headers and, in general, the blocky nature of the brick.

The omission of alternating bricks that Wright used to create most of his brick grilles is somewhat more expressive of the nature of the units than the grille detail used at the Larking Building (1903). Several grilles in the building consisted of units with rectangular holes in their centers. The holes express thickness in the units and, because of their rectangularity, express that aspect of brick's geometry. Their rhythm emulates that of the running bond of the wall. On the other hand, the slender lines of brick created between units and the holes did not express either of the face dimensions of the brick. Unlike the method of creating grilles by omitting units, this detailing requires a special brick which, by definition, expresses a variation in the basic nature of the material rather than the basic nature itself.

Curved brick grilles in the lobby and large workspace of the Johnson Wax Administration Building (1936), curved and flat grilles in the central fireplace mass of Wingspread (H. Johnson House, 1937), and a flat grille over the living room fireplace at the Stevens House (1939) are especially foreign to the image of brick. To create the grilles, all units in every other course are omitted for extended runs. Each of several courses of brick appear, consequently, to be suspended between strips of air (actually thin metal grille inserts). The image

FIGURE 4-19. Rectangular holes in brick create grilles at the Larkin Company Administration Building. (Courtesy The Frank Lloyd Wright Archives)

FIGURE 4-20. Alternating courses of brick and open space create linear grille (lower left) at the S.C. Johnson and Son Administration Building. Concrete lips under "brick spans." (Courtesy The Frank Lloyd Wright Archives)

violates the nature of brick in strength and form. Also, the large masses of brick above the openings at Wingspread and the Stevens House have no apparent support as they meet the uppermost open strips with stretchers rather than lintels. In a grille at Wingspread, the strips of brick follow the fireplace mass around its curved end. The plastic look of the linear assembly and the extreme (apparent) cantilever of the brick strips are particularly remote from the spirit of the material.

Rare, more decorative, examples appear in Wright's later work. Less utilitarian-looking grilles and patterns are distributed throughout the L. Lewis House (1940). Recesses in the patterns are the size of headers and are staggered vertically. The expression of brick is not the strongest possible but is reasonably intense and slightly elevated by the variation in the alignment of recesses that reflects a manipulation of material form for a visual effect. Because a purposeful focus on the characteristics of the brick is evident, the material sensitivity of the detail is boosted beyond that established by the information it expresses about the form of brick. A less complex, but tall and therefore somewhat imposing, checkerboard pattern is created in the entrance hall of the Zimmerman House (1952) by leaving gaps about the size of a header between the stretchers. Height and thickness of the units are emphasized by the pattern. More conventional patterns similar to a Flemish bond with the headers omitted cover nearly the entire surfaces of several small walls at the carport of the M. M.

Maxwell House (1948). The relatively large size of these is unusual in Wright's detailing.

The quasi-functional light grille to the left of the entrance to the Morris Gift Shop (1948) strongly expresses the form, if not the strength, characteristics of brick. The omission of every other unit in a vertical strip and the setting of the strip forward of the wall surface on one side nearly suspends individual units in midair. Unit rectangularity and mass are expressed to the practical maximum. The definition of unit proportions is strong, but not exact, due to the structural necessity of embedding in the adjacent walls the back corner on one end of each unit and a short segment on the other end. A stronger expression is not conceivable without the total loss of the already precarious structural integrity of the units. The grille houses lights that do little more than illuminate the grille itself, thus further enhancing the strong expression of brick form.

FIGURE 4-21. Alternating courses of brick in contrasting colors create stripes on walls at the Malcolm Willey Residence. (Courtesy The Frank Lloyd Wright Archives)

Lighting recesses in a brick mass within the interior of the Palmer House (1950) are created by omitting units so as to form a C-shaped void. The openings are three units high and about as wide as the length of a unit. A single brick cantilevers about half its length into the center of each otherwise rectangular void to create the C-shape. The detail clearly expresses the height of a unit and its rectangularity, as the cantilevered brick is framed in translucent glazing and backlit. Unit length is less precisely defined. The sense of thickness inherent in the Morris light grille is missing here, because the fixture glazing is nearly flush with the face of the brick. The lack of significant utility in the Morris and Palmer light grilles emphasizes their decorative roles. The expression of brick properties for their own sake (as decoration) indicates an elevated sensitivity to the material.

A few two-dimensional patterns exist that express various aspects of the face shape of brick but do not verify that the material has thickness. Flush horizontal stripes, for example, appear on the second level of the Heller House (1896) and throughout the Willey House (1934) (including the floors) in alternating courses of darker and lighter units. Like the projected versions, the linear patterns clarify the height of individual units, but somewhat obscure the length of each. A sense of blockiness is absent from the two-dimensional patterns, and thus expression of the nature of brick is not maximized in the surfaces.

Individual dark bricks set randomly among lighter units at the second F. Little (1913) and Schwartz (1939) houses boost the expression of form above that afforded by surfaces of a single color and above linear patterns created by two colors. Both the height and length of bricks are defined when surrounded by units of a contrasting color and are partially defined when not

FIGURE 4-22. Brick dentils at top of wall, bands of projected rowlocks, corbeled courses under upper windows, and diamond patterns at lower level of Robert M. Lamp Residence. Sparkling quality in diamond-patterned windows. (Courtesy The Frank Lloyd Wright Archives)

entirely so framed. Rectangularity is emphasized whereever the corners of units contrast in color with adjacent units. The sense of brick is elevated but not maximized by the pattern, since the randomness fails to reflect the ordered nature of brick construction.

Detailing of the brick at the Lamp House (1904) responds to the nature of brick form to various degrees. The significance of the unique detailing is in doubt, however, as John Holzhueter has observed that it resembles the style of Walter Burley Griffin, Wright's assistant.[11] Brick dentils at the cornice bring a focus to the individual units and the rhythm of rectangular projections reflects both unit shape and the orderly character of standard brick assembly. The several corbeled courses under the upper windows add a sense of unit mass although, as with any continuous course of projections, face rectangularity cannot overcome the linear pattern, which is emphasized by its shadow lines. An

FIGURE 4-23. Projected courses of brick create horizontal bands at the Rollin Furbeck Residence. Alternating projected and recessed brick in corbeled courses under columns. Expressed lintels. (Courtesy Mike Kertok)

FIGURE 4-24. Raked horizontal mortar joints and flush-pointed vertical joints at the Susan Lawrence Dana Residence. (Courtesy The Illinois Historic Preservation Agency—The Dana-Thomas House and Doug Carr, photographer, The Dana-Thomas Foundation)

image of linearity in the corbels tends to obscure the rectangularity of brick with its reference to the form of wood trim. As is typical of projected courses, the expression of brick in the corbeled strips diminishes with increased viewing distance, due to greater reduction in the visibility of the vertical joints than in the horizontal lines.

Two rare decorative features in the facade of the Lamp House bring some attention to unit form. Four sets of three bricks each are turned 90 degrees to adjacent units in two pinwheel-like patterns. Each group of twelve bricks is turned 45 degrees to the courses in the wall creating diamondlike shapes. Being derived from a only a few units (thus allowing them to maintain some individual identity) and having an overall square geometry (as opposed to the linearity of the corbeled courses), the decorative patterns reflect the spirit of brick. The 45-degree cuts of adjacent units that abut the patterns are not excessive (although otherwise unnecessary). As unusually delicate units are not produced, the working of the brick is within reasonable limits for its substance. The detailing shows an unusual manipulation of the form of brick (which may not have been initiated by Wright) but fails to significantly affect the character of the house because of its timid application. The idea was not developed further in Wright's subsequent work.

The corbeled area under the sill of the second-floor columns on the R. Furbeck House (1898) reflects to greater degree the nature of brick than does the corbeling of the Lamp facade and most other corbeled masses. The horizontal linearity that typifies most corbeling is eliminated by the setting of every other unit in each course back from the adjacent bricks. This, combined with the projection of each unit forward of the one

below, defines the face of each brick clearly as an individual rectangular unit as well as establishing a sense of depth (mass) in the material. Corbeling under brick pilasters on either side of glazing in a west elevation of the Dana House has a structural sense, given the apparent support provided to the pilasters. The pilasters carry no superimposed load, but their weight—combined with that of a concrete sill spanning across the corbels—adds legitimacy to their functional role in the facade. In spite of their sense of integration in the design (by virtue of their function), the corbels have little effect on the character of the facade due to their small size. The detail is not repeated throughout the facades, which prevents it from becoming a meaningful component in the aesthetic order.

Joints, to the degree which they are perceived, express shape and size of each brick face. His brick walls, Wright thought, were "solidified by emphasis of the horizontal joint."[12] A few notes on a presentation drawing (in a large decorative format) describe key characteristics of the Husser House (1899). Among the descriptions is a call for "Horizontal joints wide and raked out to emphasize horizontal grain—Vertical joints stopped flush with mortar the color of the bricks."[13] The

Figure 4-25. Site-cut mitered rowlock brick and specially molded stretchers at obtuse corners of the Kenneth Meyers Clinic. (Courtesy Edward A. Young)

detail characterizes Wright's brick throughout his career. His omnipresent raked horizontal joints and flush vertical joints emphasize unit height at the expense of clarity in unit length. The result is a diminishing of the faint blockiness afforded by equally emphasized joints found in traditional brick walls and the creation of a weak linearity in the long narrow strips of brick interrupted only vaguely by vertical divisions. Aside from surface sheen and color, distinction of this pattern from one created with narrow strips of wood is dependent upon the failure to entirely hide the vertical joints. Expression of brick form is inversely related to the contrast between the visual intensities of the head and bed joints. More contrast between the two joints obscures to a greater degree the form of the units.

Although construction was not always completed exactly as specified, the intent to establish the superior visibility of horizontal joints is revealed in various working drawings. The Morris Gift Shop (1948) drawings, for example, call for horizontal joints to be raked to a depth of one-half inch and painted gold.[14] Drawings for Suntop Homes (1939) specify unusually large five-eighths-inch horizontal joints and close vertical joints pointed with mortar of the same the color as the brick.[15] Except for the height of the mortar joint, this instruction is repeated in the drawings of many projects. Perhaps the strongest visual intensity of horizontal joints actually constructed occurs in the fireplaces of the May House (1908), into which gold-colored glass was inserted. The vertical joints are flush and match the color of the brick. The gold leaf rubbed into the joints of the interior brick at the D. D. Martin House (1903), Imperial Hotel (1914), and the Allen House (1917)[16] contrasts less with the brick than does the glass in the May joints. In addition to the loss of surface blockiness

in these details, the expression of the brick is further diminished by the joints' peculiarity.

The uniqueness of the mortar sheen in these examples undermines the overall sense of brick construction which does not normally have gold-colored joints. Although tradition does not, in itself, define the nature of a material, the logic commonly expressed in traditional details often does. In any case, the nature of mortar at the May, Martin, and Allen houses is obscured, which constitutes a loss to the nature of the masonry system. The attention that the joints in the houses demands is attention drawn away from the bricks themselves. The reduced dependency on the nature of the brick for the character of the architecture reflects a reduced level of its importance to the designer in relationship to other goals of the design.

WORKABILITY

Wright was willing to reshape standard brick to meet his detailing needs. The cutting of brick occurs when the building design is not compatible with the basic form of brick and the integrity of the design rather than the nature of brick governs. All cutting (and breaking) of brick might be considered a violation of its nature if it were not customary at the extrados of arches, which are so closely associated with the material. The tradition of reshaping brick does not, in itself, verify that the practice is within the nature of the material. Tradition has demonstrated, however, that the breaking of units can be achieved with simple tools and minimal disruption to the work. The measure of the material sensitivity inherent in the working of brick is, therefore, the nature of the final shape produced in combination with the amount of cutting done.

Wright used both specially molded units and cut units. They occur in the same building when the number of special stretchers needed for nonright-angled corners justifies the manufacturing of special shapes but the few rowlocks needed to cap the top of such a corner (where it is exposed) do not. The cutting of units to cover the tops of right-angled corners such as those at the Willey (1934) and Goetsch-Winckler (1939) houses was also done where the core holes in standard brick would have otherwise been exposed. Such details can be solved by a variety of cutting formats, all of which diminish the sense of mass in the masonry. The tops of obtuse corners on the battered walls at the Meyers Clinic (1956) were mitered, while two rectangular plates were cut from brick for the top of the Willey chimney and stacked to equal the height of the adjacent rowlocks. A similar detail occurs on certain rectangular corners at the Goetsch-Winckler House. Such corners, although detracting from the nature of brick form and (depending on the awkwardness of the cutting) the spirit of brick's workability, have—because of their few numbers and small sizes—little effect on the overall images of their buildings. They do suggest, however, that the level of sensitivity to the nature of the material is less than maximum, since the small negative effect prevents the expression of the nature of brick from being the strongest possible.

Wright's notes on the Morris Gift Shop (1948) working drawings give the contractor the option of producing the tapered units for the entrance arch in special molds or by grinding.[17] The molding of special units does not fall into the category of working brick, but grinding does. Given the willingness of Wright to use either method renders moot the meaning of the actual process selected by the contractor. The contractor's ultimate selection of methods reflects on his own attitude about brick but not on Wright's. Wright's offer of the option indicates that he was willing to work the brick into the shape he needed regardless of the actual method used.

Wright was willing to build hexagonal and triangular masses, as well as arches, in a rectangular material. He was willing, in many cases, to overcome the rectangularity of brick by working it in order to meet design goals unrelated to material issues. As a result, many sharp and slender shapes were produced that are incompatible with the basic form and strength of brick. His record is mixed, however, because in a number of geometrical mismatches, he did not reshape the brick. The trend in his attitude, as observed from his early to his later work, is from less to greater willingness to disregard the nature of brick form to meet his architectural goals.

STRENGTH

The product form of all masonry substances is related in large part to strength. (Compactness of units is related to strength, size to weight, and rectangularity to manufacturing and construction convenience.) Within certain limits, the elements of Wright's detailing that emphasize brick form also express the strength of the material. Brick is known as a compressive material because of its inability to resist significant other stresses. Like other masonries, its moderate compressive strength can be compensated by increased mass. Wright referred to this phenomenon in his recognition that "a stone or brick plan is heavy: black in masses."[18]

Given the greater use of rectangular piers, pilasters, and other masses of moderate scale in the brick walls of his earlier work, a trend of greater to less sensitivity to certain aspects of brick strength can be observed in his

career. These protruding masses not only bring attention to the nature of brick compressiveness in their own forms but also tend to visually stabilize the whole of the brick construction. Stabilization is also enhanced by the projected bases (or "water-tables," as Wright called them) of the earlier work. His report that he "liked to see the projecting base, or water-table, set out over the foundation walls themselves—as a substantial preparation for the building"[19] is a reference to structural stability. Although the comment was not limited to buildings of brick, the visual benefit of the detail is most significant in that material. The Dana (1902), Heurtley (1902), Robie (1906), and D. D. Martin (1903) houses characterize the many buildings with this base detail.

The physical stabilization provided by these masses is not the main issue, since they are rarely required for the function of the structure and add only to the already ample margin of safety if they physically contribute at all. The visual contribution, however, of any element that serves to spread the base of the construction is an elevated sense of compression in the brick, regardless of the physical need for it. The extreme example is a pyramid, in which the generation of tensile stress by the leaning or tipping of the structure is inconceivable. Ancient pyramids and ziggaruts have a strong sense of compression in their masonry because—among other characteristics—they look absolutely stable, with no chance of other stresses developing.

Wright spread the base of several buildings by battering the brick walls, using various techniques. The walls of the Heurtley House (1902) and Imperial Hotel (1914) have battered surfaces, with each course of brick in certain walls set back slightly from the brick below to create an approximation of a continuously sloped surface. The battered brick of the Imperial Hotel was actually cladding (which had served as the permanent formwork) of a reinforced concrete wall. Since the character of the building is established by the brick and its stone trim, the image of the brick is evaluated as if it were the structure. These buildings gain a sense of stability, and therefore compressiveness, from the battered surfaces, which are gentle but apparent.

After an absence of several years, battered brick reappeared in such projects as the Wall (1941) and Edwards (1949) houses followed by the Meyers Clinic (1956). These walls differed from the earlier battering in that they did not step back with each course. The surfaces are set back in large flush and plumb sections. The walls are divided into several segments of eight or so courses that are, as a single mass, positioned a few inches back from the top of the section below. The stabilizing effect is much the same as that of the earlier examples. The fact that the walls of the later buildings are battered is slightly more obvious, which gives the

FIGURE 4-26. Battered walls at the Imperial Hotel. (Courtesy The Frank Lloyd Wright Archives)

expression a greater certainty of effect than the earlier versions. The earlier walls, once understood as being battered, however, are more imposing than the later variations; thus, their sense of compression is slightly stronger. This difference is the result of the slight reduction in scale (and therefore the visual mass) caused by subdividing the walls of the later buildings into a few large horizontal segments of brick. A rare reverse-batter in brick occurs at the Schaberg House (1950), where the facade is divided into a few tall horizontal bands of brick, each of which projects as a flush group forward of the section below. The detail detracts from the sense of compression that is most compatible with brick, as the walls have less visual stability than do plumb or standard battered constructions.

An image of compression in brick is compatible with the nature of the material with regard to strength. To emphasize compression and to omit from the building image suggestions that brick can perform significantly in tension or in bending is to demonstrate sensitivity to the nature of the material. Although Wright's brickwork after the Allen House (1917) has an adequately stable appearance, a sense of compression in the material is not elevated by use of the buttressing elements typical of the earlier work. The fact that much of Wright's brick construction was loadbearing and necessarily responded to the physical demands of its structural role contributes to its sense of adequate stability.

The significance of buttresslike detailing as well as the absence of such can be observed in a comparison of the Larkin Building (1903) and German Warehouse (1915). In spite of its greater height, the Larkin Building has a greater sense of compressiveness through

FIGURE 4-27. Walls battered at the Kenneth Meyers Clinic in vertical sections of eight and nine courses. (Courtesy Edward A. Young)

its exaggerated stability (for a tall building) than does the German Warehouse because of the former's large pilasters and rectangular masses at the corners. The projecting concrete mass at the top of the warehouse, in contrast, serves to visually destabilize the structure with its top-heavy appearance. Because the tall planes of brick are without surface relief, they seem taut. They appear to be stretched between the base and the heavy concrete fascia that, simultaneously, seems to bear down on them. The conflicting sensations are somewhat unsettling, although the nature of brick is not violated by an appearance of actual tension in the walls.

The stacking of brick directly on a foundation is the most direct expression of compression and, therefore,

FIGURE 4-28. Blocky piers and masses at the Larkin Company Administration Building. Prominent copings. Linear pattern in iron fencing. (Courtesy The Frank Lloyd Wright Archives)

the mode most clearly reflective of brick's structural nature. Wright maintains this image for much of his brick; it often reaches from the roof, copings, and window sills directly to the foundation without the interruption of an opening. A contrast in the compressive images of brick in direct contact with grade and the brick-ground relationship interrupted by glass can be seen by comparing the City National Bank (1909) to a subsequent alteration to the building that replaced brick on the ground level with large sheets of glass. The brick wall as designed and originally built had a stronger sense of compression than it does today.

Wright routinely maintained the continuous brick-to-grade compressive flow in more complex facades. In the two main elevations of the Dana House (1902), for

example, only two openings have brick above them. The brick passes over an arch at the main entry and over an expressed lintel in the east elevation. This treatment of brick, although sensitive to the strength nature of the material, is more likely a response to intentions in building-massing and solid-void relationships rather than an intentional homage to brick.

Expressed lintels maintain the brick above them in a compressive format, since the units merely rest visually and/or physically on the lintel instead of on other brick or a foundation. Each of Wright's use of lintels is a reasonably certain indication of his respect for the compressive nature of the material, because there are other options available that violate the spirit of brick. It is not necessary for the expressed lintel to actually carry

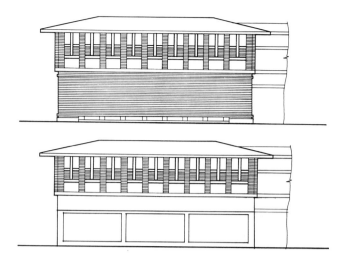

FIGURE 4-29. Elevation of the City National Bank, as originally constructed, with solid brick wall as facade base (above) and elevation as subsequently altered with display windows. (From Frank Lloyd Wright Archives drawing 0902.012 and a photograph, *Frank Lloyd Wright Monograph 1907–1913*, p. 121.)

the building loads in order to demonstrate respect for the nature of brick. It need only to appear to be load-bearing. A distinction is not made between real and false lintels here but rather between lintels that appear to be real and those that do not.

A lintel that is obviously false can still maintain the compressive sense of the brick above. If its apparent span is too long for its depth to be structural, the expressive violation is largely drawn to the lintel itself. Should the ratio of span to depth supersede that which is remotely feasible, the lintel loses some but not all ability to maintain the compressive image of the visually supported brick. Trim along the bottom edge of brick suspended above an opening can refer to the need for a lintel and to the presence of the hidden structure. Trim that serves as a visual lintel is more effective in drawing the violation away from the brick it "supports" if it has a sense of continuity—that is, minimally expressed joints and no periodic markings or decorations that seem to divide the strip into units.

A long and slender strip of stone trim along the bottom edge of the living and dining room balcony at the Robie House (1906) serves such a role in the main facade. The ability of the trim to function partially as an apparent lintel is enhanced by its association with trim of similar appearance elsewhere on the building that has shorter and more believable "spans." At the Johnson Wax Building (1936) actual structure is revealed in concrete bearing ledges below most of the suspended brick masses. The edges and lips of the concrete structure that appear in elevation as thin bands under the brick seem

to be too narrow to span a significant distance. They gain credibility by the periodic exposure throughout the building of the slabs and beams of which they are a part. Because their role can be visually clarified only by examining much of the building, their visual contribution to the nature of brick as viewed from a single vantage point is less than their actual contribution.

Wright disapproved of the hidden steel lintels in the brick over the windows of the Monadnock Building[20] but found many applications for this detail in his own work. His record of expressing the structural reality of brick above openings is mixed. Brick appears over windows and doors without expressed lintels or arches in the Francis Apartments (1895), Heurtley House (1902), Barton House (1903), the D. D. Martin Conservatory (1903), Heath House (1905), and second F. Little House (1913). Stretchers butted end-to-end seem to span in a horizontal line over the openings without visible assistance. The apparent condition is not possible in unreinforced brick and therefore violates the nature of the material. Brick appears to rest on top of long runs of glass tubing at the Johnson Wax complex (1936), although the unique appearance of the system generates more a sense of structural vagueness than a clear violation.

Upon occasion when Wright placed brick above an opening without a visual reference to a lintel, he did so on openings that were minor or in locations of lower importance. His awareness of the role of lintels in the expression of brick is suggested by this pattern. In the Dana and Robie houses, for example, structural or apparent structural members span openings in the main facades, but certain openings on the backs of the houses have no expressed lintels. The main facade of the Beachy House (1906) includes a large lintel over an important window and low louvered openings in the brick with no expressed lintels. Intent to focus on the compressiveness of brick would be more clearly indicated in an approach so disciplined as to never place brick over an opening or to never place it over an opening without a visible means of support. This is not the case in Wright's buildings.

Real or apparent lintels support brick in numerous early buildings in addition to those previously mentioned including the Heller (1896), G. Furbeck (1897), R. Furbeck (1898), the first F. Little (1902), D. D. Martin (1903), May (1908), the second F. Little (1913), H. Adams (1913), and Bogk (1916) houses, as well as the Larkin Building (1903) and E-Z Polish Factory (1905). The brick visually resting on the lintels remains in compression, a condition compatible with the nature of the material. The intermingled chronology of head details that are visually accommodating and those that are visually incompatible with the strength of brick reflects upon the degree of the issue's importance

FIGURE 4-30. Most openings extending to roofs in south and east facades of the Susan Lawrence Dana Residence. Blocky piers and masses. Prominent copings and water table. (Courtesy The Illinois Historic Preservation Agency—The Dana-Thomas House and Doug Carr, photographer, The Dana-Thomas Foundation)

FIGURE 4-31. Window openings without expressed lintels on the north side of the Susan Lawrence Dana Residence. (Courtesy The Illinois Historic Preservation Agency—The Dana-Thomas House and Doug Carr, photographer, The Dana-Thomas Foundation)

to Wright. Use of brick within its nature does not appear to have been the highest priority to Wright in his early work within the scope of this detailing. The random evidence of respect and disrespect for brick suggests that the detailing decisions were influenced by considerations other than the nature of the material with regard to strength.

Rowlock and soldier courses of brick occasionally serve as visual lintels, although, unlike false lintels of stone, cast stone, or other continuous strips, they cannot appear to be structural regardless of "span" length. Even when turned on edge or end, a brick is still a unit separated from other units by joints that interrupt the would-be structural integrity of the lintel-like band. The Francisco Terrace Apartments (1895), Waller Apartments (1895), and the Lamp House (1904) utilize such pseudolintels. Based on a criterion of literal honesty in material expression, rowlock and soldier courses are the most logical of the false lintels in that they refer to structure but cannot be mistaken as structural. Based on visual logic, however, any lintel of brick violates the spirit of masonry, to some degree, in that it causes the brick and mortar to appear to have a significant tensile strength that it does not have. The violation is abated slightly because the need for a lintel is acknowledged by the assembly.

Occasionally Wright used apparent lintels that are a part of a decorative system. This practice is compatible with his belief that ornament should be integral with design and the materials. The technique tends, however, to undermine the credibility of the assembly as a lintel. If it appears to be more decorative than structural, the brick above does not appear to have a solid place to set and would seem to span the opening itself. The white trim around the windows and entry of the Winslow House (1893) are of this type. Since the jamb and sill trim of the windows are the same thickness as the head trim, there is no sense of greater load on the head than

FIGURE 4-32. Prominent lintel expression at the Frederick C. Bogk Residence. Prominent copings and water table. (Courtesy The Frank Lloyd Wright Archives)

the sill. Without a load on the sill, it is difficult for the head trim to appear to carry the weight of the brick above. Such details are not necessarily incompatible with brick but introduce a vagueness that places the structural logic of the "supported" brick in question. A more convincing structural relationship between the parts of the trim would be for the head to have the greatest depth, the sill to have the least, and the jambs to have a width between the two extremes. The trim over the third-level windows at the Roloson Apartments (1894) is reasonably convincing as a visual support for the brick above, in spite of its faint joints. It is larger than the jamb and sill trim and appears to be superimposed on the trim system. The head trim is clearly a beamlike strip, although not clearly a beam. An intent to visually support the brick above it is apparent in the strip. The nature of brick is reasonably served, but the role of the band in the decorative system obscures slightly its actu-

FIGURE 4-33. Window openings framed with trim of equal thickness on all sides at the William H. Winslow Residence. Lapped brick yields textures at obtuse corners.

FIGURE 4-34. Stone trim refers to hidden lintels under brick in the interior of the Imperial Hotel. Repetitive patterns in stone. (Courtesy The Frank Lloyd Wright Archives)

al structural relationship to the brick. The question of whether or not the brick is carried by the apparent lintel is not clearly answered in the appearance of the detailing.

The extensive cut-stone trim on the brick of the Imperial Hotel (1914) occurs frequently where lintels or other structure is necessary. The repetitive patterns of the stone emphasize the unit-characteristic of the material, which undermines the continuity necessary to emulate a beam. These patterns, combined with the very long runs of the brick masses over openings and space, make the trim seem to hang from the brick instead of supporting it. The stone's ability to refer to the hidden structure is further diminished by its many applications unrelated to structure. The nature of brick strength is accommodated slightly more than if the stone were absent and only brick stretchers were in its place.

Brick was rarely placed over openings in Wright's later buildings. It was stacked, in most cases, directly on grade, without interruption from an opening, in its extension to the roof. Exceptions to the trend include the Mossberg House (1948), where small windows without expressed lintels appear in a field of brick on the main facade and the Olfelt House (1958), where—at the kitchen—brick passes over a tall opening without an expressed lintel.

Although highly compatible with the nature of brick, the segregation of solids and voids seems to be more of a stylistic idea than a materials idea to Wright. He favored "a simple, unbroken wall surface from foot to level of second story sill,"[21] but it was difficult to achieve because of the necessity of admitting light and air into the first floor. He admitted that, during an earlier period, he would frequently "gloat over the beautiful buildings [he] could build if only it were unnecessary to cut holes in them."[22] A distaste for holes is more likely his motivation for omitting openings from brick walls than is intention regarding the compressive integrity of the material. Because of the large number of one-story

FIGURE 4-35. Absence of expressed lintel in gallery fireplace at the Susan Lawrence Dana Residence. (Courtesy The Illinois Historic Preservation Agency—The Dana-Thomas House and Doug Carr, photographer, The Dana-Thomas Foundation)

houses, there was ample opportunity to avoid window "holes" in the brick of his latter work. Floor-to-roof and sill-to-roof glass is easily integrated into one-story walls and is spanned by the roof structure at the facade rather than by the wall material. Consequently brick abuts such windows but does not pass over them.

Wright's fireplaces often had brick over the opening of the firebox. Implications of the firebox lintel condition are the same as for exterior wall lintels. The nature of the brick above the fireplace (with regard to strength) is expressed by the presence of real or apparent lintels. The nature of the brick is violated by the absence of an expressed lintel, a circumstance that places the units in an apparent spanning mode foreign to the material.

The Heller (1896), Davenport (1901), Dana (1902), and Cheney (1903) houses have fireplaces without expressed lintels. Brick stretchers meet the top of the firebox in these and other examples. Greater consideration for the structural integrity of the brick above the hearth was demonstrated at the Robie (1906), Coonley (1906), Irving (1910), Balch (1911), and second F. Little (1913) houses where fireplaces have expressed lintels. Fireplace detailing in these two groups of buildings had no consistent relationship with the use of lintels on the exteriors of the buildings. The use of a lintel at a fireplace did not mean that exterior openings would be so detailed and vice-versa. The expression of lintels at any particular location was doubtless determined by criteria such as compositional goals rather than a consistent lintel policy. Fireplaces in the Hanna (1935) and A. Friedman (1956) houses have no expressed lintels. Brick stretchers serve in that capacity. During approximately

the same period, lintels appeared on fireplaces at the H. Johnson (1937), Zimmerman (1952), and Schultz (1957) houses. This era yielded fewer examples of brick passing over openings in exterior walls than in prior years.

In the 1930s projects, rowlock lintels appeared on a number of fireplaces including units at the Willey, Rebhuhn, Rosenbaum, Schwartz, and Sturges houses. This was followed by a repetition of the detail in 1940s houses such as Baird, Pope, Affleck, Walter, M. M. Smith, Bazett, and Mossberg. Many rowlock lintels appeared on fireplaces of the 1950s, including those of the Palmer, H. Price, Jr., and Olfelt houses. The rowlock detail would seem to be the compositionally ideal choice for Wright in an era when his brick was becoming more taut and sleek. In comparison to having no expressed lintel, the rowlocks diminished slightly the precarious image of the "supported" mass of stretchers above the firebox. On the other hand, being the same color and texture as adjacent brick, the rowlocks are not visually disruptive to the flow of the eye over the entire surface. Tautness, a condition not fostered by the spirit of brick, was thus enhanced by a detail in itself flawed with respect to the nature of the material. Expression of the nature of brick was not maximized, but unity and other compositional characteristics were served.

Although rowlocks dominated the later fireplace lintels, the chronological mixing of the various lintel options throughout Wright's career indicates some ambivalence about the importance of serving the structural nature of brick in a building element that has a vague relationship to building structure. That is to say, fireplaces in their most narrow definition are not typically allowed by code to act as building structure and, therefore, might not demand the strictest expressive structural discipline with regard to their material. Wright's large brick masses that contained fireboxes are often more than fireplaces, however. They are usually significant sections of his buildings in size, composition, and function.

Wright's early arched fireplaces and building entrances express the compressive nature of brick within and above the arch. The compressive integrity of the arch geometry is secured by adequate depth and buttressing. Wright's exaggerated arch depths appear to be able to accommodate any compressive stress flow patterns that do not exactly follow the semicircular curve of the arch. His entrance arches have adequate mass on both sides to resist the thrust of the loading that occurs if the arch is truly compressive. His fireplaces have less flanking brick but the great depth of the arches provide substantial mass between the intrados and the extreme edges of the fireplace mass at the floor line. Also, the relatively light loading from the brick above the firebox demands less flanking mass. The visual relationship

FIGURE 4-36. Arch supports mass and has buttressing at entry of Susan Lawrence Dana Residence. Taper of radial strips of brick continues across recessed arch at lower edge. Prominent copings and water table. Blocky piers and masses. (Courtesy The Illinois Historic Preservation Agency—The Dana-Thomas House and Doug Carr, photographer, The Dana-Thomas Foundation)

between load and buttressing is reasonable in these fireplaces. The structural integrity of Wright's building-arches provides the visual support necessary to maintain the brick above in a compressive state. No bending or tensile challenge to the supported masses seems possible, due to the apparent soundness of the arch supporting them. The brick above seems to have a stable support, thus relieving the units from having to perform in any structural way except compression.

A major exception to his normally structurally pure arches occurs at the Morris Gift Shop (1948). From the exterior the deep, multilayered arch at the entry conforms to expectations regarding buttressing and compression. A short distance into the entry foyer, however, half of the vault (extending inward from the facade arch) becomes glass. The loss of potential compressive resis-

tance in half of the vault renders the structural statement of the brick side essentially one of tension. The brick of the half-vault appears to cantilever from its base or hang from the ceiling (it is supported by a hidden steel structure above). While the exterior view projects an image securely within the structural nature of brick, the interior view violates the spirit of the material.

Wright's intermittent inattentiveness to the nature of brick usually occurred in details. Flagrant disregard for the strength limitations of the material at the large scale was rare. Two exceptions to this pattern occurred in his later work. A very long brick-clad balcony is suspended over the entry and much of the main facade of the Mossberg House (1948). The stretchers of its face meet the bottom edge of the mass without visible means of support. The proportions and compositional role of

FIGURE 4-37. Vault at entry of V. C. Morris Gift Shop shown to be half brick and half glass. Glass is bent in vault and cut on a curved line at door and sidelight. Curvilinear steel-framed and plastered ramp. (Courtesy The Frank Lloyd Wright Archives)

the balcony are reminiscent of the balcony in the main facade of the Robie House (1906). By comparison with the Mossberg balcony, the positive contribution to the nature of brick made by the stone trim along the bottom edge of the Robie version is clarified. The brick of the Robie balcony appears to be in considerably less

bending or tension because of the role of the stone trim as a pseudolintel. No such abatement of the visual stress in the Mossberg brick is present.

The brick-clad balcony that cantilevers beyond the end of the H. Price, Jr. House (1954) is even more challenging to the image of brick than the Mossberg example.

FIGURE 4-38. No lintel or support expressed for long cantilevered brick balcony at the Herman Mossberg Residence. (Courtesy The Frank Lloyd Wright Archives)

The length of the longer Price cantilever is magnified by the lack of a strong visual presence in several pipe-columns beyond which the balcony spans. With the near invisibility of the thin intermediate supports, the visually exaggerated cantilever of the brick becomes remarkable for any material. Unlike the Mossberg balcony, the observer can see under and beyond the Price balcony, as its long dimension extends to one side of the elevation rather being positioned in front and parallel to it. With the house as a backdrop, it is difficult to judge the magnitude of the Mossberg cantilever. The Price balcony is framed above, below, and around its extreme end by open air, thus clearly defining the curious structural achievement that appears to be solely one of brick.

The bottom edge of the Price balcony consists of the same brick stretchers as in the face. Some consistency in this regard can be observed inside the house, where a large mass of brick projects into the living room and is suspended high in the space. As in the balcony outside, the bottom edge of this "floating" brick consists of stretchers. The interior mass is high enough that a steel flange can be seen under this edge. Accidental as this seems to be, the expression of the flange abates slightly the visual "mystery" of the brick support. Adjacent to the stairwell, the Mossberg House also has "floating" brick masses with only stretchers for apparent lintels. The fireplaces of both houses have rowlock lintels, which is inconsistent with the stretchers along the bottom edges of other suspended brick in the projects. The

possibility of identifying a single policy in the works regarding the structural expression of suspended brick is thus rendered nil.

The terrace balcony at the Schultz House (1957) is somewhat similar to that of the H. Price, Jr. House in form but its detailing is remarkably accommodating to the spirit of brick strength. Cast stone trim borders the bottom (and the top) edges of the cantilevered form, thus acting as a visual support for the brick of the balcony face. The depth of the trim is far too small to be credible as the actual support, but its presence reflects the need for a support and the presence of a hidden structure for the brick. Since the brick has a place to set, it remains in a compressive mode that expresses its true structural nature. If the reference to the hidden structure made by the cast stone is not strong enough to eliminate a sense of violation to the masonry, it is the cast material that appears to have been violated rather than the brick.

In a third variation of a balcony terrace cantilevered from a brick building, the Greenberg House (1954) is the most reasonably expressive of its material. The material in this case is not brick, however. A concrete balcony, having face proportions similar to the balconies at the Schultz and H. Price, Jr. houses, cantilevers in structural harmony with its material, thus avoiding entirely the struggle to overcome or compensate for the nature of brick in the other two examples. The use of the concrete balcony here is especially significant, as the rest of

Figure 4-39. No lintel or support expressed for the cantilevered brick terrace beyond recessed steel columns at the Harold Price, Jr. Residence.

the house is brick. Wright's willingness to disrupt the brick character of the house with a rather obtrusive concrete balcony suggests a recognition of brick's limited structural potential. He was not consistent in this regard, however, as previously noted.

DURABILITY

Wright's observation that "...the material itself is admirable in quality..." and that along with other burned clay units, brick was "probably the most useful of all materials in building in our climate"[23] are references to durability. His attention was directed to the substance of units, with mortar joints essentially excluded from his judgment. Joints are neither mentioned nor implicated. Since, in the realm of weathering, the durabilities of both brick and mortar are most threatened by spalling caused by the expansion of freezing water, vulnerability to water penetration affects the measure of brick's durability. The greater probability of water penetration between brick and mortar than through the clay itself diminishes the durability level of assembled brick compared to that of a single unit. Demonstration of sensitivity to the nature of brick (meaning assembled brick) involves, then, recognition of the high durability of burned clay and the vulnerability of mortar joints. Although it is apparent that Wright's conclusions were meant to describe only individual units, there is no indication that he intended to distinguish between the durability of a brick and that of brick assembled with mortar. Wright's accommodation of the lower durability of mortar joints was greater in his work that was built before publication of his comment on the subject than after.

The significant resistance to water penetration inherent in burned clay is expressed by Wright's use of unpainted brick throughout his career. The practice did not elevate his apparent sensitivity to brick beyond the norm, and it is probable that aesthetic considerations rather than durability issues influenced his decision to leave brick exposed. Nevertheless, the long and consistent history of using bare brick on the exterior of his architecture imparts an image sympathetic to the nature of burned clay with regard to its durability. This treatment of brick indicates that Wright was at least as sensitive to this aspect of the nature of brick as are other architects. Greater insight may be gained into Wright's sensitivity to the durability of brick systems by examining his treatment of mortar joints.

Exposing standard (concave) mortar joints to the weather in vertical surfaces is compatible with the durability level of the joints. Although typically not perfectly watertight, such walls are generally adequate in this regard due to the high rate of drainage from their surfaces. Wright's frequent use of raked horizontal mortar joints in early as well as late work, however, challenges somewhat the durability level of the joints. Precipitation can collect on the small shelf that is left exposed by the raking out of some of the mortar. This places rainwater in prolonged contact with the top edges of the units as well as with the mortar, which typically contains intermittent failures of its bond to the masonry. Consequently, the raked detail increases the chances of deterioration from the freezing of water that has penetrated both the top edge of the brick and the bond failures in the joint.

The sense of violation to the durability of brick expressed by raked joints is not strong. The raked aspect of the joints has a relatively low visibility and the brick is usually dry when being viewed. Even when wet, the ramifications of the raked joint are not likely to be perceived by the casual observer. Consequently, insensitivity to the nature of brick durability is only mildly expressed by the detail. The durability issue is not pertinent to raked joints within the interior of a building.

Wright's treatment of mortar joints on the tops of walls is revealing about his materials attitude, as detailing with regard to durability is critical in that location. There, water is more threatening, because gravity tends to pull it into—instead of away from—the joints. Wright's propensity for terraces, balconies, enlarged chimney masses, and projected volumes and piers provided him with ample opportunity to address the tops of brick assemblies exposed to the weather. His willingness to extend numerous brick elements vertically and horizontally beyond the protection of the roof indicates some casualness toward the material's relationship to the elements, as detailing cannot equal the protection that the roof provides to the top of the brick. The resulting challenge to brick's durability is largely accommodated in his earlier, but not his later, work.

Prior to 1917 virtually all parapets, garden walls, balcony walls, and other brick not meeting a soffit is capped with stone or concrete copings. Although copings also have joints vulnerable to water penetration, there are typically fewer joints present than in the brick below. Protection both real and expressive is afforded to the brick. The Dana (1902), D. D. Martin (1903), Robie (1906), May (1908), and Bogk (1916) houses are among the many residences in which the role of the copings in establishing building character is particularly noticeable. Similar detailing occurred in nonresidential projects such as the Larkin Building (1903), E-Z Polish Factory (1905), and Midway Gardens (1913). The visual impact of the copings of the Larkin and E-Z Polish buildings is less intense than that of the smaller buildings because the greater height reduces the ratio of coping area to facade area. Most of these copings extend beyond the face of the brick, thus protecting the bed joint between the brick and the coping and also reducing the amount of water draining across the face of the wall. Because of their enlarged masses, shadow lines, and color that usually contrasts with the brick, these copings are highly visible. They express, consequently, a concern for the vulnerability of joints on the tops of brick walls and thus the nature of brick.

Flush copings such as at the Frank Lloyd Wright Home and Studio (1889, 1895) and the brick volume at the Gammage Auditorium (1959) express the nature of brick to a slightly lesser degree than the overhanging versions because of their reduced protection and visibility. Copings of relatively lower visibility do not offer less protection in every case but always express the nature of brick to a lesser degree. The limited contrast in color between the brick and the overhanging copings of the Heurtley House (1902) and the flush copings of the Gammage Auditorium element, for example, reduces their ability to express the nature of brick without reducing the actual protection provided. The presence of copings is visually subdued, which diminishes their importance. Consequently, the importance of the service they render to brick and, in turn, the importance of the property of brick (durability) that calls for their presence, are also diminished. To reduce the importance of brick properties in architectural expression is to demonstrate insensitivity to the nature of brick.

The water tables of Wright's early buildings provide a modicum of protection to wall materials beyond that available from a simple raised foundation. Their projection from the wall surface provides a slightly greater distance between the face of the wall and ground moisture, splashing rain, and melting snow than would a flush foundation of equal height. Where brick rests or appears to rest on a water table, it does not or does not appear

FIGURE 4-40. Prominent stone copings and water table at the Frederick C. Robie Residence.

to pass below grade. Thus, the visual contact of mortar joints to ground moisture is avoided. This issue is only critical when a basement is dependent upon the integrity of the joints for dryness. Some visual deterioration from the absorption of splashed muddy rainwater can be avoided if brick is elevated or the adjacent earth is covered by a water table. By themselves the contribution of water tables to the expression of the nature of brick would be minimal. They do not, however, appear by themselves in Wright's work.

Together, as they invariably appeared in Wright's early work, projected copings and water tables provide a "sandwich" of protection, real or expressed, to brick and its mortar joints. Although typical of virtually all of the brick work prior to 1917, the pairing of large copings and large water tables is most expressive of the nature of brick when they are close together. At the Robie House (1906), for example, a thick overhanging coping occurs only a few courses above a substantial water table in a low terrace wall adjacent to the public sidewalk in the main facade. This is complemented by a taller wall around a porch and other walls and masses in which the brick (specifically its joints) seems to be securely bracketed by protective caps above and below.

The Willey House (1934) marked an interruption to the pattern of large copings and water tables that had begun prior to the turn of the century. Flush copings occur at the Johnson's Wax Complex (1936), the H. Johnson House (1937), and the Morris Gift Shop (1948), and on the massive circular brick volume of the Gammage Auditorium (1959). Concrete and stone bases also occur at the H. Johnson House and the Morris Gift Shop. The coping and base combination does not have as significant a role in the character of Wright's brick buildings after the Allen House (1917), although the importance of the concrete coping of the Gammage Auditorium, colored a slightly lighter hue than the brick, is boosted by its association with the similar concrete trim framing the series of windows around the volume. Its similarity to the decorative window trim verifies its role as an element in the aesthetic order of the building, which makes the nature of its material more important to the architecture.

Rowlock brick copings and the direct contact of brick to grade were the dominant details in Wright's later work. Typical examples include the Hanna (1935), Walter (1945), Alsop (1948), and Laurent (1948), houses. Wright's later brick joints are generally less protected than his earlier brick joints. In this regard, the later detailing reflects the nature of brick to a lesser degree. The practical ramifications of this circumstance are revealed at such houses as the L. Lewis (1940) and Mossberg (1948) residences, where original rowlock copings were unable to perform as desired and were subsequently covered with sheet metal. The deterioration of rowlocks that were not covered with flashing is apparent at the L. Lewis House on a low band of brick along a walk. The addition of such flashing can also be found on other of Wright's later masonry buildings. An unusual return to large copings occurs at the Schultz House (1957), where cast stone covers the tops of brick constructions beyond the protection of the roof.

CONCLUSION

Wright's later brick work is characterized by fewer projected rectangular volumes and masses. It has more acute angles in brick and more mitered units. The later buildings require that brick pass over fewer openings, but when brick does occur above windows and doors, it appears to span in a way contrary to the nature of brick strength. The later examples are characterized by

reduced protection for the mortar joints compared to the earlier detailing. The detailing in the second half of his career is not entirely in violation of the nature of brick, but an item-by-item analysis reveals that it embodies the spirit of the material to a lesser degree than the earlier work. This conclusion is corroborated by the fact that the general image of the later work—taken as a whole—seems less bricklike than does his earlier architecture.

ENDNOTES

1. Wright, Frank Lloyd. 1928. "In the Cause of Architecture: V. The Meaning of Materials—The Kiln." *Architectural Record* 63(6):555–561. Reprint. 1975. *In the Cause of Architecture*, ed. Frederick Gutheim. New York: McGraw-Hill. p. 194. *ARCHITECTURAL RECORD*, (June/1928), copyright 1975 by McGraw-Hill, Inc. All rights reserved. Reproduced with the permission of the publisher.

2. Ibid. *ARCHITECTURAL RECORD*, (June/ 1928), copyright 1975 by McGraw-Hill, Inc. All rights reserved. Reproduced with the permission of the publisher.

3. Ibid., 190. *ARCHITECTURAL RECORD*, (June/1928), copyright 1975 by McGraw-Hill, Inc. All rights reserved. Reproduced with the permission of the publisher.

4. Ibid., 189. *ARCHITECTURAL RECORD*, (June/1928), copyright 1975 by McGraw-Hill, Inc. All rights reserved. Reproduced with the permission of the publisher.

5. Ibid., 190. *ARCHITECTURAL RECORD*, (June/1928), copyright 1975 by McGraw-Hill, Inc. All rights reserved. Reproduced with the permission of the publisher.

6. Ibid., 194. *ARCHITECTURAL RECORD*, (June/1928), copyright 1975 by McGraw-Hill, Inc. All rights reserved. Reproduced with the permission of the publisher.

7. Wright, Frank Lloyd. 1931. *Modern Architecture: Being the Kahn Lectures for 1930.* Reprint. 1987. ed. Bruce Brooks Pfeiffer. Carbondale and Edwardsville, IL: Southern Illinois University Press. Copyright 1987 by The Frank Lloyd Wright Foundation. p. 86. Courtesy The Frank Lloyd Wright Foundation.

8. Wright, Frank Lloyd. Frank Lloyd Wright Archives. Drawing #9305.16.

9. Wright, Frank Lloyd. 1928. "In the Cause of Architecture: V. The Meaning of Materials—The Kiln." *Architectural Record* 63(6):555–561. Reprint. 1975. *In the Cause of Architecture*, ed. Frederick Gutheim. New York: McGraw-Hill. p. 194. *ARCHITECTURAL RECORD*, (June/1928), copyright 1975 by McGraw-Hill, Inc. All rights reserved. Reproduced with the permission of the publisher.

10. Wright, Frank Lloyd. 1928. "In the Cause of Architecture: I. The Logic of the Plan." *Architectural Record* 63(1):49–57. Reprint. 1975. *In the Cause of Architecture*, ed. Frederick Gutheim. New York: McGraw-Hill. p. 155.

11. Holzhueter, John O. 1989. "Frank Lloyd Wright's Designs for Robert Lamp." *Wisconsin Magazine of History* 72(2):109.

12. Wright, Frank Lloyd. 1928. "In the Cause of Architecture: V. The Meaning of Materials—The Kiln." *Architectural Record* 63(6):555-561. Reprint. 1975. *In the Cause of Architecture*, ed. Frederick Gutheim. New York: McGraw-Hill. p. 194. *ARCHITECTURAL RECORD*, (June/1928), copyright 1975 by McGraw-Hill, Inc. All rights reserved. Reproduced with the permission of the publisher.

13. Wright, Frank Lloyd. The Frank Lloyd Wright Archives. Drawing #9901.02. Courtesy The Frank Lloyd Wright Archives.

14. Ibid., #4824.053.

15. Ibid., #3906.029.

16. Hoffmann, Donald. 1986. *Frank Lloyd Wright: Architecture and Nature*. New York: Dover Publications. p. 17.

17. Wright, Frank Lloyd. The Frank Lloyd Wright Archives. Drawing #4824.053.

18. Wright, Frank Lloyd. 1928. "In the Cause of Architecture: I. The Logic of the Plan." *Architectural Record* 63(1):49–57. Reprint. 1975. *In the Cause of Architecture*, ed. Frederick Gutheim. New York: McGraw-Hill. p. 154. *ARCHITECTURAL RECORD*, (January/1928), copyright 1975 by McGraw-Hill, Inc. All rights reserved. Reproduced with the permission of the publisher.

19. Wright, Frank Lloyd. 1931. *Modern Architecture: Being the Kahn Lectures for 1930*. Reprint. 1987. ed. Bruce Brooks Pfeiffer. Carbondale and Edwardsville, IL: Southern Illinois University Press. Copyright 1987 by The Frank Lloyd Wright Foundation. p. 71. Courtesy The Frank Lloyd Wright Foundation.

20. Ibid., 86.

21. Wright, Frank Lloyd. 1908. "In the Cause of Architecture." *Architectural Record* 23(3):155–221. Reprint. 1975. *In the Cause of Architecture*, ed. Frederick Gutheim. New York: McGraw-Hill. p. 58. *ARCHITECTURAL RECORD*, (March/1908), copyright 1975 by McGraw-Hill, Inc. All rights reserved. Reproduced with the permission of the publisher.

22. Ibid. *ARCHITECTURAL RECORD*, (March/1908), copyright 1975 by McGraw-Hill, Inc. All rights reserved. Reproduced with the permission of the publisher.

23. Wright, Frank Lloyd. 1928. "In the Cause of Architecture: V. The Meaning of Materials—The Kiln." *Architectural Record* 63(6):555–561. Reprint. 1975. *In the Cause of Architecture*, ed. Frederick gutheim. New York: McGraw-Hill. p. 194. *ARCHITECTURAL RECORD*, (June/1928), copyright 1975 by McGraw-Hill, Inc. All rights reserved. Reproduced with the permission of the publisher.

5

INTRODUCTION

Wright's observation that "in the pre-cast-block building, the method of building wholly determines the form and style"[1] was, compared to his similar comments on other materials, the most direct. His implication that the method of building relates to the nature of concrete block, renders the form and style of the building vulnerable to variations in definitions of the material. Wright defined materials by an integration of their beautiful characteristics with his larger architectural goals. Consequently, the nature of his block buildings is as much a function of design taste as of block building methods. This is not to say that his concrete block buildings are unrelated to the nature of block or its logical construction techniques. There are many relationships between his architecture and the nature of block. Although block's form was the most influential among its properties on building character, it does not appear to have governed where it was in conflict with Wright's larger design goals.

FORM

In the series of *Architectural Record* articles appearing in 1927 and 1928, Wright's placing of concrete block in his discussion of reinforced concrete instead of in its own article or with articles on stone and brick is revealing. It suggests that Wright saw block not as another type of masonry but as another way to deliver concrete. This attitude is further illustrated by his use in the concrete article of photographs showing only concrete block buildings (A. Millard, 1923; S. Freeman, 1924;

and Ennis, 1924) although examples of concrete buildings were available (Unity Temple, 1905; German Warehouse, 1915). Wright likened the image of concrete (in which he included concrete block) to certain aspects of stone, brick, tile, cast iron, and plaster but failed to expound the similar characteristics.[2] He did not acknowledge that concrete block is similar in size, form, strength, and durability to the other masonries. By ignoring certain parallels with brick and stone, his use of block remained free of their implications. Wright accepted the fact that concrete had the character of stone (presumed to mean hardness and durability) but did not suggest that it should share other aspects of stone's image.[3]

"A cast-block building," he thought, would have "such massing as is felt to be adequate to the sense of block and box,"[4] which indicates an acceptance of certain characteristics for block that are like those of brick and stone. Subsequently he referred vaguely to mass as a vehicle by which concrete block could be distinguished from terra-cotta, glass, or sheet metal,[5] reminiscent of his call for mass in brick construction. He rejected certain early concrete block as being degraded imitations.[6] This is taken, for the most part, as a reference to the units formed with lumpy faces to imitate stone, once popular for foundations and occasionally used for entire buildings. Ultimately, it is the plasticity of concrete, he observed, that is "distinguished from natural stone which has none at all."[7] The comparison is clearly logical for cast-in-place concrete, but Wright meant it to also describe concrete block. Concrete block was, he said, "a mere mechanical unit in a quiet plastic whole,"[8] thus acknowledging its sharing of plasticity with cast-in-place concrete. The "mechanical" concept was Wright's key distinction between concrete and concrete block. It refers to the "mechanical" repetition in the production of block and to the repetitive texture blocks yield in architecture.

Wright's embracing of concrete's plasticity at both the small and large scale was particularly significant in his development of a new kind of concrete block. He believed that the concrete could "be printed, 'goffered,' while fresh and wet" which "would be nearer to its nature, aesthetically, than"[9] other casting techniques. He thought impressed concrete patterns were reminiscent of those in stone from ancient leaves and other organic life. It was vaguely implied that the naturalness of the phenomenon in stone reflected favorably upon impressions in concrete block.

Brick is as mechanical (methodically produced, repetitive, and uniform) as block, although Wright did not refer to brick in this way. He favored plasticity in brick construction as he did generally for all of his materials. Brick is no less a mechanical and plastic material than the block he praised as such. Because of clear differences in size and color between standard brick and block, little effort is necessary to separate their identities in architecture. The similarity of certain stone to concrete block, however, requires precise exploitation of their differences to reflect their individual natures in architectural expression. Wright's several references to stone in conjunction with concrete and concrete block indicate that the overlap in images was of some concern to him. Wright seemed to want to maintain a separation in the images of block and stone.

Wright's most prolifically cut stone (Imperial Hotel, 1914; Yamamura House, 1918) was, like his impressed block (called textile block) of the 1923 and 1924 Los Angeles houses (A. Millard, Storer, Ennis, and S. Freeman), repetitive and geometrical in pattern. Repetition of face pattern and rectangularity of unit form occurred to some degree in the two stone examples, although the Imperial Hotel had a large variety of patterns and shapes, including masses, that were not multiples of a rectangle. In many respects, the cut stone resembled the concrete block of the four houses that would soon follow.

The greatest distinction between Wright's decorative stone and his impressed concrete units is a slightly higher sense of refinement in the stone. This may be attributed in some cases to more intricate patterns, in some cases to greater variety in pattern and form, and in general to the sharper edges of the stone relief. The difference in images between Wright's cut stone and concrete block is small. The fact that the decorative stonework meets, to a large degree, Wright's mechanical and plasticity-oriented criteria for concrete block does not indicate a deficiency in his ideal for cast units. It is the stone that has encroached on the realm of the block rather than vice-versa.

Concrete has a greater affinity for relief than does stone, since casting exploits substance tendencies whereas cutting overcomes them. This philosophical observation is compatible with the relative cost and skills required to produce patterns in the two materials in modern construction. The softness of the lava stone used in the Imperial Hotel and the relatively low cost of carving it (compared to the cost of similar carving today) compromise somewhat the reasoning that rejects the intricate cutting as being illogical. The issue is further confused by the fact that the apprehension of the owners over the use of such a soft stone proved to be well-founded, as it did not weather well. In other words, the decorative carving of the stone might be justified in this case by the same property that renders the material inappropriate for building. Sensitivity to the nature of both concrete block and stone is apparent in Wright's reluctance to produce, in subsequent stone, patterns as complex as in his concrete block. The rugged texture that

FIGURE 5-1. Concrete panels at the Midway Gardens. (Courtesy The Frank Lloyd Wright Archives)

dominated Wright's later stonework is not only highly compatible with the most basic methods of stone production (splitting, chipping, etc.) but it also clearly distinguishes the material from all concrete products, including the smooth-faced blocks that Wright commonly used.

Although in Wright's decorative block, image and substance are highly compatible, the history of his decorative masonry is not entirely materials-driven. Its evolution could be characterized as an aesthetic inspiration in search of a material. Nevertheless, the shift from stone to concrete as the vehicle for patterned masonry demonstrates a material sensitivity subsequently expressed in architecture at various levels of intensity by an assortment of design and detailing practices. Wright's patterned block expresses the nature of its substance to the degree that the pattern and other unit characteristics are emphasized in a building and to the degree that the aesthetic achievement of the architecture is dependent upon the block. Although the detailing of Wright's patterned block consistently produced a focus on unit form, slight distinctions are apparent among his works in this regard.

Numerous concrete elements appeared at the Midway Gardens (1913) in the form of structure, copings, sculptures, fascias, trim, bases, and decorative panels that resembled the decorative faces of the concrete units (textile block) that were to emerge ten years later. The role of the decorative panels at the Gardens was more limited than that of the textile block, and the units were more vague in their expression of form. Unlike the textile block—which define surfaces, corners, copings, bases, ceilings, terrace paving, window heads, jambs and sills, columns, beams and, in fact, entire buildings—the decorative panels of the Gardens provided only flat wall surfaces and vertical corners.

The walls and portions of walls clad in the decorative panels were bracketed above and below by concrete

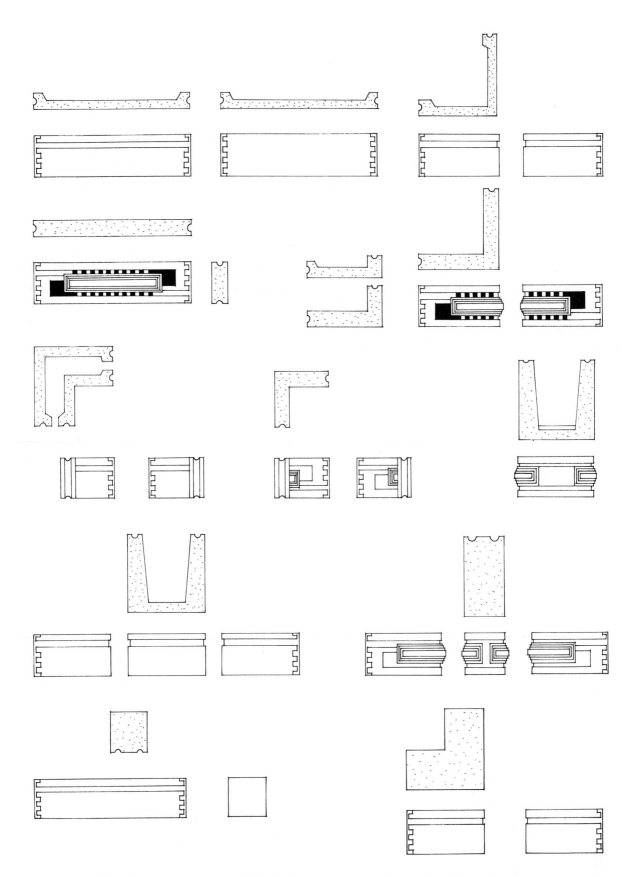

FIGURE 5-2. Details for standard concrete blocks dated 1939 proposed for use at Florida Southern College. Additional shapes were subsequently added. (From The Frank Lloyd Wright Archives drawing 3814.021.)

trim (copings and bases) and the units ran without change in pattern from trim to trim and corner to corner. The simpler format did not reveal the nature of an individual unit as clearly as did the textile units, however. Unlike the units of the A. Millard, S. Freeman, Ennis, and much of the Storer House, the patterns of the Midway Gardens panels crossed joint lines and contained jointlike lines that obscured the location of unit edges. Decorative units turned corners at the Gardens, thus providing the format that typically defines the mass of the material but, without certainty as to where one panel stopped and the next one began, the expression remained vague regarding this aspect of form.

Since repetition is usually the point of casting concrete units, the sense of greater repetition at the Gardens compared to the Los Angeles textile block houses is more aligned with the spirit of the process. Considering the variety suggested by the mixing of plain and decorative units in the Los Angeles houses and the use of more than one decorative pattern in some cases, the early textile block seems to be less standardized than the Midway Garden units. Although there was more than one face design in the panels at the Gardens, the use of each pattern in broad surfaces and/or long runs simplified their image and increased the sense of repetition of pattern and detailing. If "standardization *was* the soul of the machine…"[10] as Wright claimed, logic dictates that to maximize standardization is to maximize the spirit of the machine within the work. Although Wright promoted the machine as an appropriate influence in architecture, he also held the scope of its influence to be a matter of judgment. "Repetition carried beyond a certain point," he wrote, "has always taken the life of anything addressed to the living spirit."[11]

The variety in pattern and volumetric composition in the Los Angeles area block houses (1923–24), at the Florida Southern College campus (1938–54), and in the Usonian Automatic block house of the 1950s were achieved at some sacrifice of standardization. Over thirty molds were needed for each of the Los Angeles area houses[12] (more than forty for the S. Freeman),[13] while about the same number were initially planned to launch the campus project. The later Usonian Automatic block did not differ in this regard although it was a plainer unit. The Pappas House (1955) required 25 different molds[14] and the Turkel House (1955) had 37 different block types.[15] This indicates that at least one component of material essence (the repetitive nature of production) was compromised for artistic goals. The sense of compromise is not maximized, however, because the units as installed look far more repetitive than they actually are.

The complex profiles of the textile block as well as face patterns where they occurred made mechanized production of the units difficult. Consequently, the units were handmade involving a complex process of assembly and disassembly of the molds, tamping, vibration, curing, and stacking. The nature of the machine that Wright promoted for the production and expression of building materials was remote from the nature of his textile block. The same is true of his Usonian Automatic block, but since it was intended to be cast by the home owner, the point is moot in regard to machine spirit.

In his early textile block, Wright used plain units alongside the patterned units. The plain block, although not a standard of the industry in section or proportion, is similar in texture to ordinary block. The juxtaposition maintains the uniqueness of the patterned block by the contrast with the more standard-looking units. The impressibility of concrete is demonstrated (in the decorative units) without misrepresenting the face condition standard in the industry (expressed in the plain units). On the Florida campus, most of the blocks serving in the role of plain units are not entirely plain. They have a simple edge-pattern that contrasts with the more highly patterned units and thus together describe the range of surfaces of which concrete is capable. (Entirely plain units also appear on the campus in minor roles.)

Since adjacent units that look different define each other's edges, the mixing of plain and patterned faces also provided an opportunity to maximize the influence of the block's geometry, proportions, and size on the character of the surface. A link between the characteristics of units and the character of the facade constitutes a dependence of the architecture on the nature of materials. The intensity of Wright's block expression in this regard varies with the importance and clarity of unit characteristics in the surfaces. Unit clarity is maximized in checkerboard patterns (which are in limited use) at the Storer (1923) and S. Freeman (1924) houses. The edge definition of both decorative and plain units (alternating in both directions) is clarified by the contrasting surface texture of the adjacent blocks. In the Storer House, it is the plain units that are most clarified in these cases, as the adjacent patterned squares consist of two butted half-units. Thus, pairs of the narrow decorative units are clarified in some surfaces instead of single large square units. A few patterned blocks isolated in small fields of plain units at the S. Freeman House are clearly identified, as are alternating unit types in a series of columns.

Some loss of unit identity occurs in the early textile block houses when rows or stacks of similar units are juxtaposed against contrasting strips of block. One dimension of the units is clearly defined in the width of each strip, but the face dimension parallel to the axis of the band is subdued. The condition occurs throughout the Ennis House and is particularly prominent in the

FIGURE 5-3. Patterns of alternating decorative and plain blocks at the Samuel Freeman Residence. (Courtesy The Frank Lloyd Wright Archives)

south facade. The long strips of patterned block alternating with long runs of plain block produce a linear pattern that dominates the blockiness of the units to a degree that increases with viewing distance (because the visibility of joints diminishes faster than the visibility of the bands). This kind of identity loss is particularly counterproductive to expressing the nature of block, as the linear geometry is typical of certain other materials. Some 90 degree turns in one linear pattern are reminiscent of block geometry and thus pull the pattern somewhat away from the realm of linear materials and towards the rectangular nature of block. Less intense linear patterns occur at the S. Freeman House, where the strips are shorter.

Broad expanses of flush identical blocks define a blocklike surface character at some level of intensity, since ordinary joints tend to be recognizable, if not always strong in appearance. Architecture thus clad expresses the nature of its material without special detailing. The link of the expression to unit form, how-

ever, is only as strong as the individual identities of the blocks in the surfaces. Should unit identities be obscured (because of subdued joints, for example), the nature of the surface approaches that of concrete, stucco, or other more seamless materials. Wright's unique treatment of the joints in his decorative block reflects a sense of artistic intent typically absent from standard joints dominated by overtones of practicality, economy, and tradition. Consequently, the ramifications of his joint detailing can be evaluated for indications of sensitivity toward material form.

In textile block projects following the A. Millard House, Wright eliminated visible mortar from the joints by placing units in direct contact with each other and secured them with horizontal and vertical steel and grout in grooves on the edges of the units.[16] Consequently, the traditional three-eighths inch mortar joints with their concave surfaces and shadow lines are not present to provide their usual definition of unit perimeters. The visibility of the line of contact between flush units with no mortar would normally be dependent on irregularities in materials and workmanship. Such detailing (which can be found in certain places on the Florida Southern College campus) would not indicate a strong desire to integrate unit form into the character of the wall.

Given the relatively low visibility of flush mortarless joints, it is significant that the block of the Storer, Ennis, and S. Freeman houses and the plain units of his Usonian Automatic block system have reveals on their edges, as do the blocks of the Arizona Biltmore Hotel (1927). When stacked in tight direct contact, each block is framed by grooves and their shadows (no mortar is visible). The edge-reveals supplement decorative face patterns in establishing individual block identities and are virtually the sole method of identifying units for block with plain surfaces. The potentially materials-insensitive omission of visible mortar was countered by the creation of the edge-reveal, the use of which indicates a high level of sensitivity to material form because of its ability to define unit shape. Although the reveals are no more efficient in defining block form than raked mortar joints, their integral nature and greater permanency signify a slightly stronger commitment to the visual significance of unit form.

In addition to a loss of identity for physical reasons, individual units in a field of identical block also suffer a loss of artistic importance. Such units, unlike those forming facade patterns with contrasting units, lack special compositional roles dependent upon their individual characteristics. Since individual form characteristics are a major factor in distinguishing materials from each other, the loss of artistic importance signifies a loss in importance of material nature to the architecture. Con-

FIGURE 5-4. Linear patterns created in walls by alternating courses decorative and plain units at the Charles Ennis Residence. (Courtesy The Frank Lloyd Wright Archives)

sequently, broad expanses of identical block express the nature of the material at a less intense level than where the aesthetic order is more dependent on the form of individual units.

Although none of Wright's buildings are covered entirely by patterned units, they all include expanses of identical block. With one major exception and some minor variations, units maintain some level of individual identity by virtue of their patterns, which are complete within a single block. The faces of certain 8-inch by 16-inch units of the Storer House show three rectangular projections forming a pattern that has an inherent sense of neither completeness nor incompleteness. When stacked with similar blocks, the patterns join to form a continuous vertical series of small rectangles similar to widely spaced brick headers. The vertical identity of the blocks stacked in this way at the edges of the liv-

ing room fireplace is dependent upon the joints, as any three "headers" could constitute a single block. The horizontal joints have difficulty overcoming the visual continuity of the "headers" in order to fix the positions of blocks within the total pattern.

In a wall by the living room, these units are paired and alternated with plain blocks in a checkerboard format. What appears to be several 16-inch square patterns, each resembling three "stretchers" or "soldiers" (various units are rotated 90 degrees), are actually pairs of blocks with their header-shapes butted. Some unit vagueness results, since each 16-inch module (the standard textile block size in these houses) represents a pair of blocks instead of a single unit.

A similar phenomenon occurs in the block of the Arizona Biltmore Hotel (1927). Wright's role as a consultant on the project rather than as the architect of

FIGURE 5-5 No mortar in reveal at block joints of the John D. Storer Residence. One block face shown resembles three brick headers. (Courtesy The Frank Lloyd Wright Archives)

FIGURE 5-7. Horizontal grooves in every other block and dentil-like impressions at ends of every block at the Florida Southern College E. T. Roux Library.

FIGURE 5-6 One concentric pattern between two halves of concentric patterns created by certain orientations of four blocks at the Arizona Biltmore Hotel.

record minimizes the certainty with which significance may be assigned to its characteristics. His claim that his contribution was apparent in the appearance of the building[17] suggests that he had extensive influence on the design. In any case, it can be observed that the block patterns, although seeming to be complete within a single unit, also form complete patterns when pairs of units are inverted and joined with other pairs. Unit identity is further obscured in a field of blocks thus oriented, since the large concentric patterns that result are centered on the intersection of the joints between the four blocks and cover only half of each block. The other halves of the blocks form parts of adjacent concentric patterns. In other words, a single concentric pattern occurs on the adjacent halves of four blocks. Although one concentric pattern requires four blocks, the approximate number of units present in a field is the number of patterns divided by two, not four. Many surfaces have patterns created by pairs of blocks rather than groups of four, thus obscuring slightly less the expression of material form. The misrepresentation of the number, size, and location of blocks does not seriously divert the essential materials message. The sense of repetition and relative smallness of component imparted by the surface is within the boundaries of block spirit, if not at its center.

The pattern on the faces of the Biltmore units is the most plastic of the textile blocks, given the absence of right angles in its elevation and section. The patterns that preceded and followed are essentially rectangles and squares. The Midway Gardens panels and the S. Freeman units are minor exceptions, having some diagonal markings. Although the rectangular patterns reflect the essence of block geometry, they fail to emphasize the uniqueness of concrete's plasticity among masonry substances. In their emphasis of plasticity, however, the Biltmore units fail to acknowledge the rectangular nature of masonry. None of Wright's patterns simultaneously express to the maximum both aspects of concrete block.

While the patterns in the Florida Southern College block tend to identify individual units with some certainty, a curious shift of identity occurs in the plainer units there. A series of small square face-impressions at the ends of the plainer block (a kind of vertical strip of reverse-dentils) identify, with unusual clearness, the ends of the units and the vertical joints. The joints would otherwise have remained somewhat obscure as they are the mortarless type, with unit edges in direct contact with each other. A horizontal groove near the top of each unit appears to be a joint while the actual horizontal joints are flush. Any broad surface of the blocks (which occur periodically on the campus) shows a strong rectangular pattern reflecting the actual number and size of blocks. In a casual observation, the flush, tight, horizontal joints cannot overcome the greater visual strength of the grooves, so that the block positions appear to be a couple of inches lower than the actual positions. What seems to be one block is actually parts of two blocks.

On a wall of the Roux Library (1941), courses of blocks without the horizontal grooves are alternated with courses having the groove. The detail doubles the distance between horizontal grooves, thus changing the apparent proportion of each block by doubling its expressed height. The expressed identity of the units is a couple of inches lower than the actual position of the paired blocks, thus further obscuring the actual condition. In the strictest sense, reality is misrepresented, but the general nature of the block is not ignored. It is doubtful that the detail reflects specific materials goals rather than general artistic intent. Nevertheless, it constitutes a greater manipulation of the properties of block for a particular visual impact than the mismatch between pattern perimeters and unit perimeters at the Arizona Biltmore. The visibility of the joints, albeit low, seem to give the mismatch at the campus greater materials meaning than the mismatch at the hotel. The hotel condition seems incidental to nonmaterial goals while the slightness of the effect at the campus reflects a greater focus on the nature of block form.

The block at the Florida campus differs from that of the four California houses in ways related to the nature of the material. The 16-inch square units of the houses seem a little less stable than the 36-inch long by 9-inch high blocks (a common proportion among several unit designs) at the campus. If the special corner blocks that, in—both cases—give the illusion of very thick units are taken at face value, neither proportion seems fragile or unstable. The cubelike image of the house units seems somewhat more massive than the slablike (oriented horizontally) image of the college blocks. In both block types, some sense of unit thickness is emphasized by glazed and unglazed holes through the block. The holes in the square block tend to be slots of various configurations including small squares. The rectangular block has two sizes of openings, both of which are essentially square.

The smaller of the two hole sizes in the campus units emphasize the sense of mass in the block because of their size. A significant amount of concrete (in comparison to the hole dimension) surrounds each of these openings. Although the larger holes actually show depth in the block more clearly, the concrete omitted to create

them noticeably reduces the solid area of the face. The colored glass in some units such as at the Pfeiffer Chapel (1938) emphasizes the effect of the holes on the block image by drawing attention to them. The narrowness of the slots in the block of the houses, on the other hand, obscures somewhat, the depth they could have revealed if they were wider. In addition, the complexity of their shapes and patterns contribute to a visual and physical delicacy in the units.

Wright's most unblocklike units are found the on the Roux Library (1941). A long curved facade is divided into three horizontal bands, the upper two of which project several inches forward of the surface directly below each. Transitions are made between the offset bands by single courses of special concrete blocks. The elevation of each of these blocks is similar in pattern to the standard decorative units on the campus but the section is not. In the face pattern is a central rectangular mass framed with a series of holes. A series of small holes occurs above and below the central form and a large hole occurs at each end. Around the perimeter of the holes is a frame of concrete. The central rectangular mass is connected to the outer frame with segments of concrete passing between the small holes. Although the pattern can be described as a collection of parts, the block is actually a single entity produced in one casting.

The top of a block's outer frame is flush with the wall segment above, while the bottom of the frame is flush with the wall segment below. The transition between the two offset parts of the frame is made in the sides of each frame by six small corbeled steps. The vertical face of the central rectangular mass is aligned with the upper part of the block; thus it projects several inches forward of the lower edge of the unit. The mass of the block, already reduced by its holes, approaches fragility in the loss of unity between the frame and the central rectangular volume. The transitional blocks seem to consist of two elements with only the central form maintaining a blocklike mass. The mass of the relatively thin frame is further diminished by the stepping of its sides, which not only introduces a structural precariousness into the concrete but reduces the scale of the concrete by subdividing it into smaller segments or steps.

The central volume of each block maintains a blocky image but appears to hang from the upper part of the concrete frame, introducing a sense of tension into the unit. This aspect denies the compressive nature of concrete block and imparts an additional sense of delicacy into the image as the parts of the units seem to be on the verge of separating. The fragility established within the unit itself is magnified by the appearance that heavy sections of wall rest on the units. Visual tension is established in the elevation, which compounds the contradiction of the detailing with the spirit of the material.

FIGURE 5-8. Block in course acting as transition between offset wall surfaces at the Florida Southern College E.T. Roux Library.

FIGURE 5-9. Columns of the Mrs. George M. Millard Residence are half the width of standard wall units and have a different face pattern. Half-units serve as copings. House has blocky proportions and character. (Courtesy The Frank Lloyd Wright Archives)

The walls of the Florida campus buildings consist, for the most part, of block in fields of like face-patterns. This format contrasts with that of the Los Angeles area houses which, in addition to expanses of repetitive units, also have surface patterns of juxtaposed contrasting units as previously described. In this respect, the character of the earlier facades are dependent to a greater degree on unit form than is that of the later projects. Some loss, over time, of material sensitivity is indicated by the change in detailing. A similar change in the use of projections in elevations and surfaces is also apparent when comparing the two groups of buildings. Facades of the Florida campus have a significantly greater degree of flushness of mass and units than do the four California houses. The projection of individual units and groups of units forward of each other generates, in addition to a focus on the blocks themselves, numerous corners. The format enhances unit identity and emphasizes material mass and geometry. Consequently, the intensity of material form as a component of architectural expression is greater at the houses than at the campus. The contrast in treatments of two-dimensional patterns in the walls of the two groups is thus repeated in three-dimensional patterns with similar consequences in material sensitivity.

Like their two-dimensional counterparts, the three-dimensional block patterns express various intensities of compatibility with the nature of concrete block form. The faces of columns exposed in the facades at the S. Freeman and Ennis houses are one block wide and express clearly the width of a standard block. At the A. Millard House they are half the width of a standard unit. Those of the Storer House show paired half-blocks with a vertical joint on the column centerline; thus a standard block width is defined but not by single units. The

height of each block is obscured slightly in the Ennis columns as it always is when multiple units abut. Two patterns alternate in the Storer columns, clearly defining unit height.

The spirit of blockiness is subdued somewhat by the linearity of the stacks of units, which is strongest in the tallest columns. Although the two-story columns in the Storer facades and the Ennis living room are clearly linear, the thinner columns at the A. Millard House are even more so. A particularly intense linear image occurs in a pair of three-story columns framed by glass on the east elevation. Only slightly less strong is the linear statement of a series of six columns on the west. Since the top halves of these two-story columns are integral with a concrete block wall, the strength of their linear statement is tempered by their reduced visual definition there. One-story columns occur in an Ennis facade and in other houses. Although more linear than a single block, they are short enough to yield an image of considerable mass and are not as remote from the spirit of block as are their taller counterparts.

Given the square face shape and large size of the early textile units combined with Wright's tendency to set elements of the facade forward and back from each other, the four Los Angeles houses tend to be generally blocky and massive in character. Some are more so than others; certain details at the S. Freeman House detract from this quality slightly. Joints that occur on corners there tend to render the image of the units less massive

FIGURE 5-10. Columns at the John D. Storer Residence are composed of paired half-blocks that alternate vertically in face pattern. Half-units serve as copings. Cantilevered canopies express no support for block edges. (Courtesy The Frank Lloyd Wright Archives)

than they appear in the other houses, as their thickness is brought into question. The reasoning observer would doubtless imagine that the units do have some thickness that diminishes toward the corner in the form of a miter. Even this realistic perception leaves the block with a sense of edge-sharpness that is not a characteristic of mass. Rare nonright-angled corners that also have joints on their vertexes occur at the S. Freeman House. They do not diminish the sense of mass to the degree of the "mitered" right-angled corners but do dilute the sense of blockiness in the material.

Among the houses that are all compositions of juxtaposed and layered masses, the Ennis House has the greatest sense of volumetric massing and detailing. Volumes of various sizes project forward and back of each other and are stacked on and beside each other. Balconies, fascias, and bases project forward of wall surfaces. Windows are trimmed by projected rows of blocks that are linear in certain segments but turn right-angled corners and are intermittently interrupted by abutting single, double, or multiple units emphasizing blockiness. In addition to the presence of large and small blocklike

volumes, numerous right-angled corners are produced by the detailing that permeates the image with a sense of blocky mass.

The textural character of the Ennis House is derived almost entirely from the basic form of concrete units. Although all Wright's block buildings reflect the spirit of unit form to some degree, the strength of the relationship between the basic block form and the architectural expression at the Ennis House is equaled only at the Arizona Biltmore Hotel. The angularity in the plans on the Florida campus and the general flushness of the units renders those buildings considerably less reflective of the spirit of block form than are the early houses. Although obtuse corners increase mass at the vertex and express the plasticity of concrete, right angles define the basic geometry of concrete block masonry.

The elements of the A. Millard House interior have a particularly blocky quality. The wall by the living room fireplace steps back revealing four vertical corners, thus reinforcing several times the character of right-angled blocks. Two courses of patterned units step forward of the face of the balcony above the fireplace to create a

Figure 5-11. Smooth obtuse corners at the Samuel Freeman Residence. (Courtesy The Frank Lloyd Wright Archives)

horizontal version of the wall detail. Both the vertical and horizontal stepped masses are somewhat linear in a direction perpendicular to the stepped surface. The boundaries of the interior space prevent observation of the details from a distance great enough to obscure the joints. The joints help maintain a blockiness in the massing to a greater degree than in linear elements of the exterior for this reason.

Wright built about 60 buildings of concrete block or with major elements of block. Nearly a quarter of the buildings are of textile block (secured with steel and grout in grooved edges) that combine both patterned and plain faces and another fifteen percent are of textile block with mostly plain faces. About an eighth are Usonian Automatic units (designed to be cast and assembled by the home owner[18]) with two-foot by one-foot plain and coffered surfaces and are secured with steel as are the textile units. Nearly half are essentially standard concrete block. Categorizing the houses by the nature of block texture indicates that a quarter of the buildings are dominated by patterned units. The rest are composed mainly (but not entirely) of plain-faced blocks with exposure of the coffered side of certain blocks. Enough coffered faces are exposed in the otherwise

plain-faced Usonian Automatic group to significantly affect the images of those houses.

A kind of transitional textile block was used between the well-known version in Los Angeles of the early 1920s and the Usonian Automatics of the 1950s. Predominately plain-faced textile blocks were used at the Kalamazoo (Winn, 1948; Levin; 1948; McCartney, 1949; E. Brown, 1950) and Galesburg (Weisblatt, 1948; Eppstein, 1948; Pratt, 1948) developments The block was much like the later Usonian Automatic units except in proportion. Some decorative faces were included.

The dependence of building character on material form tends to be less when units are plain, relatively small, flush, set in running bond, or have horizontal joints emphasized and vertical joints subdued. Unit form tends to be of least consequence in Wright's standard concrete block of the 1950s and is particularly incidental in such houses as the Sweeton (1950), Brandes (1952), and Lindholm (1952) which, among others, have many of the characteristics that subdue the block in the building image. Horizontal bands created by hiding the head joints and emphasizing the bed joints such as in the Penfield House (1952) give the facades linear overtones that further pull the image away from the basic geometry of block. Linear bands are also generated by battered walls at a number of buildings including the Brandes (1952), Fawcett (1954), and Ablin (1958) houses and in the pairs of courses reverse-battered (or corbeled) at the A. Adelman House (1948).

Unlike Wright's mixtures of plain and decorative block, patterns created by special arrangements of units were not common in his plain block houses. A rare example of units set in a decorative pattern occurs in the R. L. Wright House (1953). Concrete blocks were periodically omitted for glazing in such a way as to create a blocky configuration of windows the size of a single unit or a multiple of units. Consequently, the blocks between the windows are emphasized, bringing attention to their size and shape. A similar pattern occurs in a terrace wall where omitted units leave voids that define the shape and size of the remaining as well as the missing block.

The same decade that produced weak unit-form expressions in several houses of standard concrete block also yielded the stronger form statements of the Usonian Automatic series. These blocks are larger than the standard, which helps them achieve prominence in the facade. The grid of joint-lines in the stack-bond format of this system brings a greater focus to the rectangularity of the units than would a running bond in which the vertical joints are not continuous. The beveled edges of these units when butted with others frame each block face with a deep groove and shadow line.

Exposure of coffered faces on the fascias and on occasional surfaces in the Usonian Automatics such as in

Figure 5-12. Juxtaposed masses and numerous corners at the Charles Ennis Residence. Glass corner visible at upper right. (Courtesy The Frank Lloyd Wright Archives)

FIGURE 5-13. Numerous vertical and horizontal block corners at stepped surfaces inside the Mrs. George M. (Alice) Millard Residence. Half-units serve as pseudolintel over openings. (Courtesy The Frank Lloyd Wright Archives)

the entry and living room of the Tonkens House (1955) and in the kitchen and gallery and by the entry and car-port of the Kalil House (1955), also helps establish block form as an important component of the building images. The two concentric rectangular shapes in each block echo the geometry of the units. The patterns are not as expressive of concrete's plasticity as are the early textile blocks nor are they placed, like the early block, in patterns that draw attention to unit form by their artistry. The coffered units cover small surfaces in their entirety; the simplicity and boldness effectively boost the blockiness of the architectural expression.

The perforated and glazed Usonian Automatic units, in contrast to perforated patterned textile blocks, are simple and bold. The rectangular opening of each block is set in a thick concrete frame. The thick propor-tions of the units clearly separate them from steel- or wood-framed glazing. Unlike their more delicate perfo-

rated textile-unit counterparts, the glazed Automatic units contribute mass as well as rectangularity to the col-lective statement of the masonry construction.

The periodic substitution of an operable metal sash for a glazed concrete unit in broad expanses of glazed block at the Kalil House disrupts the continuity of the vertical and horizontal lines of the unit-sized concrete frames. The somewhat visually jarring pattern thus cre-ated contributes to the blocky appearance of the walls by preventing the stack bond of glazed units from develop-ing a strong linear quality that would result from long series of aligned frames. Close examination reveals that many of the metal sashes in the large wall of the living room are set in diagonal series of various lengths, but the general sense of their placement is one of random-ness. This aspect is less reflective of the nature of block systems than would be a more rectangular pattern. A methodical placement of metal sash occurs in broad

FIGURE 5-14. Steel rods protrude from various vertical joints of double wythe walls during construction of the Robert Levin Residence. Coffered backs of blocks are visible as are decorative blocks at right center and right rear. Loose corner block on ground at left. (Courtesy The Frank Lloyd Wright Archives)

expanses of glazed block at the Tonkens House, but because the sash is equal in size to two blocks instead of one (thus forming a square), it draws more attention to itself than to the blockiness of the concrete units.

Although the character of the Usonian Automatic houses reflects the form of block to a noticeable degree, it does not achieve the level of expression at the four Los Angeles textile block houses of 1923 and 1924. The major aspect tempering the relative blockiness of the Usonian Automatics is their fewer number of juxtaposed blocky masses and the presence of their roof overhangs. The blocky fascias of the Automatic overhangs contribute more to the blockiness of the image than do the wood fascias of other concrete block houses, but the overhang itself obscures the top edges of the concrete block volume below. This forces the facade to depend on its vertical corners to establish a sense of blocky mass. These corners are usually too few in number and too far

apart to do so. The relatively lower expression of blockiness in the buildings on the Florida campus compared to the early houses may be also attributed, in part, to the effect of their roof overhangs.

The 1923 and 1924 houses expose most of the top edges of the block masses and have more corners by virtue of the presence of multiple projections of smaller volumes in the facades. Although blocky volumes could be constructed of any material, they reflect most intensely the spirit of masonry units and bring a strong sense of block into the building image when they are present. Regardless of the various intensities of blockiness in the detailing of the Usonian Automatics, they are second only to the Los Angeles textile block houses in their expression of the nature of concrete block with regard to form.

The predominantly plain-faced textile block houses (mostly of the 1940s) have images generally less related to the form of their block than do the Usonian

FIGURE 5-15. Raked horizontal joints and flush pointed vertical joints in concrete block of Louis Penfield Residence. (Courtesy The Frank Lloyd Wright Archives)

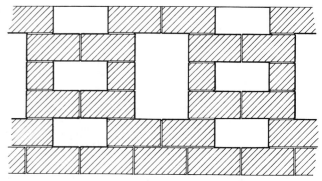

FIGURE 5-16. Partial elevation of block grille with glazed openings at the Robert Llewellyn Wright Residence. (From a photograph, *Frank Lloyd Wright Selected Houses,* vol. 7, p. 146.)

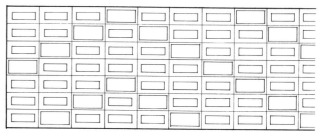

FIGURE 5-17. Partial interior elevation of glazed block and windows of Toufic Kalil Residence living room. (From a photograph, *Frank Lloyd Wright Selected Houses,* vol. 8, p. 178.)

Automatics. The difference is not large and is due in some cases to conditions peripheral to the detailing of the block themselves. Massing that does not juxtapose rectangular volumes of various heights, sloped roofs, and wood fascias tends to pull the character of certain buildings away from blockiness. Unlike the Usonian Automatics, these conditions are common among the variety of compositional strategies in these late textile block examples. The Levin (1948), McCartney (1949), and E. Brown (1950) houses have images relatively more remote from the influence of concrete block than others in this group. Their overhanging roofs and the continuity of the wood fascias subdue the sense of block in ways previously outlined. The fact that the roofs are pitched makes them more dominant in the character of the building by virtue of their high visibility and special geometry, which renders the portion of the aesthetic order attributed to the block relatively smaller.

Pitched roofs do not reinforce any sense of geometry established by the block in these examples. The absence of a visual or functional link between the block and the major visual element of the roof further separates the image of the architecture from the nature of the material. The long and seemingly smooth facades of the houses could as well be wood, brick, or other material with minimal change to the building image. In the textile block houses of midcentury, the units tend to occur below and between glazing which, especially in one-story masses, serves to diminish the sense of mass in the buildings. The planes of block juxtaposed with the planes of glass seem thin compared to the earlier versions where more block formed corners. The block becomes almost an opaque version of the glass. In the late textile block houses, the solid blocks were set beside the glazing; in the Usonian Automatics, the solid blocks are integrated with the glazing because of the characteristics they share with the glazed units. In the late textile block buildings, the block is one of several aspects in the building character. In the Usonian Automatics, the block is the building character.

Variations of these circumstances occur in some of the plain-faced textile block houses. The wood fascia of the Pratt House (1948) does not oppose the sense

FIGURE 5-18. Sloped roof with large overhangs in major visual role at the Robert Levin Residence. Concrete block in modest visual role. Stepped surface of glazed wall is just apparent. (Courtesy The Frank Lloyd Wright Archives)

FIGURE 5-19. Piers of stacked single blocks at the Richard Lloyd-Jones Residence. Decorative half-units as 'lintels' and copings. (Courtesy The Frank Lloyd Wright Archives)

of blockiness in the building to the degree found in other examples because of its large depth and relatively short roof overhang that provide some visual mass. These characteristics allow the roof to define the top of the block volume below it in a way sympathetic to its

character. The flat nature of the roof and the fact that it has more than one level is important in this regard as well. A two-story block mass at the Winn House (1948) with tall "punched" windows and no fascia is particularly blocky in itself. The large curved and glazed volume

FIGURE 5-20. Elevation of interior grille blocks at the Richard Lloyd-Jones Residence. Thin lines in center are metal. (From Frank Lloyd Wright Archives drawing 2902.029.)

FIGURE 5-21. Projecting concrete block at obtuse corners of the Wyoming Valley Grammar School. Smooth obtuse corners on chimney.

cantilevered from the block mass, however, competes with the blocky expression of the house because of its roof overhang and sense of lightness. The stack bond of these textile block houses helps maintain their sense of blockiness at a higher level that in many of the standard block houses having units in a running bond.

The R. Lloyd-Jones House (1929), a plain textile block example, is a composition of large rectangular volumes. Most of their facades, however, are highly linear, being composed block columns separated with equally wide strips of glass. The result is a strong pattern of vertical stripes. Some relief from the linearity is found in the interior where various assemblies of blocks have broader proportions. In a detail that varies from the more common flush surfaces in the house, the living room fireplace wall steps back in eight segments of stacked units. The wall has a somewhat blocky appearance from the eight right-angled corners in its surface, but the stacks of block are themselves linear in the vertical direction.

Most of the units in the building are plain. Narrow decorative units (half the height of the plain block) form linear strips as they trim elements of living room and form cornices on exterior walls. The decorative units are restrained in pattern but reflect some sense of plasticity in their substance. Particularly delicate-looking grille blocks are also used. The slender elements of the patterns in the grille block do not have the mass natural to masonry. Many appear on the corners of interior columns, which detracts from the otherwise compressive sense of the thick one-story columns. This structural incompatibility is particularly noticeable where an open, instead of solid, part of the grille occurs on a corner.

Compared to the earlier textile block houses, the R. Lloyd-Jones design is significantly less expressive of the form of concrete block. The strong linear geometry of the many columns competes with the visibility of the joints to dominate the image. Beveled edges on the units indicate an intent for the joints (and therefore, the block form) to have a visual role. The stacked bond pattern brings some focus to block's rectangularity but few solid block surfaces in the exterior have broad enough areas for the pattern to dominate the surfaces. As viewing distance to the facades increases, the visibility of the joints diminishes and linearity becomes more dominant. Inside, given the shorter columns and the closer proximity of the observer to the units, the sense of block is stronger.

The detailing of the R. Lloyd-Jones block falls below the expression of material form found in the Florida campus buildings which followed ten years later. The frequent expression of the large unit depth at the R. Lloyd-Jones House (such as at the many deeply recessed glass-strip windows) gives the masonry a greater sense of mass than on the Florida campus. The rectangular geometry of the R. Lloyd-Jones House also favors the sense of blockiness over certain more delicate block variations on the campus. Unit proportions play a larger role in the surfaces of the Florida buildings, however, as does the plasticity of the substance reflected in the patterns on individual block faces. Although the walls on the campus do not emphasize unit form in the blocky relief of the early Los Angeles Houses, neither do they have the linearity of the R. Lloyd-Jones project to detract from the geometry of each unit.

Although patterned block appeared in Wright's work throughout his career, a majority of his block buildings were built predominantly of plain-faced units. Plain units are within the nature of block, but they fail to demonstrate the uniqueness of their substance among masonries. Consequently, plain units are expressive of the nature of their material at an intensity lower than the maximum possible. The Usonian Automatic houses expose a smaller percent of coffered—compared to plain block—faces than the percent of decorative block used on the Florida Southern College campus. Nevertheless, the Automatics compete successfully with the campus buildings for second place after the Los Angeles textile block in the hierarchy of block form expression in Wright's architecture.

With the exception of the late appearance of the Usonian Automatic houses, the relationship between the form of concrete masonry and building character steadily diminished after the initial strong examples in Los Angeles. Although the downward trend seems to be, in part, budget-driven, it is pertinent that Wright was designing large-budget buildings simultaneously with the lower-budget block houses in the latter part of his career. To omit concrete block from the large projects is a design- rather than a budget-based decision. It would seem that Wright's need to explore the more expressive applications of special block had been fulfilled, leaving its more modest uses still to be developed.

The Usonian Automatic houses share with the first textile block houses a characteristic that seems to explain the revival of concrete block's influence on building character late in the chronology of block use. The two sets of houses were built with new systems devised by Wright (although the second was related to the first). With Wright's focus on original ideas, it is reasonable to conclude that each of the new ideas drew from him an attention to the material that waned in the first case once the potential of the new concept had been explored and might have eventually subsided in the second case had his career continued for a longer period. New ideas in other materials seemed to compete more effectively for Wright's attention than did concrete block, which became more commonplace with each project until the Usonian Automatic concept emerged.

The Automatic system did not reverse the diminishing presence of block form in his architecture. Wright continued his trend of ambivalence to the form of block in standard-block detailing during the Usonian Automatic period and, in fact, beyond the last Automatic house constructed. A minor variation in the detailing trend of commercial block did occur in the Wyoming Valley Grammar School (1957). At obtuse corners of the school building, units with eight-inch square faces project slightly forward of the wall plane in each course on alternate sides of the corners as they close the gap created by the right-angled stretchers that meet there at an obtuse angle. The detail provides a blockiness to the obtuse corners that they would not have had if the stretchers in each course had been cut to meet in a smooth vertical joint on the corner.

The blocky texture of the projected units ties the expression of the facade to the general nature of concrete block form, although not to its common two-to-

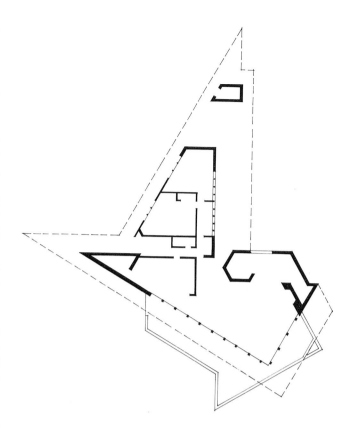

FIGURE 5-22. Floor plan of Ward McCartney Residence showing acute- and obtuse-angled corners in concrete block. (From Frank Lloyd Wright Archives drawing 4912.003.)

one face proportion. The expression is somewhat artificial compared to Wright's more direct solution of lapping bricks at obtuse corners. On the other hand, the sense of purposeful manipulation of material properties apparent in the school detail suggests a sensitivity to the material. Utilitarian links between materials and architecture lose effectiveness when they appear to be entirely casual or without artistic intent. Links based on an artistic intent lose effectiveness when practical sacrifices that are necessary for the achievement appear to be excessive. The obtuse corners of the Wyoming Valley School require no practical sacrifice that is greater than that necessary to produce smooth obtuse corners. Consequently, they express the nature of concrete block to a moderately high degree. The obtuse angles on the central chimney do not have projected block, thus weakening slightly the sense that the projected detail is an element in a comprehensive strategy for the aesthetic order of the building.

Rectangular buildings are naturally compatible with the nature of concrete block form, although their detailing has considerable influence on whether or not the nature of block is emphasized or subdued. Buildings

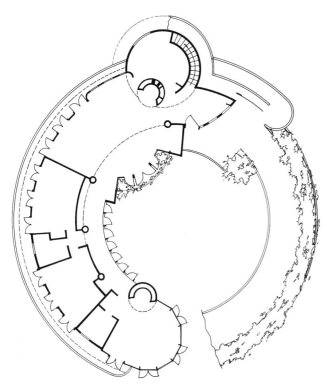

Figure 5-23. Floor plan of David Wright Residence showing long and short radius curves in concrete block. (From Frank Lloyd Wright Archives drawing 5030.012.)

that have other geometries are even more dependent on their detailing to determine the degree of harmony between building and material. A high potential for incompatibility is present when the geometries of the two do not match. In addition to the blocky masses and other rectangular volumes of buildings previously addressed, Wright's block buildings include angular geometries as well as curves. His acute-angled plans contribute the least among his designs to the spirit of block.

Acute-angled block at the McCartney (1949), Thaxton (1954), Fawcett (1954), Stromquist (1958), and other houses project a sharp and fragile sense unlike the mass and sturdiness otherwise associated with the material. The nature of concrete block with regard to its mass was overcome, in part, in the production these houses. In contrast, the obtuse angles in the block of the Davis House (1950) contributes to a sense of mass, if not blockiness, both in the overall building image and the corners, as they do in other buildings with similar geometry. Wright's use of concrete block in buildings with nonrectangular shapes indicates that the influence of building form on his choice of material was limited.

The failure of the obtuse and acute angles in Wright's work to express the rectangularity of basic block form is the result of a design decision. To build nonright-angled forms in a right-angled material under-

mines the spirit of the material in the building image in a general way but also provides the opportunity to express the rectangularity of block in the mismatch by its contrast with the larger scale geometry. That is, at corners, the rectangular block could overlap and project beyond the adjacent angled surface—as does much of Wright's early brick at obtuse corners. Since Wright typically did not overlap the block at acute or obtuse corners, the nature of block tends to be subdued in his angular plans.

Curved geometry is more compatible with the nature of block than obtuse angles in certain ways but has the major disadvantage of lacking the blockiness that corners can provide to some small degree even if they are not right angles. Any straight material can approximate a curve if the radius is long enough. Building facades, especially in houses, are too small to form an apparent curve with straight lumber of average length laid horizontally. That is to say, if the radius was long enough for the long pieces of wood to turn only slightly at their butted ends, a significant sense of curving could not be established within the length available in the wall. Should the long boards turn noticeably at their butted ends so as to form tangents on a curve of smaller radius, a polygonal rather than a curved surface would be generated.

Consequently, when wood is called upon to form a curve with its long axis laid horizontally, it is usually bent or cut. In the bending or cutting of the wood, the basic form property of straightness is physically overcome. When curves are simulated in a material of small dimension such as masonry, however, it is not necessary to physically overcome the basic property of straightness in the units. If the radius is long relative to the length of the masonry unit, an apparent smooth curve can be generated by straight units. Compared to the wood example, the relationship between the nature of material and the building geometry is reduced from being both a physical and philosophical mismatch to being only partially a philosophical mismatch. The contradiction is only partial because the curve, although it does not express the straightness of masonry, does express the relatively smallness of masonry units. A comparison of wood and block expression in this regard can be made at the R. L. Wright House (1953), which juxtaposes broad surfaces of each material on long-radius curves. The workability of wood and the smallness of block are both expressed at an expense to the basic geometry of each.

If the radius is too short relative to the length of the unit, the misalignment of unit faces becomes abrupt enough to produce a texture in the surface. Wright used unusually long-radius curves at such houses as the Winn (1948), David Wright (1950), Pearce (1951), and Rayward (1955) and thus avoided the textural problem.

As in many other cases where massing and detailing are compatible with certain materials, the long curves seem to be generated by general design inspiration rather than material needs. This conclusion is further supported by Wright's common use of block in curves with radii too small to form smooth surfaces. Both abrupt and gentle curves often occur in the same buildings. The random compatibilities and incompatibilities of the block with the building forms render unlikely the possibility of a strong relationship between material form and the architecture. Regardless of the motivation for the long curves of the previous examples, the result is architecture that accommodates the nature of concrete block with regard to its size and form.

Like the textured obtuse corners created by uncut brick, a curve textured by block edges could be seen as an expression of the blockiness of the material. Such a texture purposely created would reduce to large degree the philosophical mismatch between curvilinear geometry and the straightness of standard block. Without sense of intent in the detailing, however, such a texture reads simply as a failed attempt to force the nature of block into a mode foreign to it. Wright's textured-block curves do not have a sense of purpose about them. This is evident from the absence of additional detailing that would supplement the message of blockiness in the tight curves (i.e., exaggerating the texture), in the long curves (producing a texture when it was not necessary), and in straight walls (emulating the texture of the curves).

Curved fireplaces are particularly problematic in concrete block in that the radius of a typical fireplace is too small to generate the smooth surface that is usually desired. In lieu of a number of possible reconciliations between form of material and form of surface, recognition of the mismatch is usually limited to the use of half-units or headers at the fireplace instead of the longer block or stretchers used elsewhere in the building. The shorter block does abate the intensity of the texture that would have occurred with longer block and does affect the image of the fireplaces with its square shape. The nature of the material is, therefore, partially linked to the construction but expresses a sensitivity to material form that is limited by convenience.

One of the more unfortunate results of this circumstance occurs at the Meyer House (1950), where the bold texture and enlarged joints of the block on the curved fireplace border on crudeness. Although failures in craftsmanship bridge most detailing philosophies in their universal visual effect, it should be recognized that if blame is to be assigned for the rough result here, it is the mismatch of material nature and architectural form that is at fault. An unusually strong texture also occurs on a reverse-battered and curved wall of the house, where the ragged shadow lines under each course

emphasize the fact that the radius is too short (or the units are too long). None of these textures are presented as being desirable or purposeful by complementary detailing.

In contrast, the texture on the face of the curved fireplace at the David Wright House (1950), is brought under control by the battering of its surface. As each course steps back from the one below, the corners of the block recede from the faces of the units which they would have otherwise overhung. The dominant characteristic becomes the stepped profile of the batter in lieu of the accidental texture of flat units in a curved surface. Only the slightly enlarged vertical joints of the block reflect the mismatch of material and fireplace form. The battering of other curved walls in the building subdue their textures in the same way. At only the tops of the tapered chimneys, where the radius is very small, is the lack of attention to material form noticeable.

The philosophical contradiction of forming curves with straight block is limited somewhat by the simplicity that characterizes most of these walls in Wright's work. An exception occurs at the Lykes House (1959). The complex juxtaposition of cylindrical masses of varying radii establishes a potential for an image of plastic continuity in the block. Should the visual flow of the surface be contained within each volume as a separate phenomenon, their individual identities as stable drums of blocks could maintain a reasonably strong connection between the nature of the material and the architecture. The tendency of the masses at the Lykes House to merge into a single visual statement, however, is facilitated by the unifying effect of the prominent and long sinuous balcony. The resulting image is not that of an assembly of small blocky units. The continuity of the surface is exacerbated by the long distance from which the public typically views the building. The joints—the main characteristic upon which the identity of the material depends—are barely visible. An accidental expression of blockiness occurs at the fireplace where, as is typical of these elements, a texture is created by the corners of the flat block set in a radius too small for their size. A similar texture occurs on the exterior facade of the round storage unit at the carport.

A rare use of curved block occurs at the David Wright House in the columns within the house and on the ends of elongated piers exposed under the upper level of the building. In these cases, a new issue replaces the difficult challenge of reconciling flat block and curved surfaces. The compatibility of the curved faces with the nature of concrete block is affected by the particular characteristics of the special units, their role in the aesthetic order of the building, and the nature of concrete as a substance. The units are sympathetic to the nature

FIGURE 5-24. Numerous blocks cut to form obtuse corners at the Richard Davis Residence. Steel lintel visible at lower left. (Courtesy The Frank Lloyd Wright Archives)

casting them in a mold rather than cutting them from larger masses of concrete. Cutting is thus considered to be less in the nature of the material than is casting. This reasoning contrasts with the circumstance of wood, wherein cutting is the basis of production and is, therefore, as compatible with its nature as any kind of processing can be. Cutting does facilitate repetition in block production in an indirect way, as it eliminates the need for molds that would be used only a few times. The requirement for large numbers of molds for Wright's various custom block systems, however, reveals that maximizing repetition was not a priority to him.

Wright's early textile block houses, most of his textile block houses at Kalamazoo and Galesburg, his Usonian Automatic block houses, and much of his standard block construction are characterized by rectangular geometry. Although special sizes of rectangular units are required among these projects, the working of block to solve acute and obtuse corners is avoided in the majority of his block buildings. The presence of nonright-angled geometries in several block houses, however, reveal Wright's willingness to subjugate the form of block in pursuit of goals that have a higher priority than did maintaining the integrity of basic material form. The fact that cutting standard block at the Davis House (1950) was motivated by the angular geometry of the building, provides some basis for the violation of block rectangularity even though it is not absolutely necessary to cut the units.

Since the H. Price, Sr. House (1954) is rectangular, the motivation for some cutting of block in the project lacks the clarity of need as that in the Davis House. The battering and reverse-battering of walls there requires that courses of block have small differences in total length that typically cannot be accommodated by standard-length units in every case. Wright solved this problem in the tall battered masses of the Ennis House by using progressively shorter units on the face of the walls as the elevation increased. The result is a pasted-on appearance for the Ennis units that lacks the integral sense that he promoted for all elements of his design. His most material-sensitive solution occurs in the battered columns between the garage doors at the Lindholm Service Station (1957), where he used combinations of different size standard blocks to create the stepped faces.

More significant in the Price example is the detailing at the tops of wall ends and corners where the use of standard units would have exposed the void in the block. To solve these details, block was mitered in some places and cut, in at least one case, into a complex configuration wherein a triangular wedge fit into a triangular void in the unit. The interior nature of the cut into the unit, the high precision required, and the sharp and

of the substance in their compactness, perhaps even more so than standard units that are actually more fragile at their corners. Also, the curved faces of the special block reflects the plasticity of the substance.

The nature of their production is essentially the same as standard units except in terms of quantity, where they fall short of the maximized repetition is ideal for cast products, especially those generated by mechanized processes. The degree to which their use in the building acknowledges their special character is a measure of material sensitivity. They are not presented as the standard for concrete block but are used in special circumstances and have a radius small enough to facilitate their recognition as being special block. They are used alongside standard block so that their special form is emphasized by comparison. All things considered, their use is within the spirit of concrete block with the exception that they do not express the blockiness of the material or reveal its mass, both conditions resulting from the absence of building corners.

WORKABILITY

Cutting overcomes a block's properties; casting accommodates the nature of its substance. It is significant, in this regard, that the standard process of making units is

FIGURE 5-25. Battered concrete block walls in foreground on left and right and in background, center at the Harold Price, Sr. Residence. Corbeled concrete block at far right. Raked horizontal joints, flush vertical joints.

fragile edges produced push the cut beyond the normal workability of concrete block. Without the presence of angular geometry (as at the Davis House) or some other profound architectural concept to encourage sophisticated and difficult cutting, its presence testifies to the readiness of Wright to disregard simultaneously the nature of the material in two realms (form and workability). Around the entry drive and parking area of the H. Price, Sr. House, retaining and other walls on the site have obtuse and acute angles formed by the cutting of units. The violation of block's workability in producing the highly acute corners is apparent in the mortar patching that attempts to replace the pieces that have broken away from the sharp block, due to its inability to initially assume and maintain the shape. The battering of the courses exacerbates (by greater exposure) the expressive failure of the detail that signifies a mismatch between design and the material's nature.

Although certain detailing strategies do not require it, the ancient and contemporary tradition of cutting brick and stone at the extrados of an arch secures that extent of working as being within the nature of those masonries. Concrete block does not have such a tradition but since it is a type of masonry, a similar tolerance for working the product is justified. If a distinction is to be made between the difficulty of working reinforced concrete and the relative ease of working concrete block, some cutting of block must be accepted as being within its nature. Since the smallness of brick facilitates cutting and since the cutting is a standard process in stone production, block is deemed to be slightly less workable than those masonries.

The cutting of block is minimized in Wright's work. This is illustrated by the enlarged vertical joints in curved surfaces as at the Meyer House (1950) and David Wright chimneys and fireplace (1950). They are caused by setting blocks on a small radius. Cutting each block into a wedge (in plan) would reduce the width of the vertical joints as would reducing their depth in the wall. Tightening or otherwise obscuring the vertical joint is a detail for which Wright has shown preference in standard block of flat surfaces, so tolerating a wide joint in curved block surfaces suggests some reluctance to cut the units. Such reluctance is likely to have been driven by economics, a factor related to the nature of the material in this case—as it often is.

Decorative cutting reflects directly on one's willingness to work block, since it is not motivated by utilitarian needs that might supersede a preference to avoid cutting. Wright may not have considered the ornamental working of block to be integral with the material, to have expressive potential, or to be adequately economical. In any case, the fact that he did not cut concrete block for purely decorative uses reflects on his attitude towards the workability of the material. Wright's reluctance to work block in this realm balances somewhat his routine cutting of the material to solve problems created by building geometry. Although he also cast special block shapes that would eliminate the need for cutting, he typically did so where all the units were of his design and were cast specially for the building. Wright used special detailing to avoid cutting brick more often than he did for block. Given the greater awkwardness of cutting block, his sensitivity to the nature of concrete block

Figure 5-26. Concrete unit wedge fit into V-shaped pocket cut into top end of block in low wall at the Harold Price, Sr. Residence.

with regard to its workability is thus shown to be less than that for brick.

Strength

It could be argued that Wright's textile block, having integral light reinforcement, is structurally more similar to reinforced concrete than to unreinforced masonry. In practice, however, any flexural strength of the textile block system that approaches that of reinforced concrete does not occur by virtue of the system's standard network of steel grouted in the grooves on unit edges. Structural spans were achieved by adding reinforcing steel to the cavity between wythes in the same way that steel can be hidden in brick or stone construction to achieve similar results. The grid of thin steel rods in the joints of the textile and Usonian Automatic systems is essentially a system of lateral stabilization rather than

span. Consequently, it is logical to evaluate the expression of textile block and Usonian Automatic block with regard to its structural expression by the same criteria appropriate for standard block construction.

To accept the contribution of the steel network in these systems as an integral part of the block image is to treat the block as a composite material. It is a composite in the sense of traditional concrete block construction, which includes metal ties and wire joint reinforcement to help the assembly act as a unit. The metal components hidden in standard concrete block increase the safety factor and affect the expression of the construction through the stabilization they provide. They do not give the block significant structural span capability. Since the sectional area of steel provided by the textile and Usonian Automatic "pencil rods" falls between that of reinforcing steel and wire devices, it is reasonable to accept some level of expression in the custom block (other than flexural strength) that varies from the norm established by standard block.

As a practical matter, less variation from the norm can be tolerated in a visual analysis of the custom block than it might technically warrant, because it has the general appearance of unreinforced block. Because the stack bond used in the textile and automatic systems is necessary to provide continuity in the vertical joints, it is integral to them but unnecessary in standard commercial block. The custom systems are distinguished, consequently, from any commercial block set in a running bond. The common use of the stack bond in standard unreinforced block, however, undermines the ability of the pattern to signify with certainty the presence of steel. The special proportions and decorative patterns of the custom systems can signify their composite nature only to the historically informed. The absence of the typical textile-block steel network in the A. Millard House (1923) and, to a lesser degree, the existence of commercial block with patterned faces make difficult the identification of consistent relationships between block style and the presence or absence of hidden steel.

As reasoning becomes more convoluted, fine distinctions in structural expression that are justified by variations in the block appearance diminish in certainty and usefulness. Consequently, the structural expression of the textile and Usonian Automatic block is analyzed (with minor exceptions) as what they appear to be: unreinforced concrete block. As with any masonry expressions of compression where they are found in any of Wright's block work reflect sensitivity to the nature of block strength. Compression is the stress that concrete block most readily resists and is the stress traditionally associated with masonry. Regardless of the type of block, demonstrations in Wright's work of apparent flexural strength (or pure tensile ability) where one or more joints fall within a span violate the spirit of strength inherent in the material.

In another category of structural performance, some concessions may be made to the composite nature of Wright's textile and Usonian Automatic block. Because of the network of steel integral to Wright's custom systems, the blocks are obliged to have fewer overt signs of stability compared to standard block. Generally, visual as well as physical stability is necessary to maintain a sense of permanent compression in standard block. Some of the least visually stable of Wright's various block types occur in the large window-walls of several Usonian Automatic houses. Much of the glazing in the houses is provided by glazed block—essentially block-sized concrete frames with fixed glass inserts. Although the concrete frames express the relative mass of their substance by being thicker than the adjacent metal window frames, they lack the mass of the solid units. They seem adequately massive and therefore stable when isolated or in small groups. When they are stacked to tall heights and broad widths, however, their sense of stability diminishes.

Being the largest, the two-story glazed block walls of the Turkel House (1955) living room are the most precarious of the examples. This level of questionable stability is followed by that of broad single-story expanses at the B. Adelman (1951) and Kalil (1955) houses. The glazed units have less mass than their solid counterparts and, unlike solid block—which conceals actual wall thickness—the glazing reveals the relative thinness of the assembly. If the hidden steel network is to be allowed any expressive contribution, acceptance of these otherwise visually fragile window-walls is the logical concession to its presence.

The fact that the glazed units in the tall window-walls of the Turkel House are equal in size to two units (two feet square) instead of a single unit further diminishes the mass of the assembly. The additional loss of mass caused by doubling the size of the glazing without increasing the thickness of the frame produces a sense of linearity in the assembly. The vertical and horizontal parts of the concrete frames aligned and juxtaposed with the glass panels resemble wood mullions and muntins. Although this opposes the blockiness of masonry, it also directly reflects the linear grid of reinforcing steel embedded in the concrete frames. It is as close as Wright comes to a composite expression in any material, including concrete.

Glazed corner block is a highly visible feature in the Usonian Automatic houses. Mitered glass in each block turns the corner with the concrete frame. The frame, therefore, forms a double cantilever over the glass from its ends toward the corner. The presence of glass eliminates compression at the corners which has traditionally served to physically and visually stabilize construction.

FIGURE 5-27. Two-story glazing block under construction at the Dorothy Turkel Residence. Top and bottom sides of corner block cantilever toward corner. Steel protrudes out of each vertical joint. (Courtesy The Frank Lloyd Wright Archives)

Unlike a tall strip of mitered glass, which—if placed at a corner—would simply define the edges of the adjacent block, glazed corner block acts as a kind of reverse quoin projecting a sense of compression proposed but denied. The glazed corner units of the Walton House (1956) are relatively long and thus more remote from the image of compression than the shorter versions at the Usonian Automatic houses. The use of the slender corner units in relatively few numbers, however, limits their influence on the image of the house.

The denial of compression in the glazed corner units is acute when they are paired in every course to form columns. The contrast between the traditional compressive role of columns and the presence of glass, which undermines that role, emphasizes the mismatch between the glazed units and the nature of the material with regard to strength. Where series of such columns occur in projects such as the Tonkens (1955), Pappas

Figure 5-28. Blocks of different thicknesses used in each course of large masses for battered effect at the Charles Ennis Residence. Apparent unassisted "spans" of block of various lengths over openings and open space. (Courtesy The Frank Lloyd Wright Archives)

(1955), and Tracy (1955) houses, the image dominates the elevation. In the columns at the Tonkens carport glazed corner units alternate with solid blocks, thus exacerbating with added weight the apparent challenge to the glazed block.

The generally stable images of the four Los Angeles textile block houses of 1923 and 1924 are particularly expressive of the compressiveness of block masonry. The strongest sense of overall stability (and, therefore, compressiveness) at the large scale occurs at the Ennis House, where some walls are battered with small setbacks in each course and others battered with a few large sections, each set back from the one below by one block width (16 inches) or more. The result is a composition of many block masses that are wider at their bases than at the top of the building. The strong compressiveness of the image is reminiscent of that found in ancient ziggaruts and pyramids.

The compressive sense of the A. Millard House is generated by slightly different characteristics. The plan is compact and the volumes of the composition are relatively cubelike, especially in the west facade. Like the Ennis House, the absence of roof overhangs emphasizes the blockiness of the building. Cubes are inherently stable but no more so than volumes that are wider and shorter. Cubes have the advantage over shorter and wider forms of seeming to impose greater weight on each square inch of its footprint. Consequently, the combination of mass and stability produces a highly compressive image in the A. Millard House.

The block of the early Los Angeles houses is not compressive at the small scale, however. In the four houses (A. Millard, Storer, Ennis, S. Freeman), the block is treated like reinforced concrete in its numerous spans of multiple units over windows, doors, and open space. The image of butted units appearing to adhere to each other so as to span the openings is as visually unsettling as it is for standard block, brick, or stone in similar details. Unlike brick or stone under which a steel flange is sometimes apparent, the textile block houses show only block in the lintel-soffits, thus securing in every respect their flexural image. Contrast with the compressive spirit of block is maximized at lintels that in no way, recognize their special circumstance. The S. Freeman House sets, without celebration, some textile block over glass or space. A minimal reference to the peculiar structural condition occurs at the blocks serving as visual lintels at the A. Millard and the Storer houses in that they are eight-inch high units compared to the 16-inch high wall block immediately above. The contrast of the two types of block is minimized, however, by the face pattern of the units at the lintel, which is identical to the top half of the wall block. The eight-inch high block at the lintel, would have become a significant reference to the special flexural condition and the hidden steel that served the span if, instead of its face patterns, it had plain surfaces to contrast to a greater degree with the decorative wall units.

The strongest references among the early textile block houses to the special nature of the of the flexural strength imparted to block by hidden steel occur at the Ennis House. At most of the major openings the lintel block and jamb block project forward of the wall surface in linear strips. The projected detailing of the lintel block that contrasts with detailing of the flush wall block reflects the special use of the units in a flexural format. The compressive jamb block, having the same projected detailing, might be expected to dilute the reference to flexure in the lintel block but does not. It joins the lintel block in a single framelike expression that, as a whole, refers to the need for a support for the wall block above the windows. The positive contribution of the framelike detailing toward maintaining the compressive integrity of the wall above is made more clear by the absence of such "frames" in the corner windows of the south facade. The "bending" of the projected pseudolintel around the cantilevered corners above the glass, combined with the absence of projected jamb block to support the ends of the lintels, produces a hanging sensation in the whole mass.

The extensive use of block in the horizontal structure of the Ennis House interior generates an environment generally in violation of the compressive spirit of the material. This sense is abated somewhat by the occasional use of patterned block in lintel-like courses that appear to support plain block above. The tensile circumstance of the concrete block ceilings and soffits at the Ennis House are particularly challenging to the compressive nature of the material. The violation is exacerbated by the fact that a course of blocks often occurs at the edges of dropped ceilings, thus assuring the observer that the ceiling surface is masonry and not some thinner finish. A similar ceiling occurs in part of the dining room of the Storer House, the ceilings of which are otherwise dominated by wood beams. The block fascias of the overhanging roofs at the Storer House are particularly remote from the compressiveness of masonry. Their suspended condition is, however, so structurally vague as to slightly abate their violation of the compressiveness natural to concrete block.

Battering in a number of the later block houses visually stabilizes the walls in every case, but only in the larger volumes does this phenomenon combine with the mass to produce a significantly elevated sense of compression. The two-story drumlike volumes at the David Wright House (1950), for example, are particularly compressive by virtue of their mass and extreme sense of stability afforded by the battering and the self-buttressing aspect of the circular form. The battering is achieved in the single-wythe walls by offsetting each course of block towards the interior. Consequently, the interior surface is reverse-battered and the vertical axis of the wall leans inward. This economical technique does not capture the true spirit of battering, in which the wall is thicker at the base than at the top and wherein the interior surface is either vertical or also battered. In the circular form, however, this kind of battering does actually increase stability since any movement inward induces compression in the curve.

The apparent structural purity of the largest battered drum dominates the David Wright House only in the view from the entrance court. Nearly all other aspects of the building draw the expression away from the structural nature of block. Most of the second floor volumes are cantilevered from the circular drums and several one-story piers. The broad vista under the second story gives the house a somewhat light and airy sense. A ramp with a block rail is cantilevered from the large battered drum as it spirals up and around the mass. These conditions are counterproductive with regard to the expression of the block's massiveness and compressiveness.

The cantilevered concrete slab on which the ramp block and the block of the second story rest is implied under the units, thus providing the block with a limited visual support. Attention is drawn to this cantilevered base by the pattern of the decorative blocks at the edge, thus establishing a format that could reasonably maintain the compressive spirit of the block above. The pattern, however, is a repetitive one that reflects the spirit of periodic units rather than structural continuity. The potentially pure structural expression appears to be only a reference to the need for a material with flexural strength. The structural sense of the entire project is compromised by the detail. A nonrepetitive pattern at edges of the slabs would have avoided the structural vagueness and moved this major part of the block expression closer to the nature of the material with regard to strength.

Battering occurs in the two-story drumlike volume on the north side of the R. L. Wright House (1953). The circular mass housing the kitchen and a bathroom above contributes a sense of compression to the block in the ways similar to the battered drumlike form at the

Figure 5-29. Single- and double-block spans at openings of the Samuel Freeman Residence. Alternating courses of decorative and plain block. Stepped facade. (Courtesy The Frank Lloyd Wright Archives)

feet of block over the entrance without an apparent lintel, which somewhat undermines the compressiveness of the facade. In general, the R. L. Wright House reflects a stronger sense of compression in its block than does the David Wright House.

The sense of leaning in a straight, battered, single-wythe wall typically does not affect the image of Wright's buildings. When viewed from outside, it appears to be especially stable; when viewed from inside, its reverse batter or corbel is steep enough to avoid alarm. This fact, combined with the limited viewing distances and visual obstructions (furniture, partitions) common in building interiors, obscures the effect of the walls within the interior. Only the section that is not accessible to view seems unstable. Consequently, straight battered walls, like their curved counterparts, tend to stabilize the image of block regardless of the actual nature of the wall section. Walls that, in the exterior view, are reverse-battered are a different matter, since they can generally be viewed as a whole. The destabilizing impact of their configuration is related to their size as measured from top to bottom and between any buttressing elements in the facade.

Battered straight walls at the Davis (1950), Thaxton (1954), and Fawcett (1954) houses lend a sense of stability to the block in the exterior view as does the limited height of their structures. The compressiveness of the images is enhanced by the absence of large openings through the block. Most of the glazing occurs between block walls or between block and the roof. While increasing stability the relatively low heights of the block also temper the sense of compressiveness, as the implied weight on the footprint is limited. This effect is especially noticeable at the Davis House, where much of the block reaches only the height of the window sills.

A different approach to battering was taken at the Lindholm Service Station (1957), where bands of several flush block set back from the group below to create large tall steps each several blocks high. The visual stabilizing effect of the profile is nearly as strong as that achieved by offsetting individual courses of block from each other. The major difference is the change in scale caused by the larger steps and the greater viewing distance from which the steps of the surface maintain their identities. Individual battered courses tend to blend together at a distance to so as to appear to be a smooth leaning surface. Structurally, the two types of surfaces are similar but, in terms of material form, apparent smoothness resembles concrete more than concrete block.

Although Wright's chimneys are generally massive and often integrated into massive elements projecting above the roof, they are slender compared to the volumes of their buildings. Consequently, their potential for contributing to the image of block as a compressive

David Wright House. Although the cylindrical mass is smaller at the R. L. Wright House, the building generally carries a stronger sense of compression than the David Wright House, as the former is set securely on the ground. Both houses incorporate some "floating" block (spans without apparent lintels or references to lintels), which detracts from the structural integrity of the units at the small scale. Both fireplaces float block over the firebox, the tensile overtones of which are magnified by the fact that both are curved on short radii and would be severely challenged to accomplish a horizontal span in that configuration.

At the David Wright House a long section of the large battered cylindrical volume that is so compressive in the exterior view passes through the living room and across the fireplace with no apparent support. The tensile sensation of this "floating" block segment is strong in the living room (it appears to hang from the ceiling) but does not significantly undermine the compressive sense of the drum in the overall building image since the wall is inside the building and not readily associated with the drum volume. The R. L. Wright House "floats" 12

FIGURE 5-30. Multiple decorative half-units as lintels and sills at the John D. Storer Residence. Decorative half-units as coping. (Courtesy The Frank Lloyd Wright Archives)

material is reduced but not eliminated. The noticeable sense of compression in the tapered and broad form of the central concrete block mass of the Davis House (as viewed in the northwest elevation) is enhanced by the steep roof that surrounds it. The spreading of the roof around the block construction yields a silhouette of great mass and stability, even though the roof is clearly only light framing. (The block mass does not look the same from the opposite side as its plan is C-shaped, with its open side visible from the southeast.) The larger quantity of block projecting above the Thaxton roof gives the house a slightly greater compressive sense than in the Fawcett and Davis houses.

Concrete block's compressive nature is celebrated in the battered walls of the H. Price, Sr. House (1954), which are large enough develop a sense of significant weight. The sense is further enhanced by the fact that the block appears to play a greater role in the aesthetic order of the house than in the three previous examples, the characters of which could accommodate more readily the substitution of another material. This circumstance is related to the greater amount of block, the flat roof that reflects block's boxy form more than do sloped roofs, and certain other detailing. Any compressiveness that is projected is thus boosted in intensity because of the generally elevated importance of the nature of the material to the architecture.

FIGURE 5-31. Battered drumlike mass at David Wright Residence. Unitlike decorative edge in cantilevered slab under ramp. Enlarged vertical joints (pointed flush) at small-radius chimney top. Half-circle windows.

FIGURE 5-32. Each course sets back in battered mass at Randall Fawcett Residence. (Courtesy The Frank Lloyd Wright Archives)

Reverse battering (or corbeling), which commonly accompanies battering in Wright's work, is particularly central to the aesthetic order here because of the clarity of its role in the scheme. Unlike miscellaneous corbeling in other projects, here the detail is methodically and boldly expressed in all four faces of numerous nearly freestanding columns that dominate the central area (the court) of the south elevation and the entire north side of the house. Miscellaneous reverse battered elements such as walls at the entry, fireplaces, and walls near the parking area are also present. Because of the small bases of the columns, their broad tops, their tall dimensions, and the gap between the top of the columns and the roof, the column masses are the least stable of all of Wright's block.

The taper towards the base appears to bring a considerable amount of weight to bear on the small footprint of the columns but the suggested compression can be no more secure in the building image than the visual stability of the masses. The nearly maximum instability of the columns is tempered slightly by the partial contact of the columns with adjacent construction. The battered walls elsewhere in the project provide a stable context that psychologically provides some slight sense of stabil-

ity to the corbeled columns. The stabilizing contribution to the columns by the rest of the building is limited, however, by the absence of a clearly secure connection to the roof. The thin pipe columns protruding from the top of the block and extending to the roof are not a convincing device for the transfer of lateral loading to the building superstructure. Their integration into the glass as mullions also obscures their presence, already minimal due to their relative thinness.

The corbeled sides of the fireplace in the court area are structurally convincing. Individual block overhangs, which are relatively small compared to unit height and length, yield a steep angle in the jambs—a characteristic necessary in true corbels (unreinforced). Corbeling two sides of an opening in order to reduce the span of the lintel tends to generate tall openings if the corbels are structurally sound. Although there is no hint that this was the purpose of the corbel at this fireplace, the effect is the same. The tall opening, highly unusual for a fireplace, appears to be a function of the nature of block in a corbeled format rather than of traditional fireplace design. A corbeled fireplace in the living room has a shorter and wider firebox opening that lacks the sense of material-nature motivation embodied in the court fire-

FIGURE 5-33. Battered walls of R. W. Lindholm Service Station step back in groups of three courses. Smooth obtuse corners.

FIGURE 5-34. Tall chimney mass in northwest elevation of Richard Davis Residence. (Courtesy The Frank Lloyd Wright Archives)

place. Metal hoods obscure the nature of the lintels at both locations, thus preventing their detailing from participating in the structural message of the fireplaces.

Concrete block appearing to span by virtue of its own flexural strength occurs in the H. Price, Sr. House in a series of windows on the south facade, in several louvered openings of about the same size, and in small windows on the west. The violation of the structural spirit of block is limited by the span, which is about two concrete blocks long. The large number of openings with "floating" block lintels increases the image of insensitivity to the nature of concrete block, but the negative effect remains less than that generated if there had been fewer but wider openings. The worst case occurs in a corner window, where the cantilevering of block in the face of each wall towards the corner eliminates any sense of structural continuity available in the straight "floating" format. The block over the corner window can visually only hang as a tensile element. The limited use of the detail prevents it from significantly influencing the image of the block in the building as a whole, although it is in a prominent position by the entry.

Wright corbeled the left side of the David Wright fireplace (1950) at an angle too small (flat) for a sense of comfortable structural stability but, given the lack of structural integrity of the rest of the block in that wall, its violation of material nature is not remarkable. The corbel on the side of the Fawcett fireplace (1954) is steep enough to be structurally legitimate, but it does not significantly reduce the long span over the top of the firebox. Thus, its structural significance is limited. A

striking violation of the structural nature of concrete block occurs in the Lykes House (1959) in the form of the curvilinear cantilevered balcony. The curved walls of the building add a sense of stability to the reasonably massive volumes, thus an overall sense of compression in the block is established. The units of the balcony rail wall appear to "float" in midair, however, as a cantilevering structural material is not expressed at the bottom of the block. The block of the balcony face simply stops at its lower edge with no apparent support. Although the balcony does not constitute the entire building elevation, its importance in establishing the sense of the material is magnified by its highly visible position in the most prominent facade.

The several circular openings in block walls on the site of the Lykes House place into question the structural integrity of the units above them. The curved spans are not arches but corbels, with the edges of the block shaped so as to form a smooth curve. The low slope of the corbels as they approach the top of the curve does not reflect the nature of block with regard to its strength. In the upper part of the curve the cantilevered section becomes too long for its depth. The effect of these curious lintels is limited, however, as the spans over the openings are short and the openings do not dominate the building.

The concrete units of the Lykes fireplace "float" over the firebox opening with no apparent means of support, violating the spirit of the material with regard to its strength as they do at the J. Carr (1950), R. L. Wright (1953), Tonkens (1955), Kalil (1955), and

FIGURE 5-35. One of many columns with reverse-battered surfaces at the Harold Price, Sr. Residence. Decorated steel column at top of block supports roof.

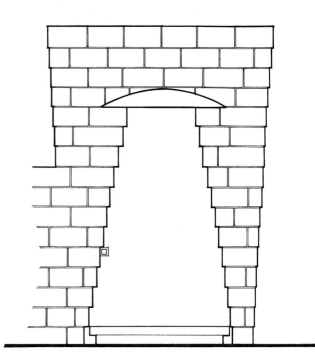

FIGURE 5-36. Corbeled jambs on court fireplace at the Harold Price, Sr. Residence. (From a photograph, *Frank Lloyd Wright Selected Houses*, vol. 8, p. 143.)

FIGURE 5-37. Curvilinear cantilevered concrete block balcony at the Norman Lykes Residence. Drumlike concrete block building mass. No structural support expressed. Smooth nonright-angle corner on balcony rail. Curved edge on cantilevered roof slab.

Erdman prefab II (1957) houses. Unlike brick, for which Wright used many lintel details, the "floating" of block over his plain block fireplaces, with no visible means of support, was the standard. Where decorative textile block was used in the building, decorative strips of block usually served as a lintel reference over the fireplace. It is curious that although Wright's custom block systems of the 1940s and 1950s show far fewer details on the facades that oppose the structural nature of block than did the early textile block houses, the structural circumstances of the fireplaces of the two groups are reversed. The fireplace lintel detailing is consistently in violation of the nature of block with regard to strength throughout his later work.

Besides the "floating" fascia block characteristic of the Usonian Automatic houses, the cantilevered balcony of the Turkel House (1955) is the exception to the otherwise generally block-sensitive facades in this series. (The

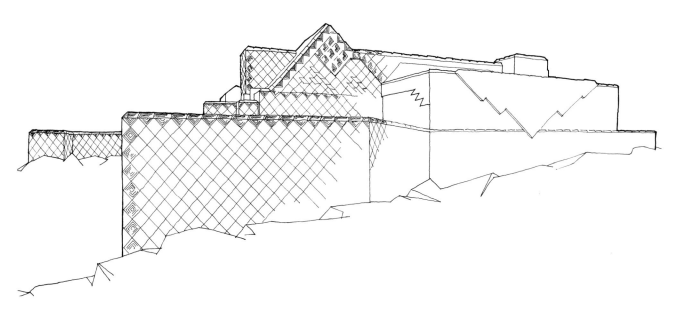

FIGURE 5-38. Concrete block rotated 45 degrees in the proposed Owen D. Young Residence (not built). (From Frank Lloyd Wright Archives drawing 2707.01.)

other houses may have been spared "floating" block at a balcony because they are only one story buildings.) The balcony shows no lintel or structure other than the unit masonry. As in the case of all floating block, the detail suggests that concrete block has a flexural strength that it does not actually have. No reference is made to the hidden structural material, which might bring the expression into alignment with the nature of block.

Single blocks are caused to span over glass in the Usonian Automatic houses when operable sash rather than glazed block is used. The span of a single unit in any kind of block is not problematic if it overlaps the supports on each side. In the case of the Automatic block, the units butt but do not overlap the jambs of the openings. The examples at the Tonkens and Kalil houses can be justified by the integral network of steel in the system that has the shear strength at the jambs necessary to keep the single block from sliding downward between the jambs (regardless of what other hidden support is provided). This tolerance is motivated by a desire to recognize, in a small way, the composite nature of the systems that have a light network of integral steel throughout as a standard feature.

Although accepting composite expressions in a material that looks like traditional masonry is questionable, the butting of a single block at the jambs of an opening is not an exaggerated challenge to the nature of unreinforced units. Although it is not within the spirit of the material, its appearance in the R. L. Wright House (1953) is not especially damaging to the compressive integrity of the standard commercial block of that build-

ing. The two-block spans over the bedroom windows of the Pappas House (1955) are philosophically too long—given the joint in the block at midspan—if not physically impossible. Some small sense of violation to the spirit of block accompanies the two-block spans there as they do in the standard units of the H. Price, Sr. House (1945).

The concrete units that cover the ceilings of the Usonian Automatic houses are philosophically troublesome with regard to the general incompatibility of masonry and tension. The issue is nearly moot, however, as the appearance of the units is not clearly that of block. Once in place, the two-foot square coffered units resemble a waffle slab. The grid of joints centered on the "ribs" does not significantly disrupt their visual continuity. They appear to span as a concrete slab rather than hang as individual pieces as they actually do. The size of the units approaches that of small precast concrete panels. Philosophically, precast products have a broader tolerance than does masonry for structural imagery but must face the same physical challenges when placed in a tensile role. The ceiling units of the Pappas House each weigh nearly 200 pounds,[19] which brings into doubt their compatibility with a ceiling finish regardless of how the product is categorized. Although the expression of the ceilings is one of mass and weight, the reality of the tensile condition is not readily apparent, abating the sense of violation to the concrete units.

The stacking of blocks for wall construction expresses compression to a greater or lesser degree depending on such detailing as battering, reverse-battering, buttressing, geometry of the footprint, etc., as has been discussed. Wright proposed a unique orientation for the concrete block of the unrealized Owen D. Young House (1929) (part of the San Marcos-in-the-Desert, Resort Hotel development), which compromises somewhat the sense of compression in the units. The square units, rotated forty-five degrees so as to become diamond-shapes with sloped bearing surfaces, lack the visual stability of traditionally positioned blocks that rest on a flat side. As a practical matter, hidden steel could secure the construction, but the expressive ramifications of the orientation are questionable for the strength-nature of block.

So long as blocks on either side of a unit are secure, each unit could transfer compression to the foundation through their sloped bearing faces. The reasoning is reassuring for all units but those at the end of a wall (a half-diamond or triangle) seem about to be pushed from the mass. Detailing that would show the construction to be clearly a composite of block and steel would help return a sense of compression to the image, as would buttressing at the ends of each wall. Such changes would not necessarily improve the architecture and would sure-ly render it unlike Wright, as this attention to the nature of the block with regard to its strength would take on a more literal sense than was typical of him.

DURABILITY

Wright's level of respect for the nature of concrete block with regard to its durability is revealed by the response of his detailing to the threat of water penetration in three realms, the face of the block in vertical surfaces, joints in vertical surfaces, and joints in horizontal sur-faces. His attention to the durability of concrete block evolved in a more or less reverse relationship with his expression of block form as the two properties generate some characteristics that are not compatible. As the strength of his expression of block form diminished after his earliest work, sensitivity to the limitations of block durability appears to have increased. The phenomenon is related to changes in aesthetic strategies that exposed fewer tops of concrete block to precipitation in the later work. Although budget and climate considerations were likely motivations for the changes, the results had rami-fications in material expression.

Wright nearly always exposed the bare faces of con-crete block in his building facades. The format express-es the high durability of the substance, which, although somewhat porous, does not need paint to survive the elements as wood does. The raked horizontal joints in a large number of Wright's houses of commercial con-crete block such as the David Wright, Davis, and

Sweeton houses of 1950, the Brandes, Lindholm, and Penfield houses of 1952, and the R. L. Wright of 1953 catch water at a particularly vulnerable location (at the bond of mortar to the unit). The challenge to the spirit of block durability is limited, however, as the shelf cre-ated by recessing the mortar is small and is unlikely to be associated with the issue of water by the casual observer. Raked joints in block construction are less confronta-tional to the durability of the masonry than is the same detail in brick, which requires three or four times as many joints depending on the size of the unit. Block is more vulnerable than brick, however, because of its greater porosity.

Prolonging the contact between water and joints challenges the durability of block because intermittent failures in the mortar bond are likely to be present. If these periodic hairline gaps are sometimes problematic, Wright's omitting of the mortar altogether in the face of his textile block and Usonian Automatic houses would seem to invite water penetration. The blocks were designed to set directly on each other with no mortar in the surface of the wall at the head or bed joints. (The steel in the voids on the edges of the block secured the system when grouted, as previously discussed.)

Reveals along the edges of the block faces have the appearance of raked joints when installed. Unlike raked mortar, however, the hairline gap that might emit water is in the center of the horizontal joint rather than at the top or bottom. This means that the vulnerable line is above the tiny shelf that could hold water. In addition, the grout that filled the channels behind the joints helped seal the joints. In the block of the Pappas House, the grout ran into the thin crevices between the blocks (resulting from irregularities in the block) and upon occasion onto the face of the units.[20] The hairline gaps were thus plugged in the grouting process. Philo-sophically, the absence of mortar in joints would seem to increase their vulnerability, but in practice, neither the image nor the actual circumstances are in significant conflict with the durability of the material.

Failing to observe the logical level of durability in block work might result only in a reduced margin of safety instead of physical failure if the units were of high quality. Because Wright's early textile block was hand-made on the site, with inferior ingredients in some cases, they have little tolerance for detailing that challenges their durability. Wright's exposure of the tops of the numerous units in parapets and projections yielded strong blocky characteristics in the 1923 and 1924 Los Angeles textile block houses but confronted the durabil-ity of the units. The 16-inch wide block shelves and parapets catch water and hold it against the block for the maximum amount of time. This violates the spirit of concrete masonry even in the mild climate of the area which, being compromised by air pollution, has been hard on the block. The problem is magnified by the fact that the horizontal surfaces are typically that of patterned block which provides, in many cases, depressions that hold water.

Patterns in the tops of terrace walls at the Storer House have lost some definition and general deterioration has occurred elsewhere. The Ennis House has shown some of the most serious signs of decay with some walls bulging, pieces of units having fallen off, and at least one entire block having crumbled away several years ago leaving a 16-inch square void in the wall. The tops of some walls at the S. Freeman House were covered with sheet metal copings in response to inadequate attention to the durability of the concrete block in the original design. Other houses such as the R. Lloyd-Jones House (1929) have had metal copings added to the tops of the block, signifying the failure of the original detail to deal effectively with the vulnerability of block system.

The practical value of mortar washes as protection for the tops of block is inversely related to visibility. Wider and flatter washes shed water less efficiently and are more likely to fail than steeper versions. Wright's call for a sloping water table on the top of exposed block in the Lindholm House (1952)[21] signifies a desire to omit from the block expression this symbol of its major durability limitation. In using low profile washes here and elsewhere, Wright failed to express or exercise respect for the nature of block in the realm of durability.

Although hidden flashing can provide some protection to a block wall near its top, more substantial protection is available from visible systems. Hidden or partially hidden protection also prevents the nature of concrete block from participating fully in the architectural expression, as the block is misrepresented with regard to its durability level. In general, Wright expressed no significant protection for the tops of block walls, thus consistently ignoring a part of the nature of concrete block. A minor reference to this aspect of block occurs occasionally where the top course of block differs in some way from the other block, thus identifying the top course as a special case and sometimes appearing to be a coping of sorts. The eight-inch high course at the top of the A. Millard House parapets (1923), is half the height of the other wall units, as are the top units at the Storer House (1923) which also differ in pattern from those below. These pseudocopings express the need for a protective strip on top the block (if not actually providing one) and, therefore, reflect to some degree the nature of concrete block with regard to its durability limitations.

Occasionally in later work, nominal two-inch thick block serves as a coping for the voids in the units below. No protection is provided to the joints in the top of the wall, as there are the same number of joints in the coping as in a typical course. A considerable amount of block at the David Wright House (1950) is so covered, as is a terrace wall at the Pearce House (1951). Given the match in color and the absence of an overhang, the expression of the nature of concrete block with regard to durability is limited but does exist.

The use of fewer projected masses and parapets in the later work exposed the tops of fewer block walls to the weather than did the earliest block houses. Buildings with fewer exposed wall tops (walls not covered by roofs) are generally more compatible with the spirit of the material's durability than those with more exposed tops. It is not suggested, that there is a relationship between the number of wall tops exposed and Wright's sensitivity to the nature of concrete block's durability. Wright showed little tendency to let the durability limitations of this material influence his design decisions. Credit can be granted for the roof protection of block where it occurs, but the greater coverage of block by roofs in his later work does not signify a growing sensitivity by Wright to the durability issue.

CONCLUSION

Wright's failure to consistently deliver a balanced expression of the nature of block at a level equal to its potential indicates that material nature, in general, was not the governing force in his concrete block buildings. His appreciation of properties appeared to be nearly limited to the realm of form. The character of his early block houses was affected significantly by their three-dimensional expressions of block form. The personalities of the Usonian Automatic houses achieved some distinction by their dependence in large part on two-dimensional expression of unit form.

A sensitivity to block's affinity for compression (at the large scale) surfaced occasionally, beginning with the relatively stable, massive, and blocky textile block houses of 1923 and 1924. The focus was not comprehensive, however, as his early and continued use of block in flexural formats diluted the compressive integrity of building masses. Some relief to this overt rejection of block's inability to perform in bending or tension is realized later in his work in the Usonian Automatic block houses. Here, mostly one-story configurations and the use of glazed block eliminated the majority of opportunities for long spans in the facades. Block was thus freed from this assignment in most cases.

Wright's approach to concrete masonry is consistent with that to other materials. He appears to have focused on the properties he thought potentially beautiful, to have violated others in lieu of larger goals, and to have never let the nature of the material in its entirety dictate the direction of the design. Compared to that of other architects of the mid-20th century, however, Wright's use of block was far more demonstrative of its nature in his strongest examples and only slightly less expressive than the norm in his weakest.

ENDNOTES

1. Wright, Frank Lloyd. 1928. "In the Cause of Architecture: I. The Logic of the Plan." *Architectural Record* 63(1):49–57. Reprint. 1975. *In the Cause of Architecture*, ed. Frederick Gutheim. New York: McGraw-Hill. p. 161. *ARCHITECTURAL RECORD*, (January/1928), copyright 1975 by McGraw-Hill, Inc. All rights reserved. Reproduced with the permission of the publisher.

2. Wright, Frank Lloyd. 1928. "In the Cause of Architecture: VII. The Meaning of Materials—Concrete." *Architectural Record* 64(2):98–104. Reprint. 1975. *In the Cause of Architecture*, ed. Frederick Gutheim. New York: McGraw-Hill. p. 208.

3. Ibid., 209.

4. Wright, Frank Lloyd. 1928. "In the Cause of Architecture: I. The Logic of the Plan." *Architectural Record* 63(1):49–57. Reprint. 1975. *In the Cause of Architecture*, ed. Frederick Gutheim. New York: McGraw-Hill. p. 154. *ARCHITECTURAL RECORD*, (January/1928), copyright 1975 by McGraw-Hill, Inc. All rights reserved. Reproduced with the permission of the publisher.

5. Wright, Frank Lloyd. 1928. "In the Cause of Architecture: VII. The Meaning of Materials—Concrete." *Architectural Record* 64(2):98–104. Reprint. 1975. *In the Cause of Architecture*, ed. Frederick Gutheim. New York: McGraw-Hill. p. 210.

6. Ibid.

7. Ibid., 209. *ARCHITECTURAL RECORD*, (January/1928), copyright 1975 by McGraw-Hill, Inc. All rights reserved. Reproduced with the permission of the publisher.

8. Ibid., 210. *ARCHITECTURAL RECORD*, (January/1928), copyright 1975 by McGraw-Hill, Inc. All rights reserved. Reproduced with the permission of the publisher.

9. Ibid. *ARCHITECTURAL RECORD*, (January/1928), copyright 1975 by McGraw-Hill, Inc. All rights reserved. Reproduced with the permission of the publisher.

10. Wright, Frank Lloyd. 1932. *An Autobiography*. Revised. 1943. New York: Duell, Sloan and Pearce. Copyright by The Frank Lloyd Wright Foundation. p. 246. Courtesy the Frank Lloyd Wright Foundation.

11. Wright, Frank Lloyd. 1927. "In the Cause of Architecture: II. Standardization, The Soul of the Machine." *Architectural Record* 61(6):478–480. Reprint. 1975. *In the Cause of Architecture*, ed. Frederick Gutheim. New York: McGraw-Hill. p. 135. *ARCHITECTURAL RECORD*, (January/1928), copyright 1975 by McGraw-Hill, Inc. All rights reserved. Reproduced with the permission of the publisher.

12. Tafel, Edgar. 1979. *Apprentice to Genius: Years with Frank Lloyd Wright*. Reprint. 1985. *Years with Frank Lloyd Wright: Apprentice to Genius*. New York: Dover Publications. p. 126.

13. Secrest, Meryle. 1992. *Frank Lloyd Wright: A Biography*. New York: Alfred A. Knopf. p. 291.

14. Pappas, Bette Kporivica. 1985. *Frank Lloyd Wright: No Passing Fancy*. St. Louis, MO: Pappas. p. 38, 39, 50.

15. Northup, A. Dale. 1991. *Frank Lloyd Wright in Michigan*. Algonac, MI: Reference Publications, Inc. p. 90.

16. Pfeiffer, Bruce Brooks, ed. 1991. *Frank Lloyd Wright Selected Houses*, Volume 8. ed. Yukio Futagawa. Text copyrighted by the Frank Lloyd Wright Foundation 1991. Tokyo: A.D.A. Edita Tokyo Co. Ltd. p. 13. Pfeiffer reports that the block of the Alice Millard house did not incorporate steel reinforcing rods like the textile block houses that followed and utilized conventional mortar joints.

17. Secrest, Meryle. 1992. *Frank Lloyd Wright: A Biography*. New York: Alfred A. Knopf. p. 354.

18. Wright, Frank LLoyd. 1954. *The Natural House*. Reprint. 1970. New York: Meridian/New American Library. p. 199.

19. Pappas, Bette Kporivica. 1985. *Frank Lloyd Wright: No Passing Fancy*. St. Louis, MO: Pappas. p. 43.

20. Ibid., 39.

21. Wright, Frank Lloyd. Frank Lloyd Wright Archives. Drawing # 5208.003.

CHAPTER 6 METAL

INTRODUCTION

Because of its potential to shape architecture through structure, steel is the metal of central interest. Wright's limited expression of steel restricts its analysis in his architecture but is, itself, revealing of his attitude toward the material. A discrete philosophy is not described here for each of his nonstructural metals. Trends in apparent sensitivity to similar properties among his metals are evaluated as are responses to unique properties in each where they are significant to architectural expression. Conclusions are drawn regarding Wright's attitude towards steel specifically and regarding the nonstructural metals in general.

In a reference to steel's aesthetic potential based on its surface characteristics, Wright observed that "in itself it has little beauty."[1] In spite of his thought that steel could provide "ideal expression as the sinews and bones of structure,"[2] he rarely allowed structural steel to have an identity in his buildings. According to Wright, its undistinguished surface was not an obstacle to steel's beauty in architecture but unlike wood and the nonferrous metals, it does not appear to have warranted exposure for its own sake. He rejected the cladding of steel structure with historic forms and heavy materials but otherwise complained of no expressive inconsistency embodied in hiding it from view. His suggestion to add only glass once the design has "honestly insured the life of the steel"[3] describes a circumstance that could minimally obscure steel's form, depending on the nature of its protection from fire and corrosion. The tactic brings to mind International Style imagery but it is doubtful that Wright entertained any such thoughts. In related testimony he promoted concrete as a logical protection for steel that, in return, could reinforce the concrete. Glass and concrete, then, defined his vision of the material instead of the glass and steel forms of Mies van der Rohe.

Steel's tensile strength profoundly affects the image of reinforced concrete, but steel's form does not. The shape of steel has no discernible impact on the form of the concrete beyond its tendency to increase the bulk of the section somewhat due to requirements for bar spacing and concrete cover. Wright's acceptance of reinforced concrete as an expression of steel falls short of a commitment to express the nature of steel as defined by its physical characteristics. It would seem to indicate the opposite intention, as it provides an opportunity to effectively hide the form of steel. It is significant that, in Wright's 1927 steel article for *Architectural Record*, several paragraphs address reinforced concrete. His thought that concrete is "more congenial to the architect than steel alone"[4] partly explains the limitation of expressed structural steel in his work.

Some distinction between cast metal form and wrought metal form can be justified. Cast metals tend to be weaker than their wrought counterparts. Introducing metal into a mold as well as removing the mold is facilitated by certain form characteristics that are not the same as those that accommodate wrought processing. Consequently, cast metal products are logically thicker, in general, than wrought components. On the other hand, cast metals can be thinner and sharper than concrete castings, molded clay, and wood intended for exposure to weathering. The nature of form in cast metals is thus more logically like wrought metals in regard to thinness and refinement than they are like cast products in the nonmetals. Generally, Wright's castings are analyzed with his wrought metals as a single group, while taking into account differences in expectations generated by the unique properties of each. The degree to which any of Wright's metal details (cast or wrought) can distinguish itself from the nonmetals constitutes a measure of his sensitivity to metals. Another measure is the degree to which his metals approach their potential to express their uniqueness.

FORM

As illustrated by flanged products and by rods, bars, sheet, and wire, it is in the nature of the wrought forms of metal to be thin and precise. This is the aspect of form that most clearly distinguishes the metals from other building materials. The degree to which detailing approaches a state of high refinement is a universal standard against which the expression of most metals in architecture can be measured. The primary structural

FIGURE 6-1. Steel columns at the Wichita State University Juvenile Cultural Study Center. Decorative steel bars curve downward between columns. Steel lattice in opening of canopy roof. (Courtesy Jennie M. Patterson)

forms of steel tend to be long and slender as do many nonstructural components in various metals. The basic form of sheet metal is broad and rectangular. Wright's sensitivity to the nature of metal can be measured by the degree to which the integrity of basic product form is respected and the degree to which it affects the aesthetic order of the architecture.

Wright's attitude toward the nature of steel form could be better understood if he favored a particular product or certain product characteristics. He embraced, however, a wide range of component forms in his observation that steel could be rolled into "any desired section,"[5] thus minimizing industry standards as well as self-imposed constraints on his detailing of steel. In his praise for the potential of steel in architecture Wright cited such products as wire, plate, and sheet among others but seemed reluctant to mention I-beams, wide-flange sections, or refer to other products with flanges. His references to "beams" and to "posts" on several occasions seem purposefully general, as these words avoid a commitment to components with flanges (although they are not necessarily excluded). This narrative pattern seems significant only in light of his reluctance to expose flanges in his facades. For example, steel pipes rather than wide flanges, channels, or angles encircle the central space of the Industrial Arts Building (1942) of Florida Southern College and are used in the facades of the H. Price, Jr. House (1954), H. Price, Sr. House (1954), Beth Sholom Synagogue (1954), Juvenile Cultural Study Center (1957), and under the ramp of the Grady Gammage Memorial Auditorium (1959). Columns in the facade of the Gammage Auditorium were specified as steel (pipelike) in presentation drawings but were constructed in concrete.

FIGURE 6-2. Flanges of steel roof structure visible in the ceiling of the court at the Harold Price, Sr. Residence.

The pipe columns of the Juvenile Cultural Study Center are among the most prominent structural steel statements in his architecture. They are freestanding and support courtyard roofs on the second level on both sides of the building thus giving them prominent positions in the facade. Their long slender proportions reflect the spirit of steel, although like all pipes, their round sections softens their image. The curved decorative bars hanging between the columns add to the softness of the image at the large scale although the thin profile of the bars adds some sharpness to the composition. A grille of both curved and straight elements spans over an opening in the courtyard roofs. The silhouette of the grille against the sky clearly defines the forms of the strips, some of which are thin and straight in the spirit of wrought metal, while others are curved and appear to thicken at their interface with curved strips. The sense of plastic flow, consequently, softens the image of the grille, thus moving it away from the sharp, straight, and angular characteristics that would have been unmistakably those of steel.

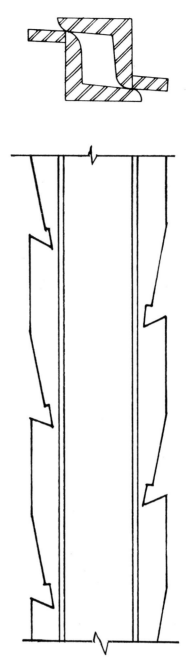

FIGURE 6-3. Plan section and partial elevation of steel post for canopy over stepped walk to Edgar J. Kaufmann, Sr. Residence Guesthouse (Fallingwater). (From Frank Lloyd Wright drawing 3812.031 and a photograph, *Frank Lloyd Wright's Fallingwater*, p.88.)

The lower flanges of the small steel beams of the roof structure are exposed in the ceilings of the H. Price, Sr. House. Because the webs and the upper flanges are not revealed, the exposed steel appears as a grid pattern of vague material identity rather than as a clearly defined system of steel beams. The thickness of the flanges shows below the ceiling but the identity of the flanges is

FIGURE 6-4. Steel columns and beams rising above exterior brick walls during the construction of the Larkin Company Administration Building. (Courtesy The Frank Lloyd Wright Archives)

obscured. The grid has a structural sense about it as it passes over the pipe columns in the exterior wall and elsewhere. The secondary support system for the edges of the roof/ceiling decking is expressed as such by its smaller width and by the fact that it appears to be supported by the larger members. The system is highly linear and steel-like, although an almost identical image could be reproduced in wood or concrete. A more clear expression of the bottom flanges and their relationship to the webs of the beams would have secured their identity as steel.

A limited exposure of flanges occurs in the living room ceiling of the S. Friedman House (1949). A single ten-inch deep wide-flange steel beam supports a section of roof as it passes through the stone chimney mass and over a balcony above the fireplace. A few feet of the high beam is visible from most vantage points in the living room. The effect on the character of the general living space is minimal but not insignificant within the balcony-space itself, where the close proximity of the steel to the observer emphasizes its presence. The absence of cladding on the beam indicates only a minimal tolerance for the image of the flanged form because of its restriction to the interior of the house and its limited importance in the composition of that realm.

Wright chose not to exploit the distinctively metallic character of flanges in his exposure of steel angles at Fallingwater. Six pairs of angles support the concrete canopy (1938) over the walkway between the main

building and the guesthouse. The inside faces of each pair of angles are turned toward each other and welded to form a hollow rectangular tube. The flanges are just visible in two faces of each column. Their minimal visibility is further subdued by the addition of steel strips along the flanges in the form of upward-jutting fins. The jagged (or leaflike) edges superimposed on the angles maintain a sharpness and thinness that is integral with the nature of steel but have effectively obscured the character of the flanges. The visual role of the steel columns in the walkway composition is minimized by their sparse distribution and thin profiles. Usually, artistic detailing boosts the importance of a component but, in this case, the plantlike edge detail facilitates a partial blend of the column silhouettes with the surrounding foliage. The concrete canopy dominates the structure, thus conforming to the material-theme of the main building.

The physical characteristics of the numerous I-beams and channels used in the Larkin Building (1903) have little effect on the building image. The slender proportions and flanges of the steel columns in the interior of the building are lost within their brick cladding. The composite columns are formed with pairs of channels that are linked with steel straps and are surrounded with fireproofing and a wythe of brick. Also enclosed with each column is a large chase. The massiveness of the brick column-forms that line the central hall does justice to the nature of brick but does not

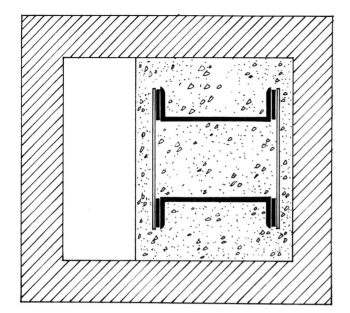

FIGURE 6-5. Plan section of steel column, chase, and brick cladding at the Larkin Company Administration Building. (From Frank Lloyd Wright Archives drawing 0403.083.)

reflect the relative thinness of the steel within. They appear to be loadbearing brick columns instead of cladding for steel.

Pairs of I-beams are positioned on either side of ductwork and are encased in a cementitious boxy form to create a beam that has an appearance similar to the concrete floor above. In his autobiography, Wright described the Larkin Building as "a simple cliff of brick"[6] and as being "built of masonry material—brick and stone."[7] His failure to mention its structural steel in describing the essence of the building is not entirely unreasonable; since the exterior of the building is load-bearing brick, the nature of brick rather than the nature of steel was reflected in the interior. This is not particularly unusual for hidden steel but it does contrast slightly with several of Wright's other uses of hidden steel, which produced remarkable demonstrations of strength in the visible construction. The relationship of the building character to its steel in the Larkin Building is particularly remote from that typical of International Style buildings, which often express both the form and strength of their structural steel without exposing the actual members themselves.

In contrast to the Larkin Building, the steel of the Beth Sholom Synagogue contributes some of its basic form characteristics to the image of the building. The 36-inch deep wide-flange sections (12-inch flanges) that form the tripod structure of the glazed roof over the sanctuary are encased in concrete and aluminum. The aluminum casing that acted as the form work for

FIGURE 6-6. Central court flanked by steel columns clad in brick at the Larkin Company Administration Building. (Courtesy The Frank Lloyd Wright Archives)

the concrete was grouted solid and left in place. The diamond shaped mass that houses the steel is several feet wide and more than twice the depth of the beam. Within the sanctuary the tripod legs appear to be especially slender, since they are 117 feet long and the greater part of their sectional mass is above the glazed roof. Consequently, the geometry of this form in the large interior is linear, like the basic form of the steel hidden within it. It has a stronger visual presence in the sanctuary than the more delicate profile of the wide-flange steel would have had if exposed. In the exterior view where more of the mass shows, the form is one of a thick linear trim on the edges of the roof glazing.

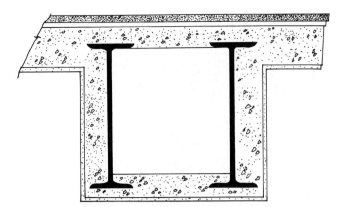

FIGURE 6-7. Section of steel beams and duct at the Larkin Company Administration Building. (From Frank Lloyd Wright Archives drawing 0403.089.)

FIGURE 6-9. Aluminum cladding with chevron patterns in leg of tripod structure (on right) at the Beth Sholom Synagogue. (Courtesy The Frank Lloyd Wright Archives)

FIGURE 6-8. Steel tripod structure visible on right and left of roof construction at the Beth Sholom Synagogue. Secondary steel elements are between the tripod legs. (Courtesy The Frank Lloyd Wright Archives)

No flanges are visible to express the thinness of steel, a characteristic property of its nature. The acute edges of the diamond-shaped tri-pod section, however, reflect the spirit of metals having some small sense of sharpness. An image of precision in the structure is bolstered in a small way within the sanctuary by the patterns on the surfaces of the tri-pod members. Periodic sets of slanted parallel lines cross each leg. As the sets of lines meet on the vertex of the aluminum cover, they form chevronlike shapes which are precise and somewhat visu-

ally sharp. The impressions on the exterior surfaces of the legs are in a different pattern and are not as sharp in their geometry. The mass of the legs combined with the nature of their surface patterns is more in the nature of concrete than aluminum. The lack of clarity in the material message of this assembly is not surprising, given the fact that it consists of three materials, each contributing some aspect of its nature to the image.

Other steel components and the secondary structure supporting the roof glazing impose their linearity on the interior composition and unlike the steel within the Larkin Building, affect the character of the synagogue interior. A similar linear network occurs on the exterior of the glazed roof, although the corrugations and the lapped horizontal connections of the glazing panels compete visually with the aluminum trim covering the panels' vertical connections. The contribution of the metal components to the image of the roof surface is less than that within the interior. The hidden structural steel has a fairly strong influence on the character of the syn-

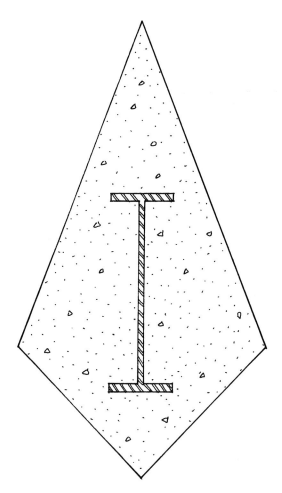

FIGURE 6-10. Section of wide-flange section embedded in concrete as tripod leg of the Beth Sholom Synagogue. (From Frank Lloyd Wright Archives drawing 5313.065.)

FIGURE 6-11. Four decorated steel columns visible above foyer roof at the entry to the Beth Sholom Synagogue. Mitered glass corner on prow of foyer.

agogue and consequently reflects sensitivity in the design to the nature of the material. The achievement is not unusual in glazed systems, however, as glazing typically defines the structure.

A circle of five pipe columns surround an opening in the floor and provide the support for a cantilevered terrace balcony at the H. Price, Jr. House (1954). The pipes express the spirit of steel in their thinness, but it would seem that this characteristic was exploited to diminish rather than integrate the presence of the steel in the architectural expression. The long brick parapet of the balcony dominates the steel columns underneath, which set back from the face of the structure. Their virtual disappearance from the facade gives the impression of a longer cantilever in the brick mass than actually exists, thus increasing the dynamacy of the image. The contribution of the steel columns to the architecture is much like that of those at the Fallingwater walkway canopy. They tend to exaggerate the apparent structural achievement of another material.

The detailing of four pipe columns at the entrance of the Beth Sholom Synagogue (1954) demonstrates an unusual level of sharpness and precision for the product. Typically, pipes do not maximize this aspect of steel because the thickness of the pipe wall is not apparent and their rounded surfaces are visually soft. Wright attached several small triangular prismatic tabs to the pipes giving their surfaces a series of sharp points, thus tempering slightly the softness of the surfaces. The pipes are visible above the top of an entrance vestibule and support an overhang above. Since the pair nearest the edge of the canopy disappear into mullions of the glazed vestibule below and since the other two are deep in the shadow of the canopy, they constitute a minor part of the building expression in spite of their location at the entrance. Nevertheless, they reflect an elevated sensitivity to the nature of steel with regard to its potential for sharpness and precision compared to pipe columns without the decorative tabs.

In the living room of the Walker House (1951) triangular prismatic tabs appear on four thin cast-iron columns (about two inches thick). The columns slope inward as they extend to the ceiling from the top of the stub-wall at the base of the windows. The posts are triangular in section and maintain a minimal presence in the space due to their slenderness. The tabs bring an additional level of sharpness to their relatively sharp profiles and increase their otherwise low visibility. The visually light and angular nature of the columns reflects the spirit of metal to a high degree. They distinguish themselves clearly from wood and concrete, the forms of which often blend with the form of metal columns.

Decorations that push the image of steel away from sharpness and thinness were applied to the pipe columns

FIGURE 6-12. Steel post with cast-iron blocks attached at the Harold Price, Sr. Residence.

The exposed chains supporting the mezzanine and several light fixtures and resisting the thrust of the rafters in the drafting room at Wright's Oak Park Studio (1895) reflect the spirit of steel form only in their relative thinness compared to the wood in the room. The common use of steel to make chains secures the identity of the chain substance but the circumstance is within the realm of product-identity rather than that strictly of material nature. It is useful to understand whether or not the detailing helps identify the material by its characteristics rather than by the traditional association of certain products with certain materials. Being entirely exposed to view, the components express the form of chains clearly enough but the product does not embody the highest potential of refinement available in steel. The profiles of the chains have a somewhat random quality about them due to the slightly varying orientations of the links. The chains are visually soft and slightly lumpy because of the roundness of the links. Cable, wire, rods, or perhaps chains with rectangular or triangular links could have represented the spirit of steel more effectively than the relatively rustic traditional chains. The product choice suggests that Wright did not require of his steel the maximum in refinement, even when exposed to view. The detailing of the system generally does not boost the limited sense of refinement established by the basic chain configuration.

The chains supporting several light fixtures hang close to the face of the mezzanine and virtually brush the wood trim along its upper and lower edges. The closeness has a haphazard quality that suggests imprecision. The odd condition is rooted in the method of securing the tops of these chains. They are hung from hooks cantilevered from the faces of spherical connecting devices on top the railing. The distance of these chains from the face of the mezzanine is defined by the length of the hooks, which is limited by their ability to cantilever. Although the light fixtures are not heavy, the fact that the hooks have little credibility as structural elements give the system a sense of casualness. The chains are slightly out of alignment with those supporting the spherical connectors, thus exacerbating the spirit of imprecision in the system.

Although the lower elements of the system are reproductions of the original components, imprecision in the assembly today reflects the character of the original construction, as old photographs indicate. It is doubtful that high precision could be achieved in the network regardless of the care applied to its construction, since the nature of the design does not facilitate accuracy. The lack of a perfectly parallel relationship in some of the paired chains hanging from the roof structure detracts slightly from a sense of precision in the system. The condition reflects inaccuracy in the connec-

of the H. Price, Sr. House (1954). Series of small equally spaced cast-iron blocks are attached to the steel pipes supporting the loggia, projecting above the concrete block piers to carry the roof over the glazing, and elsewhere. The small rectangular masses resemble, in form, blocks of wood or brick-bats. They add a blockiness to the image that confuses the identity of the steel pipes somewhat. The thinness of the columns and the common use of steel pipe for columns like these ultimately contribute some sense of steel to the identity of the material. The appearance of a similar shape on top of the living room beams of the Sturges House (1939), however, demonstrates that the shape could be reproduced in wood. (The structural wood spindles differ from the Price pipes in that their shafts, just visible between their decorative blocks, are square.) A version that is more convincing as metal occurs at the stairs in the second Erdman prefab design (1957). The block decorations on the shafts there are farther apart, thus allowing the slender form of the poles to participate more in the image of the component.

tions at each end of the chains. Even if a perfectly parallel relationship between chains could be achieved, slight variations in the orientation of the links and the irregularity of the chain profiles would dilute any sense of precision otherwise achieved. The use of open hooks to secure the chains to the mezzanine is especially primitive and incongruous with the complexity of the spheres and bar connector device to which they are attached. Fussiness in a metallic connector could yield a refined image in the achievement of precise relationships of the numerous parts. In the case of the mezzanine connector devices, however, the opposite effect prevails.

The large tolerances and the configuration of the overly wrought connections appear to tolerate movement, which in a sense reflects the spirit of chains, if not steel in general. Slight tilts of elements and slight variances in the heights of hooks are accommodated by the devices. This is sensible as a practical matter but fails to push the material to its potential of refinement. The roundness of the spheres at the connections is visually softer than the sharpness that typically distinguishes metals from other materials. The spheres reflect the spirit of the tensile network because they connect to chains that are in a variety of orientations. The spherical surface relates to each chain in the same way, regardless of its angle, thus making the geometry logical for such a network. The spherical connectors help bring the system closer than any other of Wright's built work to the ideal suggested in his reference to steel as "the spider's web."[8]

Compared to that of cable, the spirit of the chain system is primitive and small in scale. Like brick, it has a manageable quality about it at the scale of the individual. It seems that it could be assembled and adjusted by a few people with simple tools. If these qualities seem particularly appropriate for a residential context, it does not necessarily follow that the nature of steel has been served. The question of whether or not the spirit of steel at its most intense level of expression is appropriate for residential applications is beyond the scope of this analysis and does not affect conclusions regarding the degree to which the nature of steel has been exploited. This installation of steel in Wright's home-based drafting room suggests a compromise to the nature of the material on behalf of the needs of the architecture. The circumstance is common in his work.

Expressing the great strength of steel in small-scale projects is difficult because spans, heights, and loads are limited. The relatively small mass of typical steel components diminishes with the reduced loading common in small projects, thus providing the opportunity for thinner members and increased refinement. Wright does not appear to have exploited this opportunity for the expression of form in a proposed design for a development of all-steel houses in Los Angeles (1938). Since the houses were not intended to be all steel—as their name suggests—but concrete and steel, it is possible that the composite nature of the building prevented it from being highly reflective of the spirit of steel. The character of steel at the small scale would not have been established until the detailing for the actual construction of the project was finalized. Based on a preliminary sketch, however, it does not appear that the character of steel in the house would have been much different than that of wood. In a perspective drawing, the house looks like wood construction in the character of its surface, detailing, and structure. The proportions of the siding are those of boards. Fins, flanges, wires, cables, and other devices expressing the unique thinness of metal are absent.

Although the complete exposure of the metal parts of gates, fences, grilles, and screens typically renders their image to be clearly that of metal, pattern geometries and other detailing further clarify Wright's attitude towards the nature of metals. Some distinction can be made between the relative linearity, angularity, and sharpness of the components that in general distinguish metals from masonry, concrete, and wood. Compared to gates at the Francis Apartments (1895) and Ennis House (1924), the Larkin Building (1903) fence, for example, has a greater sense of sharpness and precision. The Larkin fence consists of straight iron bars forming parallel lines, composed in groups having varied spacing and lengths. The composition is based on the most basic geometry of metal bars (rectilinearity), thus expressing their nature. Although the bars form rectangles, as they always will when parallel lines cross perpendicular lines, they are close enough together that the rectangular spaces between bars do not dominate the image. The closely spaced parallel lines create voids that also have a linear quality because they are long and narrow.

The fence composition contrasts with that of the Francis Apartments wrought-iron gate in which the focus of the composition is a juxtaposition of voids in the form of circles and squares supplemented by ovals. The solid lines present are dominated by the voids they define. The curved lines are visually soft, which does not reflect metal's basic characteristic. Such softness is readily associated with the plasticity of concrete and the workability of wood (although the thinness of the lines is not like those materials). If the significance of the gate composition is diminished by any influence of Louis Sullivan that it might reflect, a later example also illustrates Wright's willingness to let other goals supersede the nature of metals in governing design.

The design of the Ennis House gate is securely integrated into the character of the building. Since the spirit of the building is dominated by the form of concrete block, the metal of the gate reflects certain form

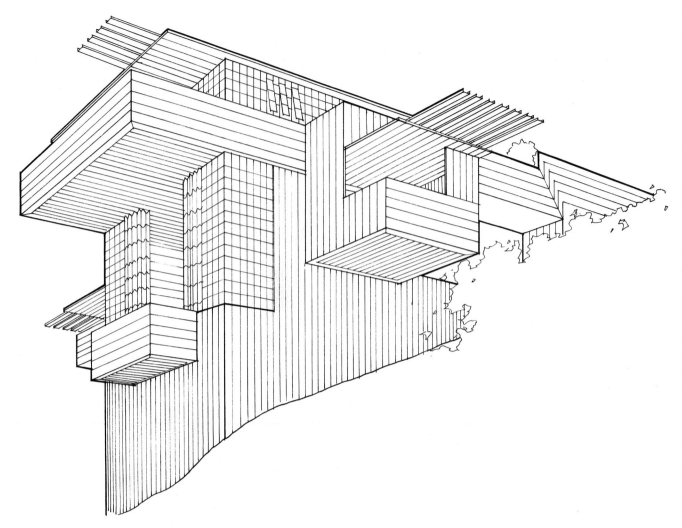

FIGURE 6-13. Perspective drawing of an All Steel House. (From Frank Lloyd Wright Archives drawing 3705.003.)

characteristics of the masonry to the degree that a thin line can emulate a blocky mass. The character of the gate composition is based, to large degree, on rectangular shapes positioned so as to form stepped profiles. The right-angled stepped edge is a characteristic of masonry construction and is a profile found throughout the Ennis facade. Several opaque squares and rectangles occur in the gate and contribute to the blockiness of the pattern. The shape of the free-form leafy decoration positioned at the center and top of the gate, as well as in side panels, is remote from the rectilinearity associated with basic metal components. The gate generally lacks the rectilinearity of metal bars.

Wright's expression of metals in decorative elements falls into a distinct hierarchy of sensitivity to the nature of the material. The variations appear to respond to different stylistic approaches to architecture rather than to an evolving attitude towards metals. The trend suggests that the material is not the central concern. Highly metallic designs at Taliesin West (1953) and at the

Riverview Terrace Restaurant (1956) bracket moderately strong statements at the H. Price, Sr. (1954) and Lovness (1955) houses. With some exceptions, subsequent steel and aluminum appurtenances at the Annunciation Greek Orthodox Church (1956), The Marin County Civic Center (1957), and the Grady Gammage Memorial Auditorium (1959) were among the most visually soft metallic images of his work. The Taliesin West gate and the Riverview Terrace Restaurant sign are unusual among Wright's steel detailing in their demonstration of the metal's thinness through the use of flanges and flangelike projections. Both constructions are angular in nature and expose the edges of plate. The acute angles of the gate and the parallelogram-shaped fins of the sign also add to the sense of metallic sharpness.

The gates at the H. Price, Sr. House and the Lovness House lack the angularity of the previous examples but establish a strong sense of basic metal form in the rectilinearity established through the use of closely spaced,

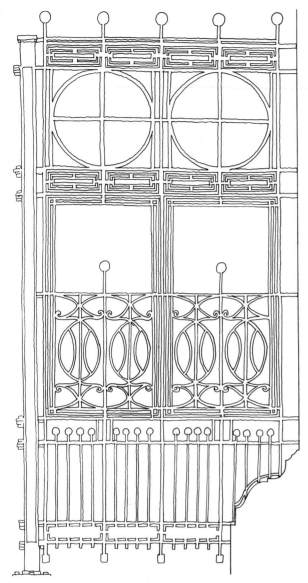

FIGURE 6-15. Gate at the Charles Ennis Residence.

FIGURE 6-16. Flanged-steel construction in a Taliesin West gate.

FIGURE 6-14. Wrought iron gate at the Francis Apartments. (From a photograph, *Frank Lloyd Wright Monograph 1887–1901*, p. 78.)

long parallel lines absent from the Taliesin West and restaurant devices. Both gates contain plate, the edges of which can express sharpness, but most plate edges are obscured by their alignment with linear elements. The sharpness of the Price gate is elevated by the exposure of several plate edges and bar ends. Although the ends of the bars are cut at right angles, they are thin and, therefore, sharp compared to typical exterior wood. The sharpness achieved in this exposure of unadorned bar ends contrasts with earlier bar terminations in the Francis gate where they were blunted by spheres, in the Larkin fence where they were blunted with long rectangular blocks, and in the Ennis gate where many termi-

nations are slightly enlarged and rounded. The roundness of the pipe in the Lovness gate and the absence of exposed ends soften the image of the metal in the close view, although they are adequately thin to carry the metallic message in spite of this. The blocklike shapes on the posts rising above the top of the Lovness gate confuse the image, as do similar decorations on posts at the H. Price, Sr. House, a Taliesin gate in Wisconsin, and elsewhere. They introduce a blocky sense into the image that compromises the thin sleek character of iron and steel.

The circles and semicircles that dominate the metallic accessories within the interior of the Greek Orthodox Church reflect a plasticity compatible with the concrete and geometry of the building. In doing so, the basic rectilinearity and sharpness of metals are not emphasized as the central theme of the components. Exceptions occur in the metallic icon screen behind the pulpit, in certain

FIGURE 6-17. Flanged-steel and plate construction in the Riverview Terrace Restaurant sign.

FIGURE 6-18. Steel bars and plate construction in the Harold Price, Sr. Residence gate.

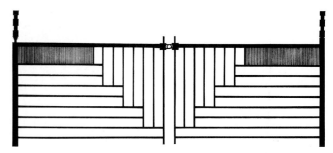

FIGURE 6-19. Wrought-iron pipe construction in the Don Lovness Residence gate. Blocky decorations on top of posts. (From a photograph, *Frank Lloyd Wright: Preserving an Architectural Heritage*, p. 121.)

FIGURE 6-20. Metallic screen in the Annunciation Greek Orthodox Church.

diamondlike shapes, and in the aluminum brackets that radiate from the fascia on the exterior. The thinness of metallic sheet is often expressed only at its edges, but the extensive perforations in the decorative icon screen reveal the thinness of the metal along every inch of its surface. Patterns formed by tangent arcs in the metal sheet create between them curved-sided diamond shapes. The four vertices of the shapes are visually sharp and precise. This pattern occurs both in the decorative screen and in larger elements.

The aluminum brackets that radiate from the building just below the fascia and precast sun screen are phys-

ically and visually sharp. In its cross section, each bracket is an angle which, in side elevation, tapers to a point from a broader dimension at its connection to the building. At its cantilevered end each bracket is cut at an acute angle, thus creating a series of lancelike points around the building. The devices reflect, to a near maximum level, the sharpness that is associated with the spirit of aluminum and metals in general.

Rectilinearity and plasticity are expressed in the aluminum gates and large steel grilles at the Marin County Civic Center. These building elements consist of straight parallel pipes that curve into semicircular shapes at both ends and connect to other parallel pipes in the assembly. The central part of the grilles expresses the basic rectilinearity of pipes; the top and bottom edges express a plasticity that is visually softer than the sharpness natural at the ends of aluminum or steel components in their basic form. Between the pipes are small spheres that further soften the image of the aluminum and steel. Large hollow aluminum spheres line the fascias of the building. Unlike the tiny spheres of the gates

FIGURE 6-21. Aluminum brackets cantilevered from face of the Annunciation Greek Orthodox Church.

FIGURE 6-22. Aluminum gates at the Marin County Civic Center.

and grilles, these are large enough to be duplicated in a variety of materials and thus establish their material identity only by their metallic sheen. This may be enough to carry the metallic message to observers nearby but, since the circumstance does not capitalize on the basic form characteristics of metal, the design is not sensitive to this aspect of the nature of aluminum. Instead of the sharper sense that would come from revealing the thickness of the material, a visually soft image is presented.

Part of the aluminum cladding on the triangular radio tower consists of visually soft (curved) and blunt aluminum decorations, the forms of which could be reproduced in concrete, clay, or wood. An exception to the tendency of the detailing in this building to compromise metal's spirit of sharpness also occurs on the tower. Its anodized aluminum trim strongly reflects the thinness, sharpness, and precision of metals. Horizontal strips of aluminum are applied to the surface of the tower. The strips are positioned with their broader surfaces horizontal and their edges projecting outward. The thin

strips meet at mitered connections on each of the acute corners. Running vertically through each mitered corner is an aluminum strip that juts outward beyond the horizontal bands at each connection. The knifelike corners and the thin parallel lines across the surface establish their metallic identity by both form and sheen. A nonmetallic material could not substitute for the aluminum in these details.

Two curved light-pole systems outside the Gammage Memorial Auditorium promote a soft image for steel at the large scale. The large C-shaped poles along the sidewalk express the linearity (but not the straightness) of structural steel and some degree of thinness by their long slender proportions. The light poles on long ramps to the building create series of arches. Their soft image is abated slightly in the close view by the three metal fins that surround each lamp. (The top fin is actually a pair of fins with the lamp support passing between them.) The fins are welded inside the perimeter of a pipe circling each lamp and project toward the lamp. The thinness of these plates is revealed

FIGURE 6-23. Aluminum cladding on concrete tower at the Marin County Civic Center.

FIGURE 6-24. Curved steel pipe lamppost at the Grady Gammage Memorial Auditorium.

but not emphasized by their exposed edges. Since they project inward rather than outward, the view of their thin edges is somewhat obscured. The curved shape of each fin prevents any sense of sharpness in the side elevation of the assembly.

Contrasting expressions of steel occur in Wright's chairs at the S. C. Johnson and Son Co. Administration Building (1936) and those he designed for the Midway Gardens. The two chairs are similar in the shape of their round backs but the nature of their undercarriage construction contrasts in response to their differing steel components. Because the steel tubing of the Johnson chairs has a diameter large enough to develop rigidity at the joints, no cross bracing was necessary. The Midway chairs (not built) were intended to be constructed of twisted wire,[9] thus could not remain rigid at the joints by virtue of their section. Each leg was diagonally braced, creating a miniature version of a traditional triangulated steel structure. The effect of triangulation on structure is revealed in the far thinner lines of the Midway chairs compared to the thicker lines of the

Johnson chairs. Each chair expresses the nature of steel from a slightly different viewpoint. The Johnson chair expresses the great strength of steel through its moderately thin elements and rigid joints. The Midway chairs express the potential of the material to achieve extreme thinness and still support a load.

The backs of the Midway chairs were to contain a vertical gap filled with a series of small triangular plates. The triangles add a sense of sharpness within the circular perimeter of the chair back, the effect of which can be observed by comparing them to similar chairs at Taliesin West that do not contain the series of the triangles. The round section of the tubes, the round seat and back, and the curved undercarriage of the Johnson chairs soften the image of the steel. In unifying the chair forms with that of the concrete structure and brick walls of the building, the design has caused the steel to assume the geometry of other materials. Consequently, the sharpness of steel is not expressed in the Johnson Wax chairs.

Angularity in section and elevation is generally maintained in cast aluminum chairs designed for

FIGURE 6-25. Steep pipe supports for ramp with arched-pipe lamp supports at the Grady Gammage Memorial Auditorium. Semicircular steel plate fins project inward toward each globe, which is centered in a circular pipe surround.

the Price Tower (1952). Since the chair has the equivalent of two rather than four legs, the thicker base and spine of the Price chair accommodate the strength limitations of the cast aluminum. The decorative surface at the top of the aluminum spine reflects the surface plasticity of cast materials. It is appropriate that such plasticity is missing from the wrought steel chairs at the Johnson Wax building. The thick proportions of the Price Tower chair are more appropriate for the material than are the relatively thin profiles Wright proposed in cast aluminum for his original design of the Johnson Wax chairs. The form of the chairs was the same and the sizes of their components were similar to that eventually constructed in steel. The cruciform section proposed for the cast aluminum reflects the sense of thinness appropriate for steel but the mass of the sections seem small for aluminum. One prototype chair that was constructed of aluminum pipe had bandlike brackets at the joints that were absent from the steel chairs eventually manufactured. The detail distinguishes aluminum from steel by virtue of its expression of lower strength but fails to meet the high level of refinement inherent in metals and exhibited in the cleaner steel connections. These particular aluminum joints give the legs of the prototype a somewhat lumpy appearance.

WORKABILITY

Metal components designed primarily for resistance to force (structural stock, bars, rods, strips, plates) have a relationship to workability that is different from components designed primarily for coverage of an area

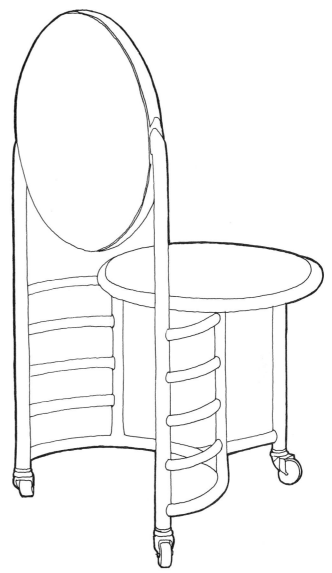

FIGURE 6-26. Steel tube chair for the S. C. Johnson and Son Administration Building. (From a photograph, *The Wright State: Frank Lloyd Wright in Wisconsin*, p. 77.)

(sheet). The two types of components warrant separate examinations, begining with structural members and similar shapes. Changes to the basic forms of metals after the first manufacturing process constitutes working the metal. Cutting a pipe so that it may be removed from the manufacturing line and may be reasonably handled and shipped is not an act of working the pipe but the final step of manufacturing. Further cutting of the pipe for installation or fabrication purposes is considered working the material. Bending is a type of working, as is any other change to the first manufactured form.

Wright's enthusiastic claim of steel's nearly unlimited workability is curious, considering his unwillingness

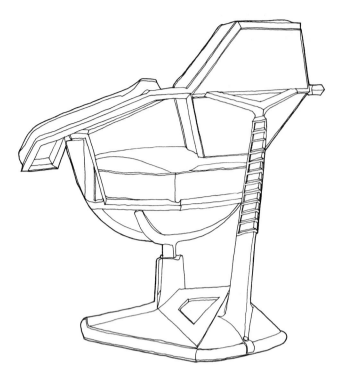

Figure 6-27. Cast aluminum chair for the H. C. Price Company Tower. (From a photograph, *Frank Lloyd Wright at The Metropolitan Museum of Art*, p. 47.)

to exploit the greater workability of wood. The greater strength of steel requires more sophisticated equipment, greater skill, more time, and more prior planning to work than does the more moderate strength of wood. Nevertheless, he thought that steel could be "easily bored, punched, planed, cut, and polished" like wood. It is, he claimed, "more easily and cheaply curved or bent or twisted or woven to any extent."[10] In a discussion of steel's workability, his references to its rigidity (taken to mean '*strength*') and ease of fastening offer some insight into his otherwise inexplicable position regarding this property.

Wood, although easily shaped, does not have the strength or durability to maintain thin shapes when exposed to the weather. Steel is more difficult than wood to reshape but offers smaller minimum and larger maximum sizes in section and elevation. It offers more precise connections and a greater variety of connection types and configurations. Consequently, there is a wide range of worked shapes in steel that are viable in exterior installations if one is willing to pay the cost of overcoming steel's natural resistance to reshaping. Although certain iron constructions of the 19th century were highly decorative and historically reminiscent, Wright did not dwell on their offensiveness to the degree that he did regarding wood's role in Victorian architecture. He could have hardly supported the working of wood after his strong rejection of the Victorian treatment

of it. On the other hand, Wright's rejection of the International Style did not hinder his embracing of worked steel, as it was not characteristic of that style. He tended to favor an environment of more rather than less latitude in his design decisions and the working of steel provided more options to him than did the working of wood.

Wright's limited concern for cost made the variety of forms available from the working of steel more accessible to him than to designers who feel more restricted by budgets. Wright's high tolerance for cost, however, does not elevate the level of workability that is actually reasonable for steel. Since steel products commonly used in structural applications (virtually all but sheet) are designed to resist bending, to bend them seems opposed to their essence. Greater tolerance for bending non-structural products and for bending products with thinner sections seems reasonable. To bend pipe, a product that must resist buckling but is not a product primarily designed to resist bending stresses, seems more reasonable than to force a flanged component into a curved shape against its strong axis.

The reasoning for the other metals is similar except that, because they are weaker than steel and not primarily designed for building structures, their nature logically tolerates a greater degree of working than does that of steel. A specific degree of bending cannot be identified that indicates the level of working appropriate for each metal. Extremes can be described that constitute excessive working or that are clearly within the logical limits. Since steel's workability is not extremely high, buildings that have a character based entirely or to large degree on the bending of steel have superseded the nature of the material. On the other hand, the nature of steel would seem to tolerate the expression in a building of some incidental bending. Much of Wright's bent metals have round sections, several examples of which occur in his later work. Among miscellaneous worked products, steel pipe and rods are curved at the Greek Orthodox Church (1956), and much aluminum and steel pipe are bent at the Marin County Civic Center (1957). A considerable amount of flat bar and glazing-frame stock is bent at the Juvenile Cultural Study Center (1957). The quantity of curved pipe at the Grady Gammage Memorial Auditorium (1959) is not large but it constitutes most of the metal expressed at that building. A large quantity of flat aluminum bars is bent at the Marin building. Although the character of these buildings is not primarily derived from their metals, the character of the metals is derived almost entirely from their bending. This tends to fall somewhat beyond the nature of the metals, in spite of the fact that many of them are not steel and that the sections are round or relatively weak.

Since steel products are not designed specifically to resist cutting, to cut steel would seem to be less contrary to the nature of the material than to bend it. Since steel is more difficult to cut than is wood, it seems reasonable to accept less cutting in steel than in wood. Reasoning for setting natural limits on the cutting of steel and other metals follows that for bending. A building's artistic message that depends entirely on the cutting of steel would seem to express more working than is within its nature. Although Wright would not agree, the high workability of wood is compatible with the extent of cutting common in Victorian detailing. The lesser workability of steel and other metals is not.

Wright did not cut metals to an extent that draws attention in his architecture to the act itself. The greatest sense of cutting occurs in his most angular detailing. Cuts made at an angle constitute a modestly higher level of working than right-angled cuts, as they are longer and slightly more complicated to perform. The acute angled fins on the Riverview Terrace Restaurant sign, and the angular plate on the Taliesin West gate (previously addressed) are among the details in Wright's work expressing to a high degree the working steel by cutting.

The limited number of angular fins in each composition prevents the sense of working from dominating the image of the appurtenances or the architecture. Part of the reason for this circumstance is that the angularity that results from the cutting emphasizes the spirit of steel with regard to sharpness and precision and thus draws attention from the expressive ramifications of the cutting that produced it. The cutting of the curved metal fins in the arched light-standard system at the Gammage Auditorium does not seem excessive, as the small thickness of the plate facilitated the cutting and expresses the thinness, and therefore sharpness, of the otherwise soft image of steel in the component.

Wright's claim that sheet metal "may be stamped to any desired form"[11] indicates that he saw no philosophical limit on the extent to which the material could be worked. Characteristically, he thought that sheet metal could be worked to inappropriate ends, which was the case if it was made to resemble another material. He lamented the "imitation in metal of a wood paneled door," which "was usually 'grained' to complete the ruse."[12] He sought the use of "sheet metal...as a fine material for its own sake."[13] His rejection of material imitations and his desire to exploit the essence of sheet metal suggests that properties unique to the material would be expressed in his work. Given his record with other materials, however, it is likely that he defined sheet metal's nature by its ability to yield beauty rather than by some combination of physical properties.

An extensive use of sheet metal occurs in the copper cladding of the Price Company Tower (1952). The

FIGURE 6-28. Small copper panels of the H. C. Price Company Tower in the foreground. Large panels in the background.

panels, glazing louvers, and fins constitute a major part of the building's aesthetic order. The horizontal and vertical fins express the thinness and sharpness of the metal that is difficult to achieve with cladding panels alone, the edges (thicknesses) of which are not typically expressed. The production of the sheet into slender louvers and fins is a relatively routine level of working, involving simple cuts and joinery. The less traditional working occurs in the faces of the panels where two different patterns appear. Large panels have a boardlike pattern suggesting the proportions and thickness typical of wood cladding, although not in its traditional configuration. No imitation is suggested, but the patterns could be reproduced on the building relatively easily in wood. To accept the linear patterns as reflecting the unique spirit of the sheet metal would require viewing the nature of sheet metal and lumber as being similar. Since the essence of sheet metal is thought to differ from that of wood, the working of this sheet falls short of its potential to express the unique nature of the material. Wright believed in the individuality of materials, which if rigorously expressed would not yield images in which the exchange of substances was relatively easy.

Smaller panels are imprinted with trapezoids, triangles, parallelograms, and other shapes that are reminiscent of the concrete block patterns of the S. Freeman House (1924). The acute angles impressed in the surfaces of both the concrete units and the metal panels reflect a sense of sharpness like metal and unlike concrete's natural bluntness. The relative shallowness of the metal impression reflects the limitations, in this regard, of stamping compared to casting. The ductility of the copper makes stamping viable but limits the depth that can be achieved. Depth in casting does not depend on ductility, thus is not limited by it.

The depth in the block pattern also reflects greater mass than does the shallowness of the patterns in the sheet. In both cases these are accurate reflections of the material's character. Although some linearity is present in both components, its failure to dominate either pattern reflects a circumstance common to casting and stamping. Neither is subject to the form limitations of rolling, extrusion, or other linear processes. If the patterns in the block and sheet are more similar than demanded by the nature of the materials, the greater fault lies with the block. More bluntness and less refinement would be logical in the concrete. The small panels on the Price Tower express the workability of the material without superseding its practical limitations.

The use of more than one pattern in the sheet metal at the tower fails to maximize "standardization" which Wright claimed, "is in the nature of both sheet-metal process and material."[14] Since Wright tended to avoid extremes defined by literal applications of a concept, the two patterns in the sheet metal of this building are typical of his general approach to design. It would appear that he failed to exploit the nature of sheet metal including the nature of its processing—to the maximum possible for larger architectural (nonmaterial) goals.

The copper sheet on the fascias of the Florida Southern College campus buildings (1938–54) and on the Price Tower facade (1952) and the aluminum cladding on the tripod structure of the Beth Sholom Synagogue (1954) are similar in their use as formwork for concrete. In these applications concrete was poured against the sheet metal, taking the shape of the stamped patterns. The detail is compatible with Wright's observation that "all 'spread' materials need reinforcement,"[15] although he was referring to steel as the stiffening element. The use of the solid backing behind the sheet metal is within the nature of the thin material but it yielded, in Wright's installations, no visual characteristic in which the composite nature of the assembly is expressed. Given the fact that entirely concealed concrete need not fill every crevice of the pattern in the back of the panel, the shape of the sheet is free to respond to the full potential of metal. That is to say, if the presence of the concrete is ignored, narrow projections can be formed in the metal into which the concrete would not flow from behind.

Recognition of the concrete in the expression would encourage simpler, wider, and more shallow impressions. No claim is made that the configuration of the metal panel necessarily reflect the presence of the hidden concrete as the issue is within the realm of expressive honesty, not within to scope of this study. Reinforcement of the metal panel faces at the Price Tower was necessary during the placement of concrete. This took the form of wood pieces fitted into the pattern of the metal in addition to the usual formwork bracing. The tendency of the concrete to deflect the impressions in the metal illustrates the workability of the sheet but brings into question its use in a structural role to support the wet concrete. The sense of labor-intensiveness in the cutting and fitting of the small wood pieces into the pattern reflects the mismatch of the nature of sheet metal and its use as formwork.

The repetitive triangular pattern in the Florida campus fascias reflects the sharpness of metals in a philosophical way and simulates no other material. The simple pattern is not central to the nature of concrete because it fails to maximize a sense of plasticity and challenges the matrix to completely fill numerous corners. The subsequent loss of many metal fascias revealed the ability of the concrete to assume the shape of the pattern in most cases. The exposure of the concrete fascias revealed an expression that was more in the nature of metal than concrete because of its angularity and sharp points. Criticism cannot be leveled at this slight mismatch of material and texture, since the concrete was not intended to be exposed.

The linearity and sectional rectangularity of the patterns in the aluminum cladding of the tripod structure at the Beth Sholom Synagogue resemble slender lumber strips juxtaposed to create a stepped surface. The lack of refinement in the aluminum accommodates the forming of concrete to the extent that, in spite of the silver color on the sheet metal, it is not entirely clear from simple observation whether the surface is concrete or metal. The working of the aluminum used at the synagogue failed to express the unique nature of the metal. In contrast, the working of the copper fascias at the Florida campus yielded an appearance more like metal than like other materials. Repetition of the same small rectangular impressions around the copper fascia of the Dana House (1902) captures the spirit of standardization that Wright thought to be in the nature of sheet metal. The pattern creates forms that are rather delicate for exterior wood but are not especially sharp or otherwise distinguished from wood except at the corners. Fascia corners form knifelike profiles as each corner slopes upward to a point. The many corners of the roof combined with the fine texture, afforded by the slotlike impressions give the fascia system a sense that is ultimately more like metal than wood.

STRENGTH

Instead of product form, which dominated Wright's attention to other materials, strength was his focus in steel. His claim that steel had "a miracle of strength"[16] echoed a recurring theme in his discourse on the mate-

FIGURE 6-29. Decorative aluminum cladding on tripod leg (at right) of the Beth Sholom Synagogue. Corrugated wired glass cladding.

FIGURE 6-30. Copper fascia of the Susan Lawrence Dana Residence. (Courtesy The Illinois Historic Preservation Agency—The Dana-Thomas House and Doug Carr, photographer, the Dana-Thomas Foundation)

rial. Given his admiration for this property, demonstrations of great strength could logically be anticipated in his steel work. More specifically, he admired the tensile strength of steel most, claiming that "lightness, openness and tenuous strength combined are its building characteristics."[17] His reference to strength reflects his focus on certain physical characteristics that, although not a commitment to a particular form, calls for thinness of form. He thought that these characteristics "ought to be associated never with heavy stone or concrete"[18] in tall buildings, believing that glass and metal panels were the logical cladding for a steel structure.

Wright was not referring to reinforcing steel in his rejection of concrete as a cladding for steel structure. He thought that reinforced concrete was an expression of the tensile ability of steel (in the form of strands) and an ideal vehicle for steel to fulfill its unique potential in this realm of strength. This attitude, combined with an apparent ambivalence toward the aesthetic potential of

steel form, resulted in vague expressions of steel strength in his built work. Wright thought that during his lifetime steel had been largely manufactured into the form of lumber and used as lumber.[19] The complaint was essentially in regard to strength, as he saw steel as a tensile element and apparently saw lumber as a bending element. Although Wright often depended upon steel's great bending strength and occasionally upon its pure tensile ability, he most often expressed the compressive strength of the material when he exposed structural steel.

Since the ability to support compressive loads is not unique to steel, demonstrations that steel's compressive strength is greater than that of wood, masonry, and concrete are necessary to distinguish (structurally) from those materials. The expression of the slenderness typical of steel columns helps achieve this end, as the steel is shown to carry its loading with a small cross section. Other detailing can ignore or boost the sense of steel's strength that is usually reflected in simple exposure of the columns. The steel pipes exposed at the H. Price, Jr. House (1954), H. Price, Sr. House (1954), Beth Sholom Synagogue (1954), Juvenile Cultural Study Center (1957), and under the ramps of the Grady Gammage Memorial Auditorium (1959) are appropriately slender but are not shown to carry heavy loading. The support of small terraces, canopies, roofs, and ramps does not offer the same structural challenge as carrying building masses. Consequently, the expression of strength in these examples is not maximized.

An interior expression of relatively high compressive strength occurs at the Walker House (1951) where four slender (two-inch thick) cast-iron posts support the roof over the living room. Since the roof is pitched, its profile has greater mass than the thinner-looking, and therefore seemingly lighter, flat roofs supported by steel columns elsewhere. The strength expression of the columns is intensified by the glass surrounding the living space, which shows clearly that the exterior wall is not providing support to the roof. A greater demonstration of steel's compressive strength occurs at Beth Sholom Synagogue in the large steel tripod structure that supports the sanctuary roof. Although the general form of the structure can be seen both inside and outside the building, the cladding of the wide-flange members first with concrete and then aluminum pushes the strong compressive statement slightly away from the image of steel. Given the slope of the members and the lateral loading of the roof, steel's great ability to resist bending stresses is also reflected.

Where Wright hid structural steel entirely from view, the burden of its expression falls upon the property of strength because the form of the material is not part of the image. If the strength of steel is to affect the image of a building in a way that brings steel to mind without seeing it, the structural achievement must be extreme. The thoughtful professional can discern the presence of hidden steel with certainty in some of Wright's work but only suspect it where alternatives are viable. Although entirely obscuring its presence does not necessarily violate the spirit of steel, it seems reasonable to expect that architecture purported to be designed within the nature of its materials would be affected by them in some visually discernable way.

Because of concrete's significant strength, its presence in a building where structural steel is hidden obscures steel's contributions to the spatial qualities of the building. While great spans in wood or masonry buildings might be correctly attributed to hidden steel simply because they are too great for the visible material, such is not the case in such buildings as the Barnsdall House (1917), Johnson Wax Administration Building (1936), the Pfeiffer Chapel (1938), and the Marin County Civic Center (1957) due to the confusion between the contributions of the concrete and the steel. Structural steel is present in each of the buildings but is neither expressed nor violated because of the vagueness that surrounds it. Hardly less vague is steel's (or iron's) contribution to the interior volumes of the Dana (1902), Willits (1902), Cheney (1903), Robie (1906), Coonley (1906), Tomek (1907), May (1908), Gilmore (1908), and other houses as well as the Unitarian Church (1947), the Riverview Terrace Restaurant (1956), and the Kundert Medical Clinic (1956) where concrete is not an issue. The spans and/or loads assigned to the steel are excessive for lumber in these buildings and others but not necessarily to the degree

FIGURE 6-31. Cantilevered roof of the R. W. Lindholm Service Station. Battered column at garage visible at left.

recognizable by most observers. Only the most remarkably vast spaces such as the H. Johnson House (Wingspread, 1937) living room, express the presence of hidden steel with any degree of certainty.

The remarkably cantilevered roof of the Lindholm Service Station (1957) expresses the presence of hidden steel with reasonable clarity. The steel trusses in the roof of the service station appear to have affected the architectural expression beyond just the dynamacy they lend to the structural statement. An early sketch shows the roof with a much flatter pitch and thus a lower profile than the one built. It would seem that large depth of the two trusses within the roof that was required by the cantilever forced the peak of the roof up from the earliest images contemplated, thus tying the final image of the architecture to the nature of steel with regard to its strength. Without some hint of the truss geometry in the roof elevation, however, the resulting form does not express the specific forms of the hidden steel trusses.

A disadvantage of failing to express hidden steel in some way is that the weaker material visible in the construction might appear to be stronger than it is. Hidden steel causes the brick of the cantilevered terrace balcony at the H. Price, Jr. House (1954) and that of the half vault at the Morris Gift Shop (1948) to seem to perform structurally beyond its nature. In such cases, it could be said that the steel is violated because it appears in the architecture with another material's form characteristics, but this is not the larger issue. The greater concern regarding the nature of materials is the misrepresentation of the visible material's strength. The structural statement of the assembly violates the nature of the visible material if it appears to be the structural material and is not. This is usually not a problem in roofs where only the fascia and shingles are visible in the elevation. Although the roof structure might be correctly thought

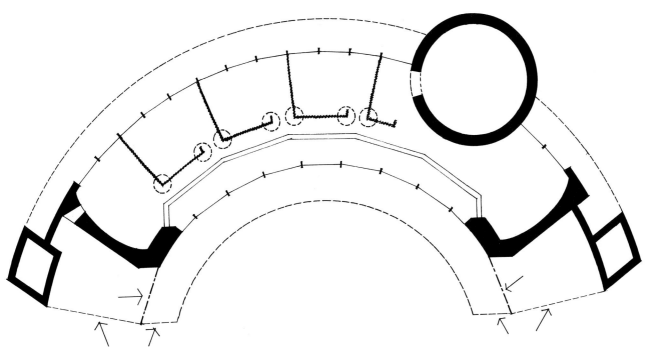

Figure 6-32. Floor plan of the Herbert Jacobs Residence II. Positions of hanger rods shown with dotted circles. Beams and fascias with flitch plates shown with arrows. (From Frank Lloyd Wright Archives drawing 4812.015.)

to be wood, the reality of the structure is often too vague to clearly misrepresent the strength of wood.

An exception occurs at the second Jacobs House (1943), due to the visibility of the wood joists under the overhangs (one of the less common soffit details in Wright's work). Flitch plates occur in the beams cantilevered from the stone toward the end fascias and in the end fascias themselves. They make the double cantilevers of the roof at each end of the building possible given the depth of the system. They give the visible wood a boost in apparent strength as the roof structure is thin for the cantilever and the steel is not noticeable. The double cantilevers in the roof of this house would be especially problematic without steel in that the end fascias make two gentle turns thus preventing their full length from being utilized as a single spanning element. The result is an apparent structural performance by the wood which misrepresents its nature with regard to strength. On several occasions, Wright used steel to solve the structural challenge to wood in long roof overhangs most of which lack the clarity of violation to the nature of wood found at the second Jacobs House because the structural wood is not visible.

The Larkin Building (1903) and Gammage Auditorium (1959) are examples at extremes of Wright's career that are, to a great degree, steel but in almost no way express the presence of the material. Brick and concrete are likely to be assigned credit for the structural work of steel in the former and perhaps in the latter as

well. The variety of materials at the auditorium, combined with some vagueness of identity of several of them, leave the role of the steel largely shrouded in mystery.

Wright expressed steel in a few minor tensile roles, a stress condition for which he thought steel to be particularly suited. The structural expression of the chain system in his Oak Park Studio (discussed previously) is clear but lacks the scale and loading that steel needs to fulfill its potential for expressing great strength. The low intensity of the strength expression is especially noticeable because of the rather large section of the chains compared to the smaller section needed in cable for the same loads. Series of thin bars and thin rods are expressed in tension as supports for hanging stairs at Fallingwater (1935) and the Mossberg House (1948). Although the thinness and tensile mode of the hangers establish themselves as clearly metallic, the loading is light for the potential of steel.

Steel in pure tension was used for larger loads on several occasions but was not expressed. The Willits and Heurtley Houses (1902), for example, have tensile rods concealed among the wood framing. It is unlikely that the spaciousness or other physical manifestation that are facilitated by such tensile applications would be recognized as resulting from steel by an uninformed observer. The failure of the upper floor of the second Jacobs House to connect to the exterior wall on the court side combined with the absence of columns suggest that a hanging system is present. The small distance between

FIGURE 6-33. Hanging stairs at the Edgar J. Kaufmann, Sr. Residence. Large concrete piers supporting the main cantilevered balcony visible to left of stair. (Courtesy The Frank Lloyd Wright Archives)

the edge of the second floor and the exterior wall obscures slightly the fact that it does not connect, however. The seven steel rods that support the floor from the roof rafters were visible during the earliest days of occupancy as the walls of the upper floor were installed at a later date. Eventually the rods were enclosed within the partitions, thus eliminating their expressive role in the interior.

Although the focus is on Wright's built work, certain unbuilt projects are of interest because of their response to his verbal focus on the tensile ability of steel. The use of steel as reinforcing for concrete was not the only outlet he envisioned for the use of the material in pure tension. He admired the Brooklyn Bridge as a legitimate expression of the tensile strength of steel.[20] In a similar spirit, the proposed tensile steel structures of the Twin Suspension Bridges for Pittsburgh Point Park Civic Center (1948) and the Self-Service Garage for E. J. Kaufmann, Pittsburgh (1949) would have reflected a sense of refinement and strength greater than that of the chains at his Oak Park Studio. Although the sizes of the cables would have had to be thicker than the studio chains and the connections more massive, they would have seemed thin

and precise in relationship to the great sizes of the garage and bridge.

Thin lines are difficult to see if not expressed in groups. The expression of the cables in the bridge would have been enhanced by the large number used. Their convergence to high points of support in both projects increases their visual density as they move farther from the eye, thus helping maintain their presence in the composition. The decorative devices hung on the bridge lines are of special interest because of their nonutilitarian nature and their rarity among the tensile systems of other designers. They would have further secured the identity of the steel lines in the elevation by drawing attention to them and increasing their importance beyond the minimum established by their structural role. The high profile of the garage mass would have tended to obscure the presence of the steel, since— when viewed in perspective—the tensile lines would be foreshortened and partially hidden by the parapet of the facade. The shorter spans in the garage and the strength of the concrete masses would have diminished the apparent structural importance of the cables. In drawings of the structure, the cables do not look as if they are as necessary as they appear to be in

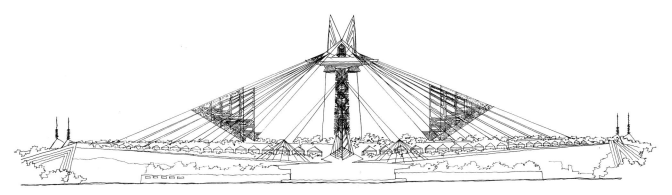

FIGURE 6-34. Elevation of the Twin Suspension Bridges for Pittsburgh Point Park Civic Center (not built). (From Frank Lloyd Wright Archives drawing 4836.003.)

the drawings of the bridge. It is likely that the spirit of steel would have been stronger in the bridge but also present in the garage.

DURABILITY

Wright's comment that steel's tendency to rust was "a fatal weakness"[21] indicates a level of interest in the phenomenon different from that typical of other architects. Most designers deal with steel's vulnerability to corrosion as a technical problem rather than a design issue. The routine nature of the circumstance has drawn little public comment from others. In contrast Wright observed, almost with enthusiasm, that "owing to its nature it may be plated with other metals or protected by coverings."[22] It would seem that the nature of steel with regard to durability justified hiding its surface from view to a degree to be determined by the designer. The circumstance is compatible with Wright's lack of interest in flanged components and the surface of steel in general.

His reference to combining steel with a protective material is taken to mean reinforced concrete, which begs the question of expressing the durability of steel. Plating steel with a metal of similar color (zinc, tin, aluminum, chrome) would minimize the expression of steel's durability limitations due to the similarity in appearance of the protective metal to the surface of clean bright steel. This never became an issue, however, as Wright did not express steel that was plated for protection. His proposal to cover steel pipe and plate in the nave of the Greek Orthodox Church (1956) with gold leaf is not a durability issue, as weathering is not involved. The covering of steel offers a wide range of intensities at which steel's durability limitations can be expressed.

Embedding steel within the framing or behind the cladding of other materials protects it from weathering to a near maximum degree. In these cases, however, the expression of steel typically is lost entirely, thus preventing any expression of its durability limitations. Covering the metal with paint provides significant protection and reveals the coating, its role, and steel's durability limitations to the degree that the paint is apparent. Paint offers the greatest potential for expressing the durability of steel as, among the options for covering the surface of the material, it obscures the characteristics of the metal the least.

The terra-cotta red color on the Taliesin West gate (1953) and the Riverview Terrace Restaurant (1956) sign are reasonably noticeable hues. Although they are earth tones, it does not appear that the color is meant to entirely disappear into the background nor does the steel seem to be unpainted. A similar color appears on large grilles of steel pipe over certain windows at the Marin County Civic Center (1957). Although it is not a strong color, it has a sense of deliberateness that prevents it from fading into the background. Wright's partiality to the hue and its use by him upon occasion as part of the aesthetic order of a building elevates its importance and therefore its ability to express steel's need for protection from the elements.

The gold paint on the pipe supports at the ramp of the Gammage Auditorium (1959) draws attention to itself and, consequently, to the fact that the steel has a protective coating. This contrasts with his use of darker colors on the steel pipes under the H. Price, Jr. terrace balcony (red) and over the entry to the Beth Sholom Synagogue (black). Because the dark pipes tend to recede into the shadows, the expression of steel's durability as well as form is subdued. The working drawings for the H. Price, Sr. House call for Wright's favorite reddish hue to be painted on the gate, columns, and window grilles. Although the two tones of blue paint that were ultimately applied to the metals seem foreign to Wright's typical color schemes, they are more expressive of the durability limitations of steel than is his typical terra-cotta red color. The brighter and more unusual

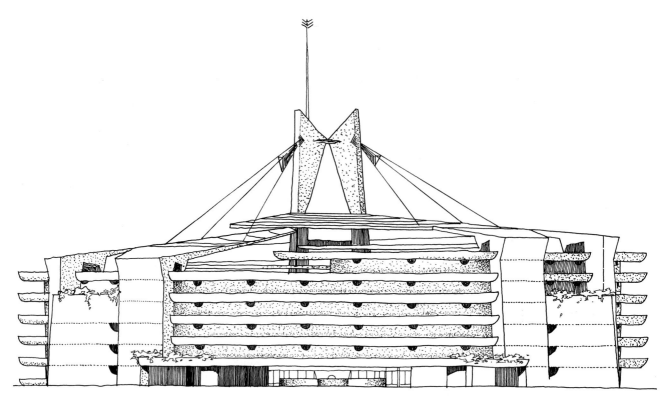

FIGURE 6-35. Elevation of the Self Service Garage for Edgar J. Kaufmann. (From Frank Lloyd Wright Archives drawing 4923.051.)

colors celebrate more intensely their presence and thus protective role.

Wright's tendency to exploit the strength of steel more than its appearance clouds the issue of durability expression. He recognized steel's limitations in durability and seems to have considered it to various degrees in his design strategies. It does not appear that steel's durability governed his larger design decisions.

Conclusion

Outside the International School, the utilitarian and impersonal character of flanged steel was generally considered to be appropriate only for industrial applications. In his prediction that to future archaeologists "only our industrial buildings could tell anything worth knowing about us,"[23] Wright embraced the industrial image but did not necessarily commit to the desirability of industrial-looking steel outside that realm. His limited use of the material as a vehicle of expression might be attributed in part to the size and nature of his commissions. His limited expression of steel must also be recognized as largely a matter of choice, however, as demonstrated by the extensive residential as well as commercial use of steel by Mies van der Rohe, Philip Johnson, and other contemporaries.

Wright's focus on steel's strength over its other properties is revealed in his comment on the common practice in the early 20th century of cladding steel skyscrapers with historical forms and masonry in general. "Steel, behind it all," he observed, "still nobly stands up to its more serious responsibilities."[24] The responsibility to which he refers is steel's structural role. Although it would seem in his discourse that he was complaining about the failure of skyscraper architects to express the form of the steel, he did not demonstrate a commitment in his own work to rectify the insult to the material. The Music Pavilion (1956) at Taliesin West is, given its exposed steel bents, a near exception. The identity of the steel is more obscured by its rectangular tubular form, however, than is usually typical of the lumberlike shape because of its similarity to wood of a similar profile and color elsewhere in the complex. The pavilion notwithstanding, Wright never brought a commission to fruition wherein the nature of steel was expressed at a high intensity.

Endnotes

1. Wright, Frank Lloyd. 1927. "In the Cause of Architecture: Part III. Steel." *Architectural Record*

62(2):163–166. Reprint. 1975. *In the Cause of Architecture*, ed., Frederick Gutheim. New York: McGraw-Hill. p. 139. *ARCHITECTURAL RECORD*, (August/1927), copyright 1975 by McGraw-Hill, Inc. All rights reserved. Reproduced with the permission of the publisher.

2. Ibid., 140. *ARCHITECTURAL RECORD*, (August/1927), copyright 1975 by McGraw-Hill, Inc. All rights reserved. Reproduced with the permission of the publisher.

3. Ibid., 141. *ARCHITECTURAL RECORD*, (August/1927), copyright 1975 by McGraw-Hill, Inc. All rights reserved. Reproduced with the permission of the publisher.

4. Ibid. *ARCHITECTURAL RECORD*, (August/1927), copyright 1975 by McGraw-Hill, Inc. All rights reserved. Reproduced with the permission of the publisher.

5. Ibid., 139. *ARCHITECTURAL RECORD*, (August/1927), copyright 1975 by McGraw-Hill, Inc. All rights reserved. Reproduced with the permission of the publisher.

6. Wright, Frank Lloyd. 1932. *An Autobiography*. Revised. 1943. New York: Duell, Sloan and Pearce. Copyright by The Frank Lloyd Wright Foundation. p. 150. Courtesy The Frank Lloyd Wright Foundation.

7. Ibid., 151. Courtesy The Frank Lloyd Wright Foundation.

8. Wright, Frank Lloyd. 1928. "In the Cause of Architecture: VI. The Meaning of Materials—Glass." *Architectural Record* 64(1):10–16. Reprint. 1975. *In the Cause of Architecture*, ed., Frederick Gutheim. New York: McGraw-Hill. p. 198. *ARCHITECTURAL RECORD*, (July/1928), copyright 1975 by McGraw-Hill, Inc. All rights reserved. Reproduced with the permission of the publisher.

9. Lipman, Jonathan. 1986. *Frank Lloyd Wright and the Johnson Wax Buildings*. New York: Rizzoli International Publications, Inc. pp. 84–91. These pages describe the development of the furniture for the Johnson Wax Building and provide some information on the Midway Gardens furniture.

10. Wright, Frank Lloyd. 1927. "In the Cause of Architecture: Part III. Steel." *Architectural Record* 62(2):163–166. Reprint. 1975. *In the Cause of*

Architecture, ed., Frederick Gutheim. New York: McGraw-Hill. p. 139. *ARCHITECTURAL RECORD*, (August/1927), copyright 1975 by McGraw-Hill, Inc. All rights reserved. Reproduced with the permission of the publisher.

11. Wright, Frank Lloyd. 1928. "In the Cause of Architecture: VIII. Sheet Metal and a Modern Instance." *Architectural Record* 64(4):334–342. Reprint. 1975. I*n the Cause of Architecture*, ed. Frederick Gutheim. New York: McGraw-Hill. p. 216. *ARCHITECTURAL RECORD*, (October/1928), copyright 1975 by McGraw-Hill, Inc. All rights reserved. Reproduced with the permission of the publisher.

12. Ibid., 216–217. *ARCHITECTURAL RECORD*, (October/1928), copyright 1975 by McGraw-Hill, Inc. All rights reserved. Reproduced with the permission of the publisher.

13. Ibid., 213. *ARCHITECTURAL RECORD*, (October/1928), copyright 1975 by McGraw-Hill, Inc. All rights reserved. Reproduced with the permission of the publisher.

14. Ibid., 217. *ARCHITECTURAL RECORD*, (October/1928), copyright 1975 by McGraw-Hill, Inc. All rights reserved. Reproduced with the permission of the publisher.

15. Ibid., 213. *ARCHITECTURAL RECORD*, (October/1928), copyright 1975 by McGraw-Hill, Inc. All rights reserved. Reproduced with the permission of the publisher.

16. Wright, Frank Lloyd. 1927. "In the Cause of Architecture: Part III. Steel." *Architectural Record* 62(2):163–166. Reprint. 1975. *In the Cause of Architecture*, ed., Frederick Gutheim. New York: McGraw-Hill. p. 139. *ARCHITECTURAL RECORD*, (August/1927), copyright 1975 by McGraw-Hill, Inc. All rights reserved. Reproduced with the permission of the publisher.

17. Wright, Frank Lloyd. 1932. *An Autobiography*. Revised. 1943. New York: Duell, Sloan and Pearce. Copyright by The Frank Lloyd Wright Foundation. p. 317. Courtesy The Frank Lloyd Wright Foundation.

18. Ibid. Courtesy The Frank Lloyd Wright Foundation.

19. Pfeiffer, Bruce Brooks, ed. 1987. *Frank Lloyd Wright, His Living Voice*. Fresno, CA: California State

University Press. Copyright by The Frank Lloyd Wright Foundation. p. 172.

20. Ibid., p. 173.

21. Wright, Frank Lloyd. 1927. "In the Cause of Architecture: Part III. Steel." *Architectural Record* 62(2):163–166. Reprint. 1975. *In the Cause of Architecture*, ed., Frederick Gutheim. New York: McGraw-Hill. p. 139. *ARCHITECTURAL RECORD*, (August/1927), copyright 1975 by McGraw-Hill, Inc. All rights reserved. Reproduced with the permission of the publisher.

22. Ibid. *ARCHITECTURAL RECORD*, (August/1927), copyright 1975 by McGraw-Hill, Inc. All rights reserved. Reproduced with the permission of the publisher.

23. Wright, Frank Lloyd. 1931. *Modern Architecture: Being the Kahn Lectures for 1930*. Reprint. 1987. ed. Bruce Brooks Pfeiffer. Carbondale and Edwardsville, IL: Southern Illinois University Press. Copyright 1987 by The Frank Lloyd Wright Foundation. p. 115. Courtesy The Frank Lloyd Wright Foundation.

24. Ibid., 95. Courtesy The Frank Lloyd Wright Foundation.

7

INTRODUCTION

Wright's comment that "aesthetically," concrete had "neither song nor story"[1] indicates that he saw little more artistic potential in the surface of concrete than he saw in the surface of steel. Concrete's great strength, durability, and potential for a variety of forms, however, gave him more design flexibility and left more latitude for defining the character of the material than did the properties of steel. His thought that it was "endlessly subject to [his] will"[2] explains why he was more willing to expose concrete in his architecture than he was steel. Wright's fondness for plasticity in architecture motivated his citing of plasticity as a property of nearly every material he encountered. Concrete, however, is the one structural material which truly embodies plasticity in the traditional sense, that is, an affinity for visually soft imagery. Although concrete's compatibility with curvilinear forms was not lost on Wright, this type of plasticity did not find expression at the large scale until his later work.

FORM

To Wright, concrete was a material that a designer could use in "whatever shape he may desire."[3] Not all shapes were acceptable to Wright, however, for reasons that were not directly related to the material's nature. In keeping with his disdain for imitation, he rejected forms that were similar to those common in wood, for example. Referring to concrete, he lamented that it was the material's "misfortune to project as wooden beams," and could "unluckily...take the form (and texture too) of wooden posts and planks."[4] Wright's use of concrete

FIGURE 7-1. Concrete structure of the Harold C. Price Company Tower cantilevers over concrete base. Concrete planes project above building volume at top. Balconies cantilever beyond curtain wall at right. Vertical and horizontal copper fins.

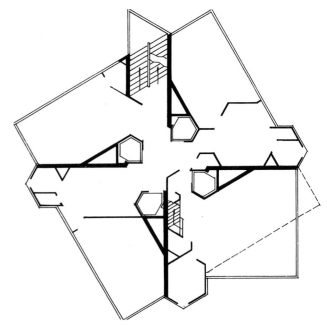

FIGURE 7-2. A floor plan of the Harold C. Price Company Tower showing vertical concrete planes between spaces, cantilevered floors, cantilevered balcony (dotted), and cantilevered stair landing. (From a drawing, *The Story of the Tower, p. 31.*)

in woodlike forms at the Kaufmann House (1935), on the Florida Southern College campus (1938–54), and elsewhere, suggests that his definition of wood imagery was not based on a literal interpretation of the material's properties.

Wright believed that the form of concrete was a function "of casting rather than a matter of anything at all derived from its own nature."[5] His exclusion of casting from the concrete's nature in the remark narrows the range of aspects he thought to be within the nature of the material. Since he credited reinforced concrete's strength to steel and saw no inherent beauty in the substance, there was little left among concrete's properties to define its nature according to his criteria. He saw aggregate as being a unique characteristic of concrete but thought that it was not aesthetically significant in defining concrete's nature.[6] The idea indicates that Wright saw the nature of a material as being defined only by characteristics that had aesthetic potential rather than by all of its properties.

Although he complained of difficulty in identifying form that was uniquely concrete, Wright was able to suggest several possibilities including its ability to "hang as a slab...or lie low and heavily in mass upon the ground."[7] He also accepted concrete in the form of a perforated screen, evidence of which can be found in the Pfeiffer Chapel (1938). The continuity of surface and physical solidity of a structural slab separates the image of concrete from that of framed floors and roofs. Concrete's sense of continuity in this regard is different from the sense of assembly inherent in framing. The absence of cladding, trim, and numerous joints in concrete significantly contributes to this distinction between monolithic and framed construction. Unlike linear forms such as beams and columns found in wood and steel, the monolithic structural plane is unique to concrete.

Vertical planes resting on a base do not distinguish concrete's structural properties from those of masonry, as such planes are in simple compression like any brick wall. If bending is introduced into the system, the slabs would express more clearly concrete's unique combination of form and strength. The large vertical planes extending above the building mass at the Price Company Tower (1952), for example, express concrete's ability to form continuous slabs. The height of the planes compared to their relative thinness indicates

FIGURE 7-3. Cantilevered roof planes and balconies juxtaposed against stacked stone at the Edgar J. Kaufmann, Sr. Residence (Fallingwater). Massive concrete piers just visible in the recess under the main balcony. (Courtesy of the Western Pennsylvania Conservancy. Photo by Harold Corsini.)

FIGURE 7-4. Ribs of balcony floor slab visible prior to installation of deck at the Edgar J. Kaufmann, Sr. Residence. Perforated cantilevered canopy. Vertical planes of railings. Rounded edges on all planes. (Courtesy The Frank Lloyd Wright Archives)

that they have the strength to resist wind loading which, with some angularity in their edge profile, distinguishes them slightly from masonry walls.

Wright expressed a combination of concrete's structural potential and its ability to form continuous planes in several large roof overhangs and other cantilevers. For a slab to read as such, its thickness and a significant part of its length and width must be revealed in a facade. Exposing only the edge of a slab in a flush relationship with adjacent surfaces does not verify that the concrete is wider than a beam (measured perpendicular to the exposed surface). A cantilevered slab maximizes the exposure of its proportions, as well as its surfaces, if the edges and soffit are not clad. The roof and canopy slabs at the Kaufmann House make strong planar statements because of their large sizes and double cantilevers. Concrete is better suited to cantilevering simultaneous-

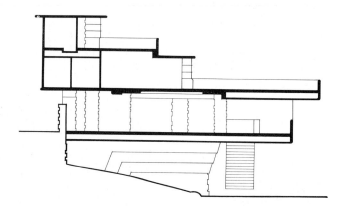

FIGURE 7-5. Building section of the Edgar J. Kaufmann, Sr. Residence. Molded surface of pier under building shown as designed. (From Frank Lloyd Wright Archives drawing 3602.011.)

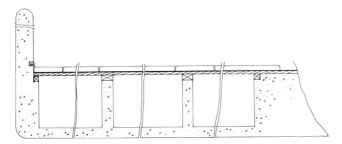

FIGURE 7-6. Section of cantilevered balcony at the Edgar J. Kaufmann, Sr. Residence showing beams, decking, and rounded edges. (From Frank Lloyd Archives drawing 3602.094.)

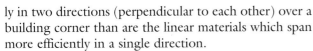

FIGURE 7-7. Stepped concrete railing by stair at the Edgar J. Kaufmann, Sr. Residence. Beams in balcony floor prior to installation of decking. Stone lintels over openings. (Courtesy The Frank Lloyd Wright Archives)

FIGURE 7-8. Perforated overhanging roof slab at the Florida Southern College Emile E. Watson Administration Building.

ly in two directions (perpendicular to each other) over a building corner than are the linear materials which span more efficiently in a single direction.

The concrete railings of the many balconies at the Kaufmann House are vertical slabs that do not read clearly as such except from high viewing positions. Since the house affords routine opportunities to view the balcony railing-slabs from above, they participate more extensively in the image of the building than would be the case in a simpler project. The slabs of the balcony floors are not clearly expressed, as their edges are merged with the concrete railings. Consequently, they do not directly contribute to concrete's image in the building as a structural plane. The large balcony cantilevers incorporate ribs, which typically add a linear quality to the concrete. In this case, however, the ribs are above the slab rather than below and are covered by balcony flooring. The ribs, therefore, do not interrupt

the continuity of the concrete surface as they would if exposed below the slab.

Concrete takes a partially masonrylike form in a stair rail on one end of the house. The undulations on the top and bottom of the rail have a sense of plasticity about them, especially in light of their round edges, but their stepped profile in elevation is reminiscent of brick or concrete block. The angle of the bottom edge is not steep enough to establish credibility as a masonry corbel so the strength of reinforced concrete is expressed there rather than the compressiveness of masonry. The continuity of the surface helps the construction distinguish itself from brick or block, ultimately drawing the upper configuration away from the sense of masonry.

A number of cantilevered roof slabs and canopies appear on the Florida Southern College campus. The planar expression of concrete is compromised slightly by the copper fascias—the case whenever the concrete edge

Figure 7-9. Perforated cantilevered slabs at the Midway Gardens. Decorative impressions in concrete copings. (Courtesy The Frank Lloyd Wright Archives)

is clad with another material. The loss to the monolithic sense caused by the trim is regained somewhat by the untrimmed edges of perforations in the slabs that occur throughout the campus. The holes and slots in the roofs and canopies also reinforce the image of the slabs as being planar, rather than massive, because thickness is revealed at each opening. The geometry of polygonal openings distinguishes somewhat the image of the construction from that of framing, in which rectangularity would be logical in such perforations.

Periodic series of parallel slots in the roof slabs tend to define beamlike concrete strips. Linear strips of concrete that are solid and rectangular in section share an image with wood beams, a phenomenon about which

Wright complained in general on more than one occasion. Slotted concrete slabs, prominently cantilevered at the Midway Gardens (1913), had a linear infrastructure with some woodlike characteristics. The solid rectangular sections of the beams in the slab plane were the aspect most like wood with the significant structural achievement of the highest cantilevers at the Gardens being the least like that available in wood. Decorative grooves in the surfaces of the beams, although reproducible in wood are not particularly associated with that material and consequently reflect some concrete-plasticity in the surface. The surfaces of the numerous bases and copings which embody a sense of concrete in their role as protection for the brick are similar in appearance

FIGURE 7-10. Perforated canopy slab at the Florida Southern College Polk Science Building.

to some of the slotted slabs and, therefore, help pull the image of the beamlike cantilevers away from wood and towards concrete.

The sense of wood is limited in perforated slabs where the slots are not the same length such in the triangular groupings within the Watson Administration Building (1945) overhangs. The sense of wood is maximized where the depth of the beamlike strips differs from adjacent concrete because it gives them an identi-

ty separate from that of the slab. In the Esplanade (1938) and Watson Administration Building, for example, closely spaced parallel concrete strips approximate sizes and spans typical of timber. Certain slots in the roof overhang of the Roux Library (1941) are unique in that the solid strips between them have beveled edges. The strips are relatively broad compared to their thickness which is the same as the slab thickness. Because of their tapered edges they lack the rectangularity of section typical of wood planks. Among the strips defined by slots on the campus, these are the most concretelike. The openings in a canopy at the Polk Science building (1953) are so large that the solid concrete strips between them become large beams structurally as well as visually. Their sections are within the size range possible in laminated timber. They are slightly wider than they are deep and are the same thickness as the adjacent slabs into which they merge. These proportions help them share an identity with the slab system, rather than stand alone as a traditional beam system.

The Esplanade canopies project a clear image of concrete as a structural plane since their edges are largely free of obstructions and typically cantilever several directions at once. The clarity of the slab identity is maximized when canopies change elevations as separate slabs (not continuous across the change). The canopy slab over the steps from the Kaufmann House (1935) to the Guesthouse (1938) enjoys a similar clarity as a single

FIGURE 7-11. Canopy over stepped walk from the Edgar J. Kaufmann, Sr. Residence to the Guesthouse. One decorative steel post at far side of each vertical segment. (Courtesy The Frank Lloyd Wright Archives)

FIGURE 7-12. Concrete beams as trellis over walk to entry (lower right) at the Edgar J. Kaufmann, Sr. Residence. Third and seventh beams curve around trees at connection to wall. Cantilevered roof slabs at left and throughout. (Courtesy The Frank Lloyd Wright Archives)

continuous slab, in spite of its change of elevation. While the Esplanade is supported by massive concrete piers, a few slender steel columns support the Kaufmann canopy and thus interfere with its image to a minimal degree. The Kaufmann canopy has strong plastic sense as, in plan, it curves along a semicircular arc and in elevation the horizontal slab sections turn downward periodically so as to descend the sloped grade as a continuous stepped plane. The vertical sections of the canopy obscure the thickness of the horizontal sections at their juncture, but the curve of the continuous stepping plane reveals its thickness in every elevation. Consequently, the material identity of the slab is never in doubt.

Woodlike concrete beams are used at the Kaufmann complex in much the same way as at the Florida campus. The least likeness to wood occurs in a slotted canopy of the guest house. Because much of the canopy is solid, the beams defined by the slots have less of a separate

FIGURE 7-13. Concrete bents exposed above roofs of the Florida Southern College Ordway Industrial Arts Building. Cantilevered circular roof slab at junction of building wings.

identity than elsewhere in the complex. Although they are long, slender, and rectangular in section, they appear to be part of the adjacent concrete plane. A canopy by the living room of the main house is completely perforated with slots and is thus similar to a trellis of wood

FIGURE 7-14. Concrete columns in the main workroom of the S. C. Johnson and Son Administration Building. (Courtesy The Frank Lloyd Wright Archives)

beams. The two exposed edges of this perforated plane are rounded like the edges of other slabs in the project. This helps the series of beams seem somewhat like a slab by association and gives its perimeter an identity different from the long edges of the beams within the plane, which are essentially rectangular in section. (Rectangular reveals at the top edges of the beams prevent the sections from being simple rectangles.) The last beam in the series (the edge beam) is slightly wider that the interior beams thus referring somewhat to the presence of a slab.

The series of concrete beams that is least able to maintain an identity as a perforated slab occurs over the walk to the entry. Since these beams span from the rough hillside to the irregular facade, they cannot establish a clear edge identity on either side. The first beam encountered as one approaches the series from the bridge (east of the house) has a rounded edge like other slabs in the project while the interior beams, like others in the project, have (essentially) rectangular sections. Two of the concrete beams in this trellis distance themselves from the image of wood as they curve around

trees. These two details capitalize on concrete's plasticity and strength to appear more like concrete than like wood. It would seem that Wright intended these and other beams in the canopies to be no more than the solid segments of perforated slabs. The variety of circumstances in which the beams appear support this possibility with inconsistent efficiency, however.

Wright's use of concrete frames visible above the roof of the Florida Southern College Ordway Industrial Arts Building (1942) resembles the linearity of steel, as do those above the Roux Library (1941). Because the beams are difficult to see on the roof of the library, however, they have little effect on the image of the building. The highly visible concrete frames over the Pilgrim Congregational Church (1958) are especially thin, and although the loads they carry are not large, their proportions suggest steel. Without the presence of flanges, however, mistaking the sections for steel is not possible.

The slender concrete columns of the S. C. Johnson and Son Administration Building (1936) are reminiscent of tapered steel pipe (such as light-poles turned

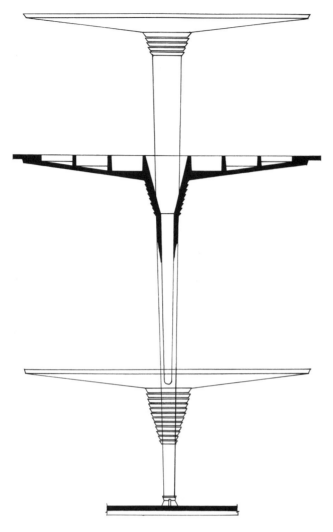

FIGURE 7-15. Superimposed elevations and section of columns in the (top to bottom) lobby, main room, and carport of the S. C. Johnson and Son Administration Building. (From Frank Lloyd Wright Archives drawing 3601.012.)

FIGURE 7-16. Cantilevered roof slab with curved edge at the Lowell Walter Residence. Glazed wall with glass corners. (Photo courtesy State Historical Society of Iowa—Des Moines.)

FIGURE 7-17. Ornamental impressions cast integrally with concrete columns at the Unity Church. (Courtesy Mike Kertok)

FIGURE 7-18. Precast concrete ornament at the Aline Barnsdall Residence (Hollyhock House) as stylized hollyhocks.

upside down). The flared and corrugated capital at the top of each column shaft has the plasticity of concrete and is unlike any shape common in steel The continuity and plasticity of the disklike slabs supported by the columns are highly expressive of concrete. The physical relationship of the column shafts with their capitals and slabs combined with the similarity of their finishes helps pull the image of the column shaft toward that of concrete. By themselves, the column shafts lack the breadth of surface or overall mass to establish a strong concrete image. Slender concrete columns at the Gammage Memorial Auditorium (1959) have a similar overlap with the image of steel but lack the supplementary detailing to clarify the image of their material.

FIGURE 7-19. Decorative concrete fascia on the Albert D. German Warehouse.

FIGURE 7-20. Concrete piers, typical of the Florida Southern campus, at the College Ordway Industrial Arts Building. Repetitive rectangular patterns at the top. Horizontal linear patterns at the bottom.

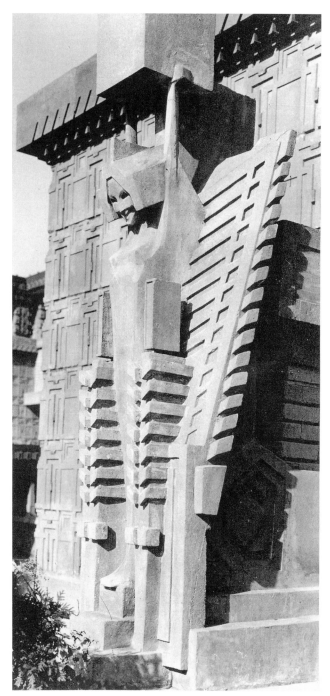

FIGURE 7-21. Concrete sculpture, "Queen of the Gardens," cast on the site at the Midway Gardens. (Courtesy The Frank Lloyd Wright Archives)

The similarities between Wright's concrete beams and columns to wood and steel do not necessarily reveal hypocrisy in Wright's discourse. It is doubtful that Wright considered his linear concrete to be like wood or steel even though similar sizes and spans often occur in those materials. His use of concrete in the form of wood and steel suggests that shapes and structural achievements were not, to Wright, significant aspects in the nature of these materials. If Wright, as evidence sug-

gests, considered the nature of wood to be largely defined by its surface, the concrete beams of the Florida campus and the Kaufmann buildings would not have seemed, in his view, similar to wood. Nevertheless, it must be observed that Wright's use of linear concrete

FIGURE 7-22. Perforated concrete wall in the Florida Southern College Annie Pfeiffer Chapel. Linear pattern in concrete at upper left. No visible support for the concrete blocks in the fascia of the balcony. (Courtesy The Frank Lloyd Wright Archives)

FIGURE 7-23. Blocky concrete masses of Unity Church.

FIGURE 7-24. Angular concrete bastion at the Beth Sholom Synagogue. Patterned aluminum cladding on tripod leg of roof structure above.

does not clearly separate the image of the material from wood or steel to the maximum degree possible.

Wright thought that "concrete is essentially a plastic material…" that ultimately could be expressed with "the shapes characteristic of drifted snow or sand or the smooth conformation of animals."[8] He claimed economics as the reason he did not express concrete in this way during the first half of the 20th century. In his early work, Wright exploited the plasticity of concrete only at the small scale. He explored surface plasticity through decorative concrete block, precast elements, and cast-in-place concrete. He demonstrated concrete's plasticity in section by expressing rounded slab edges at such buildings as the Johnson Wax complex (1936, 1944), the Kaufmann House (1935), and the Walter House (1945).

His patterned concrete expresses plasticity perpendicular to the surface but not all of his designs demonstrate plasticity in the configuration of the pattern. The concrete block of the Midway Gardens (1913), S. Freeman House (1924), and Arizona Biltmore Hotel (1927), and columns in the Taliesin West Cabaret Theatre (1949) have angular impressions in their faces. Although not free-form or curvilinear, they express plasticity in their demonstration of concrete's freedom from the rectangularity imposed by manufacturing economies upon basic forms of other materials. Stronger expressions of plasticity occur in the curves of the pattern in the cast units on the Barnsdall living room fireplace

(1917) and on the edges of the cantilevered slabs at the David Wright House (1950).

Many patterns that Wright cast, however, are rectangular in nature and could be imitated by a composition of wood parts. The impressions cast in the columns of Unity Church (1905), the concrete at the top of the German Warehouse (1915), the stylized hollyhock ornaments at the Barnsdall House (1917), the surface of the Pfeiffer Chapel tower (1938), the surfaces of the piers at throughout the Florida campus (1938–54), and the surface on the northeast corner of the Guggenheim Museum (1943, prior to the latest addition) are of this type. Because the geometric patterns have an image that is within the potential of wood does not mean that they are incompatible with the nature of concrete. It does mean, however, that they neither maximize the expression of concrete's plasticity nor verify its uniqueness among materials. Early concrete castings reflecting a greater sense of plasticity include certain sculptural figures at the Midway Gardens (1913), which have angu-

FIGURE 7-25. Cantilevered and rounded concrete volumes at the Dallas Theatre Center (Kalita Humphreys Theater).

FIGURE 7-26. Concrete spiral and other cantilevered volumes at the Solomon R. Guggenheim Museum. Curved dividing bars visible in glazing above rail.

FIGURE 7-27. Curvilinear ramps in the interior of the Solomon R. Guggenheim Museum.

lar and stylized human forms, and the assembly of precast units over the fireplace at the Barnsdall house with angular and circular shapes in its pattern and curves in its section.

The perforated concrete choir screen in the Pfeiffer Chapel is among the most plastic of Wright's noncurvilinear patterned concrete. The complex outline of each hole, although consisting of straight lines, seems almost curvilinear. Patterned surfaces above the perforated area are less unique to concrete as they have linear patterns similar in proportion to wood siding. Unlike a solid plane that is distinguished from a mass only at its edges, the openings in the screen frequently reveal the concrete's thickness, which verifies the construction as being a slab like form.

Curved slabs (in plan) express the plasticity of concrete at the S. C. Johnson and Son Administration

Building (1936) and Research Tower (1944) and the Kaufmann canopy for the guesthouse walk (1938). The cantilevered roof slabs of the S. Friedman House (1949) clearly express themselves as structural planes but are not quite as plastic because their edges consist of many short straight segments rather than a continuous curve. The slab expression at the Johnson Wax complex is diluted slightly by the fact that most of the tops of the slabs are not exposed. It is not necessary to actually see the tops of slabs for their exposure to contribute to the clarity of the image. If both their tops and soffits are exposed, however, the edges will not blend with adjacent materials when viewed from any angle and will have a stronger identity as a slab. Although, in other projects, slab thickness is revealed for some distance back from the outer edge, most of the Johnson Wax slabs show their thickness only at the edge. The round slabs centered on each column taper and slope upward as they cantilever. The configuration expresses plasticity while maintaining the identity of the disks as planes rather than masses

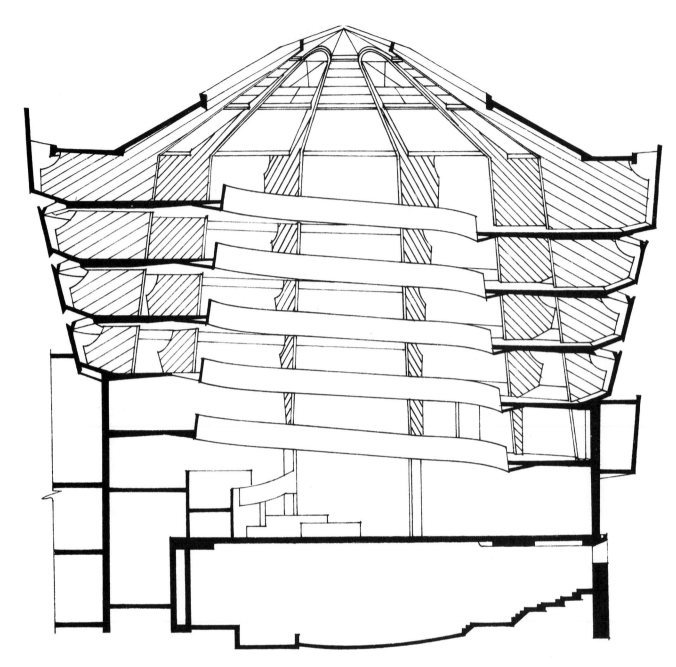

Figure 7-28. Building section of the Solomon R. Guggenheim Museum showing large vertical planes (shaded) oriented on radial lines and supporting floor system. (From Frank Lloyd Wright Archives drawing 4305.625.)

(although they actually have concentric and radial ribs on their upper sides).

A distinction is made between concrete expressed as a slab or as a mass. Although Wright thought that concrete was essentially a massive substance,[9] it shares this characteristic with masonry, which (without reinforcing) has the greater reason to be massive. For concrete to express its uniqueness when in the form of a mass, properties unlike masonry must be emphasized. Surface texture is always a distinction between masonry and concrete but does not define the entire nature of either

material. Plasticity and structural achievement can distinguish concrete from masonry if expressed in formats not readily available to stone, brick, or concrete block.

Unity Church (1905), Wright's first large-scale expression of concrete, is a composition of rectangular masses. The degree of plasticity in the building form is not different from that of masonry as illustrated by the ease with which brick could be substituted without significant change to the building profile in plan or section. Wright recognized this characteristic of the building, referring to the masses as "great concrete blocks"[10] and

FIGURE 7-29. Concrete dome, bowl-shaped soffit, and walls at the Annunciation Greek Orthodox Church. Curved dividing bars in windows. Glass "spheres" under edge of dome.

FIGURE 7-30. Curved concrete roof with precast ornaments at the Marin County Civic Center. Metal spheres attached to lower edge of fascia.

FIGURE 7-31. Concrete, masonry, and stuccoed wood framing at the Aline Barnsdall Residence (Hollyhock House). (Courtesy The Frank Lloyd Wright Archives)

to the sanctuary as "a cube—a noble form in masonry."[11] Wright attributed the character of the building, in large part, to the influence of the wood formwork. Early in his career, he acknowledged a considerable influence from the formwork on the shape of concrete. The material of the formwork itself, he thought, would "modify the shape the concrete naturally takes, if indeed it does not wholly determine it."[12]

Wright's opinion that concrete "may be continuous or monolithic within certain very wide limits,"[13] however, reveals that he accepted only certain influences from formwork. He disliked the joint marks that formwork tended to leave in concrete and promoted scrubbing the surface with acid to achieve uniformity.[14] In this regard he went so far as to recommend lining forms with paper.[15] In every broad concrete surface Wright produced, he endeavored to obliterate the expression of the formwork's lack of continuity as well as the marks of any form-ties used. Wright's definition of the formwork characteristics he found acceptable in concrete excluded those aspects he thought unattractive. The lumpy and faintly scarred surfaces of the Guggenheim Museum (1943) and Kalita Humphreys Theater (1955) reveal failed struggles to overcome the nature of the concrete in its high sensitivity to impressions and the nature of formwork in its lack of continuity.

The role of formwork in Wright's concrete shapes diminished as his career progressed. In his later work, the rectangularity he had accepted from the formwork of the Unity Church gave way to angularity and eventually to curved geometries. With each step of increased plasticity, the image of his concrete moved further from that of masonry. The angularity of the massive desert rubble masonry (or desert concrete) of Taliesin West (1937) is a characteristic of concrete that the substance imparted to the hybrid material. Where reverse-battered masses yield acute-angled points of concrete at the upper corners of several walls, the refinement and sense of precision in the concrete seems too great for the material. On the other hand, any failure for such points

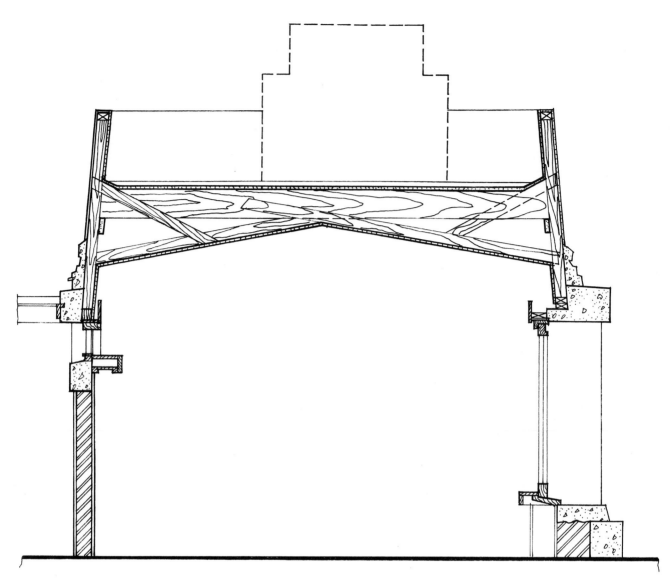

FIGURE 7-32. Section at the Aline Barnsdall Residence showing wood framed roof and parapets. (From Frank Lloyd Wright Archives drawing 1705.013.)

to be perfectly formed or to maintain their form in spite of miscellaneous impacts that occur over the life of a building would not be particularly noticeable because of the rugged texture of the system. Since the system visually accommodates, to some degree, failures in attempts to produce refinement in the concrete, such as partially grouted edges or missing segments, the production of sharpness is less offensive to the material than in circumstances where every failure is obvious.

The bastions (masses of concrete) on the corners of the Beth Sholom Synagogue (1954) are angular to the extent of having sharp points in which imperfection would be highly noticeable. The formation of concrete in nonright-angled geometries is a plastic concept although, in this case, the execution shares with steel an image of sharpness and precision. The angularity separates the masses from the traditional sense of brick, con-

crete block, ashlar stone, and common rubble. The projection outward of the upper parts of the bastions beyond their footprints visually destabilizes the masses, separating the image somewhat from that of masonry, which requires maximum stability for its most natural image. A considerable amount of angularity occurs in concrete on the Florida Southern Campus. It appears in the form of cantilevered slabs and perforations of slabs but is also found in the massive forms of piers throughout the site. Some curved concrete can be found on the campus as well, most notably in the base of the Roux Library (1941). The angular plan of the Hughes House (1949) expresses concrete's plasticity at the large scale while at the small scale it finds expression in a few widely spaced horizontal reveals.

The combination of circular and angled masses at the Kalita Humphreys Theater (1955) provides a transi-

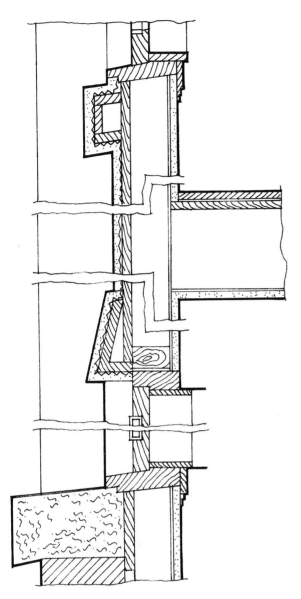

Figure 7-33. Wall section of the first Francis W. Little Residence showing concretelike trim formed in wood and stucco. (From Frank Lloyd Wright Archives drawing 0009.014.)

tion to a higher level of plasticity in his last major uses of concrete, the Guggenheim Museum (1943, construction completed in 1959), Annunciation Greek Orthodox Church (1956), and elements of the Marin County Civic Center (1957). All of his later major concrete works expressed concrete as the mass material that he had claimed it to be 30 years earlier. The most plastic concrete buildings of his career showed to the least degree the influence of formwork (flatness) that he had also embraced earlier. Even in their elevated plasticity, however, the church, museum, and civic center did not exploit to the maximum concrete's potential as a plastic material.

One of Wright's strongest expressions of concrete's plasticity occurs at the Guggenheim Museum. The exterior walls of the ramp around the main volume simultaneously spiral, slope, and lean outward to produce a complex curvilinear form, but because of its straight lines in section, one that could be reproduced in steel and stucco. (The highly plastic curved ramp in the Morris Gift Shop, 1948, for example, is plaster on steel framing.) Within the interior, concrete is expressed as a planar material of various intensities of plasticity. When the railings of the spiral ramp are viewed from above (as they commonly are), their planar character is revealed. Large vertical concrete planes, tapering from a wider dimension at the top of the building to a more narrow base, fall on lines radiating from the center of the large interior space and support the ramped floor system. Although partially obscured from some vantage points, several of the vertical slabs can be seen at one time, thus maximizing for the observer their uniquely concrete proportions, shapes, and structural achievement.

The domes of the Greek Orthodox Church and Marin County Civic Center and the vaultlike shapes of the civic center reflect concrete's plasticity as does the bowl-shaped volume of the church. Plasticity is reflected in the church at the small scale in semicircular openings in the sloped precast visor and its scalloped edge impressions and in the roof overhangs at the civic center. Semicircular windows and impressions in the concrete elsewhere in the facade further supplement the plastic image at the church. The arched openings over the roads at the civic center are plastic but not distinguished in their geometry from masonry arches. The arched windows at the church have beveled edges, separating themselves slightly from the rectangularity that would be expected in the edges of masonry arches.

The expression of concrete is much obscured and misrepresented in several of Wright's buildings because of its visual confusion with stucco. The Barnsdall House (1917) is a complex assortment of concrete, masonry, steel, and wood-framed elements. Given the variety of materials used, the facades of the house are remarkably uniform in appearance due to their resemblance to a single material, concrete. The detailing of the Barnsdall House elevates the sense of mass and juxtaposes structural concrete, decorative concrete, and stucco, all with similar surfaces, thus adding credibility to the appearance of the stucco as a structural and cast material. The odd fact that the entry door is concrete diminishes the usefulness of logic in understanding which parts of the house are concrete and which are not.

The simpler role of the stucco—as well as the use of wood trim—prevents the stucco from appearing to be anything but cladding in most of Wright's earlier houses. The working drawings for the first Little House

FIGURE 7-34. Concrete and stuccoed concrete block at the Florida Southern College Annie Pfeiffer Chapel.

FIGURE 7-35. Concrete columns and stucco-clad steel framing at the Grady Gammage Memorial Auditorium. Large glass curtain wall.

(1902) show an exception wherein stucco trim is detailed so as to have an appearance similar in texture and proportion to stone or concrete trim. Wright recognized that in the Barnsdall House, (Hollyhock House) he had strayed from the principles of materials and construction he had promoted throughout his career. Although his conscience resisted the respite from discipline, he admitted that the "Hollyhock House was to be another holiday for me."[16] Some of the materials

confusion might be explained by the fact that the house was originally intended to be concrete.[17]

There were to be other such holidays. The expression of concrete is ambiguous on the campus of Florida Southern College, particularly in the Pfeiffer Chapel (1938) and Roux Library (1941). The concrete and stuccoed concrete block on the buildings are indistinguishable. Structural characteristics of certain masses hint at the presence of concrete upon occasion as do impressed patterns in their surfaces but, without consistency in such detailing distinctions, a clear sense of one material or the other cannot be established with certainty. For example, in the tower of the chapel, the broad, plain, central surfaces are stuccoed concrete block while the patterned surfaces of the flanking elements are concrete. Other plain surfaces on the chapel are also concrete. Certain cantilevered masses are concrete, but masses of concrete block also have cantilevered elements. Wright's failure to clearly distinguish between the properties of stuccoed block and reinforced concrete reflects a level of material sensitivity below the maximum possible. It appears that, in the projects on this campus, issues other than the nature of materials governed the design decisions.

The Gammage Memorial Auditorium (1959) is a building of some plasticity and, except for a large brick element, has a concretelike appearance. The building is,

FIGURE 7-36. Concrete columns and steel framing of the Grady Gammage Memorial Auditorium. (Courtesy The Frank Lloyd Wright Archives)

for the most part, however, a steel-framed structure. The tall concrete columns (precast on the site) surrounding the round volume of the main structure reflect the slender proportions of steel that they were once intended to be. The aggregate in their finish has an applied look thus preventing the surface from verifying the true nature of the material. Given the slender proportions of the columns, which detract from the sense of concrete, ver-

ification of their substance by an aggregate with an integral appearance would have been helpful to the expression of the material.

The stuccoed steel-framed fascia panels appear to bear on the tops of the columns, transmitting compressive stresses across their arched forms. In actuality, the arched fascia hangs from the steel structure behind it. The deep fascia is curved in section as well as in plan

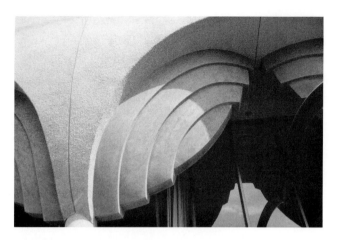

FIGURE 7-37. Precast petal ornaments and stucco fascia at the Grady Gammage Memorial Auditorium.

FIGURE 7-38. Concrete walls and bastions at ground level of the Beth Sholom Synagogue. Aluminum clad tripod legs on roof ridges. Corrugated glass cladding on roof.

FIGURE 7-39. Concrete walls and vault at ground level of the Marin County Civic Center. Walls above are stucco on steel framing. Pointlike bearing contacts at intersections of arches.

a reversal of expressions suggested by the nature of the materials. The steel framing resembles concrete and the concrete columns resemble steel. Since the similarities are not absolute, material vagueness rather than imitation prevails in the image of the building.

WORKABILITY

The term *workability* is used here to refer to the ease with which the shape of a finished material can be changed. By this definition, the workability of cured concrete is extremely low compared to that of other substances. Wright's treatment of the surface of his first concrete building, Unity Church (1905), fits the definition of "working" as used here if the concrete is considered to be essentially cured at the time the forms were removed. After the forms were removed the concrete was scrubbed, which revealed the aggregate and provided a more uniform surface. Wright was to seek uniform surfaces in his subsequent concrete by working the surface, but the aggregate would not again be exposed. Wright's working of cured concrete after the Unity Church was focused on the removal or hiding of form marks and blemishes by both scrubbing and the application of coatings. These efforts were essentially attempts to subdue the nature of concrete with regard to its high impressionability (or surface plasticity). Wright recognized this aspect of concrete's nature as a legitimate property when it yielded aesthetically acceptable results but rejected it when it did not. His inability to entirely eliminate form marks in every case attests to the low workability of the material.

Wright did not work concrete at a more intense level, that is, to a degree that produced noticeably new

because its lower edge curves inward to meet the tops of the columns. Under each arch are two petal-like cast elements that have curved and stepped profiles on both their long and short axes. The structural sense of these highly plastic components is one of hanging. This accurately reflects their structural condition—except that they do not hang from the arches as they appear to do but from hidden steel struts rising from the column.

The roof, visible above and behind the fascia, curves inward (the reverse of a dome) as it follows the circular plan of the building. The compound curve is constructed with steel trusses in a radial plan. The curved top chords of the trusses and the relatively smooth roof finish provide the plasticity and surface quality that together resemble a concrete. As any cladding does, the stucco on the Gammage Auditorium tends to obscure the expression of the structural material it covers. This stucco warrants attention, however, because it participates in

FIGURE 7-40. Concrete base with steel framing above at the Marin County Civic Center. (Courtesy The Frank Lloyd Wright Archives)

textures or shapes. To avoid a more extensive cutting or chipping of cured concrete would not seem to require a high level of material sensitivity as the practical limitations are considerable and obvious. The fact that other designers have worked concrete more intensely indicates that some credit is due to Wright for showing restraint in this regard. Small fins cast in the surface of the Yale Art and Architecture Building (1959–63) by Paul Rudolph, for example, were broken by hand a few years after Wright's death in 1959, establishing that practice as nearly contemporary to Wright's career. Other examples by other architects followed. Wright superseded the nature of concrete workability only in his attempt to remove form marks. Surface marks and other imperfections resulting from the formwork in some of Wright's concrete signifies a

recognizable but not maximized level of insensitivity to the material.

STRENGTH

Although Wright observed that concrete had "great strength in compression,"[18] he was more focused on the structural potential afforded by its reinforcing steel. His view of concrete's contribution to the composite material seems to have been not so much the compressive role it played, but the protection from corrosion it provided to the steel as well as the new structural forms that were possible. Wright's use of concrete in compression rarely elevated the sense of compression in the structural expression of the building. The blocky proportions,

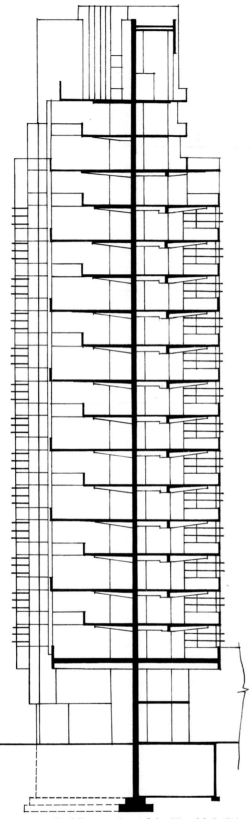

Figure 7-41. Building section of the Harold C. Price Company Tower showing cantilevered floor system. (From Frank Lloyd Wright Archives drawing 5215.018.)

general mass, and stable form of Unity Church (1905) has a compressive image but one that is typical of masonry rather than unique to concrete. The low, spread-based, and massive desert concrete of Taliesin West (1937) expresses compression as a major part of its aesthetic order. The masses are more plastic than those of Unity Church, but—as a hybrid of stone and mostly unreinforced concrete—Taliesin West cannot represent Wright's attitude toward compression in reinforced concrete.

Perhaps the closest Wright came to expressing the compressiveness of concrete in its own right occurs in the Beth Sholom Synagogue. Although the concrete walls of the building are over a story in height, they appear to be a low-slung base for the enormous roof structure. Combined with the triangular geometry of the plan, the relatively low profile of the concrete suggests great stability and compression. The angularity of the material distinguishes it from masonry, although the sharp points of the corners lack the bluntness associated with concrete. Some sense of compression exists in most of Wright's arched concrete structures, as the stress is traditionally associated with those forms. Arched concrete typically fails to draw attention to compression if it is not clearly buttressed in the manner of unreinforced masonry arches.

The apparent support of the dome at the annunciation Greek Orthodox Church (1956) by a series of glass globes undermines the sense of weight and thrust that would have boosted the image of compression in the building. The arched windows around the sanctuary of the church are reasonably convincing as compressive elements since they buttress each other. Some intensity is lost in the compressive image because the arches follow the curved perimeter of the building, thus reducing the efficiency of their mutual thrust resistance. The bowl of the church expresses a resistance to bending stresses, verifying that concrete is more than a compressive mass.

The base of the Marin County Civic Center (1957) is cast-in-place concrete. The arcades lining the upper floors of the building are visually integrated with the concrete base. Their arches establish a progression of sizes and numbers beginning with the few large arches in the base through intermediate sizes and numbers to the smallest and most plentiful at the top floor. The color and texture of the upper surfaces are essentially the same as those of the concrete base. Except for one particular detail, it would appear that the material of the facade is concrete. The arches of the upper levels are, in fact, steel-stud framing clad with stucco. They hang from the structure in a tensile mode entirely compatible with the nature of steel and the lightness of stuccoed cladding. Their appearance, however, is largely one of compression, which—combined with its other characteristics—emulates the concrete below.

The steel-framed arches are only distinguished from concrete in their bearing details. The lower series of framed arches meet each other and their (apparent) base support at points defined by the intersection of their curved jambs. The triangular aluminum brackets that occur at the intersections provide visual bearing points. The contact point is uncomfortably small for the transfer of building loads in concrete. The smaller arches in the next higher arcade intersect above the visual bearing level provided by the railing. Thin aluminum brackets bridge the gap between the intersection of the arches and the railing below. The sense of load transfer is nearly nonexistent in this detail. The aluminum, which is too thin to carry building loads, overlaps the surface below rather than appearing to bear on it—thus further limiting its ability to carry weight.

It could be argued that the absence of believable bearing details prevents any imitation of concrete by the stuccoed framing. This might be true if only professionally trained persons who take the time to analyze the facade were to see the building. It is likely that a far greater number of visitors, not versed in structural theory, see it as a concrete building. In any case, it can be observed that the minimal distinction between the two major materials does not reflect a maximum sensitivity to the individuality of material nature in either. If some violation of the spirit of material has occurred, it is in the realm of framing and stucco rather than of the concrete. Nevertheless, the identity of the concrete in the building is adversely affected by the presence of the stucco, which causes a sense of materials vagueness in the facades.

The false arcades of the Civic Center confuse the structural circumstance in the real arches of the facade, thus undermining the ability of the large concrete vaults at the base of the building to express the considerable compression that they are carrying. The potential of the vaulted and domed concrete roofs to express compression is limited by their overhangs, which are clearly in a bending mode and have no visible devices for resisting thrust. The fact that there is a network of hidden structure supporting the vaults does not affect expectations of its expression as the structure beneath it is not visible in the facade.

Several of Wright's buildings that have concrete in compression in their facades neither deny the condition nor exploit it as an expressive device. Among these, the Kalita Humphreys Theater comes the closest to a purposeful compressive statement because of the massive volumes of the building. The compression, however, fails to seem more than incidental to the building image. Some attention to compression is directed to the lower-level concrete of the Guggenheim Museum by the great

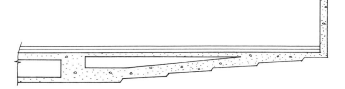

FIGURE 7-42. Section of cantilevered floor at the Harold C. Price Company Tower showing stepped soffit. (From Frank Lloyd Wright Archives drawing 5215.080.)

spiral mass appearing to rest on it. The compressive sense cannot compete with the remarkable nature of the spiral and other features of the building; thus, compressions remains essentially inconsequential in the aesthetic order of the building.

Perhaps the most remarkable elements of the Johnson Wax Administration Building (1936) are its interior concrete columns. Featuring columns as a major component of the aesthetic order of the interior, however, has not resulted in a focus on compression as a phenomenon integral with the image of concrete. The slender proportions of the columns and their taper from a broader top to a narrower base are characteristics opposite from those expressing the presence of great compression. The columns seem light with a sense of uplift rather than a downward push. Without their visual association with the cantilevered slabs they support, their structural identity would be confused with that of steel.

The massive concrete piers under the cantilevered living room and balcony of the Kaufmann House (1935) slope outward at their tops and have smooth faces and thus, due to their plasticity, maintain forms within the realm of concrete rather than masonry. The slight reliefs or changes in thickness shown for the piers in early drawings were eliminated prior to construction. Thus, some potential plasticity was lost. The resulting effect, although highly compressive and securely within the image of concrete, has virtually no visual role in the building. The piers are held back in the dark recess under the cantilever so as to boost the sense of enormity in the balcony cantilever. The expression of concrete compression is forfeited here for the expression of concrete as a cantilevering material.

Given his reference to cantilevering in concrete as "the most romantic of all structural possibilities,"[19] it is not surprising to see extensive use of the device in Wright's work. In addition to its contrasting texture, Wright distinguished the expression of concrete from stone in the Kaufmann House by the nearly consistent use of concrete in bending (mostly cantilevers) and stone in compression. The clarity of the distinction between the limitations of stone strength and the potential of concrete strength contributes a strong sense of logic to the architecture, as the role of each material

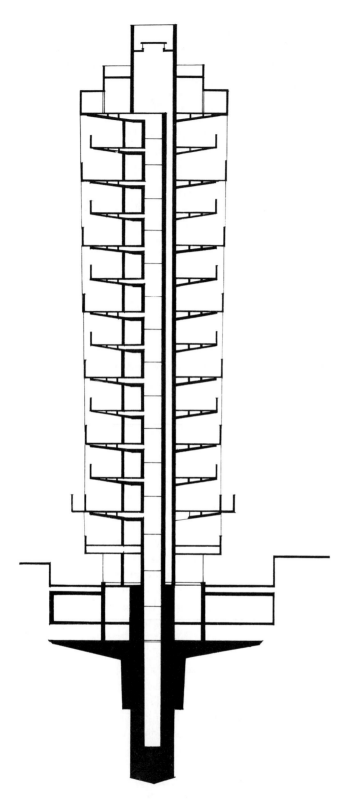

FIGURE 7-43. Building section of the S. C. Johnson and Son Research Tower showing long and short cantilevered floors with sloped soffits. (From Frank Lloyd Wright Archives drawing 4401.094.)

appears to be derived directly from the characteristic qualities of its nature.

This clarity in the demonstration of concrete's unique ability to form structural planes contrasts with the less specific demonstration of form and strength at the Humphreys Theater. Although the use of concrete in both bending and compression at the theater provides a broad and accurate demonstration of concrete's nature, it fails to express the material's strength as being more than incidental to the aesthetic order. The Guggenheim Museum comes as close to any of Wright's buildings in bringing a simultaneous focus to both compression and bending in concrete. The remarkable character of the large spiraled volume draws attention to the cantilevered aspect of its forms, while the mass of the form suggests a sense of great weight on the building base. As previously mentioned, the compressive aspects are overshadowed by the unusual structural circumstance of the spiral.

The moderate masses of concrete cantilevered over the ground floor of the Price Tower (1952) appear to carry the tall volume of the building above and thus accurately express the material to be strong in resistance to bending stresses. The fact that each floor is actually cantilevered from a central spine is not apparent, however, so the special condition fails to contribute to the image of concrete or the image of the building. The numerous cantilevered balconies and stair landings supplement the strength-in-bending message but the cantilevered nature of the slabs is obscured in the facade by the glazing which is flush with the extreme perimeter of most floor slabs. As seen from within the building, the bottom surfaces of the cantilevered floors express a sense of plasticity as they step from a thicker dimension near the center of the building to a thinner dimension at the outer edge. The stepping of the surface does not occur at right angles but at obtuse angles, thus increasing its visual flow. The compressive expression of the shaft is overshadowed by the more dynamic cantilevering of the building volume and other details. The tree metaphor often used to describe the structure seems particularly appropriate, since the trunk of a tree is more often thought of as a vertical cantilever than as a compressive mass.

Wright's structural achievement in the Price Tower is similar to that in the concrete system of the S. C. Johnson and Son Company Research Tower (1944). The cantilevered floors have the potential to express the strength and plasticity of concrete, but the glazing system—which is flush with the outer edges of the larger floors—obscures the nature of the system. Bands of concrete bracketing the brick cladding in the facade suggest that concrete is the structural support, as no other means is visible. The remarkable cantilevers of the concrete, however, are not apparent. In the interior view, every other floor that stops short of the outer wall expresses its cantilever as well as the plasticity of concrete, since these floors are circular in plan. The effect of this concrete image is limited, because only part of one cantilever can be viewed at one time. Prior to the installation of the glazing, the entire system was visible from points outside the tower, thus expressing to a near maximum the nature of concrete with regard to strength and form. Like the Price Tower, the Johnson Research Tower embodies the spirit of concrete but fails to express it to a level of intensity within its potential.

Given the need to enclose space, the obscuring of structural reality by cladding and glazing is a common. Balconies such as the very large ones at the Kaufmann House can help project the structural message of concrete, but integral concrete railings like the Kaufmann examples tend to obscure the slab edge and, to some degree, the sense of cantilevered plane. Roof overhangs free of railings, glazing, and cladding can clearly express the structural potential of concrete in the form of a continuous plane. Several such examples occur in Wright's work, including the Kaufmann (1936), Grant (1945), Walter, (1945), and S. Friedman (1949) houses. Numerous cantilevering roof slabs are apparent on the Florida Southern campus including the remarkably thin and long example at the Danforth Chapel. Although angular to the extreme of sharpness, the roof strongly reflects the spirit of concrete's bending strength. Its change of thickness (in a single step) responds to the diminishing magnitude of stresses toward the slab edge and boosts the sense of strength in the material by minimizing its thickness at the most visible and expressive point, the outer edge.

Wright's focus on concrete's bending rather than compressive strength as a vehicle of expression is compatible with the concept that exploitation of a material's uniqueness brings the architecture into a clearer alignment with the nature of the material than does expressing characteristics common to several materials. Although compression is within the capability of all the structural materials, bending ability is not a significant property of masonry; thus, the expression of bending distinguishes concrete from masonry. Manifested in the form of a slab, the expression of bending demonstrates a combination of properties unique to concrete. The dynamacy of the cantilever magnifies concrete's characteristics, thus elevating the spirit of the material in the building image. Where Wright maximized his use of cantilevered concrete and minimized other formats that would dilute the uniqueness of the structural message, the architecture seems most aligned with the spirit of concrete.

FIGURE 7-44. Cantilevered roof slab at the Florida Southern College William H. Danforth Chapel with stepped soffit.

DURABILITY

Wright saw concrete as a highly durable material. Most of his comments on this aspect of concrete referred to its ability to protect steel from rust. "The more bulky material protects the slighter material from its enemy, disintegration," he observed.[20] In practice, however, his aesthetic needs superseded the expression of concrete's durability. He painted virtually all of his concrete buildings after Unity Church (1905). (The concrete of Unity Church was originally unpainted, which left exposed unsightly pour lines between the concrete lifts. The surfaces have since been coated.) Thus, in applying his preferred color and texture to concrete, he also seemed to protect the material from the elements. The practice fails to distinguish the concrete from wood or steel with regard to their differing abilities to withstand weathering. As previously noted, it also brings the appearance of the surface closer to that of stucco.

As a practical matter Wright's placing of concrete in contact with the grade (including paving) exploits and therefore expresses its high durability. This detail at all-concrete buildings such as the Guggenheim Museum (1943) and Kalita Humphreys Theater (1955), however, does not express to an elevated degree the durability of the material. The message is diluted because concrete occurs in high as well as low positions, thus rendering its contact with grade apparently incidental.

When the concrete serves as a base for other materials at grade (regardless of the motivation for the detail), some focus is brought to its durability. The concrete bases or water tables at the Dana and Heurtley Houses (1902) separate the brick (and, more significantly, the mortar joints) from the moisture in the earth and—to some degree—snow. Its service to the brick in this regard suggests that it has a greater durability than the brick (even if it is only because of its fewer joints.) Concrete copings on the brick carry the same durability message. The expression of concrete's durability is inversely related to the durability of the material it protects. The particularly vulnerable wood-framed and stuccoed walls of the W. Martin (1903) and Coonley (1906) houses, for example, express the durability of their concrete water tables more intensely than does the brick of the Dana and Heurtley houses, because the concrete is more important to the preservation of the framed walls than of the masonry walls.

The water table and coping details are limited in their ability to express the durability of concrete due to their similar appearance to stone. Concrete's durability significantly differs from that of stone only if it has fewer joints. This distinction is minimized in some of Wright's concrete water tables, which are installed in sections rather than in continuous strips. The ability of concrete's proximity to grade to express its durability is diluted in Wright's work by his installation of wood very close to the earth in some buildings. The wood siding of the River Forest Tennis Club (1905) and G. Millard House (1906) was installed nearly in contact with grade, as was the wood base trim of the Boynton (1907), Davidson (1908), and Stockman (1908) houses. The implication is either that the durability of concrete and wood are similar or that the earth offers no threat to materials. Both messages are incorrect.

The small size of concrete bases prevents them from playing a large role in a building's image, even if they are noticed. A concrete base would have to be several feet high to impose with certainty its message regarding concrete on the building image. The concrete walls of the Beth Sholom Synagogue (1954) are high but act as a base for the very tall roof system. The visual message imparted by the relationship is largely structural but it also has durability overtones. The more durable material is on the ground while the more vulnerable construction is raised above it. The large concrete base of the Marin County Civic Center (1957) is especially significant for utilitarian purposes because the building merges with the flanking hillsides. The contact of the earth to the building at points higher than the traditional horizontal foundation line magnifies the need for protection from its hazards. The potential expression of concrete's service in this regard is lost, however, due to its similarity in appearance to the stuccoed framing of the upper floors. Because it is not clear that concrete is protecting a more fragile system, concrete's contact with grade appears to be more incidental than it actually is.

CONCLUSION

If considered in isolation, Wright's praise of concrete's potential as the stylistic solution to modern architecture as well as to numerous technical problems would suggest that concrete was Wright's most favored material. Although he spoke of most materials as if each was his favorite, his adulation of concrete has a tone different from his praise for wood, masonry, and steel. Wright often told his apprentices, Edgar Tafel reports, that concrete provided greater freedom than wood, steel, or brick, which he considered to be essentially straight-line materials.[21] Concrete offered to Wright, in one material, the structural freedom afforded by the great strength of steel and the true plasticity inherent in casting. These qualities, combined with the neutral personality that he observed in its surface and the lack of a traditional image, provided to Wright the greatest opportunity among his materials to define a material's nature without interference from external influences.

Of Wright's materials, concrete seemed to come the closest to having the capabilities that he wanted it to have. As was typical, his discourse on concrete's nature was aligned more closely with its properties than was his use of the material in architecture. In spite of his failure to express concrete's unique qualities to the maximum level possible, the character of his concrete architecture was related to the nature of the material to a high degree. While his intensity of expression in the nature of other materials remained static or diminished throughout his career, his expression of concrete's nature increased in purity and scope until his final buildings. The Marin County Civic Center and the Gammage Memorial Auditorium disrupted this trend. The ability of these two buildings to define his attitude toward concrete, however, is impaired by the fact that they were constructed after his death. Although his supervision of the construction might have yielded results similar to those that were built, the buildings lack the sense of final acceptance that his other concrete works enjoy.

ENDNOTES

1. Wright, Frank Lloyd. 1928. "In the Cause of Architecture: VII. The Meaning of Materials— Concrete." *Architectural Record* 64(2):98–104. Reprint. 1975. *In the Cause of Architecture*, ed. Frederick Gutheim. New York: McGraw-Hill. p. 205. *ARCHITECTURAL RECORD*, (August/1928), copyright 1975 by McGraw-Hill, Inc. All rights reserved. Reproduced with the permission of the publisher.

2. Wright, Frank Lloyd. 1928. "In the Cause of Architecture: III. The Meaning of Materials—Stone." *Architectural Record* 63(4):350–356. Reprint. 1975. *In the Cause of Architecture*, ed. Frederick Gutheim. New York: McGraw-Hill. p. 171. *ARCHITECTURAL RECORD*, (April/1928), copyright 1975 by McGraw-Hill, Inc. All rights reserved. Reproduced with the permission of the publisher.

3. Wright, Frank Lloyd. 1928. "In the Cause of Architecture: VII. The Meaning of Materials—Concrete." *Architectural Record* 64(2):98–104. Reprint. 1975. *In the Cause of Architecture*, ed. Frederick Gutheim. New York: McGraw-Hill. p. 208. *ARCHITECTURAL RECORD*, (August/1928), copyright 1975 by McGraw-Hill, Inc. All rights reserved. Reproduced with the permission of the publisher.

4. Ibid. *ARCHITECTURAL RECORD*, (August/1928), copyright 1975 by McGraw-Hill, Inc. All rights reserved. Reproduced with the permission of the publisher.

5. Ibid. *ARCHITECTURAL RECORD*, (August/1928), copyright 1975 by McGraw-Hill, Inc. All rights reserved. Reproduced with the permission of the publisher.

6. Ibid., 210.

7. Ibid., 208. *ARCHITECTURAL RECORD*, (August/1928), copyright 1975 by McGraw-Hill, Inc. All rights reserved. Reproduced with the permission of the publisher.

8. Wright, Frank Lloyd. 1927. "In the Cause of Architecture: IV. Fabrication and Imagination." *Architectural Record* 62(4):318–321. Reprint. 1975. *In the Cause of Architecture*, ed. Frederick Gutheim. New York: McGraw-Hill. p. 146. *ARCHITECTURAL RECORD*, (October/1927), copyright 1975 by McGraw-Hill, Inc. All rights reserved. Reproduced with the permission of the publisher.

9. Wright, Frank Lloyd. 1928. "In the Cause of Architecture: VII. The Meaning of Materials—Concrete." *Architectural Record* 64(2):98–104. Reprint. 1975. *In the Cause of Architecture*, ed. Frederick Gutheim. New York: McGraw-Hill. p. 208.

10. Wright, Frank Lloyd. 1927. "In the Cause of Architecture: IV. Fabrication and Imagination."

Architectural Record 62(4):318–321. Reprint. 1975. *In the Cause of Architecture*, ed. Frederick Gutheim. New York: McGraw-Hill. p. 146. *ARCHITECTURAL RECORD*, (October/1927), copyright 1975 by McGraw-Hill, Inc. All rights reserved. Reproduced with the permission of the publisher.

11. Wright, Frank Lloyd. 1932. *An Autobiography*. Revised. 1943. New York: Duell, Sloan and Pearce. Copyright by The Frank Lloyd Wright Foundation. p. 154. Courtesy The Frank Lloyd Wright Foundation.

12. Wright, Frank Lloyd. 1927. "In the Cause of Architecture: IV. Fabrication and Imagination." *Architectural Record* 62(4):318–321. Reprint. 1975. *In the Cause of Architecture*, ed. Frederick Gutheim. New York: McGraw-Hill. p. 146. *ARCHITECTURAL RECORD*, (October/1927), copyright 1975 by McGraw-Hill, Inc. All rights reserved. Reproduced with the permission of the publisher.

13. Wright, Frank Lloyd. 1928. "In the Cause of Architecture: VII. The Meaning of Materials—Concrete." *Architectural Record* 64(2):98–104. Reprint. 1975. *In the Cause of Architecture*, ed. Frederick Gutheim. New York: McGraw-Hill. p. 208. *ARCHITECTURAL RECORD*, (August/1928), copyright 1975 by McGraw-Hill, Inc. All rights reserved. Reproduced with the permission of the publisher.

14. Pfeiffer, Bruce Brooks, ed. 1992. *The Collected Writings of Frank Lloyd Wright*. Volume I (1894–1930). New York: Rizzoli International Publications. p. 83.

15. Ibid., 70.

16. Wright, Frank Lloyd. 1932. *An Autobiography*. Revised. 1943. New York: Duell, Sloan and Pearce. Copyright by The Frank Lloyd Wright Foundation. p. 228. Courtesy The Frank Lloyd Wright Foundation.

17. Pfeiffer, Bruce Brooks. 1991. *Frank Lloyd Wright Selected Houses*. Volume 8, ed. Yukio Futagawa. Text copyrighted by the Frank Lloyd Foundation 1991. Tokyo: A.D.A. Edita Tokyo Co. Ltd. p. 8.

18. Wright, Frank Lloyd. 1927. "In the Cause of Architecture. Part III. Steel." *Architectural Record* 62(2):163–166. Reprint. 1975. ed. Frederick Gutheim. In the Cause of Architecture. New York: McGraw-Hill.

p. 141. *ARCHITECTURAL RECORD*, (August/ 1927), copyright 1975 by McGraw-Hill, Inc. All rights reserved. Reproduced with the permission of the publisher.

19. Ibid., 142. *ARCHITECTURAL RECORD*, (August/1927), copyright 1975 by McGraw-Hill, Inc. All rights reserved. Reproduced with the permission of the publisher.

20. Ibid., 141. *ARCHITECTURAL RECORD*, (August/1927), copyright 1975 by McGraw-Hill, Inc. All rights reserved. Reproduced with the permission of the publisher.

21. Tafel, Edgar. 1979. *Apprentice to Genius: Years with Frank Lloyd Wright*. Reprint. 1985. *Years with Frank Lloyd Wright: Apprentice to Genius*. New York: Dover Publications. p. 120.

CHAPTER ⬛8 GLASS

INTRODUCTION

Glass, Wright observed, is the "most precious of the architect's new material."[1] Although he praised nearly every material that caught his attention, he proposed for modern glass the most profound of his justifications. "It amounts to a new qualification of life in itself,"[2] he claimed, because it could change the traditional relationship between man and nature. The nature of glass, he believed, was that of an invisible device to control the interior environment: "air in air to keep air out or keep it in."[3] Its near invisibility minimized the distinction between inside and outside, he thought, and by its opening of vistas and its admission of light glass allowed people to mentally and visually escape from the cavelike darkness that had dominated their dwellings in the past. Wright appreciated the near invisibility of glass in the way he admired steel's great strength. These properties allowed him to create beautiful effects but were not in themselves beautiful. Modern glass is, he lamented, "chiefly a perfect 'clarity' or nothing very delightful."[4]

Given his focus on properties that are beautiful, it is not surprising to find that the transparency of glass was not enough for Wright to define the potential of the material. Coexisting with his concept of glass as a something to see through was his view that it was also a material to be seen, "as a brilliance, catching reflections and giving back limpid light," he thought.[5] The ability of glass to modify light was, in his view, the root of its beauty as a visible substance. He envisioned the aesthetic potential of the substance as "light itself in light, to diffuse or reflect, or refract light itself."[6] Consequently, Wright used glass as a nonmaterial, in the service of vision and light, and also as the light and the vision itself.

FORM

Although there are products incorporating opaque glass, transparency is the property that defines the material as building glazing. All levels of transparency (as well as translucency) are within the nature of glass but are not equally intense in their expression of glass essence. High translucency can be achieved in such materials as fabric, wood, and even stone, which has been used in thin sheets to modify and transmit light to the interior of buildings—thus making the low end of the transparency range the least remarkable. High transparency is the more sophisticated property, the one in greatest demand for glass and the one that distinguishes glass from the most materials. To maximize transparency is, therefore, to achieve the ultimate expression of the nature of glass. (It is not claimed that maximum transparency is necessarily maximum beauty, which is an issue beyond the scope of this analysis.)

Since the sheen of glass that produces reflections is an inherent characteristic, it logically constitutes a property representing the nature of the material. The fact that transparency and reflectiveness cannot be maximized in the same expression of glass is the kind of conflict found among properties in all materials. Wright's praise of "great polished surfaces for reflections, leaving openings as though nothing closed them"[7] indicates his appreciation of reflections in glass while failing to acknowledge their compromise to the invisibility of the material. In large plain glass, however, no attempt by Wright to emphasize reflections is apparent. For the most part, it would seem that reflections in broad surfaces were, to him, a fortunate by-product of the material but not a property warranting purposeful exploitation for its own sake.

Small diamond-shaped panes of clear glass set in a lattice of thin glazing bars were used in a large number of his early houses, including the Emmond (1892) and W. Gale (1893) houses. The accidental misalignment of the panes produce a sparkling effect from their varied reflections. The phenomenon can be also be seen in Wright's Oak Park Home (1889), the McArthur House (1892), and the Davidson House (1908). Although the varied reflections are part of the charm in this kind of window, his use of the glazing is logically attributed, in large part, to its popularity rather than any focus on the reflective nature of glass. A similar but less intense effect occurs in the clear pieces of glass in his art glass windows but the phenomenon was unavoidable and therefore incidental. It does not appear that Wright attempted to exploit the reflective property of small pieces of clear glass beyond the standard effect that naturally occurred in every installation.

Some sense of the forms that are appropriate and unique to materials can be achieved by observing which shapes are the result of standard manufacturing processes, which are common in construction, and—when several forms are available—which are the least typical of other materials. The manufacturing processes for building glass at Wright's disposal routinely produced flat rectangular sheets as their first product. Although the configuration is typical of several cladding products, it constitutes a component of the nature of glass, that of primary material form.

Wright's work can, therefore, be examined to determine the degree to which it emphasizes, subdues, ignores, or depends on the basic form of building glass. Variations from rectangularity in Wright's glass are deviations from the shape most central to the nature of the material as a building product. This is the same evaluative tack taken for the other materials, in which degrees of deviation are identified as a way to determine to what intensity the basic form of the product has been respected. The transparency of glass makes it somewhat dependent on the shape of adjacent construction (including its frame) for the expression of its form. Nevertheless, the visibility of adjacent materials—combined with the reflective quality of its surface—makes the form of Wright's transparent glass discernable in architectural expression and thus subject to evaluation.

Most of Wright's glass is rectangular but the geometry is rarely celebrated in its own right. Trim around fenestration emphasizes the rectangularity of the glass to the degree that it draws attention to it. In Wright's early stuccoed houses, such trim was common. It often extends beyond the borders of the windows, thus becomes visually associated with more than the glazing and, therefore, loses some ability to emphasize the rectangularity of the glass. A particularly strong reference to the rectangularity of an opening and, therefore, its glazing occurs in the west facade of the Fricke House (1902). The dark wood trim is positioned several inches from the opening, so that a rectangle of stucco is visible between the trim and the window frames. The concentric light and dark rectangles surrounding the glass seem to focus on it more than they do on other aspects of the facade. The rectangularity of the glass is thus elevated to a degree above the average expression in Wright's architecture.

A similar phenomenon occurs in the white trim set in the field of orange brick at the Winslow House (1893). The trim design contrasts with most of Wright's other masonry openings, which incorporate a lintel and sill (or just a sill) that do not form a continuous border around the opening. The white bands around the windows at the Winslow House seem to focus entirely on the windows and thus emphasize the rectangularity of the glass. A similar trim pattern was used around the

FIGURE 8-1. Wood trim and stucco band frame windows at the William G. Fricke Residence. (Courtesy Mike Kertok)

FIGURE 8-2. Sloped top on glazing at roof soffit at the Paul Olfelt Residence. Glazing dividing strips in decorative orientation. (Courtesy Frank Lloyd Wright Archives)

windows on the top level of the Charnley House (1891). The stone trim at the Roloson Apartments (1894) provides a weaker version of this kind of emphasis. Each of four groups of six windows is surrounded with stone that is not of equal width on all sides. The stone trim—being a large form in a relatively small field of brick—tends to dominate the facade and thus seems more focused on establishing a particular building character than paying homage to the form of the glass.

A rare three-dimensional expression of glass rectangularity occurs at the Levin House (1948). Individual glass sheets are offset in the west facade so as to a create stepped (saw-tooth in plan) surfaces in the glazed wall. Consequently, the widths—as well as heights—of the sheets are clearly defined by the change in plane, as is the rectangular shape of each panel. (The glass panels in the south wall step also but meet the sloped roof line and are, therefore, not rectangular). Wright's tendency to extend glass to the roof produced a number of nonrectangular shapes under sloping roofs. Most of these are more or less incidental to the larger architectural goals and thus fail to define an attitude about the form of glass. The parallelograms, trapezoids, and other polygonally shaped glass at the Jiyu Gakuen Girl's School (1921), Taliesin (1925), Mossberg House (1948), and the Olfelt House (1958) are slightly less incidental than other examples, because the strips dividing the glass into complementary shapes suggest a sense of purpose in the nonrectangular panes. The trapezoids at numerous sloped roofs such as the Levin (1948), Alsop (1948), Harper (1950), and Zimmerman (1952) houses are not divided into smaller polygonal shapes,

thus their slanted tops seem to respond to the slope of the roof rather than to some strategy based on the nature of glass in its own right.

Wright's use of glass with curved edges is a more significant departure from the basic form of the material than is his use of straight slanted edges. The small semicircular glass above the windows of the second floor in the west facade of his Oak Park Home (1889) draws some attention directly to the geometry of the glass, as it was not derived from a curvilinear building shape. A larger version of this shape occurs in the high window in the east wall of the Dana House gallery wing (1905). Except for the slope of its roofs, the Dana House is essentially rectangular in elevation and plan, thus the curve of the glass appears to occur largely for its own sake when viewed from outside. The inside view, however, reveals the close relationship between the shape of the glass and the vault of the gallery ceiling, thus diminishing the directness of the link between substance and form established by the exterior view. The small semicircular window at the Oak Park House only loosely relates to the polygonal ceiling of the space inside and thus stands more on its own as an expression of glass form rather than building form.

The semicircular form of glass under an arch does not assure a free choice of geometry for the glass. Like the slanted top of glass meeting a sloped roof, the curved glass responds to the geometry of the arched

FIGURE 8-3. Semicircular window in east wall of gallery wing of Susan Lawrence Dana Residence. (Courtesy The Illinois Historic Preservation Agency—The Dana-Thomas House and Doug Carr, photographer, The Dana-Thomas Foundation)

construction. The curved tops on the glass in the front door of the Dana House (1902) and in the entry door and side light of the Morris Gift Shop (1948) are examples of such curved-edge glass. In each of these buildings a flat band of glass also curves over the tops of the doors resulting in a unique double concentric-curve geometry for the material. The glass bands, semicircular on both their upper and lower edges, express a degree of plasticity higher than is natural to a material that is manufactured as a straight-edged product.

The sense of plasticity in the arched bands of decorative glass over the Dana entry doors (on opposite sides of the foyer) is elevated by their strong individual identities. They are separated from the door glass below by wide trim and the glass bands extend beyond the width of the door, thus further separating themselves from the identity of the doors. Their plasticity is abated somewhat by the fact that they are art glass made of small flat pieces rather than from a single curved-edge sheet. The decorative glass vault over the foyer expresses greater plastic-

ity than the arched bands because its plane is curved rather than its edges. Its curved plane is achieved with small flat pieces, however, which ultimately limits the plasticity it expresses for glass compared to curves produced with a single unit.

The sense of plasticity in each of the clear glass bands above the door and the side light of the Morris entry is boosted by the fact that they are each a single sheet. They are visually separated from the glass below by only a thin metal frame, however, which obscures slightly their identities as individual units. That is to say, they almost blend with the door to become its top edge. Nearly appearing to be a single expanse of glass diminishes the identity of the double curved edges and thus some of their visual plasticity. As the plasticity of these examples is diminished slightly by their detailing, they are drawn closer to the nature of basic flat rectangular form of standard building glass.

The semicircular bottoms of the otherwise rectangular sheets of glass at the S. Friedman House (1949)

FIGURE 8-4. Butterfly pattern in curved art glass band over (interior) entry door at the Susan Lawrence Dana Residence. (Courtesy The Illinois Historic Preservation Agency—The Dana-Thomas House and Doug Carr, photographer, The Dana-Thomas Foundation)

and the downward-curving semicircular windows at the David Wright House (1950) relate to the circular plans of their buildings, as the structures do not have curvilinear forms in elevation. Because they neither emulate curvilinear building forms in the vertical plane nor serve arched construction, the curved glass has a small degree of expression independent of the building massing. Consequently, Wright's willingness to ignore the basic rectangularity of glass in these structures is slightly more pronounced than his willingness to do so in the Annunciation Greek Orthodox Church (1956), where the glass in the arched openings clearly responds to the geometry of the structure.

As detailing pushes glass towards invisibility, the nature of its form loses significance. Perfectly invisible glass could be criticized as misrepresenting reality, although this circumstance is not necessarily problemat-

ic in the expression of the material's nature. Glass could achieve complete invisibility in Wright's day (as today) only under special circumstances. Nevertheless, the ramifications of his detailing, which reduces the visibility of glass, warrant examination as a component of his material's attitude.

Wright believed that, in addition to great clarity, great size was a defining characteristic of modern glass. He thought that entire walls could become glass "and windows as we used to know them as holes in walls will be seen no more."[8] He incorporated isolated windows as holes in walls, however, as well as groupings of windows as entire walls throughout his career. The Winslow House (1893) is an early example dominated by the hole-in-wall type windows in the main facades but also having a continuous series of windows around the semicircular conservatory on the back of the house. Long

FIGURE 8-5. Vaulted art glass ceiling in the entry foyer of the Susan Lawrence Dana Residence. Curved butterfly-patterned art glass band over (exterior) entry door. (Courtesy The Illinois Historic Preservation Agency—The Dana-Thomas House and Doug Carr, photographer, The Dana-Thomas Foundation)

bands of windows were common in his prairie houses, often stretching across entire sections of facades. These windows tend to be about half a story in height and thus, while covering a long expanse as a group, are not large as individual units.

Early examples of tall windows in series can be found at the Dana House and gallery wing (1902), the second Hillside Home School (1901), and at the back of the Hardy House (1905). The large expanses of windows are a story or more high but occur in two-story facades thus fail to define the entire exterior wall. Although isolated windows continued to appear in Wright's buildings, his window series quickly grew in length and height to become a prominent feature in his facades. The sense of transparency in clear glass planes is directly related to the size of the glazing and inversely

related to the interruptions of framing and dividing bars. Given Wright's appreciation of the transparency of the material and his dislike of its use as holes in walls, very large glazed surfaces could be anticipated in his work. Such surfaces do occur but coexist with a variety of sizes and detailing that further illustrates Wright's reluctance to consistently follow a particular line of reasoning to its extreme.

One- and two-story glass volumes projecting from the R. Lloyd-Jones House (1929) are enclosed by floor to ceiling glazing and are highly transparent but are clearly intended to contribute to the building composition by their visual presence. Horizontal glazing bars are inserted into the glass expanses at a spacing equal to the height of the large concrete block of the building. Many horizontal lines are produced in the glazed surfaces,

FIGURE 8-6. Series of tall windows in the gallery wing of the Susan Lawrence Dana Residence. (Courtesy The Illinois Historic Preservation Agency—The Dana-Thomas House and Doug Carr, photographer, The Dana-Thomas Foundation)

which contrast with the verticality of the tall block piers lining the facades of the building. In plan, these glass boxes have stepped sides as if to emulate the right-angled nature of the block in the facade. As a result of the detailing, the several glass volumes at the R. Lloyd-Jones House are highly integrated into the block-oriented theme of the building. The sheetlike quality that routinely distinguishes the form of glass from the form of concrete block and other materials has been subdued to maximize a sense of unity with the concrete block. The transparency of the system is boosted by the thinness of the frames and the mitered glass at the outside corners. It is diminished by the presence of more glazing bars than necessary (given the larger sizes of glass available at the time).

Long sections of wall at the Hanna House (1935) are floor to ceiling glass (which tends to maximize invisibility) but clearly intended to participate in the building image in their own right. The hexagonal undulations of the glass walls are visually purposeful rather than neutral. The numerous horizontal dividing bars in the undulating sections maintain the presence of the glass in the facade composition far beyond what its reflective surface could achieve alone. Lengthy bands of narrow floor to ceiling glass occur in the Rosenbaum (1939), Goetsch-Winckler (1939), Baird (1940), and Penfield (1952) houses, as well as in numerous others. Like the Hanna House, the detailing of these examples fails to maximize the transparency of the glazing systems. The sheets of glass are relatively narrow, introducing into the glazed

FIGURE 8-7. Projected glazed volumes with horizontal dividing bars and glass corners at the Richard Lloyd-Jones Residence. (Courtesy The Frank Lloyd Wright Archives)

wall many mullions and thick frames, which establish the presence of a barrier. The exaggerated narrowness of the glass at the Baird and Penfield houses produce a visual element of unique proportions and thus a prominent component of the building image.

At the other extreme, numerous cases of near maximized system transparency can also be found in Wright's work. A two-story glass wall (although not two-story sheets of glass) reaches across almost the entire south facade of the second Jacobs House (1943). Since it follows the curve of the plan, it has a slightly stronger presence than it would have had as a straight wall more neutral in its image. Its presence is further maintained by the thick mullions and frame stock as well as the massive stone walls flanking the facade. Two semi-circular pools appear to join as a single circular pool with the glass wall crossing its center. The apparent disregard of the pool configuration by the wall tends to blur the distinction between inside and outside, thus diminishing slightly the visual presence of the glass wall, at least near the pool.

The one-story sheets of glass cover the entire south and west elevations of the living room of the Walter House (1945). Not only does the glass reach from the floor to the ceiling but the sheets are unusually wide.

FIGURE 8-8. Serpentine glazed wall in hexagon-based geometry at the Paul and Jean Hanna Residence. (Courtesy The Frank Lloyd Wright Archives)

FIGURE 8-9. Closely spaced mullions in glazed wall at the Louis Penfield Residence. (Courtesy The Frank Lloyd Wright Archives)

FIGURE 8-10. Living room (on left) surrounded on three sides by glazed walls at the Douglas Grant Residence. Glass corners. Cantilevered concrete slab roof. (Photo courtesy State Historical Society of Iowa—Des Moines)

The number of mullions interrupting the expanse are thus minimized. The mitered glass corners contribute further to the transparency of the wall, as no mullions exist on the corners. The trio of tall glass walls with thin mullions and mitered glass corners surrounding the living room of the Grant House (1945) seem particularly transparent, as from a position outside the house the sky can be seen through any two of the walls at one time. A similar circumstance occurs at the hexagonal living room of the Glore House (1951), over half of which is surrounded by tall glass walls.

Wright's residential glazing continued to vary throughout his career with regard to the sizes of the glass sheets, the widths of mullions and trim, the corner detailing, and the percentage of the wall covered. Although he clearly desired to use glass in wide expanses, there was no trend in his design and detailing towards an extreme demonstration of transparency. Some glass installations are more transparent than others, but there appears to be no methodical progress toward bringing plain glass to the brink of invisibility. Invisibility is enhanced by frameless detailing where it occurs, but Wright typically limited it to only part of the glazing. It appears that, like the expression of other materials in his architecture, Wright determined the specific expression of the glass with regard to the transparency of its assembly according to the needs of each design as a separate phenomenon. A common detail in Wright's glass is the mitered corner, which occurs in numerous projects including the S. Freeman (1924), R. Lloyd-Jones (1929), Walter (1945), Palmer (1950),

Zimmerman (1952), R.L. Wright (1953), and H. Price, Sr. (1954) houses.

As in the other houses, details coexist at the Kaufmann House (1935) that elevate or diminish the visual presence of the glass. The mitered frameless corners of the fixed glass and its direct contact to the stone without benefit of frame stock contribute to the transparency of the glazing system, as does the thinness of the steel frames where they occur. In opposition to transparency are the red color of the frames, the presence of frame stock where operating sash meets the stone, and the presence of frame-stock where fixed glass meets concrete. The glass is extremely wide in some places—which reduces the number of vertical frame elements—but it is relatively short (measured vertically) thus greatly increasing the number of horizontal frame strips present. The slender horizontal strips of glass and their many horizontal bars are clearly compositional devices meant to visually participate in the building character.

The direct contact of glass without a frame to the wall material is not as common in Wright's work as are the mitered corners. Certain fixed glass at the H. Price, Sr. House (1954) meets the concrete block without a frame and is mitered at other locations. The effect on the architecture is noticeable but limited by the amount of glass involved.

Wright's expression of glass transparency in nonresidential architecture is mixed. The strong contrast between the punched-hole window format of the Larkin Building (1903) and the glazed wall detailing of his last several nonresidential works is predictable, given the differing stylistic environments at the beginning and middle of the 20th century. Contrasting glass treatments can also be found among Wright's later works.

The large prow of the Unitarian Church (1947) is unique among Wright's glass for several reasons. The plain clear glass is divided by closely spaced sloped wood

FIGURE 8-11. Horizontal dividing bars in glazing with glass corners at the Samuel Freeman Residence. (Courtesy The Frank Lloyd Wright Archives)

pit, thus allowing the glass to serve as a partial transmitter of light to the church. Its dominant role, however, is that of building form, which complements the angular geometry of the roof.

Clear glass forms walls at the Guggenheim Museum (1943), Marin County Civic Center (1957), Juvenile Cultural Study Center (1957), and Gammage Memorial Auditorium (1959). The long expanses of glass at the museum and civic center are dominated by building form. The glass around the office pod at the north end of the Guggenheim is just visible above the railings of the cantilevered terraces. Other glass there is deep in shadow. The glass walls that run nearly the entire length of the civic center wings are set back from the arcades of the facades. The glass is visible but somewhat obscured by its recessed position, the arcades that cover the upper part of the glass, and the shadows of the arcades.

In contrast, the glass walls of the Juvenile Study Center and the Gammage Auditorium occupy a large part of the elevations. The large sheets of clear glass at the auditorium minimize the number of mullions, thus increasing the transparency of the system. The gold color of the mullions, and their unequal spacing (alternating narrow and wide spaces) have the opposite effect, since they draw attention to themselves and therefore to the presence of glass. Ultimately, the glass wall is visible or virtually invisible depending on whether or not the sun is shining on it. In direct sun, the white curtain behind the glazing minimizes reflections, making the glass nearly invisible. In shade or shadow, the contrast of tree reflections superimposed on the reflection of the sky makes the glass visible. Except for the choice of the large sheets, the circumstances that subdue the presence of the glass are incidental rather than purposeful, thus minimizing their significance in the architectural expression.

Downward-curved dividing bars define semicircles of glass at the tops of glazed walls at the Guggenheim Museum and the Juvenile Cultural Study Center. These, like other glazing bar patterns, indicate that Wright did not intend for the glass systems to be invisible. He also installed a similar bar pattern but without glass along the open sides of the elevated and roofed courtyards of the study center. The rare detail seems to define a glazed wall without the glass, thus illustrating in a literal way Wright's reference to glass as a kind of air. The detail suggests the possibility that his glass is incidental to its dividing bars rather than vice-versa. Downward curved bars also occurred in clear (before the subsequent substitution of stained glass) semicircular glass under the arches of the Greek Orthodox Church (1956). Like those of the Guggenheim, these respond to the geometry of the building and thus lack a sense of being selected for reasons relating to the properties of glass. Those at the Juvenile Cultural Study Center have no such basis,

strips cut from 2 by 12s, laid flat, and extended somewhat forward of the glass. Several thin metal bars are set inside the glass and run vertically the full height of the system. Mitered glass on the vertex of the acute angled corner, the low visibility of the metal bars, and the projected and gently sloping wood strips give the system a distinct image, not typical of glass meant to be invisible. Its unique proportions and geometry establish it as an important element of the building character, clearly intended to play a visual role in the composition of the facade.

The transparency of the glass and its importance in the facade misrepresent the role of the glazing, as they suggest a stronger visual connection between the exterior and an important interior space than actually exists. The glass wall does not directly border the nave—as would be expected—but a narrow circulation space behind the pulpit, choir, and organ. Upon occasion, this hall has been used for storage. The construction that separates the glass prow from the nave does not reach the ceiling or the glass wall on either side. The partial barrier allows light to enter the nave over the choir loft and around the edges of stone masses flanking the pul-

FIGURE 8-12. Windows isolated in field of brick at the Larkin Company Administration Building. (Courtesy The Frank Lloyd Wright Archives)

as the building is rectangular. Consequently, their expression reflects more clearly on Wright's attitude toward the nature of glass.

In most cases, using glass in forms other than flat rectangles indicates a desire for the glass to participate in the facade composition, that is, to be seen. Glazing can be curved in certain ways (as occasionally seen in a store window) to eliminate reflections thus making it virtually invisible. Wright's rare curved glass, however, clearly has a compositional role in his architecture. His curving of glass challenges the material's primary form and diminishes its distinction from plastic glazing.

A significant sign of sensitivity to materials is the detailing of materials that have similar but not identical properties in such a way that their identities are distinguishable from each other. A small difference between glass and plastics (perhaps not as great as the name implies) is the greater *plasticity* of plastics. Although glass, like steel, can be bent when heated (routinely

done in automobile glass), plastic materials, by their molecular structure and manufacturing processes, embody a sense of flow. Expressing plastic glazing in curved planes and glass in flat planes would conform to their property differences with regard to plasticity.

The curved glass enclosure above the roof of the H. Johnson House (1937) preceded the routine availability of plastic glazing for building construction. (The acrylics, Plexiglass and Lucite, were developed in the mid-1930s). The superior scratch resistance of glass made the material a reasonable choice in lieu of plastic (on a functional basis) for use in the entry foyer of the Morris Gift Shop (1948). On the other hand, the curved shapes for the glazing in both buildings was a design choice that could have been rejected in lieu of forms more suitable to flat glass. Strict adherence to the use of glass in its basic flat form in these buildings would have demonstrated a disciplined focus on the nature of basic glass form. Wright used flat glass in the vast majority of

FIGURE 8-13. Glass corner on the glazed prow of the Unitarian Church. (Courtesy The Frank Lloyd Wright Archives)

FIGURE 8-15. Curved glass encloses "lookout" above the roof of the Herbert F. Johnson Residence (Wingspread). (Courtesy The Frank Lloyd Wright Archives)

FIGURE 8-14. Curved dividing strips in glazed wall at the Wichita State University Juvenile Cultural Study Center. (Courtesy Jennie M. Patterson)

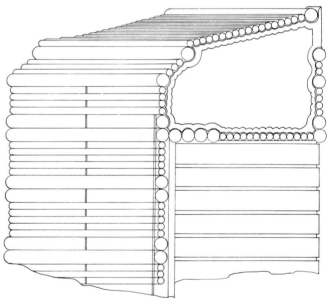

FIGURE 8-16. Section and elevation of glass tube glazing at the S. C. Johnson and Son Administration Building. (From Frank Lloyd Wright Archives drawing 3601.323.)

his work. These minor variations from the norm do not define Wright's attitude about glass beyond a propensity for experimentation. Eventually, Wright, did specify plastic for curved glazing. A notation appears, for example, in an elevation drawing for a plastic skylight dome on the sunken chapel proposed for the Greek Orthodox Church (1956).[9]

The glass tubing at the Johnson Wax complex (1936, 1945) is more plastic than flat sheet in both its form and ability to accommodate curvilinear configurations. Consequently, it seems more philosophically suited than flat glass for the plasticity expressed by the curves in the walls and ceilings. The curves and angles in the cross sections of the glazed surfaces are also served by the circular tube sections in a practical way. As the tubes are stacked in curved or angled profiles, the rela-

tive configurations of tube surfaces on either side of each joint remain constant. That is to say, the perimeters of circles that are a constant distance apart relate to each other in the same way regardless of their relative positions. Such a constant relationship facilitates forming connections. The diameter of the tubing is small compared to the size of the openings, however, thus requir-

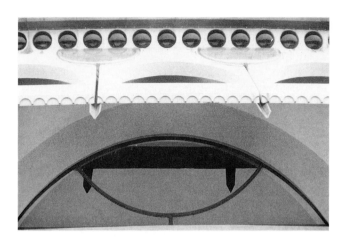

FIGURE 8-17. Glass "spheres" under edge of dome at the Annunciation Greek Orthodox Church. Curved dividing bar in semicircular window (before installation of stained glass).

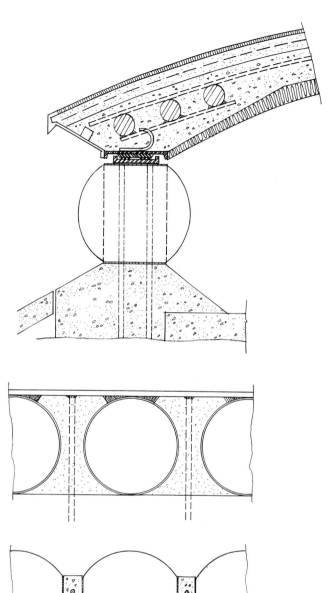

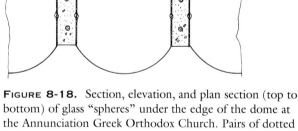

FIGURE 8-18. Section, elevation, and plan section (top to bottom) of glass "spheres" under the edge of the dome at the Annunciation Greek Orthodox Church. Pairs of dotted lines indicate steel support rods connected to steel plate above glass. (From working drawings: Church for the Milwaukee Hellenic Community, Frank Lloyd Architect, sheet 15, revised May 23, 1959, The University of Oklahoma College of Architecture Collection.)

ing numerous joints in the glazing. Joints in glass have not generally been a problem in architecture but their combination with the round shape of the tubes is contrary to the essence of glazing as continuous watertight membrane. The issue is one of durability, subsequently addressed in that section.

The plasticity of the spherical masses of glass surrounding the top of the sanctuary at the Annunciation Greek Orthodox Church (1956) is philosophically compatible with the plasticity of the building. It would appear that a constant relationship between spherical surfaces is repeated around the circular plan, thus verifying the logic of the sphere as the appropriate form for the geometry of the installation. In this case, the configuration of the joint between spheres would remain constant, facilitating the formation of a connection. Working drawings, however, show adjacent surfaces of the glass masses to be flat, thus undermining any minor practical advantage of a sphere over a cube. Since concrete fills the joints between the "spheres" (which also have flat tops and bottoms), the point is moot. The plasticity of the concrete accommodates the loss of plasticity in the glass globes caused by their flat surfaces. The plasticity of the glass tubes and spheres diminishes their philosophical distinction from acrylic or other plastics. Since these particular shapes are rare in architecture, familiar products in either material are not present to impart a greater sense of appropriateness to one or the other.

The corrugations of the glass sheets that clad the roof of the Beth Sholom Synagogue (1954), however, blur the distinction between plastic and glass in a practical as well as philosophical way. The corrugated glass, a rare form for the material, closely resembles corrugated plastic panels, which are far more common. The confu-

sion of materials identity is exacerbated by the fact that corrugated plastic sheets cover the inside of the roof structure that is visible in the sanctuary. (The corrugated plastic panels on the interior were not Wright's first

FIGURE 8-19. Corrugated wired glass on the roof of the Beth Sholom Synagogue.

choice but were eventually selected by him for safety reasons.) The wire embedded in the corrugated glass panels and the slightly reflective surface of the glass do not significantly separate their image from that of the plastic sheets inside. Both the plastic and the glass are translucent, thus further obscuring the identity of the glass.

Wright rarely used translucent or partially transparent glass in large sheets. The Beth Sholom cladding and the gold-tinted glass at the Price Tower (1952) are rare examples of these types. His most well-known windows, however, involve glass with a variety of transparencies and colors in small pieces. His decorative glazing—often called art glass—combines characteristics at opposite ends of the visual spectrum, near invisibility and high visibility. The mixture of glass types (clear and translucent) in the same panel serves to emphasize by contrast the special qualities of each: Colored glass looks particularly colorful beside the clear glass; the clear—in turn—looks particularly transparent next to its tinted counterpart. The assembly is thus distinguished from materials that do not have the unique range of light-transmitting properties expressed by glass.

Wright preferred geometrical patterns in his decorative glass as he did in other materials. He rejected the depiction of realistic subjects in window glazing as it tended "to get mixed up with the view outside."[10] He was not opposed to abstractions of realistic subjects, however, as demonstrated by the butterflylike shapes over the entry and the sumac-inspired patterns in other glass of the Dana House (1902), the tuliplike designs in glass at the Lake Geneva Inn (1912), and the balloon and confetti references in the Coonley Playhouse glazing (1912). The American flag in the playhouse glass may be Wright's closest brush with realism although the tiny replica does not have enough stars or stripes to qualify as the real thing. The integrities of the glass itself and the view beyond are thus secured. Like the two con-

cepts of glass coexisting in the windows, the two kinds of patterns (glass pattern and view pattern) generally maintain their individual identities.

In his architecture, Wright thought that glass acted as a kind of jewel.[11] Among his glass work, decorative glass comes the closest to this ideal—yielding at once a sense of surface and depth, color and clarity, as well as a variety of reflections. He used various strategies that produced patterns having qualities ranging from more jewel-like to less jewel-like, from that largely to be seen to that largely to be seen through. Windows at the Davenport House (1901), for example, are divided by glazing bars but contain very little glass that is not clear. The small number of faintly colored inserts in the Tomek House (1907) windows has a similar effect except that the pattern of the glazing bars has more variety, which draws attention to the glass as an artistic object. The visual presence of the glass is secured in both cases by the dividing bars but ultimately the view is not dominated by the pattern. Wright's extensive use of glazing bars to create decorative patterns in the clear glass portions of his stained glass compositions establishes the importance of the metal devices as compositional elements in their own right. In referring to his focus on the nature of glass in his decorative windows, Wright acknowledged that he also considered the nature of "the metal bar used in their construction," the majority of which "are treated as metal 'grilles' with glass inserted."[12]

In addition to the high percentage of clear glass present, the importance of transparency in Wright's decorative windows is illustrated by the nature of the distribution of colored and clear glass as well as glazing bars. Concentrations of colored glass and glazing bar patterns often occur at the top of the window, thus leaving a lower area of clear glass relatively open to the view. The Dana House (1902), D. D. Martin House (1903), Robie House (1906), and Coonley Playhouse (1912), are a few of the many houses that have examples of this common practice. The concentration of patterns high in the glazing also occurs in groupings of windows such as in the living room of the Bradley House (1900), a bedroom of the Dana House (1902), and the living room of the second Little House (1913) where higher windows in a wall have more dense patterns than do the lower windows. A similar pattern distribution can also be seen in the high and low windows of the Boynton dining room, although the wall of lower windows is offset from the wall of the higher group and, consequently, the windows are juxtaposed only from certain vantage points.

Somewhat less common is the distribution of colored glass and glazing bars at the perimeter of the panel composition. Glass of this nature can be seen at Wright's Oak Park Home and Studio (1889, 1895),

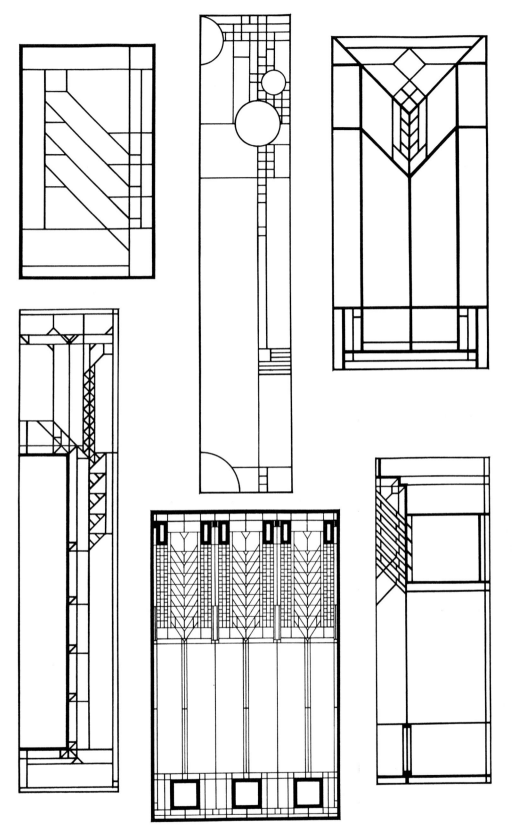

FIGURE 8-20. Art glass at the (top left to right) Stephen M. B. Hunt Residence II, Avery Coonley Playhouse, Lake Geneva Inn, and (bottom left to right) Francis W. Little Residence II, Darwin D. Martin Residence, Oscar Steffens Residence. (From photographs, *The Prairie School Tradition*, p. 94; *Frank Lloyd Wright*, Taschen, p. 77; *The Prairie School Tradition*, pp. 79, 84; *Frank Lloyd Wright*, Taschen, p. 71; *The Prairie School Tradition*, p. 73.)

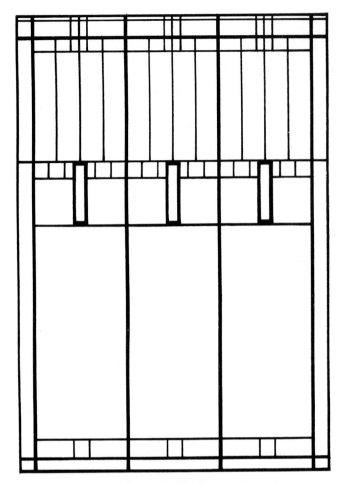

FIGURE 8-21. Art glass at the Ferdinand F. Tomek Residence. (From a photograph, *Frank Lloyd Wright Monograph 1907–1913*, p. 34.)

FIGURE 8-22. Gallery entrance windows at the Susan Lawrence Dana Residence. (Courtesy The Illinois Historic Preservation Agency—The Dana-Thomas House and Doug Carr, photographer, The Dana-Thomas Foundation)

Willits House (1902), Gilmore House (1908), and elsewhere. The top- and edge-concentrated patterns are clear separations of glass to be seen from glass to be seen through, which also reduce the possibility of the glass pattern from blending with the view. Certain windows at the Coonley House (1906) incorporate glass with the pattern focused along one edge (if individual panels are considered) thus leaving the other side of the window clear. Since the edge-focused units are paired with sash having the mirror image of the composition, pairs of windows yield a symmetrical composition with the pattern at the center.

A similar but more aggressive blending of art and view occurs in the centrally positioned patterns in single panels of glass at the Boynton House (1907). The Boynton glass demonstrates the least common execution of the concentrated-pattern strategies. Although the sides of these panels are transparent, any view beyond the glass is split by the pattern in the center of the panel. Consequently, it is difficult for the view to compete with the simple central pattern. The symmetry of the clear glass panels hinders the focus of the eye on the view to one side while ignoring that on the other side of the center line. It is also difficult to see the split view as a single entity. The low density of the pattern facilitates its blend with the view as the widely spaced colored glass does not entirely obscure that upon which it is superimposed. The Boynton glass is a strong integration of Wright's two seemingly opposed attitudes of glass that accept the material as something to be seen and something to be seen through. The result is more disruptive to the visual experience, however, than his windows which integrate less efficiently the two concepts of glass.

The effect of the view on Wright's decorative window glass is made apparent by its comparison to his skylight glass and ceiling fixture glass beyond which there is

FIGURE 8-23. Art glass at the Frank Lloyd Wright Studio. (Courtesy The Frank Lloyd Wright Archives)

FIGURE 8-24. Art glass in the dining room at the Edward E. Boynton Residence. (Courtesy The Frank Lloyd Wright Archives)

no view. Decorative panels of glass mounted in ceilings such as at Wright's Oak Park Home and Studio (1889, 1895), the Dana House and gallery wing (1902), the Heurtley House (1902), and Unity Church (1905) are dominated by translucent glass. The absence of visual interest above the glass coincides with the greatly diminished presence of clear glazing. Thus the role of the clear glazing in his art glass windows is further verified as that of glass to be seen through.

WORKABILITY

Wright worked glass by both bending and cutting. The time and cost involved in obtaining curved glass as well as replacing broken curved glass illustrate the limited workability of the material in the realm of bending. High skill, sophisticated machinery, and preplanning are required, driving down the ease of bending glass compared, for example, to bending wood. Consequently, the bending of glass for the H. Johnson House (1937) and Morris Gift Shop (1948) somewhat challenges the workability of the material. Their simplicity and small quantity, however, fail to establish a pattern of significant disrespect for the limitations of glass in this regard.

Without an industry standard for the form of glass tubing as building glazing, the bending of the glass tubing at the Johnson Wax complex (1936, 1944) is not distinctly an exercise in working rather than manufacturing. In any case, the production of curved tubing—because of its limited use—cannot define Wright's attitude about the working of glass in general.

Cost can reflect on the relationship between the nature of glass and a particular kind of working as it is related, in part, to difficulty and inconvenience. Wright's thought that "pattern is made more cheaply and beautifully effective when introduced into the glass of the windows"[13] than in any other material is pertinent to the workability issue. Since his claim is couched in terms of beauty, however, more than the relative workabilities of materials is being compared. The extensive cutting of glass necessary to produce his numerous art glass windows constitutes Wright's most intense working of a material. Although it is difficult to establish a unit for measuring the extent to which Wright worked wood, it can be readily observed that he worked it far less than its potential. In comparison, his working of glass came closer to the physical limits of that material.

Since the trimming and dividing of sheets into smaller sizes is standard in the manufacture and fabrication of

FIGURE 8-25. Glass tube glazing at the S. C. Johnson and Son Research Tower.

building-glazing, some level of cutting must be accepted as falling within the natural limits of the material's workability. Those cuts that are most similar to the initial trimming of sheets are logically within the nature of the material; those that are particularly troublesome are logically beyond the level routine working. To accept all working that is physically possible as natural to the material is not useful in defining material sensitivity and leads ultimately to a denial that detailing can be less or more sensitive to material nature.

Simple straight cuts, consequently, are candidates for normal working and other geometries of cutting are potentially beyond the norm. This reasoning places virtually all of Wright's large flat straight-sided clear glazing within the nature of the material with regard to workability. Triangular glass, which falls into this category, can however, be problematic as acute-angled corners are particularly fragile. Both the cutting and subsequent handling of the product are affected by this circumstance. No specific angle is recommended as the one separating cuts that are within from cuts that are beyond the nature of glass, because the matter is one of

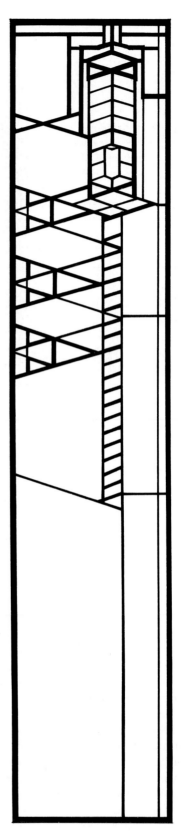

FIGURE 8-26. Right side of double door glazing at the Frederick C. Robie Residence. (From a photograph, *Frank Lloyd Wright Monograph 1902–1906*, p. 203.)

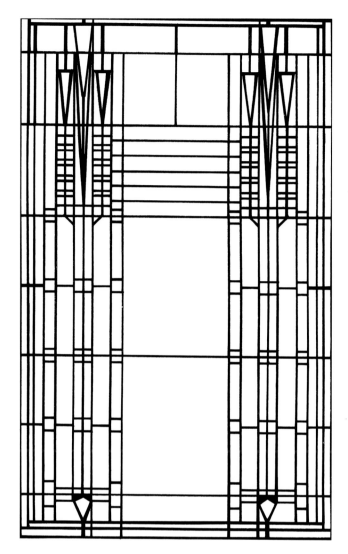

FIGURE 8-27. Art glass at the Frank Thomas Residence. (From a photograph, *Frank Lloyd Wright*, 1982. St. Martin's, p. 29.)

image rather than of pure technology. The acute angles of the numerous diamond-shaped pieces in Wright's Oak Park Home (1889) and other houses around the turn of the century seem routine and easily handled because of their small size. Although they do not have a clear sense of being overworked, significant working is apparent. As the glass pieces decrease in size and increase in number, the limit of logical workability is approached.

Glass cut into shapes with smaller angles seem less routine. Small triangular panes flanking the entry of the Annunciation Greek Orthodox Church (1956) are particularly sharp. Their moderate size, however, facilitated their cutting and handling, which would have been more difficult for larger pieces or very small pieces of equal sharpness. The workability of glass is most severely challenged by acute-angled pieces in certain of Wright's decorative windows because of their sliverlike

FIGURE 8-28. Inside corner cut in semicircular glass at the Annunciation Greek Orthodox Church.

form and small size. The decorative glass at the Dana House (1902) is particularly complex and intricate. Included in much of the glass are numerous small but elongated triangular pieces with sharp points. The extensive use of such pieces imparts to the glass some sense of being overwrought. (The observation does not address aesthetic quality but only the nature of the material—in contrast to Wright's view that they are the same thing.)

Glass at the Robie House (1906) has a similar although less intense image. The patterns there are less sliverlike than those at the Dana House and are in general simpler. All of Wright's triangular glass does not have the same effect on images of the windows. The sense of overworking in the particularly sharp segments in the glass of the Thomas House (1901) is subdued by the limited number of the pieces. The triangles in the glass of the second Hunt House (1917) remain relatively neutral in this regard by virtue of their 45-degree angles and compact proportions.

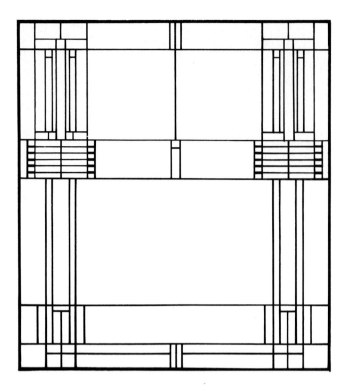

FIGURE 8-29. Art glass at the Ward W. Willits Residence. (From a photograph, *Frank Lloyd Wright Monograph 1887–1901*, p. 201.)

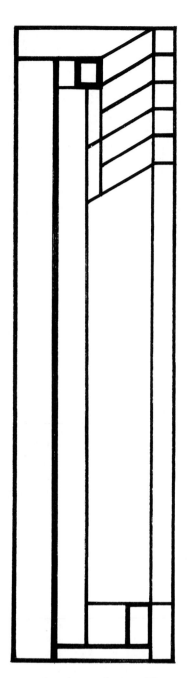

FIGURE 8-30. Art glass at the Mrs. Thomas Gale Residence. (From a photograph, *Frank Lloyd Wright*, 1982. St. Martin's, p. 53.)

The straight cuts most challenging to the workability of glass are those projecting inward from the perimeter toward the center of a shape. Inside cuts, although not impossible, are physically difficult to produce. The fact that they rarely occur in Wright's glass suggests that he recognized this limitation of workability, although it is possible that the shapes resulting from such cuts may not have appealed to him either. An inside cut occurs in an otherwise semicircular window of the Greek Orthodox Church, making the shape particularly troublesome in its expression of the nature of glass with regard to workability. The fact that the cut responded to the wall configuration abates the challenge only slightly, as other solutions were possible that would not require an inside cut to the interface of glass and wall.

Curved cuts define a marked increase over straight cuts in the intensity of working glass. Their difficulty and thus their challenge to the nature of glass is inversely proportional to their radii. Because of their large radii, the top edges of the (original) clear semicircular glass at the Greek Orthodox Church were among the least challenging of Wright's curved glass to the workability of the material. Their challenge was elevated, however, because the amount of curved cutting necessary for each window was tripled by the use of a downward curving dividing bar through the glazing. Downward-curved dividing bars also appear in window-walls at the

Guggenheim Museum (1943) and the Juvenile Cultural Study Center (1957). The confrontation with the workability of glass in these examples is slightly elevated by the fact that the curves do not respond to wall openings that are curved in the plane of the glass. The geometry of the dividing bars at the museum relate to curves in plan while those at the study center appear to exist entirely for their own sake. The study center glass thus

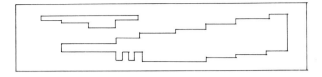

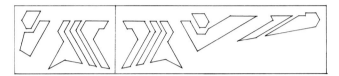

FIGURE 8-31. Perforated glazing boards at the Melvin M. Smith (top) and I. N. Hagan residences. (From photographs, *Frank Lloyd Wright Selected Houses*, vol. 6, p. 171, *Architectural Monograph No. 18: Frank Lloyd Wright*, 1992. p. 127.)

FIGURE 8-32. Metal grilles set in front of glass at the Harold Price, Sr. Residence. Two concrete blocks above the corner window and the block below it are mitered. Raked horizontal mortar joints and flush vertical joints. No lintel expressed at block over glass.

reflects the most intensely Wright's attitude about the workability of glass, since it appears to be driven entirely by a desire for a particular image in the glazing.

Several of Wright's buildings have curved glass with smaller radii. Among the smallest are the circles and partial circles of colored glass representing balloons in the Coonely Playhouse windows (1912). The "balloons" which appear throughout the series, are a rare example of curved cutting in Wright's decorative glass. In contrast to the complexity introduced into the working of glass by curved and angular geometries, several of Wright's art glass windows are based entirely on rectangular forms. Certain windows of the Willits House (1902), D. D. Martin House (1903), Tomek House (1907), and Barnsdall House (1917) are of this type, which minimize the challenge to workability based on geometry. (These examples do not necessarily minimize the appearance of working as measured by other criteria.)

Although straight cutting is in the nature of glass, some distinction can be made in the convenience of cutting according to the size of the unit produced. In the sizes typical of decorative glass, cutting and reassembling the smallest pieces is more labor-intensive and time-consuming than producing an equal area with larger pieces. Some windows incorporating a particularly large number of very small pieces of glass such as those in certain windows of the first D. D. Martin House seem nearly overwrought, if not actually in violation of the nature of glass. Rectangular pieces of glass that are particularly long and slender seem especially fragile and awkward to cut compared to rectangles with more balanced dimensions. Much of Wright's decorative glass includes such slender pieces, especially along the edges of patterns. Windows at the D. D. Martin House (1903), Robie House (1906), Steffens House (1909), the last house for Mrs. T. Gale (1909), and the second Little House (1913) are examples.

Various decorative elements in Wright's buildings give simple sheets of clear glass an image of excessive working. Certain of Wright's perforated wood panels express the single sheets of glass between the boards as being many smaller pieces cut and fitted into the odd configurations of the wood. Such would require cutting of extreme difficulty, including numerous inside corners. The rectangular perforated boards of the M. M. Smith House (1948) are of this type; those at the I. N. Hagan House (1954) are an angular example. In spite of the fact that the glass is not actually cut into the complex assortment of pieces, the boards express the workability of glass as being equal to wood which, given the ease of cutting the odd shapes in wood and the difficulty in glass, it is not. In contrast, window grilles at the H. Price, Sr. House (1954) do not adversely reflect on the workability of glass. The rectangular patterns in the grilles, although slender, could be cut with relative ease compared to the shapes in the perforated wood that would be necessary to fit them into the grille pattern. More important, however, the grilles clearly are set forward of the glass and are not repeated inside the glazing. The fact that the glass passes behind the grilles as a single pane is reasonably clear.

Steel pipe mullions at the H. Price, Sr. House are decorated with cubical cast-iron shapes that overlap both faces at the edges of the glass so as to give the impression that the glass is notched. The square notches would have been most difficult to cut and would have constituted excessive working. An arched steel pipe appears to pass through a large panel of glass in the Gammage Auditorium (1959) facade but actually stops at the surface. An arched pipe inside the building stops

FIGURE 8-33. Cast-iron decorative blocks as glass stops on a steel mullion of the Harold Price, Sr. Residence.

at the inside of the glass and appears to be the continuation of the pipe outside. The implied hole in the glass would have been more difficult to cut than are straight cuts on the edges of glass. The level of working expressed by the configuration is elevated, but because the aesthetic order of the facade does not depend on the isolated detail, the intensity of its expression is diminished in all respects. Although working was not actually performed in these examples, the degree to which cutting appears to have been done establishes the degree to which the expression of glass is affected by the detailing. A thoughtful observer would not be misled, but to casual observers—the majority of those who experience buildings—it is the general impression of the glass that establishes the relationship between the architecture and the nature of its materials.

The working necessary to produce the mitered corners in glass that are so common in Wright's work is at a level far more intense than that of common scratch-and-break type cutting. The cuts are at 45 degrees to the face of the glass and must achieve near-perfection. Roughness and slight misalignments of the cuts cannot be tolerated to the degree that they are in edges that are to be hidden by frames. Given the fragile nature of the material, this level of perfection is beyond a comfortable workability level in spite of Wright's many successful applications of the detail. The intensity of the challenge to the nature of glass can be measured both by length and quantity of the mitered corners.

Although mitered glass corners appear in numerous houses, there are typically only a few in each project. The largest numbers of the details, if each separate unit is counted, occur in glazed corner blocks of the Usonian Automatic houses such as the Tonkens and the Kalil (1955). Numerous floor-to-ceiling mitered corners were also used in Wright's buildings. Those of the Grant House (1945) living room seem to be particularly long because they continue across horizontal dividing bars to reach a high roof soffit. The Kaufmann House (1935) combines both quantity and length to yield one of Wright's most intense challenges to the workability of glass in this format. Moderate and short lengths of glass align vertically in many locations to give an impression of longer miters.

These corners increase the transparency of the glazing system that places the expression of two properties in conflict with each other. As workability is pushed beyond a comfortable limit, the essence of glass as a transparent substance is maximized. This type of conflict is common among materials and requires that the designer emphasize one or the other property or reach a balance in their expressions. It appears that with regard to mitered corners, Wright favored boosting the transparency of his glazing at the expense of expressing its limitations in the realm of workability. Consequently, the architectural effect generated by these corners does not result from a routine expression securely within the nature of glass. It is the result of elevated transparency and visual tension derived from pushing the workability of the glass beyond its logical limit.

STRENGTH

Since glass is not a structural material (for the support of building loads), its nature is most efficiently served in architectural expression by avoiding the appearance of having superseded its strength limitations. Purposeful demonstrations of its strength potential is not effective in making the substance seem more glasslike. Wright's use of large sheets of glass expresses a greater sense of strength in the material than do his small pieces, but the smaller units seem no less like glass as a result of the strength distinction. In fact, the fragile nature of the material calls for units smaller and thicker than the thin broad sheets in which glass is traditionally used. In Wright's call for "due allowance [to be] made for its fragility,"[14] he acknowledged the limitations of glass strength. His work, however, shows no overt concessions to this property such as consistent moderation in the size of his plain glazing.

The desire to maximize transparency has driven glass to sizes requiring care in handling at an extreme beyond that tolerable in other materials. This is not to

FIGURE 8-34. Large sheets of glass at the Anderton Court Shops lean outward. (Courtesy The Frank Lloyd Wright Archives)

say that large sheets violate the nature of glass in every respect as it has been shown that they maximize transparency. Large sheets clearly challenge the nature of glass in the realm of strength, however, a property secondary to transparency in defining the material as a unique substance. Conflicts between the expressions of properties are common as have been periodically illustrated. Enormous sheets of glass in a building are structurally remarkable, not because of clear harmony with the strength of the material, but because this property is challenged to an extreme degree. The symptoms of the violation are the special handling required and the inherent sense of vulnerability to lateral loading such as wind and miscellaneous impact.

The glazing of the Gammage Memorial Auditorium (1959) although among Wright's largest is not so large that its strength plays a significant role in the its image. Although the size of the glass is exaggerated by the stacking of sheets, the apparent strength of the frame relieves, to some degree, the sense of challenge to the glass. The fact that the system sits directly on the ground also helps abate the apparent structural challenge. The

use of several sizes of glass in the building dilutes any sense that the maximizing of glass size was, itself, a focus of the design. The structural integrity of the glazing on the facade of the Anderton Court Shops (1952) is challenged by the large size of the sheets and their outward lean. Although the angle from the perpendicular is not great, any destabilizing effect introduces bending stresses into the glass, which unlike those induced by wind are both permanent and apparent.

The challenge to strength plays a larger role in smaller examples of Wright's glass. Mitered corners, the largest of which are about a story in height, seem particularly vulnerable without the support and protection of frame stock. Their delicacy is further elevated because of the high precision at risk. The smallest failure would be readily apparent in the detail. Stacking of mitered corners at the Grant House (1945), boosts the sense of challenge. Like the challenge to workability afforded by the mitered corners, the challenge to the strength of the material makes the detail even more visually remarkable. Whether or not this has a positive effect on the architecture is not the issue. The point is that the detail is not

FIGURE 8-35. Art glass at the B. Harley Bradley
Residence. (Courtesy The Frank Lloyd Wright Archives)

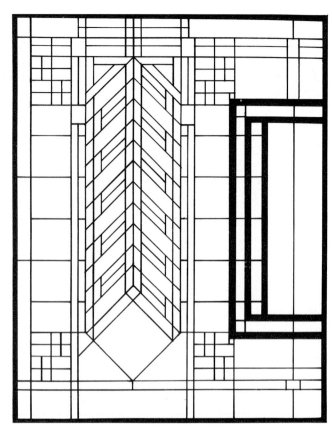

FIGURE 8-36. End window at the W.R. Heath Residence
in group of three over which a single pattern is
distributed. The dependance of the pattern on all three
windows is emphasized by viewing a single unit in isolation.
(From a photograph, *Frank Lloyd Monograph 1902–1906*,
p. 149)

entirely in harmony with the nature of glass regarding
material strength. The fact that these corners have sur-
vived over many years of service does not nullify the violation but tends to define the issue as being more of a
philosophical question than a practical problem.

Decorative glass depends largely on the nature of
the glazing bars for its structural integrity. Although
some structural continuity is afforded by tight-fitting
joints to the separate pieces of glass, the span of bars

across entire glass surfaces is typically haphazard in his
various patterns. The intermittent continuity of the bars
combined with their small cross sections render decorative glass weaker than single-piece glazing. It is appropriate, therefore, that Wright's decorative windows are
smaller than his plate glass. Although factors more profound than strength doubtless dictated the sizes of his
decorative windows, the compatibility of their expression with the nature of glass is enhanced by their moderate sizes. Occasional bulges in old and large stained-
glass church windows testify to the challenge that size
brings to patterned glass. Bulges in the glass at the Dana
House (prior to restoration) indicates that Wright
pushed the limits of strength in this format of glazing.

Patterns that are distributed across several units of
decorative glazing serve to draw the individual sections
into one unified whole, thus subduing the sense of each
window as a separate hole in the wall. The most basic
examples of this are found in many double doors and
operable windows as in the Robie House (1906) and the
second Little House (1913) which, among other

FIGURE 8-37. Decorative glazing in windows and doors around the fountain at the Susan Lawrence Dana Residence. (Courtesy The Illinois Historic Preservation Agency—The Dana-Thomas House and Doug Carr, photographer, The Dana-Thomas Foundation)

numerous other examples, share single glazing patterns that are symmetrical about the vertical center lines of the openings. A variation occurs in windows at the east end of the living room in the Bradley House (1900) where windows are paired vertically rather than side by side. The pattern for each vertical pair of windows is symmetrical about their vertical center lines but the windows are separated horizontally through the pattern. Thus a sense of large glazing is achieved without challenging the strength of the glass as the pattern is formed by relatively small windows.

A series of three windows in the den on the second floor of the Heath House (1905) form a symmetrical pattern about the center window but are linked by more than symmetry. A large rectangle defined by a bold border of colored glass crosses the three windows thus requiring all three for its identity. The end units look especially odd if viewed without the other windows as the ends of the large rectangle have little to do with the patterns in the end panels.

Since one window cannot stand on its own, the larger pattern is unified and reads nearly as one large expanse of glass without bringing the strength of the material into question. A variety of glazing details at the Dana House (1902) bring certain issues of strength to mind. Individual panels of the glass doors on either side of the fountain in the reception area contain patterns with complete compositions. The fact that the pattern in

each pair of doors is not symmetrical about their individual vertical center lines is not common in Wright's glass doors and seems to define the glazed expanse as a series of individual units. A view of the entire wall, however, reveals that the mirror image of the asymmetrical patterns of one pair of doors can be found in the pair of doors on the other side of the fountain. Combined with two windows over the fountain, the symmetry of the group draws it together into a single large expanse of glass. A third pair of doors at one end of the wall does not participate in the symmetry but, nevertheless, adds a few more feet of transparency to the wall. Thus, a large entity of glass is achieved without visually challenging the sense of strength in the system. Also, the sense of "holes" in the wall is somewhat diminished by the continuity established by the relationships of the glazing patterns.

Although the glazing of the east bedroom on the second floor of the Dana House consists of a large expanse of decorative glass, the composition is spread across several windows separated both horizontally and vertically by substantial wood elements. None of the sections stand on their own as complete patterns, thus their identity as a single entity is enhanced. The sturdy wood framing system that divides the whole into sections prevents even the larger pieces from seeming too large for the strength of the patterned glazing. The window is not rectangular, a rare circumstance in Wright's decorative

FIGURE 8-38. A single pattern distributed across several windows in a bedroom at the Susan Lawrence Dana Residence. (Courtesy The Illinois Historic Preservation Agency—The Dana-Thomas House and Doug Carr, photographer, The Dana-Thomas Foundation)

glass, as the top of the glazing follows the slope of the roof. The semicircular window at the end of the dining room ceiling vault is another example of nonrectangular patterned glass uncommon in Wright's work. This very large panel is not subdivided by a wood structure, which places its size in strong contrast with the numerous very small pieces of glass in its pattern. Although the panel is tall and wide, the semicircular form reduces the amount of glass contained compared to a rectangular panel of the same dimensions. The apparent challenge to the strength of decorative glass is thus abated to some degree. The size of the window remains, however, as one of Wright's least accommodating of the strength of patterned glass.

The greatest challenge to the strength of art glass is its use in a horizontal position. When mounted horizontally, the load perpendicular to the surface from the

weight of the glass is constant, thus the challenge to the structural integrity of the glazing rises rapidly with increases in the glass width. Horizontal and sloped patterned glass is common in Wright's early buildings in the form of lighting covers and skylights. Typically, their widths are small enough so as to not seem to threaten the spanning capability of the systems. The decorative glass ceiling of a sitting area in the west end of the Dana House gallery is philosophically troublesome, however, because of its large size. In contrast, the vaulted shape of the decorative glass ceiling in the main entry foyer does not seem structurally precarious. Conceptually, the vault of small glass units is not unlike a vault of small masonry units. The sense of compression in the vaulted glass challenges the integrity of the unit assembly far less than the sense of bending challenges that of flat glazing in ceilings elsewhere. In addition, the pattern in the foyer

FIGURE 8-39. Art glass ceiling under balcony in gallery of the Susan Lawrence Dana Residence. (Courtesy The Illinois Historic Preservation Agency—The Dana-Thomas House and Doug Carr, photographer, The Dana-Thomas Foundation)

ceiling glass has a grid of glazing bars with a relatively high degree of continuity in both directions. They contribute further to the reasonable expression of strength in the glazing.

The nature of glass includes a sense of compressive ability necessary to carry its own weight but no superimposed gravity loads. The frames in which Wright set much of his plate glass abates somewhat the sense of challenge to the compressive ability of the glass. The frames appear to carry or at least help carry the superimposed weight of higher glass. One of the most conservative mullion systems occurs at the Blair House (1952), where relatively small rectangular panels of glass are set in a substantial wood mullion system. The transparency of the system is reduced by the mullions and horizontal framing but the highly visible wood absorbs the structural demands of the large glass walls, leaving the glass free of any significant challenge to its strength. The expression of glass rectangularity is particularly strong in this example also.

At the other extreme of glass size, excessive compressive challenge is not apparent in the tall glazed wall of the Gammage Auditorium (1959). Although the

FIGURE 8-40. Grid of mullions and muntins at glazed walls of the Quentin Blair Residence. Glass corners. (Courtesy The Frank Lloyd Wright Archives)

sheets are large (about 6 by 12 feet in some cases) they are secured in substantial metal frames and stacked only to a moderate height. When mullions are widely spaced and the horizontal frames are thin, as at the Kaufmann House (1935), the sense of superimposed weight on the lower glass increases. Here, the circumstance does not draw attention, however, because the height of glazing is not great in most cases.

The sense of compression in the glass at mitered corners is slightly elevated when several strips of stacked glass meet as at the Kaufmann House and the S. Freeman House (1924). Without a corner mullion for support, the horizontal frame stock appears to cantilever toward the corner in an attempt to carry the glass. The thinness of the frames at these two houses undermines their credibility as cantilevered supports, thus rendering them essentially dead weight on the system. The lower strips experience virtually the same amount of compression as do the lower parts of single sheets, which are the same height overall. However, the sense of weight is greater in the strips, because of their stacked format. The limitation of the total height of these glass corners prevents them from seriously challenging the compressive strength of the glazing.

The great height of the glass prow of the Unitarian Church (1947) challenges the level of compression (including resistance to buckling) that is philosophically comfortable in glass. The long, gently sloping strips of glass that meet at a mitered corner are stacked 10 panels high. Three vertical bars cut from one-half-inch by two-inch stock are visible in certain lighting behind each plane of the glazing. By their placement inside the glass and by their small size, it is apparent that their visual presence was intended to be much subdued compared to the sloped wood dividing strips (cut from 2 by 12s). Had the metal bars been as prominent as the wood strips, a sense of framing would have prevailed in the glass. With the subdued vertical elements, a sense of stacking suggests a significant magnitude of compression in the system.

Herbert Jacobs reports that when Wright ordered the removal of the construction bracing of the glazed prow, the contractor protested—fearing that the system would collapse.[15] The fact that the glass did not collapse upon removal of the braces does not diminish the system's philosophical challenge to the nature of glass with regard to strength. Few details that challenge the spirit of material strength are expected to physically fail. The issue is not whether the safety factor is entirely consumed or not. The issue concerns the relationship of architectural expression to material nature at a conceptual level. The alarm of the builder in this case is symptomatic of discord in the expression of strength in the glazing. As is always the case, no claim is made that the discord detracts from the architecture.

The detailing of the glass spheres just under the edge of the dome at the Annunciation Greek Orthodox Church (1956) fails to clarify their structural role. The close spacing of the glass globes and their tight fit against the edge of the dome suggests high compression in the glass from the weight of the dome. The apparent structural role is so unnatural for glass that the presence of a hidden support system is suggested. The revelation afforded by the interior view that no columns are present confounds intuitive rejection of the glass as the dome support. In fact, the dome rests on 267 pairs of three-quarter-inch steel rods set vertically in concrete between the spheres.

The round faces of the glass framed by the concrete infill suggest that the glazing is entirely spherical. If this was true, there would be virtually no room for steel between the spheres. Since the elevation gives this impression, the burden of the dome seems to fall entirely on the glass. What cannot be seen within the concrete infill, however, is that the sides of the spheres are actually flat. Consequently, two and three-quarter inch gaps occur between the units that house the steel support rods. The fact that the concrete infill appears to be structural exacerbates the challenge to the glass. Since the spheres appear to be embedded in the concrete, compressive stresses would seem to be routinely transferred through the glass as part of the matrix. The result is that, in the facade, structural vagueness competes for dominance with a sense of excessive compression in the image of the glass. The nature of the material is not served by either circumstance.

It is unlikely that the apparent delivery of a building's gravity loads into sheets of glass can be mistaken for reality in Wright's work. Philosophically, however, such an appearance challenges the nature of glass with regard to its strength. Wright took some pleasure in noting this awkward circumstance forced onto designers of historical facades by merchants demanding large show-windows. His ridicule of "giant stone Palladian 'orders' overhanging plate glass shop fronts"[16] refers to the philosophical incongruity of glass as the apparent support for masonry.

Wright's use of hidden steel lintels, which give the illusion that masonry rests on glass, violates the spirit of strength in both materials. He sometimes avoided the issue by extending his glass to the roof, thus permitting no masonry to pass over it. This was often done with the longer expanses of glazing, thus minimizing the intensity of the hidden-lintel violations by restricting them to the smaller windows. As stylistic changes in his work eliminated expressed stone and concrete lintels from his facades, however, and the frequency of masonry "resting" on glass increased. The phenomenon is addressed in the masonry chapters.

A unique (apparent) delivery of building loads into plate glass occurs at the entry of the Morris Gift Shop (1948). Half the entry vault is brick and half is curved glass thus implying that the glass shares compression with the brick. The fact that the brick half of the vault extends the short distance to a ceiling above establishes a sense of hanging, thus maximizing the violation to the nature of the brick while minimizing the challenge to the glass. The absence of logic in the hanging brick, however, never entirely frees the glass from the apparent structural challenge.

Without a clearly defined beam of credible size positioned above glass, the material is nearly always subject to criticism as the apparent support for materials above it. However, at least two of Wright's glazing details clearly report the material to be nonstructural. A sense of hanging occurs in the shinglelike lapped translucent glazing panels of the proposed Rogers Lacy Hotel project (1946). With each panel extending over the face of the panel below, it seems apparent that the units are independently hung and support neither the panel above nor any building element. The parallelogram-shaped panels are turned so that their acute-angled corners point down. Any sense of bearing is thus further diminished in the glazing expression.

The window walls surrounding the living room of the Walker House (1951) are divided horizontally into three bands of glass. Each band sets forward (toward the exterior) of the one below by several inches. A few thin iron posts set a couple of feet inside the glazing slope inward to support the roof, thus further increasing their distance from the glass. The nature of the glass support is vague as the stepped section fails to provide the vertical continuity that is useful in hanging and bearing systems. As a result of the apparently precarious circumstance (as viewed from the exterior), any philosophical participation of the glass in the support of building loads is out of the question. Although the glass is clearly not structural, the vagueness of its own support fails to establish with certainty that the strength of glass is free from other challenges. The nature of glass would be more efficiently served if its detailing clearly expressed the presence of a large safety factor. Such a factor would indicate significant respect for the nature of glass with regard to its strength.

DURABILITY

Wright appreciated the high durability (weatherability) of glass as indicated by his belief that "a precious feature of the material is that it does not disintegrate."[17] Like the durability of masonry, however, the otherwise high durability of the substance is compromised by the greater vulnerability of joints and connections in the system. This is not an issue in the traditional divisions of glass by muntins or in Wright's introduction of numerous joints into his decorative glass. Wright's glass is typ-

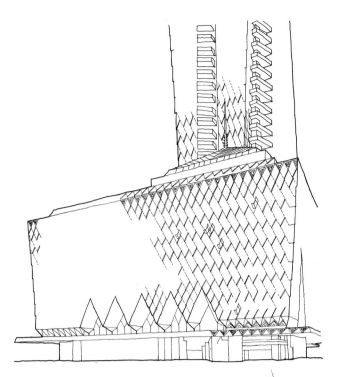

FIGURE 8-41. Translucent glazing panels on the proposed Rogers Lacy Hotel (not built). (From Frank Lloyd Wright Archives drawing 4606.001.)

FIGURE 8-42. Corbeled bands of horizontal strips of glazing at the Mrs. Clinton Walker Residence. Reverse-battered stone wall. (Courtesy The Frank Lloyd Wright Archives)

ically set in a vertical position and protected by overhangs. Consequently the contact of water to the glass is reduced and water is shed quickly when contact occurs. The numerous divisions in the glass prow of the Unitarian Church (1947) seem particularly vulnerable because the wood dividing strips project forward of the glass and do not seem able to remain watertight indefinitely. The sense of violation is abated somewhat by the fact that the wood strips slope downward (albeit in the

FIGURE 8-43. Glass tube glazing over bridge at the S. C. Johnson Wax and Son Administration Building. Original sealant has been removed and tubing has been covered with sheets of plastic.

long direction), thus providing positive drainage from the system.

Wright's most notorious disregard for the potential compromise by joints to the weathering integrity of glazing occurs at the Johnson Wax complex (1936, 1945). The use of glass tubing instead of single sheets of glass introduced dozens of joints into the glazing where only a few would otherwise have been required. In this case, the problem superseded the philosophical realm as expansion and contraction of the tubing periodically broke the seals of the caulked joints and plagued the building with leaks for years.[18] Eventually, much of the exterior glass of the Administration building was replaced with plastic sheets shaped to resemble the tubes. Smooth plastic sheets were installed over the tubing of the vaulted top of the pedestrian bridge.

The aforementioned Lacy Hotel project proposed a use of glazing simultaneously responsive to the high durability of glass and the greater vulnerability of joints. Cladding the entire building in translucent glass panels exploited, to the maximum degree, the excellent weatherability of the material while lapping the panels like shingles provided positive mechanical and gravity protection for the joints between units.

CONCLUSION

Wright defined glass as a material having two personalities, both related to the transmission of light. In his work he repeatedly exploited the potential of glass in both realms. He intensified the role of glass as an invisible material by incorporating large expanses of clear glazing and minimizing elements that define its presence. He magnified the role of glass as a visible object by assembling a remarkable variety of compositions in pieces of colored and clear glass. His challenges to the nature of glass through philosophical and practical confrontations with its various properties were limited except in certain experimental cases. The character of Wright's architecture is often defined, in part, by the unique properties of his glass, thus establishing a record of his dependence on glass to complete his architectural message. Often the expression benefits from detailing harmonious with the material but—upon occasion—confrontation with the nature of glass yields a visual impact useful to Wright's goals for the architecture.

ENDNOTES

1. Wright, Frank Lloyd. 1928. "In the Cause of Architecture: VI. The Meaning of Materials—Glass." *Architectural Record* 64(1):10–16. Reprint. 1975. *In the Cause of Architecture*, ed. Frederick Gutheim. New York: McGraw-Hill. p. 202. ARCHITECTURAL RECORD, (July/1928), copyright 1975 by McGraw-Hill, Inc. All rights reserved. Reproduced with the permission of the publisher.

2. Wright, Frank Lloyd. 1932. *An Autobiography.* Revised. 1943. New York: Duell, Sloan and Pearce. Copyright by The Frank Lloyd Wright Foundation. p. 338. Courtesy The Frank Lloyd Wright Foundation.

3. Ibid. Courtesy The Frank Lloyd Wright Foundation.

4. Wright, Frank Lloyd. 1927. "In the Cause of Architecture: II. Standardization, The Soul of the Machine." *Architectural Record* 61(6):478–480. Reprint. 1975. *In the Cause of Architecture*, ed. Frederick Gutheim. New York: McGraw-Hill. p. 137. ARCHITECTURAL RECORD, (June/1927), copyright 1975 by McGraw-Hill, Inc. All rights reserved. Reproduced with the permission of the publisher.

5. Wright, Frank Lloyd. 1928. "In the Cause of Architecture: VI. The Meaning of Materials—Glass."

Architectural Record 64(1):10-16. Reprint. 1975. *In the Cause of Architecture,* ed. Frederick Gutheim. New York: McGraw-Hill. p. 197. *ARCHITECTURAL RECORD,* (July/1928), copyright 1975 by McGraw-Hill, Inc. All rights reserved. Reproduced with the permission of the publisher.

6. Wright, Frank Lloyd. 1932. *An Autobiography.* Revised. 1943. New York: Duell, Sloan and Pearce. Copyright by The Frank Lloyd Wright Foundation. p 338. Courtesy The Frank Lloyd Wright Foundation.

7. Wright, Frank Lloyd. 1927. "In the Cause of Architecture: II. Standardization, The Soul of the Machine." *Architectural Record* 61(6):478–480. Reprint. 1975. *In the Cause of Architecture,* ed. Frederick Gutheim. New York: McGraw-Hill. p. 137. *ARCHITECTURAL RECORD,* (June/1927), copyright 1975 by McGraw-Hill, Inc. All rights reserved. Reproduced with the permission of the publisher.

8. Wright, Frank Lloyd. 1932. *An Autobiography.* Revised. 1943. New York: Duell, Sloan and Pearce. Copyright by The Frank Lloyd Wright Foundation. p. 340. Courtesy The Frank Lloyd Wright Foundation.

9. Wright, Frank Lloyd. Frank Lloyd Wright Archives. Drawing #5611.32.

10. Wright, Frank Lloyd. 1928. "In the Cause of Architecture: VI. The Meaning of Materials—Glass." *Architectural Record* 64(1):10–16. Reprint. 1975. *In the Cause of Architecture,* ed. Frederick Gutheim. New York: McGraw-Hill. p. 201. *ARCHITECTURAL RECORD,* (July/1928), copyright 1975 by McGraw-Hill, Inc. All rights reserved. Reproduced with the permission of the publisher.

11. Ibid., 200.

12. Wright, Frank Lloyd. 1908. "In the Cause of Architecture." *Architectural Record* 23(3):155–221. Reprint. 1975. *In the Cause of Architecture,* ed.

Frederick Gutheim. New York: McGraw-Hill. p. 59. *ARCHITECTURAL RECORD,* (March/1908), copyright 1975 by McGraw-Hill, Inc. All rights reserved. Reproduced with the permission of the publisher.

13. Wright, Frank Lloyd. 1928. "In the Cause of Architecture: VI. The Meaning of Materials—Glass." *Architectural Record* 64(1):10–16. Reprint. 1975. *In the Cause of Architecture,* ed. Frederick Gutheim. New York: McGraw-Hill. p. 200. *ARCHITECTURAL RECORD,* (July/1928), copyright 1975 by McGraw-Hill, Inc. All rights reserved. Reproduced with the permission of the publisher.

14. Ibid., 197. *ARCHITECTURAL RECORD,* (July/1928), copyright 1975 by McGraw-Hill, Inc. All rights reserved. Reproduced with the permission of the publisher.

15. Jacobs, Herbert. 1965. *Frank Lloyd Wright: America's Greatest Architect.* New York: Harcourt, Brace & World, Inc. p. 173.

16. Wright, Frank Lloyd. 1931. *Modern Architecture: Being the Kahn Lectures for 1930.* Reprint. 1987. ed. Bruce Brooks Pfeiffer. Carbondale and Edwardsville, IL: Southern Illinois University Press. Copyright 1987 by The Frank Lloyd Wright Foundation. p. 9. Courtesy The Frank Lloyd Wright Foundation.

17. Wright, Frank Lloyd. 1928. "In the Cause of Architecture: VI. The Meaning of Materials—Glass." *Architectural Record* 64(1):10–16. Reprint. 1975. *In the Cause of Architecture,* ed. Frederick Gutheim. New York: McGraw-Hill. p. 197. *ARCHITECTURAL RECORD,* (July/1928), copyright 1975 by McGraw-Hill, Inc. All rights reserved. Reproduced with the permission of the publisher.

18. Lipman, Jonathan. 1986. *Frank Lloyd Wright and the Johnson Wax Buildings.* New York: Rizzoli International Publications, Inc. This book contains a comprehensive description of the glass tube glazing system.

CHAPTER **9** CONCLUSION

INTRODUCTION

It has been shown that, although Wright's materials were important to his architectural expression, his imagery was not always harmonious with the nature of substances and products as defined by technical properties. This circumstance can be reconciled with his artistic success and his claim to have focused on the nature of materials if two premises are accepted. First, it is proposed that artistic success is not dependent upon harmony with the (technical) nature of materials. Certain expressive advantages can be achieved by the informed violation of material nature. The quality of the result of doing so is dependent upon the skill of the designer. Second, it is claimed that Wright did not define the nature of materials by their technical properties but by their ability to yield beauty. It is not surprising, therefore, to find greater consistency throughout his work in the expression of beauty than in the expression of literal material nature.

It is also apparent that Wright's focus on materials was diluted by his dedication to more comprehensive principles. He once called "the Nature of Materials," "the Third-Dimension," and "Integral Ornament" a "neglected Trinity" that he believed constituted "the beating heart of the whole matter of Architecture so far as Art is concerned."[1] The statement appears to equate the three issues and elevate their importance above that of other ideals. However, Wright's prior and subsequent discourse did not support this message as his attention to simplicity, plasticity, honesty, nature, horizontality, and originality surpassed that given to the third dimension and to integral ornament. The organic ideal appears to have been Wright's ultimate principle

237

in service to beauty, usually providing the basis for defining the others.

General design principles can be compatible or incompatible with the expression of material properties. If a material's nature is violated in order to meet the demands of a general design principle, a lack of material sensitivity is indicated. If Wright's expression overcomes the influence of an incompatible design principle to positively reflect the nature of materials, he demonstrates a particularly high commitment to material essence. On the other hand, positive material expression incidentally generated by the application of general design principles to other goals does not verify material sensitivity with certainty.

The following summaries of the relationships between selected design principles and material properties supplement specific examples cited in the text in which material expression was vulnerable to the influence of nonmaterial parameters. It is doubtful that Wright saw the possibility of conflict between his general and material principles. In an organic architecture it would be expected that all elements relate to each other and to the whole in positive ways. This is only possible if all components are derived from a single concept. Such was the case in Wright's approach, as a quest for beauty provided his central theme. However, material nature defined by technical properties, generates the possibility of incompatibility between Wright's general principles and the nature of materials.

GENERAL DESIGN PRINCIPLES

Organic Ideal. Wright called his work "Organic" Architecture and made numerous references to organic principles when discussing architecture. He used organic characteristics as a standard for judging the quality of architectural elements. It is apparent, therefore, that—in spite of any claim Wright made that they are one—the achievement of materials goals was secondary to the achievement of the organic ideal. In his definition of organic principles, he rejected the literal biological interpretation of the word. Organic, as Wright used the term, referred to "a structure or concept wherein features or parts are so organized in form and substance as to be, applied to purpose, *integral*."[2] Design that was not organized so that all the parts served a central purpose was not organic by Wright's definition. Given their influential role in Wright's commentaries, organic objectives could be expected to govern if conflicts with materials purity should occur in practice.

The purity of material expression (based on a literal interpretation) is related to the degree of clarity with which the relationships between material properties and external forces are revealed. Detailing so as to express properties could be called organic because a central purpose is served, albeit one limited to materials issues. The purpose on which Wright was focused, however, was external to materials. In order to design organically, he advised, one must first "find the characteristic qualities in both [materials and tools] that are suited to your purpose." These should be united according to the organic ideal, he continued, "to serve that purpose [so that] what you do has integrity."[3] In placing a material's nature in service to a larger purpose, Wright makes materials use subject to goals that could be counterproductive to the expression of properties. Such is the circumstance for any architecture not derived from the nature of materials as the primary motivation for form and detailing.

Nature. In Wright's encouragement for designers to have "an ideal of organic nature as a guide,"[4] it is the underlying principles of nature to which he refers rather than its forms. Wright's observed that in nature "the individuality of the attribute is seldom sacrificed" to benefit other aspects of the entity.[5] The observation suggests that because contradictions rarely occur in the natural environment (where organic principles are defined), neither would conflicts develop between material essence and other principles in the constructed environment of organic architecture. Wright's focus on the principles of nature and organic architecture would generate harmony in materials use so long as his definitions of the nature of materials were universally embraced.

Simplicity. Wright's many references to simplicity verify its significance in his thinking. He rejected traditional definitions of simplicity, however, claiming that "plainness was not necessarily simplicity."[6] Neither did the elimination of detail (which he thought was as meaningless as embellishment for its own sake) define simplicity. He embraced organic harmony as a measure of simplicity, believing that elements of architecture cannot be simple unless they harmonize with the whole. This tact moved any debate about what is simple and what is not toward subjective criteria rooted in Wright's ideology. Wright thus established himself as the ultimate definer of simplicity because he defined the criteria for it.

Wright's praise of unadorned wood beams because they were without affectation[7] would seem to encourage directness and straightforwardness in material use. It is likely that Wright would have considered detailing which did not conform to organic principles, however, to be "affected." Thus, attempts to reconcile his proclamations and applications by any criteria but Wright's own is likely to be frustrated. His reference to simplicity as "the gift of the Machine"[8] was a traditional view of simplicity, as it suggests that the straight uniform products typical of machine production are simple. Maintaining material simplicity by never reshaping basic manufactured forms could thwart the expression of material nature, however, if material essence was defined to include a material's affinity for reshaping.

Ultimately, Wright's desire for simplicity should have affected the expression of materials more positively than negatively, given his belief that true simplicity can be achieved in only one way, "and that way is, on principle, by way of *Construction* developed as Architecture."[9] The reference to construction implicates the practical aspects of assembling building parts. In the absence of aesthetic concerns, construction logic often harmonizes with material properties. Consequently, efficiency in construction as a motivation for material use can yield material expression that is harmonious with material nature. Exceptions occur when long-standing traditional practices make certain illogical details economical. His thought that the key to simplicity is "to know what to leave out and what to put in, just where and just how"[10] suggests a sobering possibility. If Wright achieved simplicity by intuitive judgment rather than by conscious application of principle, the usefulness of simplicity as a vehicle for understanding Wright's material use is severely limited.

Plasticity. Wright reference to plasticity "as Machine-aesthetic in modern designing for wood-working, stone-work, metal-casting and reproductive processes"[11] suggests that, to him, the characteristic was less a property of material substance than of technology. His tendency to find a potential for plasticity in nearly every material prevents the property from characterizing specific substances. His desire for plasticity in all his architecture seems to place the characteristic into the realm of choice, regardless of the materials used. Wright's description of plasticity as "light and continuously flowing"[12] conforms to the common meaning of the term insofar as continuity is concerned, but the reference to lightness conflicts with the compressive expression natural to the masonries that he also believed to be plastic. Although he described the curvilinear form of Erich Mendelsohn's Einstein Tower (1920) as a "purely 'plastic' structure,"[13] he did not restrict the characteristics of "continuous" and "flowing" to curved, jointless surfaces.

Continuously flowing surfaces emphasize the identity of the whole rather than the parts. In materials installed as individual units such as wood, masonry, steel, and precast concrete, the importance and clarity of unit form is diminished as plastic detailing facilitates the movement of the eye across the surface. Consequently, as plasticity increases, the contribution of product form to architectural character diminishes. Each component visually flows into the next, "'flowing or growing' into form instead of seen as built up out of cut and joined pieces."[14] Material form as manifested in individual products is thus obscured. Wright often achieved directional plasticity by emphasizing horizontal joints and subduing vertical joints. Such plasticity is partially dependent on a unit trait (height) and thus expresses one product characteristic. Unit proportion is obscured. This boosts the expression of material nature in some cases and subdues it in others. In directional plasticity (always horizontal in Wright's work), the characteristic proportion of long units such as boards is exaggerated. A linear material is expressed as a highly linear material. The proportion of short units such as masonry is misrepresented. Consequently, plasticity forces blocky units also to be expressed as linear materials.

Horizontality. A sense of horizontality may be achieved in architecture by manipulating proportions and detailing so as to subdue the vertical dimension and exaggerate the horizontal dimension. This effect can occur with entire buildings, building elements, or building materials. The presence of horizontality in much of Wright's work verifies the seriousness of his praise for that characteristic. He predicted that "the citizen of the near future preferring horizontality…will turn and reject verticality as the body of any American City."[15] In his own effort toward this end he reported that, "I brought the whole house down in height to fit a normal man…I broadened the mass out, all I possibly could."[16] He reported of his architecture that, "The house began to associate with the ground and become natural to its prairie site."[17]

Horizontality could conflict with materials principles should a material, because of certain properties, logically call for freedom from the ground. Associating with the earth suggests a close proximity and a prairielike levelness. For example, materials of light airy forms, great tensile and bending strength, or limited durability would be less compatible with the ground than massive, compressive, and durable materials. Emphasis of the horizontal tends to promote a linear quality in materials that boosts the expression of that characteristic in wood and steel but subdues the blockiness of stone, brick, and concrete block.

Originality. Wright promoted the original ideas from one's imagination as the appropriate basis for architectural design. "It is natural to be 'original',," he declared, "for we are at the fountain-head of all forms whatsoever."[18] "Supreme Imagination is what makes the creative Artist,"[19] he believed. Although he accepted certain sources outside one's own mind (building function, machine processes, structural integrity) to be interpreted by the creative imagination, he consistently rejected one particular source of inspiration, historic styles. "INSTINCTIVELY, I think, I hated the empty, pretentious shapes of the Renaissance,"[20] he admitted—among similar proclamations regarding other styles.

Although he rejected imitation in general, his enthusiasm for originality was, in large part, an anticlassical crusade. He also rejected the International Style in his declaration that, "Any 'international style' would probably be a cultural calamity fit for Fascism but intolerable to democracy."[21] However, Wright did not accept the International Style—unlike classical architecture—as being legitimate in its own time. It was rejected on its own merits rather than because its time had passed. His curious temporary fascination in Mayan influences resulted in both material harmony and discord, which varied depending on the material and the faithfulness of the detailing to the original concepts of the style.

Wright's focus on originality was one of the larger obstacles he faced in finding the true essence of materials. This attitude tended to limit his range of material expression to only new images. (His least pure material expressions among his Mayan inspired designs were his more original interpretations.) It is unlikely that he could have accepted massing and detailing characteristics of the International or Neoclassical styles in his materials even if an objective analysis of a material's properties justified it. This could be particularly limiting with regard to the property of material strength because historic styles (and consequently their revival styles) often had a logical structural expression due to technological necessity.

Wright observed that, "The Architect is no longer hampered by the stone arch of the Romans or by the stone beam of the Greeks." "Why then," he wondered, "does he cling to the grammatical phrases of those ancient methods of construction."[22] If a literal interpretation of stone's properties revealed a compatibility with Romanlike arches, rejection of this conclusion would be a denial of the nature of stone because the ancient arches responded accurately to stone's properties. Wright's claim that "every new material means a new form, a new use if used according to its nature"[23] is logical if the properties of new materials are different from those of old materials. Few of Wright's materials qualified as new, however, least of all his stone. They had new potentials in Wrights' hands, which might have qualified them in his mind as new materials. Wright's rejection of material conclusions of the Classical period would not necessarily generate violations of material nature if there were equally pure details available among new alternatives. In any case, the exclusion of historic but pure expressions reduced the range of harmonious options and thus was more likely to generate material discord

than acceptance of the broadest range would have been.

Judgment relating to workability can also be affected by rejection of historical forms. Detailing produced by hand tools can, because of the nature of the hand, have a high level of complexity. Consequently the intricate and convoluted detailing occurring prior to the widespread use of the machine (and later copied by the machine) had become, to Wright, associated with historic styling as well as the hand. Wright's admonition to "forget ancient models that are especially made to suit freedom of the hand"[24] is a rejection of a particular range of surface characteristics with historic overtones. Because of its association with hand work, this type of detailing is highly expressive of workability. Should it be rejected because of its historical association, the nature of certain highly workable materials might be denied unless equally expressive alternatives could be found.

Designing lighting that was integral with architecture he thought was relatively easy "because there was no precedent to impede progress."[25] The comment reveals his perception of a design freedom inherent in new circumstances and that is absent from traditional practices. There was less danger of appearing to be imitative when using detailing that had no preexisting images associated with it. Materials with less of a tradition in architecture provided more latitude to Wright in developing material form and detailing.

Honesty. Wright's promotion of architectural honesty permeates his writing. Honesty in architectural expression is compatible with the literal expression of material properties and should not cause their violation. Wright's thought that truth was subject to interpretation, however, eliminates the direct connection between literal honesty and the literal expression of material nature. Consequently, Wright's promotion of honesty in architecture does not assure that the nature of materials would be expressed. On the other hand, dishonesty in expression does not necessarily mean that the nature of material would be violated.

Wright sometimes misrepresented the nature of a material by expressing it as a substance with properties that it did not have. Edgar Tafel's recollection that Wright would explode upon any suggestion that certain materials might not act as Wright wished they would[26] verifies his tendency to idealize a material's nature rather than derive it from actual properties. This commonly took the form of Wright's wanting weak materials to be strong. He sometimes hid a strong material behind a weak one, which caused the visible substance to seem stronger than it was. The nature of the weaker material was thus misrepresented. Wright also often denied the low durability of certain materials. His detailing, which gives the impression that vulnerable materials need no protection from the elements, misrepresents their nature. This occurs when the systems that protect the material from deterioration are invisible, visually subdued, or missing.

Misrepresenting enough properties to cause one material to resemble another is a less subtle type of dishonesty. Generally, Wright rejected material imitation. "How dangerous imitation always is!"[27] he remarked. "Materials everywhere are most valuable for what they are—in themselves—," he insisted, "no one wants to change their nature or try to make them like something else."[28] Since Wright defined material essence by subjective criteria, his expression of material nature could be entirely honest in his way of thinking but dishonest upon occasion according to an objective interpretation of properties.

MATERIAL SENSITIVITY

Frank Lloyd Wright is known as an architect who designed within the nature of his materials. His numerous challenges to material nature, however, reveal that his sensitivity was neither maximized nor greater, in every case, than that of other architects. His expression of wood reflects its properties less intensely than that of Charles and Henry Greene and E. Fay Jones. His use of masonry embodies the spirit of the material to a lower degree than does the architecture of Frank Furness and H. H. Richardson. His limited expressions of steel and aluminum fail to capture the essence of the metals at the level found in the work of Mies van der Rohe and Skidmore, Owings, and Merrill. His concrete expressed the nature of its substance to no greater degree than did the concrete of Le Corbusier. What then, could be the basis of his reputation for material sensitivity?

A number of circumstances contribute to the common association of Wright with the nature of materials. Probably the most significant aspect of his reputation is his record of repetitive and forcefully stated claims as to the importance of the nature of materials and his devotion to materials in his architecture. In addition, the supporting commentary of admirers and critics continues to supplement Wright's claims. Other architects have not engaged in such claims about themselves and authors rarely address the issue when writing about other architects. Consequently, there is a remarkable contrast between the extensive commentary supporting Wright's materials sensitivity and the virtually nonexistent commentary addressing the materials use of other designers.

Claims alone cannot account for Wright's reputation, however. As it happens, Wright's claims, although exaggerated, are not unfounded. He frequently detailed materials so as to express some or all of their properties, as described in the previous chapters. The most consistently expressed property is product form. The linearity of wood, the blockiness of masonry, and the plasticity of concrete were often central to the character of his buildings in those materials. Workability, however, was a phenomenon limited to serving certain design intentions but not a property that he explored in its own right. He was highly restrained in his working of the most workable material—wood—thus leaving one aspect of its nature largely without expression. The materials he worked the most extensively were copper and aluminum sheet—not unreasonable, considering their ductility and thinness.

Wright expressed strength in a way most compatible with the nature of a material when he used concrete. Some masonry was expressed according to its strength properties but not as consistently as was concrete. The strength of the strongest material, steel, was rarely expressed in its own right, often being used to cause masonry and wood seem stronger than they are. Wright expressed material durability in rudimentary ways without allowing material limitations in this regard to obstruct his design intentions. Many of his decisions relating to material durability were logical only in a context of ideal circumstances. For much of his detailing to remain watertight and to resist deterioration, the optimum performance was necessary from the materials, the craftpersons, and nature. He seemed to view materials and their context as they should be rather than as they are in reality.

Wright's reputation of materials sensitivity doubtless benefits from his comparison to typical International Style architects. International Style detailing, however, was not as confrontational to the nature of materials as criticism in recent years has made it seem. Its rigid and impersonal image maintains an air of general insensitivity, but this image is due in large part to the use of steel and aluminum in ways that are sympathetic to their properties. Because Wright expressed relatively little steel and aluminum, the contrast of his less sensitive use of these metals by comparison goes largely unnoticed. The expression of properties in International Style, masonry is on a par with Wright's work of the same time-period but his more purely expressed early masonry typically dominates any such comparison. His concrete is more plastic than its counterpart in the International Style, thus giving Wright a legitimate advantage in this realm.

The evidence does not indicate that the nature of materials ever governed Wright's design decisions as a conscious application of a theory-based methodology. Given the inconsistencies in his expression of materials, it would appear that the force most consistently influencing Wright's design was his intuitive judgment of

Figure 9-1. Idealized sumac tree in art glass windows of the Susan Lawrence Dana Residence. (Courtesy The Illinois Historic Preservation Agency—The Dana-Thomas House, Maynard Parker, photographer)

beauty. The high but not maximum level of material sensitivity in Wright's work suggests that integrated into his intuitive thinking was a sense of material nature that revealed itself in his work only when it could provide the greatest beauty.

Conclusion

Many would agree that the artistic goals of architecture are not means- but ends-oriented. That is, the point is not to perfect the implementation of a particular theory but to strive for an expressive ideal in the final product. While methodologies are typically employed in the search for such ideals, it is generally understood that faithful adherence to the precepts of a methodology is not the measure of success. Consequently, the remark-

able artistic success of Wright's architecture is not verification of a consistent implementation of any single materials principle. The greatness of Wright's work does not prove that he designed within the nature of materials (defined by a literal interpretation of properties) in every case, in most cases, or more frequently than other architects. On the other hand, to observe that his accommodation of material nature was not consistent does not detract from his artistic achievements.

It is not necessary to design within the nature of materials for materials to be important to architectural expression. A variety of combinations of material harmony and discord are possible on which a building can depend for its artistic message. Most of Wright's architecture is characterized by the purposeful role of materials in the design—whether or not their nature is expressed. The visual success of his buildings gives the materials a sense of correctness. Their nature was treated in a way that produced moving and significant architecture. Wright's tendency, upon occasion, to see in his materials a greater potential than their properties justified pushed them towards an ideal state in his architecture. Idealization, he insisted, "is precisely what architecture does and is when it is really architecture."[29]

Endnotes

1. Wright, Frank Lloyd. 1931. *Modern Architecture: Being the Kahn Lectures for 1930*. Princeton: Princeton University Press. Reprint. Carbondale and Edwardsville: Southern Illinois University Press. Copyright 1987 by The Frank Lloyd Wright Foundation. pp. 5–6. Courtesy The Frank Lloyd Wright Foundation.

2. Ibid., 27. Courtesy The Frank Lloyd Wright Foundation.

3. Wright, Frank Lloyd. 1914. "In the Cause of Architecture." Second Paper. *Architectural Record* 35(5):405–413. Reprint. 1975. ed. Frederick Gutheim. *In the Cause of Architecture*. New York: McGraw-Hill. p. 129. ARCHITECTURAL RECORD, (May/1914), copyright 1975 by McGraw-Hill, Inc. All rights reserved. Reproduced with the permission of the publisher.

4. Ibid. ARCHITECTURAL RECORD, (May/1914), copyright 1975 by McGraw-Hill, Inc. All rights reserved. Reproduced with the permission of the publisher.

5. Wright, Frank Lloyd. 1908. "*In the Cause of Architecture*." *Architectural Record* 23(3):155–221.

Reprint. 1975. ed. Frederick Gutheim. In the Cause of Architecture. New York: McGraw-Hill. p. 58. *ARCHITECTURAL RECORD*, (March/1908), copyright 1975 by McGraw-Hill, Inc. All rights reserved. Reproduced with the permission of the publisher.

6. Wright, Frank Lloyd. 1931. Modern Architecture: Being the Kahn Lectures for 1930. Princeton: Princeton University Press. Reprint. Carbondale and Edwardsville: Southern Illinois University Press. Copyright 1987 by The Frank Lloyd Wright Foundation. p. 75. Courtesy The Frank Lloyd Wright Foundation.

7. Wright, Frank Lloyd. 1928. "In the Cause of Architecture: IV. The Meaning of Materials—Wood." Architectural Record 63(5):481–488. Reprint. 1975. ed. Frederick Gutheim. In the Cause of Architecture. New York: McGraw-Hill. p. 182.

8. Wright, Frank Lloyd. 1931. Modern Architecture: Being the Kahn Lectures for 1930. Princeton: Princeton University Press. Reprint. Carbondale and Edwardsville: Southern Illinois University Press. Copyright 1987 by The Frank Lloyd Wright Foundation. p. 19. Courtesy The Frank Lloyd Wright Foundation.

9. Ibid., 80. Courtesy The Frank Lloyd Wright Foundation.

10. Ibid., 76. Courtesy The Frank Lloyd Wright Foundation.

11. Ibid., 30. Courtesy The Frank Lloyd Wright Foundation.

12. Ibid., 72. Courtesy The Frank Lloyd Wright Foundation.

13. Wright, Frank Lloyd. 1928. "In the Cause of Architecture: I. The Logic of the Plan." *Architectural Record* 63(1):49–57. Reprint. 1975. ed. Frederick Gutheim. In the Cause of Architecture. New York: McGraw-Hill. p. 155. *ARCHITECTURAL RECORD*, (January/1928), copyright 1975 by McGraw-Hill, Inc. All rights reserved. Reproduced with the permission of the publisher.

14. Wright, Frank Lloyd. 1931. Modern Architecture: Being the Kahn Lectures for 1930. Princeton: Princeton University Press. Reprint. Carbondale and Edwardsville: Southern Illinois University Press. Copyright 1987 by The Frank Lloyd Wright Foundation. p. 30. Courtesy The Frank Lloyd Wright Foundation.

15. Ibid., 91. Courtesy The Frank Lloyd Wright Foundation.

16. Ibid., 70. Courtesy The Frank Lloyd Wright Foundation.

17. Ibid., 71. Courtesy The Frank Lloyd Wright Foundation.

18. Wright, Frank Lloyd. 1927. "In the Cause of Architecture: IV. Fabrication and Imagination." *Architectural Record* 62(4):318–321. Reprint. 1975. ed. Frederick Gutheim. *In the Cause of Architecture.* New York: McGraw-Hill. p. 148. *ARCHITECTURAL RECORD*, (October/1927), copyright 1975 by McGraw-Hill, Inc. All rights reserved. Reproduced with the permission of the publisher.

19. Wright, Frank Lloyd. 1931. *Modern Architecture: Being the Kahn Lectures for 1930.* Princeton: Princeton University Press. Reprint. Carbondale and Edwardsville: Southern Illinois University Press. Copyright 1987 by The Frank Lloyd Wright Foundation. p. 29. Courtesy The Frank Lloyd Wright Foundation.

20. Ibid., 47. Courtesy The Frank Lloyd Wright Foundation.

21. Wright, Frank Lloyd. 1952. "Organic Architecture Looks at Modern Architecture." *Architectural Record* 111(5):148–154. Reprint. 1975. ed. Frederick Gutheim. *In the Cause of Architecture.* New York: McGraw-Hill. p. 238. *ARCHITECTURAL RECORD*, (May/1952), copyright 1975 by McGraw-Hill, Inc. All rights reserved. Reproduced with the permission of the publisher.

22. Wright, Frank Lloyd. 1931. *Modern Architecture: Being the Kahn Lectures for 1930.* Princeton: Princeton University Press. Reprint. Carbondale and Edwardsville: Southern Illinois University Press. Copyright 1987 by The Frank Lloyd Wright Foundation. p. 20. Courtesy The Frank Lloyd Wright Foundation.

23. Wright, Frank Lloyd. 1928. "In the Cause of Architecture: IV. The Meaning of Materials—Glass." *Architectural Record* 64(1):10–16. Reprint. 1975. ed. Frederick Gutheim. *In the Cause of Architecture.* New York: McGraw-Hill. p. 198. *ARCHITECTURAL RECORD*, (July/1928), copyright 1975 by McGraw-Hill, Inc. All rights reserved. Reproduced with the permission of the publisher.

24. Wright, Frank Lloyd. 1927. "In the Cause of

Architecture: II. Standardization, The Soul of the Machine." *Architectural Record* 61(6):478–480. Reprint. 1975. ed. Frederick Gutheim. *In the Cause of Architecture.* New York: McGraw-Hill. p. 137. *ARCHITECTURAL RECORD,* (June/1927), copyright 1975 by McGraw-Hill, Inc. All rights reserved. Reproduced with the permission of the publisher.

25. Wright, Frank Lloyd. 1928. "In the Cause of Architecture: IV. The Meaning of Materials—Glass." *Architectural Record* 64(1):10–16. Reprint. 1975. ed. Frederick Gutheim. *In the Cause of Architecture.* New York: McGraw-Hill. p. 202. *ARCHITECTURAL RECORD,* (July/1928), copyright 1975 by McGraw-Hill, Inc. All rights reserved. Reproduced with the permission of the publisher.

26. Tafel, Edgar. 1979. *Apprentice to Genius: Years with Frank Lloyd Wright.* Reprint. 1985. *Years with Frank Lloyd Wright: Apprentice to Genius.* New York: Dover Publications. p. 180.

27. Wright, Frank Lloyd. 1932. Revised. 1943. *An Autobiography.* New York: Duell, Sloan and Pearce. p. 335. Courtesy The Frank Lloyd Foundation.

28. Wright, Frank Lloyd. 1927. "In the Cause of Architecture: V. The New World." *Architectural Record* 62(4):322–324. Reprint. 1975. ed. Frederick Gutheim. *In the Cause of Architecture.* New York: McGraw-Hill. p. 149. *ARCHITECTURAL RECORD,* (October/ 1927), copyright 1975 by McGraw-Hill, Inc. All rights reserved. Reproduced with the permission of the publisher.

29. Wright, Frank Lloyd. 1928. "In the Cause of Architecture: IV. The Meaning of Materials—Glass." *Architectural Record* 64(1):10–16. Reprint. 1975. ed. Frederick Gutheim. *In the Cause of Architecture.* New York: McGraw-Hill. p. 202. *ARCHITECTURAL RECORD,* (July/1928), copyright 1975 by McGraw-Hill, Inc. All rights reserved. Reproduced with the permission of the publisher.

CITED BUILDINGS
AND PROJECTS

Dates represent the year that each project became a commission in Wright's office. They are derived from project numbers as listed in the Frank Lloyd Wright Archives, Taliesin West, except where subsequent research by archive staff and others has dictated revision.

Year	Project	Location
1887	Hillside Home School I (demolished)	Spring Green, WI
1889	Frank Lloyd Wright Residence	Oak Park, IL
1890	William S. MacHarg Residence (demolished)	Chicago, IL
1891	James Charnley Residence	Chicago, IL
1892	Warren McArthur Residence	Chicago, IL
1892	George Blossom Residence	Chicago, IL
1892	Robert G. Emmond Residence	LaGrange, IL
1893	William H. Winslow Residence	River Forest, IL
1893	Lake Mendota Boathouse (demolished)	Madison, WI
1893	Walter M. Gale Residence	Oak Park, IL
1894	Robert W. Roloson Apartments	Chicago, IL
1894	Frederick Bagley Residence	Hinsdale, IL
1895	Frank Lloyd Wright Playroom Addition	Oak Park, IL
1895	Edward C. Waller Apartments	Chicago, IL
1895	Francisco Terrace Apartments (demolished)	Chicago, IL
1895	Frank Lloyd Wright Studio	Oak Park, IL
1895	Francis Apartments (demolished)	Chicago, IL
1896	Romeo and Juliet Windmill	Spring Green, WI
1896	Isidore Heller Residence	Chicago, IL
1896	Charles E. Roberts Residence	Oak Park, IL
1897	George Furbeck Residence	Oak Park, IL
1897	Chauncey Williams Residence	River Forest, IL

Year	Project	Location
1898	Rollin Furbeck Residence	Oak Park, IL
1899	Joseph Husser Residence (demolished)	Chicago, IL
1900	E. H. Pitkin Residence	Sapper Island, Desbarats, Ontario, Canada
1900	Warren Hickox Residence	Kankakee, IL
1900	B. Harley Bradley Residence	Kankakee, IL
1900	Fred B. Jones Boathouse (demolished)	Lake Delavan, WI
1901	Fred B. Jones Gatehouse	Lake Delavan, WI
1901	Fred B. Jones Residence	Lake Delavan, WI
1901	F. B. Henderson Residence	Elmhurst, IL
1901	Hillside Home School II	Spring Green, WI
1901	E. Arthur Davenport Residence	River Forest, IL
1901	Frank Thomas Residence	Oak Park, IL
1901	Edward R. Hills Residence	Oak Park, IL
1902	Ward W. Willits Residence	Highland Park, IL
1902	William G. Fricke Residence	Oak Park, IL
1902	Francis W. Little Residence I	Peoria, IL
1902	Susan Lawrence Dana Residence	Springfield, IL
1902	Arthur Heurtley Residence	Oak Park, IL
1903	George Barton Residence	Buffalo, NY
1903	Larkin Company Administration Building (demolished)	Buffalo, NY
1903	William E. Martin Residence	Oak Park, IL
1903	Edwin H. Cheney Residence	Oak Park, IL
1903	Darwin D. Martin Residence	Buffalo, IL
1904	Robert M. Lamp Residence	Madison, WI
1904	Frank L. Smith Bank	Dwight, IL
1905	William R. Heath Residence	Buffalo, NY
1905	A. P. Johnson Residence	Lake Delavan, WI
1905	Thomas P. Hardy Residence	Racine, WI
1905	Mrs. Thomas H. Gale Summer Residence	Whitehall, MI
1905	River Forest Tennis Club	River Forest, IL
1905	Hiram Baldwin Residence	Kenilworth, IL
1905	Charles E. Brown Residence	Evanston, IL
1905	Mary Adams Residence	Highland Park, IL
1905	Unity Church	Oak Park, IL
1905	William A. Glasner Residence	Glencoe, IL
1905	E-Z Polish Factory	Chicago, IL
1906	Frederick C. Robie Residence	Chicago, IL
1906	Avery Coonley Residence	Riverside, IL
1906	George Madison Millard Residence	Highland Park, IL
1906	Peter A. Beachy Residence	Oak Park, IL
1907	Andrew Porter Residence	Spring Green, IL
1907	Ferdinand F. Tomek Residence	Riverside, IL
1907	Edward E. Boynton Residence	Rochester, NY
1908	Walter V. Davidson Residence	Buffalo, NY
1908	G. C. Stockman Residence	Mason City, IA
1908	Meyer May Residence	Grand Rapids, MI
1908	Isabel Roberts Residence	River Forst, IL
1908	Eugene A. Gilmore Residence	Madison, WI
1908	Robert Evans Residence	Chicago, IL
1909	Bitter Root Inn (demolished)	Darby, MT

Year	Project	Location
1909	City National Bank	Mason City, IA
1909	Oscar Steffens Residence (demolished)	Chicago, IL
1909	J. Kibben Ingalls Residence	River Forest, IL
1909	Mrs. Thomas Gale Residence	Oak Park, IL
1909	George Stewart Residence	Montecito, CA
1910	Edward P. Irving Residence	Decatur, IL
1911	Taliesin I (demolished)	Spring Green, WI
1911	Oscar B. Balch Residence	Oak Park, IL
1912	Lake Geneva Inn (demolished)	Lake Geneva, WI
1912	Avery Coonley Playhouse	Riverside, IL
1912	William Greene Residence	Aurora, IL
1913	Francis W. Little Residence II (demolished)	Wayzata, MN
1913	Harry Adams Residence	Oak Park, IL
1913	Midway Gardens (demolished)	Chicago, IL
1914	Imperial Hotel (demolished)	Tokyo, Japan
1915	Albert D. German Warehouse	Richland Center, WI
1916	Frederick C. Bogk Residence	Milwaukee, WI
1917	Aline Barnsdall Residence (Hollyhock House)	Los Angeles, CA
1917	Stephen M.B. Hunt Residence II	Oshkosh, WI
1917	Aisaku Hayashi Residence	Tokyo, Japan
1917	Henry J. Allen Residence	Wichita, KS
1918	Tazaemon Yamamura Residence	Ashiya, Japan
1921	Jiyu Gakuen Girls' School	Tokyo, Japan
1923	John D. Storer Residence	Los Angeles, CA
1923	Alice Millard Residence	Pasadena, CA
1923	Nathan G. Moore Residence (Reconstruction)	Oak Park, IL
1924	Samuel Freeman Residence	Los Angeles, CA
1924	Charles Ennis Residence	Los Angeles, CA
1925	Taliesin III	Spring Green, WI
1927	Arizona Biltmore Hotel	Phoenix, AZ
1929	Owen D. Young Residence (San Marcos-in-the-Desert) (not built)	Chandler, AZ
1929	"Ocatillo" Desert Compound (demolished)	Chandler, AZ
1929	Richard Lloyd-Jones Residence	Tulsa, OK
1934	Malcolm Willey Residence	Minneapolis, MN
1935	Paul and Jean Hanna Residence	Stanford, CA
1935	Edgar J. Kaufmann, Sr. Residence	Mill Run, PA
1936	S. C. Johnson and Son Administration Building	Racine, WI
1936	Herbert Jacobs Residence I	Madison, WI
1937	Herbert F. Johnson Residence	Wind Point, WI
1937	Taliesin West	Scottsdale, AZ
1937	Edgar J. Kaufmann, Sr., Office (demolished)	Pittsburgh, PA
1938	Florida Southern College, Esplanades	Lakeland, FL
1938	Florida Southern College Annie Pfeiffer Chapel	Lakeland, FL
1938	Ben Rebhuhn Residence	Great Neck Estates, NY
1938	All Steel Houses (not built)	Los Angeles, CA
1938	Edgar J. Kaufmann, Sr. Guesthouse	Mill Run, PA
1938	John C. Pew Residence	Shorewood Hills, PA
1939	Goetsch-Winckler Residence	Okemos, MI
1939	C. Leigh Stevens Residence	Yemassee, SC
1939	Stanley Rosenbaum Residence	Florence, AL
1939	Clarence Sondern Residence	Kansas City, MO

Year	Project	Location
1939	Suntop Homes	Ardmore, PA
1939	Rose Pauson Residence (demolished)	Phoenix, AZ
1939	Bernard Schwartz Residence	Two Rivers, WI
1939	George Sturges Residence	Los Angeles, CA
1939	Andrew Armstrong Residence	Ogden Dunes, IN
1940	Theodore Baird Residence	Amherst, MA
1940	Loren Pope Residence	Mount Vernon, VA
1940	Stanley Bazett Residence	Hillsborough, CA
1940	Lloyd Lewis Residence	Libertyville, IL
1941	Carlton Wall Residence	Plymouth, MI
1941	Florida Southern College E. T. Roux Library (Thad Buckner Building)	Lakeland, FL
1941	Arch Oboler Retreat	Malibu, CA
1941	Gregor Affleck Residence	Bloomfield Hills, MI
1942	Florida Southern College Ordway Industrial Arts Building	Lakeland, FL
1943	Dairy Shed	Spring Green, WI
1943	Herbert Jacobs Residence II	Middleton, WI
1943	Solomon R. Guggenheim Museum	New York, NY
1944	S. C. Johnson and Son Research Tower	Racine, WI
1945	Douglas Grant Residence	Cedar Rapids, IA
1945	Florida Southern College Emile E. Watson Administration Building	Lakeland, FL
1945	Lowell Walter Residence	Quasqueton, IA
1946	Rogers Lacy Hotel (not built)	Dallas, TX
1946	Chauncey Griggs Residence	Tacoma, WA
1947	Unitarian Church	Shorewood Hills, WI
1948	Robert Levin Residence	Kalamazoo, MI
1948	Herman Mossberg Residence	South Bend, IN
1948	Robert Winn Residence	Kalamazoo, MI
1948	Albert Adelman Residence	Fox Point, WI
1948	David Weisblatt Residence	Galesburg, MI
1948	Eric Pratt Residence	Galesburg, MI
1948	Samuel Eppstein Residence	Galesburg, MI
1948	Kenneth Laurent Residence	Rockford, IL
1948	Melvin Maxwell Smith Residence	Bloomfield Hills, MI
1948	V. C. Morris Gift Shop	San Francisco, CA
1948	Charles T. Weltzheimer Residence	Oberlin, OH
1948	Twin Suspension Bridges for Pittsburgh Point Park Civic Center (not built)	Pittsburgh, PA
1948	Carroll Alsop Residence	Oskaloosa, IA
1949	J. Willis Hughes	Jackson, MS
1949	Edward Serlin Residence	Pleasantville, NY
1949	Self Service Garage for Edgar J. Kaufmann (not built)	Pittsburgh, PA
1949	Ward McCartney Residence	Kalamazoo, MI
1949	Howard Anthony Residence	Benton Harbor, MI
1949	Sol Friedman Residence	Pleasantville, MI
1949	James Edwards Residence	Okemos, MI
1949	Taliesin West Cabaret Theatre	Scottsdale, AZ
1950	Robert Berger Residence	San Anselmo, CA
1950	William Palmer Residence	Ann Arbor, MI
1950	J. A. Sweeton Residence	Cherry Hill, NJ
1950	Seymour Shavin Residence	Chattanooga, TN
1950	Richard Davis Residence	Marion, IN
1950	David Wright Residence	Phoenix, AZ

1950	Patrick Kinney Residence	Lancaster, WI
1950	Arthur Mathews Residence	Atherton, CA
1950	Ina Harper Residence	St. Joseph, MI
1950	Eric Brown Residence	Kalamazoo, MI
1950	Henry J. Neils Residence	Minneapolis, MN
1950	Curtis Meyer Residence	Galesburg, MI
1950	John O. Carr Residence	Glenview, IL
1950	Alvin Miller Residence	Charles City, IA
1950	Donald Schaberg Residence	Okemos, MI
1951	Wilbur Pearce Residence	Bradbury, CA
1951	Charles Glore Residence	Lake Forest, IL
1951	Karl Staley Residence	North Madison, OH
1951	Russell Kraus Residence	Kirkwood, MO
1951	Benjamin Adelman Residence	Phoenix, AZ
1951	Roland Reisley Residence	Pleasantville, NY
1951	Gabrielle Austin Residence	Greenville, SC
1951	Mrs. Clinton Walker Residence	Carmel, CA
1951	S. P. Elam Residence	Austin, MN
1952	Louis Penfield Residence	Willoughby Hills, OH
1952	Isadore Zimmerman Residence	Manchester, NH
1952	R. W. Lindholm Residence	Cloquet, MN
1952	Harold C. Price Company Tower	Bartlesville, OK
1952	Ray Brandes Residence	Issaquah, WA
1952	Anderton Court Shops	Beverly Hills, CA
1952	Quentin Blair Residence	Cody, WY
1952	Archie B. Teater Residence	Bliss, ID
1953	Jorgine Boomer Residence	Phoenix, AZ
1953	Robert Llewellyn Wright Residence	Bethesda, MD
1953	Florida Southern College Polk Science Building	Lakeland, FL
1953	Taliesin West Gate	Scottsdale, AZ
1954	Randall Fawcett Residence	Los Banos, CA
1954	William B. Tracy Residence	Normandy Park, WA
1954	William Thaxton Residence	Bunker Hill, TX
1954	Florida Southern College William H. Danforth Chapel	Lakeland, FL
1954	Harold Price, Sr. Residence	Paradise Valley, AZ
1954	Maurice Greenberg Residence	Dousman, WI
1954	I. N. Hagan Residence	Chalkhill, PA
1954	Beth Sholom Synagogue	Elkins Park, PA
1954	Harold Price, Jr. Residence	Bartlesville, OK
1955	Theodore A. Pappas Residence	St. Louis, MO
1955	Dallas Theatre Center (Kalita Humphreys Theater)	Dallas, TX
1955	Maximilian Hoffman Residence	Rye, NY
1955	Arnold Jackson Resicence (Marshall Erdman Company Prefab I)	Madison, WI
1955	Dorothy Turkel Residence	Detroit, MI
1955	Frank Iber Residence (Marshall Erdman Company Prefab I)	Stevens Point, WI
1955	Gerald Tonkens Residence	Amberley Village, OH
1955	Toufic Kalil Residence	Manchester, NH
1955	Don Lovness Residence	Stillwater, MN
1955	John Rayward Residence	New Canaan, CT
1956	Allen Friedman Residence	Bannockburn, IL
1956	Riverview Terrace Restaurant	Spring Green, WI

Year	Project	Location
1956	Kundert Medical Clinic	San Luis Obispo, CA
1956	Kenneth Meyers Clinic	Dayton, OH
1956	Frank Bott Residence	Kansas City, MO
1956	Annunciation Greek Orthodox Church	Wauwatosa, WI
1956	Robert Walton Residence	Modesto, CA
1956	Taliesin West Music Pavilion	Scottsdale, AZ
1957	Wichita State University Juvenile Cultural Study Center	Wichita, KS
1957	Marin County Civic Center	San Raphael, CA
1957	Wyoming Valley Grammar School	Wyoming Valley, WI
1957	R. W. Lindholm Service Station	Cloquet, MN
1957	Carl Schultz Residence	St. Joseph, MI
1957	Marshall Erdman Company Prefab II	Madison, WI
1957	Herman Fasbender Medical Clinic	Hastings, MN
1957	Conrad E. Gordon Residence	Aurora, OR
1958	Pilgrim Congregational Church	Redding, CA
1958	George Ablin Residence	Bakersfield, CA
1958	Seth Petersen Cottage	Lake Delton, WI
1958	Paul Olfelt Residence	St. Louis Park, MN
1958	Don Stromquist Residence	Bountiful, UT
1959	Grady Gammage Memorial Auditorium	Tempe, AZ
1959	Norman Lykes Residence	Phoenix, AZ

REFERENCES

Abernathy, Ann, and Fieroh, Len. 1989. "Restoring Frank Lloyd Wright's Oak Park Home." *Fine Homebuilding* 56:82–87.

Beach, John. 1983. "Lloyd Wright's Sowden House." *Fine Homebuilding* 14:66–73.

Brandes, Susan J., ed. 1991. *Affordable Dreams: The Goetsch-Winckler House and Frank Lloyd Wright. Kresge Art Museum Bulletin* 6:xiii–xviii.

Charles E. Tuttle Co., Inc. 1968. *Imperial Hotel.* Reprint. 1988. *Frank Lloyd Wright's Imperial Hotel,* ed. Cary James. Mineola, NY: Dover Publications.

Chicago Portland Cement Co. 1910. *Beauty and Utility in Concrete.* Chicago: Chicago Portland Cement Co.

Cohen, Daniel. 1985. "Hollywood Discovers the Wright Stuff." *Historic Preservation* 37(4):20–25.

Connors, Joseph. 1983. *The Robie House of Frank Lloyd Wright.* Chicago: The University of Chicago.

Costantino, Maria. 1991. *Frank Lloyd Wright.* New York: Crescent Books.

Davis, Patricia T. 1974. *Together They Built a Mountain.* Lititz, PA: Sutter House.

Eifler, John. 1993. "Restoring the Jacobs House." *Fine Homebuilding* 81:78–82.

Fisher, Thomas. 1993. "Seth Peterson Cottage." *Progressive Architecture* 4:109.

Ford, Edward R. 1989. *The Details of Modern Architecture.* Cambridge, MA: The MIT Press.

Gebhard David. 1988. *Romanza: The California Architecture of Frank Lloyd Wright.* San Francisco: Chronicle Books.

Gill, Brendan. 1987. *Many Masks: A Life of Frank Lloyd Wright.* New York: G. P. Putnam's Sons.

———. 1990. "Frank Lloyd Wright." Keynote address for the Association of Collegiate Schools of Architecture Western Regional Meeting, 18–20 October 1990, University of Colorado, Denver, Colorado.

Green, Aaron G., and De Nevi, Donald P. 1990. *An Architecture for Democracy: The Marin County Civic Center*. San Francisco: Grendon Publishing.

Gurda, John. 1986. *New World Odyssey: Annunciation Greek Orthodox Church and Frank Lloyd Wright*. Milwaukee, WI: The Milwaukee Hellenic Community.

Hanks, David A. 1979. *The Decorative Designs of Frank Lloyd Wright*. New York: E. P. Dutton.

———. 1989. *Frank Lloyd Wright: Preserving an Architectural Heritage*. New York: E. P. Dutton.

Hanna, Paul R. 1981. *Frank Lloyd Wright's Hanna House: The Clients' Report*. Reprint. 1982. Cambridge, MA: The MIT Press and The Architectural History Foundation.

Heinz, Thomas A. 1981. "Frank Lloyd Wright's Jacobs II House." *Fine Homebuilding* 3:20–27.

———. 1982. *Frank Lloyd Wright*. New York: St. Martin's Press.

———. 1992. *Frank Lloyd Wright*. Published as *Architectural Monographs No. 18*. London: Academy Editions. Reprint. 1992. New York: St. Martin's Press.

———. 1993. *Frank Lloyd Wright Furniture*. Salt Lake City, UT: Gibbs Smith.

Hildebrand, Grant. 1991. *The Wright Space: Pattern and Meaning in Frank Lloyd Wright's Houses*. Seattle: The University of Washington Press.

Hoffmann, Donald. 1978. *Frank Lloyd Wright's Fallingwater: The House and Its History*. New York: Dover Publications.

———. 1986. *Frank Lloyd Wright: Architecture and Nature*. New York: Dover Publications.

Holzhueter, John O. 1989. "Frank Lloyd Wright's Designs for Robert Lamp." *Wisconsin Magazine of History* 72(2):82–125.

———. 1989. "Frank Lloyd Wright's 1893 Boathouse Designs for Madison's Lakes." *Wisconsin Magazine of History* 72(4):273–291.

Jacobs, Herbert. 1965. *Frank Lloyd Wright: America's Greatest Architect*. New York: Harcourt, Brace & World, Inc.

———. 1978. *Building with Frank Lloyd Wright*. San Francisco: Chronicle Books.

Johnson, Donald L. 1990. *Frank Lloyd Wright Versus America: The 1930s*. Cambridge, MA: The MIT Press.

Kalec, Donald G. 1982. *The Home and Studio of Frank Lloyd Wright in Oak Park, Illinois 1889–1911*, ed. Jean P. Murphy. Oak Park, IL: Frank Lloyd Wright Home and Studio Foundation.

Kaufmann, Edgar. n.d. *Frank Lloyd Wright at the Metropolitan Museum of Art*. New York: Metropolitan Museum of Art.

Kinch, Richard. 1981. *Wingspread the Building*. Racine, WI: Johnson Foundation.

Laseau, Paul, and Tice, James. 1992. *Frank Lloyd Wright: Between Principle and Form*. New York: Van Nostrand Reinhold.

Lind, Carla. 1992. *The Wright Style*. New York: Simon and Schuster.

Lipman, Jonathan. 1986. *Frank Lloyd Wright and the Johnson Wax Buildings*. New York: Rizzoli International Publications, Inc.

Lipman, Jonathan, and Levine, Neil. 1992. *The Wright State: Frank Lloyd Wright in Wisconsin*. Milwaukee: Milwaukee Art Museum.

McArthur, Shirley DuFresne. 1983. *Frank Lloyd Wright: American System Built Homes in Milwaukee*. Milwaukee, WI: North Point Historical Society.

McCarter, Robert, ed. 1991. *Frank Lloyd Wright: A Primer on Architectural Principles*. New York: Princeton Architectural Press.

Meehan, Patrick J., ed. 1984. *The Master Architect: Conversations With Frank Lloyd Wright*. New York: John Wiley & Sons, Inc. Interview by Hugh Downs at Taliesin (Spring Green, Wisconsin) for the National Broadcasting Company, May 8, 1953. Television broadcast, May 17, 1953 as a program titled, "Wisdom: A Conversation with Frank Lloyd Wright."

Morton, Terry B. and Bullock, Helen D., eds. 1969. *The Pope Leighy House*. Washington, D.C.: National Trust for Historic Preservation.

National Concrete Masonry Association. 1976. *The Work of Frank Lloyd Wright in Concrete Block*. McLean, VA: National Concrete Masonry Association.

Northup, A. Dale. 1991. *Frank Lloyd Wright in Michigan*. Algonac, MI: Reference Publications, Inc.

Pappas, Bette Kporivica. 1985. *Frank Lloyd Wright: No Passing Fancy*. St. Louis: Pappas.

Patterson, Terry L. 1990. *Construction Materials For Architects and Designers*. Englewood Cliffs, NJ: Prentice-Hall.

Pfeiffer, Bruce Brooks. 1984. *Frank Lloyd Wright: Letters to Architects*. Fresno, CA: California State University.

———, ed. 1986. *Frank Lloyd Wright: Letters To Clients*. Fresno, CA: California State University Press.

———. 1986. *Frank Lloyd Wright Monograph* (12 volumes), ed. Yukio Futagawa. Text copyrighted by the Frank Lloyd Wright Foundation 1986. Tokyo: A.D.A. Edita Tokyo, Ltd.

———, ed. 1986. *Frank Lloyd Wright: The Guggenheim Correspondence*. Carbondale and Edwardsville, IL: California State University Press.

———, ed. 1987. *Frank Lloyd Wright, His Living Voice.* Fresno, CA: California State University Press. Copyright by The Frank Lloyd Wright Foundation.

———. 1991. *Frank Lloyd Wright*, eds., Peter Gossell and Gabriele Leuthauser. Germany: Taschen.

———. 1991. *Frank Lloyd Wright Selected Houses* (8 volumes), ed. Yukio Futagawa. Text copyrighted by the Frank Lloyd Wright Foundation 1991. Tokyo: A.D.A. Edita Tokyo Co. Ltd.

———, ed. 1992. *The Collected Writings of Frank Lloyd Wright. Volume I (1894–1930).* New York: Rizzoli International Publications

———, ed. 1992. *The Collected Writings of Frank Lloyd Wright. Volume II (1930–1932).* New York: Rizzoli International Publications

Pfeiffer, Bruce Brooks and Nordland, G. 1988. *Frank Lloyd Wright in the Realm of Ideas.* Carbondale and Edwardsville, IL: Southern Illinois University Press.

Quinan, Jack. 1987. *Frank Lloyd Wright's Larkin Building: Myth and Fact.* Cambridge, MA: The MIT Press and The Architectural History Foundation.

Randall, John D. 1983. *Frank Lloyd Wright: Six Buffalo Houses. A Louis Sullivan Museum Guide.* Buffalo, NY: Louis Sullivan Architecture Museum.

Secrest, Meryle. 1992. *Frank Lloyd Wright: A Biography.* New York: Alfred A. Knopf.

Senkevitch, Jr., Anatole. 1991. "Usonia II and the Goetsch-Winckler House: Manifestations of Wright's Early Vision of Broadacre City." *Affordable Dreams: The Goetsch-Winckler House and Frank Lloyd Wright. Kresge Art Museum Bulletin* 6:12, 25.

Skidmore, Owings and Merrill Foundation. 1986. *The Charnley House.* Chicago: Skidmore, Owings and Merrill Foundation.

Spencer, Brian A., ed. 1979. *The Prairie School Tradition.* New York: Whitney Library of Design.

Steelcase, Inc. 1987. *The Meyer May House, Grand Rapids Michigan.* Grand Rapids, MI: Steelcase, Inc.

Steiner, Frances H. (n. d.). *Frank Lloyd Wright in Oak Park and River Forest.* Chicago: Sigma Press.

Storrer, William Allin. 1974. *The Architecture of Frank Lloyd Wright.* Cambridge, MA: The MIT Press.

Storrer, William Allin. 1993. *The Frank Lloyd Wright Companion.* Chicago: The University of Chicago Press.

Sweeney, Robert L. 1978. *Frank Lloyd Wright: An Annotated Bibliography.* Los Angeles: Hennessey & Ingalls, Inc.

Tafel, Edgar. 1979. *Apprentice to Genius: Years with Frank Lloyd Wright.* Reprint. 1985. *Years with Frank Lloyd Wright: Apprentice to Genius.* New York: Dover Publications.

Tanigawa, Masami. 1980. *Measured Drawing by Frank Lloyd Wright in Japan.* Tokyo: Graphic Co.

Wright, Frank Lloyd. 1908. "In the Cause of Architecture." *Architectural Record* 23(3):155–221. Reprint. 1975. *In the Cause of Architecture*, ed. Frederick Gutheim. New York: McGraw-Hill.

———. 1911. *Ausgefuhrte Bauten und Entwurte von Frank Lloyd Wright.* Reprint. 1984. *The Early Work of Frank Lloyd Wright: The "Ausgefuhrte Bauten" of 1911*, with a new introduction by Grant Carpenter Manson. New York: Dover Publications.

———. 1914. "In the Cause of Architecture: Second Paper." *Architectural Record* 35(5):405–413. Reprint. 1975. *In the Cause of Architecture*, ed. Frederick Gutheim. New York: McGraw-Hill.

———. 1927. "In the Cause of Architecture: II. Standardization, The Soul of the Machine." *Architectural Record* 61(6):478–480. Reprint. 1975. *In the Cause of Architecture*, ed. Frederick Gutheim. New York: McGraw-Hill.

———. 1927. "In the Cause of Architecture: Part III. Steel." *Architectural Record* 62(2):163–166. Reprint. 1975. *In the Cause of Architecture*, ed. Frederick Gutheim. New York: McGraw-Hill.

———. 1927. "In the Cause of Architecture: IV. Fabrication and Imagination." *Architectural Record* 62(4):318–321. Reprint. 1975. *In the Cause of Architecture*, ed. Frederick Gutheim. New York: McGraw-Hill.

———. 1927. "In the Cause of Architecture: V. The New World." *Architectural Record* 62(4):322–324. Reprint. 1975. *In the Cause of Architecture*, ed. Frederick Gutheim. New York: McGraw-Hill.

———. 1928. "In the Cause of Architecture: I. The Logic of the Plan." *Architectural Record* 63(1):49–57. Reprint. 1975. *In the Cause of Architecture*, ed. Frederick Gutheim. New York: McGraw-Hill.

———. 1928. "In the Cause of Architecture: III. The Meaning of Materials—Stone." *Architectural Record* 63(4):350–356. Reprint. 1975. *In the Cause of Architecture*, ed. Frederick Gutheim. New York: McGraw-Hill.

———. 1928. "In the Cause of Architecture: IV. The Meaning of Materials—Wood." *Architectural Record* 63(5):481–488. Reprint. 1975. *In the Cause of Architecture*, ed. Frederick Gutheim. New York: McGraw-Hill.

———. 1928. "In the Cause of Architecture: V. The Meaning of Materials—The Kiln." *Architectural Record* 63(6):555–561. Reprint. 1975. *In the Cause of Architecture*, ed. Frederick Gutheim. New York: McGraw-Hill.

———. 1928. "In the Cause of Architecture: VI. The Meaning of Materials—Glass." *Architectural Record* 64(1):10–16. Reprint. 1975. *In the Cause of*

Architecture, ed. Frederick Gutheim. New York: McGraw-Hill.

———. 1928. "In the Cause of Architecture: VII. The Meaning of Materials—Concrete." *Architectural Record* 64(2):98–104. Reprint. 1975. *In the Cause of Architecture*, ed. Frederick Gutheim. New York: McGraw-Hill.

———. 1928. "In the Cause of Architecture: VIII. Sheet Metal and a Modern Instance." *Architectural Record* 64(4):334–342. Reprint. 1975. *In the Cause of Architecture*, ed. Frederick Gutheim. New York: McGraw-Hill.

———. 1928. "In the Cause of Architecture: IX. The Terms." *Architectural Record* 64(6):507–514. Reprint. 1975. *In the Cause of Architecture*, ed. Frederick Gutheim. New York: McGraw-Hill.

———. 1931. *Modern Architecture: Being the Kahn Lectures for 1930*. Reprint. 1987. ed. Bruce Brooks Pfeiffer. Carbondale and Edwardsville, IL: Southern Illinois University Press. Copyright 1987 by The Frank Lloyd Wright Foundation.

———. 1932. *An Autobiography*. Revised. 1943. New York: Duell, Sloan and Pearce. Copyright by The Frank Lloyd Wright Foundation.

———. 1948. "Frank Lloyd Wright." *The Architectural Forum* 88(1):65–156.

———. 1952. "Organic Architecture Looks at Modern Architecture." *Architectural Record* 111(5):148–154. Reprint. 1975. ed. Frederick Gutheim. *In the Cause of Architecture*. New York: McGraw-Hill.

———. 1953. *The Future of Architecture*. New York: Horizon Press.

———. 1954. *The Natural House*. Reprint. 1970. New York: Meridian/New American Library

———. 1956. *The Story of the Tower*. New York: Horizon Press.

———. The Frank Lloyd Wright Archives. Taliesin West, Scottsdale, AZ.

INDEX

Illustrations are indicated by italicized page numbers.